·WHEN·
IDEAS
MATTER

MICHAEL D. HIGGINS has been a university teacher, a broadcaster, a published poet and a member of both houses of the Irish legislature. He was Minister for Arts, Culture and the Gaeltacht from 1993 to 1997.

Born in Limerick, he was educated at University College Galway, where he later taught sociology and political science. He was a Labour TD for Galway for many years and has been President of Ireland since 2011.

·WHEN·
IDEAS
MATTER

Speeches for an
Ethical Republic

MICHAEL D.
HIGGINS

First published in the UK in 2016 by Head of Zeus, Ltd.

9 7 5 3 1 2 4 6 8

A catalogue record for this book is available from
the British Library.

ISBN (HB): 9781784978273
ISBN (E): 9781784978266

Typeset by Adrian McLaughlin

Printed and bound in Germany by
CPI Books GmbH

Head of Zeus Ltd
Clerkenwell House
45–47 Clerkenwell Green
London EC1R 0HT

WWW.HEADOFZEUS.COM

Contents

Preface

|||||||||||||||||||||||||||||||||||||||

I T WAS IN response to interest and requests from a number of members of the public, some of whom had either attended, or read about, some of my public addresses, and had asked where they might be found, that I agreed to the suggestion that publication of a selection of speeches might be worthwhile.

Those chosen are selected from a very much larger number that I have delivered since my inauguration as President of Ireland, on November 11th 2011. They were chosen by the editors of this volume to whom I am grateful.

For their assistance in preparation of those speeches chosen, may I thank those staff who worked within the Áras, and others from outside, who have contributed by suggestion, draft, amendment and, above all, with the challenging task of interpreting my handwriting. For all of my speeches, those included here and others, I of course take full and sole responsibility.

In doing so I want to say just a word about the speeches which have been chosen by the editors. If you sense a concern with the intellectual and social crisis, you are correct. Simply recognising the challenges of the deep changes of our times is, I believe, insufficient. We need to create the capacity to understand, critique and offer options and alternatives to those changes, ones that will sustain and deepen democracy. It is important to sustain, claim or defend a space of discourse that allows for this, and draw such shared conclusions from that understanding that it will be emancipatory for humanity.

My journey to being President of Ireland has been a long, complex and informative experience. Given the background that I brought to my present position I regard it as a further privilege that I had the opportunity to deliver these speeches. Words are a great gift. They are all the power that some people, and often even entire peoples and classes have. To be given the opportunity to offer a critique of current circumstances, with their threats and their possibilities, is a great privilege. I am grateful for that privilege and I respect it. Words matter.

Soon after my inauguration, I said that I would seek to make my tenure a Presidency of ideas. In truth what I have written I would have sought to write, irrespective of circumstance. What the speeches contain are just my response to current circumstances, no more than that, and they are offered, in humility, as invitations to a shared discourse and debate.

For some who live and struggle in an unequal world, ideas and words are all they have at their disposal. Their ideas express their common humanity, their aspirations for what is fair, just, and emancipatory. They constitute what is, for them, the realm of hope.

In the course of preparing and delivering some of the speeches which follow I have often found myself thinking in this year of commemoration – 2016 – of those who dreamed of and struggled for Irish Independence a century ago, among them my father, John Higgins.

During this year I have often thought of his hard life, his illness and his death, accompanied by a fall into poverty, an experience shared by so many former participants in the birth of the State of which I now have the honour to be President.

For such people social security and health care were far from sufficient, in their ageing years, in the Republic for which they gave so much of the energy of their young lives. I think too of my mother who shared his views with a quiet fortitude and my sisters who emigrated when they were twenty years old, and my brother who kept his courage in challenging circumstances. So much has been achieved in modern Ireland but our fully inclusive, equal version of a republic is very much an unfinished task.

My own family, Sabina, Alice Mary, Michael, John and Daniel have shared all the public life that has led up to the position I now fill. The discussion of public affairs and public rhetoric has been central to their experience of our lives together. We have had great friends, allies, comrades. To them all I dedicate this book.

I have come to regard the ethics of friendship as the beautiful, most enduring prospect that remains available to this and coming generations. Discussing, debating, making the case for change, is best achieved within the ethics of friendship. To all those who welcomed me to their causes, I am so grateful.

I acknowledge with gratitude the assistance of my agent Jonathan Williams, my editor Neil Belton and his skilful and patient colleagues Georgina Blackwell, Clémence Jacquinet, Simon Hess and Declan Heeney. I am also grateful to Declan Kiberd for his friendship and advice. For use of their work may I thank artists Brian Bourke and Ger Sweeney.

I hope that you find what follows of interest and continue the debate on the issues they raise.

There is so much more to be said, so much more reflection to be made, for a world not merely made better than before, but built on a freedom that will release the joy of a shared life on our fragile planet.

Beir beannacht

MICHAEL D. HIGGINS

PRELUDE

Inaugural Speech

C ITIZENS OF IRELAND, you have chosen me to be your ninth President, to represent you at home and abroad, and to serve as a symbol of an Irishness of which we can all be proud, and which together we must forge anew.

I enter the ninth Presidency with a sense of humility, but also with confidence in the great capacity of our people not only to transcend present difficulties but to realize all of the wonderful possibilities that await us in the years ahead.

I wish to acknowledge the immense contribution of those who have previously served in this office, particularly the two great women who immediately preceded me. They have developed our consciousness of human rights, of inclusion, and the important task of deepening and sustaining peace within and between communities in every part of our island. It is work I will endeavour to continue and to build upon.

As your President, I am grateful for the extent of the support, the strong mandate, you have given me. I also realize the challenges that I face, that we face together, in closing a chapter of our history that has left us fragile as an economy and wounded as a society, with unacceptable levels of unemployment, mortgage insecurity, collapsing property values and many broken expectations. During my campaign for the Presidency, I encountered that pain, particularly among the most vulnerable of our people.

However, I also recognize the will of our people to move beyond anger, frustration or cynicism and to draw on our shared strengths. To close the chapter on that which has failed, that which was not the best version of ourselves as a people, and open a new chapter based on a different version of our Irishness will require a change in our political thinking, in our view of the public world, in our institutions, and, most difficult of all, in our consciousness.

In making that transformation, it is necessary to work together for a different set of values that will enable us to build a sustainable economy and a society which is ethical and inclusive; a society and a state that will restore trust at home and act as a worthy symbol of Irishness abroad, inviting relationships of respect and co-operation across the world.

We must seek to build together an active citizenship, one based on participation, equality, respect for all and the flowering of creativity. A confident people is our hope, a people at ease with itself, a people that grasps the deep meaning of the proverb *ní neart go cur le chéile* – our strength lies in our common weal.

Sin iad mór-théamaí na hUachtaránachta atá curtha romham agam, agus mé lán-dóchasach go bhfuilimid ar tháirseach ré nua d'Éirinn agus d'Éireannaigh, sa bhaile agus i gcéin. Ré nua ina mbeidh bunluacha na cothroime agus an chirt, agus spiorad na cruthaíochta, faoi bhláth: poblacht, a mbeidh Éireannaigh de gach aicme agus traidisiún bródúil aisti.
(Those are the major themes of the Presidency set before us; and I am fully confident that we are on the brink of a new age for Ireland and for Irish people, at home and abroad. An age in which the values of equality and rights, and a spirit of creativity, will all flourish; and a Republic of which all Irish people of all classes and traditions will be proud.)

My Presidency will aim to be one that recognizes and builds on the many positive initiatives already under way in communities, in the economy, and in individual and collective efforts throughout our land. It will seek to encourage investment and job creation, innovation and original thinking.

I will seek to make this a Presidency of ideas. It will aspire to turn the best ideas into living realities for all of our people, realizing our limitless possibilities – *ár feidireachtaí gan teorainn*.

In implementing the mandate you have given me, I will seek to achieve an inclusive citizenship where all can participate and everyone is treated with respect. I will make it a priority to visit and to support the participation of the most excluded in our society, including those in institutional care.

I will champion creative communities who are bringing about positive change at local level by giving recognition to their achievements on the national stage. I believe that when we encourage the seedbed of creativity in our communities and ensure that each child and adult has the opportunity for creative expression, we also lay the groundwork for sustainable employment in creative industries and enrich our social, cultural and economic development.

In promoting inclusion and creativity, I will be inviting citizens of all ages to make their own imaginative and practical contribution to the shaping of our shared future. Active citizenship requires the will and the opportunity to participate in every way – to be the arrow, not the target.

Next year Bunreacht na hÉireann is seventy-five years old and a Constitutional Convention is planned by the Government. As President, I encourage citizens at home and abroad to engage with this important review as an opportunity to reflect on where we have come from and on how we might see ourselves in the future.

During my Presidency, I also intend to hold a number of seminars which will explore themes important to our shared life that are separate from and wider than legislative demands, themes such as the restoration of trust in our institutions, the ethical connection between our economy and society, and the future of a Europe built on peace, social solidarity and sustainability.

The first of these seminars will focus on being young in Ireland. It will address issues of education, employment, emigration and mental health. I hope also that the seminars during the next seven years might also address more global issues, stressing the importance of the ethical connection between politics, the economy and society.

I recognize that our long struggle for freedom has produced a people who believe in the right of the individual mind to see the world in its own way, and indeed that independence of mind has given Ireland many distinguished writers, artists and scientists, who are often insufficiently celebrated.

However, in more recent years we saw the rise of a different kind of individualism – closer to an egotism based on purely material considerations – that tended to value the worth of a person in terms of the accumulation of wealth rather than their fundamental dignity. That was our loss – the source, in part, of our present difficulties. Now it is time to turn to an older wisdom that, while respecting material comfort and security as a basic right of all, also recognizes that many of the most valuable things in life cannot be measured by monetary success.

Our successes, after all, in the eyes of the world have been in the cultural and spiritual areas – in our humanitarian, peace-building and human rights work, in our literature, art, drama and song – and in how that drama and song have helped us cope with adversity, soothed the very pain they describe so well, and opened the space for new possibilities.

James Connolly said: 'Ireland without her people means nothing to me.' Connolly took pride in the past but, of course, felt that those who excessively worshipped that past were seeking to escape from the challenge of the present. He believed that Ireland was a work in progress, a country still to be fully imagined and invented – and that the future was exhilarating precisely in the sense that it was not fully knowable.

A decade of commemorations lies ahead – a decade that will require us to honestly explore and reflect on key episodes in our modern history; that will require us to draw on memory in a way that will enable us not only to be sensitive to differing and incomplete versions of that history, but also to remain open to reconciliation and the acceptance of different versions of memory.

A common shared future built on the spirit of co-operation and real participation in every aspect of the public world is achievable. In our rich heritage some of our best moments have been those that turned towards the future and a sense of what might be possible. That imagination of a better time to come brought us our independence. It is what has enabled us to overcome adversity and it is what will enable us to transcend our present difficulties and celebrate the real Republic that is ours for the making.

Every age, after all, must have its own Aisling and dream of a better, kinder, happier world.

Ní díomas ach dóchas a bheidh ag teastáil uainn ins na blianta dúsh-lánacha atá amach romhainn. Dóchas as ár n-oighreacht shaibhir, as ár ndúchas iolrach; dóchas as ár n-acmhainn samhlaíochta agus cruthaíochta; as an daonnacht choiteann a fáisceadh as stair chasta ár muintire i ngach cúinne d'Éirinn.
(It's not chauvinism but hope which will be necessary in the challenging years before us. Hope in our rich heritage, in our plural culture; hope in our capacity for imagination and creativity; in the common humanity generated from the complex history of our people in every corner of Ireland.)

It is my wish to be a President for all of the Irish, at home and abroad. We Irish have been a diasporic people for a great part of our history. The circumstances that have impelled and continue to force many citizens to seek a better life elsewhere are not ordained by some mysterious hand of fate. They challenge our capacity to create a sustainable economy and an inspiring model of the good society. We, in our time, must address the circumstances that cause involuntary emigration, and resolve that in the years ahead we will strive with all our energy and intellect, with mind and heart to create an Ireland which our young people do not feel they have to leave and to which our emigrants, or their children, may wish to return to work and live in dignity and prosperity. I invite all of the Irish, wherever they may be across the world, to become involved with us in that task of remaking our economy and society.

Agus, ár muintir atá lonnaithe i dtíortha ar fuaid an domhain mhóir, bíodh a gcás, a gcearta agus a ngaiscí siúd ar ár n-aire againn. Tá rian a saothair agus a ndíograis fágtha acu ar gach tír inar lonnaigh siad: ar an gcultúr polaitíochta agus creidimh, sna réimsí oideachais agus sláinte, san eolaíocht, san saol gnó agus sna h-ealaíona ar fad: agus i ngluaiseachtaí éagsúla ar son chearta daonna agus dínit an duine. Ní suarach iad na gaiscí seo mar thaisce inspioráide dúinne sa bhaile.
(And, may the plight, the rights and the achievements of our people living in countries across the wide world remain in our care. The fruits of their work and dedication have been left by them in every country where they resided: in culture, politics and faith, in areas of education and health, in science, business and in all of the arts; and in the various movements for human rights and for the dignity of the person. These are not inconsiderable achievements to inspire us here at home.)

Let these, then, be our shared hopes, our common purposes, as we face the future. We Irish are a creative, resourceful, talented people, with a firm sense of common decency and justice. Let us address the next seven years with hope and courage as we work together to build the future for our country.

Muintir na hÉireann, ar aghaidh linn le chéile leis an dóchas agus an mis-neach sin a bhí is ba choir a bheith i gcónaí in ár gcroí.

A Toast

A*Shoilse Banríon, A MHÓRGACHT RÍOGA:*
Your Majesty, Your Royal Highness:

Thank you for your kind and generous welcome and for the warm hospitality you have extended to me, to Sabina and to our delegation.

That welcome is very deeply felt and appreciated by me, and by the people of Ireland, whom I represent. However long it may have taken, Your Majesty, I can assure you that this first State Visit of a President of Ireland to the United Kingdom is a very visible sign of the warmth and maturity of the relationship between our two countries. It is something to be truly welcomed and celebrated.

Your Majesty:

You famously used some words of Irish during your State Visit to Ireland. Today I would also like to turn again to the oral tradition of our ancient language, and to quote a *seanfhocal*, or wise saying, often applied to the mutuality of relationships. It observes simply: *ar scáth a chéile a mhairimíd.*

Because *scáth* literally means shadow, this phrase is sometimes translated as 'we live in the shadow of each other'. However, there is a more open and more accommodating meaning. *Scáth* also means shelter.

The word embodies the simple truth that physical proximity makes mutual influence and interaction almost inevitable. But more importantly, I believe, it implies the opportunity, even the obligation, for reciprocal hospitality and generosity – the kind of generosity reflected in your words this evening when you encouraged us to embrace the best version of each other.

Ireland and Britain live in both the shadow and in the shelter of one another, and so it has been since the dawn of history. Through conquest and resistance, we have cast shadows on each other, but we have also gained strength from one another as neighbours and, most especially, from the contribution of those who have travelled over the centuries between our islands, and particularly in recent decades.

The contribution of Irish men and Irish women to life in Britain, which Your Majesty has acknowledged with such grace, is indeed extensive and lends itself to no simple description. It runs from building canals, roads and bridges in previous decades to running major companies in the present, all the while lending Irish personality and imagination to the English language and its literature.

Like so many of our compatriots, Sabina and I feel very much at home when visiting Britain, which should be the case with our nearest neighbour and our close friend. Tonight we celebrate the deeply personal, neighbourly connection which is embodied in the hundreds of thousands of Irish and British people who have found shelter on each other's shores.

Your Majesty:

When we are fortunate, history evolves into greater mutual understanding between peoples. The welcome that is so naturally afforded to British visitors in Ireland today was, I think, wholeheartedly expressed on the occasion of your State Visit in 2011. Your gracious and genuine curiosity, your evident delight in that visit, including its equine dimension, made it very easy for us to express to you and, through you to the British people, the warmth of neighbourly feelings. It laid the basis for an authentic and ethical hospitality between our two countries.

Admirably, you chose not to shy away from the shadows of the past, recognizing that they cannot be ignored when we consider the relationship between our islands. We valued your apt and carefully considered words when you addressed some of the painful moments of our mutual history, and we were moved by your gestures of respect at sites of national historical significance in Ireland.

These memorable moments and these moving words merit our appreciation and, even more, our reciprocity. While the past must be respectfully recognized, it must not imperil the potential of the present or the possibilities of the future – *ar féidireachtaí gan teorainn* – our endless possibilities of working together.

This present occasion, which completes a circle begun by your historic visit three years ago, marks the welcome transformation in relations between our countries – a transformation that has been considerably helped by the advancement of peace in Northern Ireland.

We owe a great debt to all of those who had the courage to work towards, and make manifest, that peace. I wish to acknowledge here the remarkable contributions of my predecessors Mary Robinson and Mary McAleese. I am especially pleased that former President McAleese, and her husband Martin, are here with us this evening.

We must, however, never set aside or forget those who died, were bereaved, or injured, during a tragic conflict. As the French philosopher Paul Ricoeur wrote, to be forgotten is to die twice. We owe a duty to all those who lost their lives, the duty to build together in peace; it is the only restitution, the only enduring justice we can offer them.

We share, also, the imperative to be unwavering in our support of the people of Northern Ireland as we journey together towards the shelter and security of true reconciliation. We celebrate what has been achieved but we must also constantly renew our commitment to a process that requires vigilance and care.

YOUR MAJESTY:

We have moved on from a past where our relations were often troubled, to a present where – as you have said – Ireland and the United Kingdom meet each other in mutual respect, close partnership and sincere friendship. That friendship is informed by the many matters of mutual interest in which we work together and support one another.

In recent times we have seen our two Governments working ever more closely together in the European Union and in the United Nations. We have seen deepening partnership in the area of trade, but also in development aid where we share a common commitment to tackling hunger and improving nutrition.

The future we each desire, and seek to work towards, is one where Ireland and the United Kingdom stand together to seek common opportunities and to face common global challenges as partners and friends.

YOUR MAJESTY:

Ar scáth a chéile a mhairimíd. The shadow of the past has become the shelter of the present. While we grieve together for lost lives, we will not let any painful aspect of our shared history deflect us from crafting a future that offers hope and opportunity for the British and Irish people.

We again thank you for the hospitality that allows us, on this most joyous occasion, to celebrate the bonds of mutual understanding between our two peoples, and the warm, enduring friendship on which we have so happily embarked.

I therefore invite you, distinguished guests, to stand and join me in a toast:

To the health and happiness of Her Majesty and
His Royal Highness, and the people of the United Kingdom;

To a creative co-operation and a sustainable partnership
between our countries and our peoples; and
To valued neighbours whose friendship we truly cherish.

Go raibh maith agaibh go léir.

State Visit to Britain, 2014

St Mary's Guildhall, Coventry

11 APRIL 2014

I AM DELIGHTED TO bring a memorable State Visit to a close in a city with so many Irish connections, and in a place that enjoys such great renown as a symbol of peace and reconciliation.

I have had a very long personal association with Britain, and have been visiting the country for over fifty years. I first came as a university student seeking work during the college holidays. My two sisters emigrated to England at the age of twenty, and worked for British Rail at Central Station and Victoria Station in Manchester. They both married in Manchester, one to a railwayman from Oldham whose family had worked on the railway for generations. My sister and her family still live there. My other sister married an Irishman from Mayo, whose family – with one exception – all lived in England.

When I came as a postgraduate student to Manchester University in 1968, and stayed with my sister in Corby Street near Belle Vue, I regularly moved between the two worlds of an Irish construction worker's family in Manchester and the realm of British academia. My field of research was apt – migration.

Over the years I have come here to stay in touch with my siblings and their families; to visit Irish community centres; to maintain fraternal contacts in the labour movement; and, as a parliamentarian, to advance inter-parliamentary links with my colleagues in Westminster. During all this time, including the decades of the 1970s and 1980s when the conflict in Northern Ireland cast a dark shadow over British–Irish relations, I was always impressed by the resilience of the Irish community in Britain.

In the 1960s, in Manchester and across Britain, monuments to the labour of Irish workers could be seen in the cities and throughout the countryside, especially the motorways but also on the building sites where Irish tradesmen and labourers were often the backbone of the workforce. The phrase 'the men who built Britain' was more than an idle boast. It was a statement of pride in the reputation for industry and capacity for hard work earned by our people.

There are other sectors of the economy, too numerous to list here but including agriculture, teaching and nursing, where routes of labour migration were carved especially deeply. Indeed, it was a great privilege for me this week to see the continuing contribution of Irish nurses and doctors to British medicine during my visit to University College Hospital in London.

During the 1950s, around half a million Irish men and women made the journey to Britain, my sisters among them. When we think of the circumstances in which these earlier generations of Irish emigrants moved to Britain, it is a joy to note that there is virtually no aspect of British civic or political life that has not been enriched by contributions from the Irish community. That success is due in no small part to the determination and character of those who settled here in more difficult times.

Today the Irish community has become one of the most dynamic in Britain. In my speech at the Guildhall in London earlier this week, I pointed to the contribution now being made, by our many highly skilled graduates, to British industry, to the professions, in commerce and in education. For this generation, migration is often temporary, or may even take the form of commuting, and many of these young people will return to Ireland enriched by the experience and education they gained here.

In marking the successes and achievements of those Irish men and women who have made those journeys and built new lives in Britain we must also, of course, recognize that for some of our people migration from Ireland was painful and traumatic. Many left difficult circumstances behind and some found hard lives in their new home. The story of the Irish in Britain has many dimensions, but as President of Ireland I am immensely proud today to bear witness to your continuing centrality in our national identity.

Of course British people too made the journey in the opposite direction, to Ireland – some for reasons of employment; others for reasons of family or romantic attachment; and others again because they just felt an affinity for the smaller island.

Since the time of Saints Patrick and Colmcille, there have been countless journeys in both directions across the Irish Sea. This afternoon, I would like to recall just two that have direct relevance to Coventry.

In September 1950 a young poet, born and raised in Coventry, moved to Belfast to take up a new job as Librarian at Queen's University. He was, by any definition, a migrant. His name was Philip Larkin, and over the next five years in Belfast he wrote some of the finest poetry of his career. Later, drawing on a migrant's sensibility, he described his family home. It is one of the most beautiful evocations of the memory of an emptied house:

> Home is so sad. It stays as it was left.
> Shaped to the comfort of the last to go
> As if to win them back.
> As if to win them back.

So, while we rightly celebrate the legacy of the contribution of Irish emigrants to this country, we should not forget the terrible human cost exacted by this aspect of our history on our own people, the leaving and the left, and the emptied landscape of possibility.

Two years after Philip Larkin returned to England, another poet left his native Belfast to take up a job as Director of the Herbert Art Gallery and Museum here in Coventry. John Hewitt would call this city his home for the next fifteen years and would memorably capture Coventry's great generous spirit as it rebuilt itself after the Blitz:

> *... this eager city,*
> *the tolerance that laced its blatant roar,*
> *its famous steeples and its web of girders*
> *as image of the state hope argued for*

Transience is the circumstance at the heart of these great poets' work, as it is at the heart of the experience of all migrants. When they arrived here, many Irish men and women did indeed find 'the state hope argued for', and we will never forget the generosity of those who held out the hand of friendship to them.

Standing here in this ancient Guildhall, in the shadow of your great Cathedral and under the watchful gaze of those two protagonists at the Battle of the Boyne, Kings William and James, I am reminded of the words of Nelson Mandela, at whose funeral I was honoured to speak: 'Courageous people do not fear forgiving, for the sake of peace.' What is true of great people might also be said of great cities. This great city has lived and continues to live by those words. In 1944, with the Second World War still raging and only a few years after Coventry had been devastated in the Blitz, and in an act of great empathy on your part, you reached out to another devastated city and twinned with Stalingrad, now Volgograd.

You rebuilt and dedicated your Cathedral to reconciliation and forgiveness – reminding the world, at a dark time, that humanity and compassion had not been extinguished. I was therefore honoured to be welcomed to Coventry Cathedral by Dean Witcombe and to have a number of its symbolic features associated with peace, reconciliation and ecumenical dialogue pointed out to me. I was particularly pleased to meet representatives of other Christian faiths in the Chapel of Unity.

Coventry is rightly respected for its outstanding work in the art of healing the wounds of past conflicts. Its story provides a powerful inspiration for those in Northern Ireland who are continuing to struggle with the legacy of conflict, and trying to make sure that the toxins of a divisive past do not poison our hopes for a shared future.

The lesson of Coventry is that peace will only be embedded when we each have the generosity to recognize the common humanity of the other, including former enemies, and to give respect to their differing perspectives and narratives.

In Coventry you have extended your hand in solidarity to cities all over the world, twinning with, among many others, Warsaw in 1957, Dresden in 1959 and, recognizing those strong Irish connections, Cork in 1958. Cork was, of course, the final stop for Queen Elizabeth during her visit to Ireland three years ago. Her Majesty's State Visit to Ireland was a groundbreaking event for Britain and Ireland. Our two nations have come a very long way in recent years in terms of mutual understanding and co-operation. It is a journey not yet complete, but we are both strongly committed to facing current and future challenges together. It has been my privilege during this State Visit to continue stretching the hand of friendship across the Irish Sea and, I hope, strengthening its grip. Sabina and I would like to take this opportunity to thank our hosts, Her Majesty the Queen and His Royal Highness, the Duke of Edinburgh for the warmth of their welcome and their kindness and hospitality over these past few days.

The programme of events during the visit has demonstrated the depth, authenticity and warmth of the relationship between our two countries. In virtually every area of life, the people of the United Kingdom and Ireland are co-operating with each other, learning from each other and supporting each other practically on a daily basis.

I cannot think of a better place to bring this State Visit to a close than among the Irish community: with the Irish in Britain, with the St Patrick's Club in Leamington Spa, which has just celebrated its fiftieth year; with the Coventry Irish Society; the Coventry Cork Poets Group; and the Coventry County Associations. You play a vital role by providing a 'home from home' for our community. I thank you for your fidelity to your homeland; for your solidarity with each other; and for the contribution you have made to the warm friendship that now exists between Ireland and the United Kingdom.

This State Visit has had its essential share of ceremonial formality, but at its heart it has been about the warmest of relations between close neighbours.

If I may be allowed a note of regret, it is that the late Seamus Heaney was not with us to witness this visit. Seamus and Marie rightly shared the table of honour at the State Dinner in Dublin Castle during Her Majesty's visit in May 2011. It was an honour merited not just by Seamus's poetic genius, but also by his reconciling influence within what he called the *Republic of Letters* and the *Republic of Conscience*, and above all by his enthralling, companionable presence.

In reflecting on what Seamus might have made of this State Visit to the United Kingdom, I thought of his lines:

> *Our pioneers keep striking*
> *Inwards and downwards,*
> *Every layer they strip*
> *Seems camped on before.*

The historical terrain shared by our two peoples has been the site of many and different struggles over the years. We, in this generation, are now the pioneers who are stripping away the old layers of the troubled past and creating a new path of hope and opportunity. As I conclude this first

State Visit by an Irish President to the United Kingdom, my earnest hope is that our two countries will continue to tread the path of neighbourly friendship together.

Go raibh míle maith agaibh agus rath Dé oraibh go léir.

State Visit to Britain, 2014

MIGRATION, DIASPORA AND THE FAMINE

Liverpool and Its Irish Migrants

THE JOHN KENNEDY LECTURE IN IRISH STUDIES, INSTITUTE OF IRISH STUDIES, UNIVERSITY OF LIVERPOOL

21 NOVEMBER 2012

I DOUBT THAT ANYONE in this room today would argue that there is any forum better suited than the Institute of Irish Studies at the University of Liverpool at which to consider together questions of Irish identity and the Irish migrant experience.

It is fitting in this most Irish of British cities, that the Institute of Irish Studies has developed, during its almost twenty-five years of existence, into an institute of the highest rank. It has made, and continues to make, a major contribution to understanding between these islands.

The first obvious fact is that geography itself made it inevitable that there would always be strong connections between this city and Ireland. And the travel was not only in one direction. When King John in 1207 granted Liverpool its charter, he cemented its status as the main port through which soldiers and administrators left England for the garrison in Ireland.

For centuries past, Liverpool has represented the first glimpse of Britain for generations of Irish migrants and travellers. The mighty docks of Liverpool symbolized a gateway; the mouth of the Mersey became a point of transition to a new life, much as Ellis Island and the Statue of

Liberty were for those men and women who travelled west, to New York and beyond. How appropriate, then, that one of the many plaques placed by the Great Hunger Memorial Committee should be at the Liverpool docks. As to the migration from Ireland to Britain, there has never been any single Irish migratory experience. There was always an element of circular migration in the movement of Irish people between Ireland and Britain; and this made such migrations different to the migrations of a classical kind to America or Australia.

When we think of the past, we must give the migrant experience its space; we should remember those Irish migrants who peopled that past, who came to Britain in vast numbers and in so much more difficult times than at present. They came regularly and seasonally at first, and then, between 1847 and 1857, became a flood and part of a struggle for survival. To give some idea of numbers, a witness before the British Parliament's Select Committee on Emigration commented on the pre-Famine Irish migration that, as long ago as 1827, he would not feel the least surprised to find that of a hundred men employed as labourers, ninety were Irish.

The Irish navvies occupy a central place in the history of Britain. First they built the canals, then the railways, then the roads and, in a recent century, the Channel Tunnel. Ultan Cowley titles his history of the Irish navvies well – *The Men Who Built Britain*. Between 1745 and 1830 4,000 miles of navigable water were constructed in the British Isles. Railway-building began and between 1830 and 1845 200,000 navvies were employed as 20,000 miles of rail were laid in Britain alone. In the building of the Manchester Ship Canal, which took six years, Irish labourers made up almost a third of the workforce of 16,000.

The sociologist Liam Ryan[1] has written of how emigration acted as a safety valve at times when Ireland struggled to cope with the economic

---

1   Liam Ryan, 'Irish Emigration to Britain since World War II', in *Migrations: The Irish at Home and Abroad*, edited by Richard Kearney (Irish American Book Company, 1991).

and social problems of its population. The post-Famine 'adjustment' meant that one son inherited at a very mature age, one woman married and the rest had to 'travel' or settle for a life as 'relatives assisting' on the family farm. In the decades that followed, emigration came to be a fact of life. It became accepted that at times of transition the promise of a modern way of life in Ireland could only be offered to 75 per cent of its population, as Ryan says:

> The remaining 25 per cent have had, for a long time past, a choice of unemployment at home or migration abroad... there is scarcely a single political, social, economic, intellectual or religious problem which has not been influenced directly or indirectly by emigration. Emigration is a mirror in which the Irish nation can always see its true face.

The 1950s alone would see a quarter of a million people emigrate, mostly to Britain – never less than 50,000 in any given year.

Irish emigration to Britain had, of course, been going on since the Middle Ages. Over time, this led to the existence of Irish communities in some large towns including London, Liverpool, Bristol, Canterbury and Norwich, and in garrison towns such as York. As a proportion of the population of such towns, they were not perceived as the threat they would later become. John Jackson estimates that the Irish in Britain numbered 419,256 in 1841, 727,326 in 1851 and 806,000 by 1861.

Irish seasonal migrants' lives were governed by the form and the cycles of British agricultural economics. Some Irish moved south and settled when the season was over. Economic hardship and lack of work pushed many people towards the ports. Even the one son inheriting what was often an unsustainable farm holding had to emigrate, at times. The prospect of comparatively well-paid employment in Britain's industrialized urban centres, letters of encouragement home from family members who had already emigrated, and the propaganda of shipping companies that told of the prosperous and beautiful life to be had abroad, all helped dislodge the potential migrants. And we must acknowledge that the sense of one's personal life being stifled and restricted at home also surfaces in migrant accounts.

It was in 1818 that the first steam packet service (the *Rob Roy*) linked Belfast to Glasgow. Within ten years, ships were also ferrying passengers from Dublin and Cork. The majority of those heading for Liverpool were destined for onward travel to North America. Growing competition among the shipping companies saw fares drop to as low as 10d. in steerage and 3d. on deck. This meant that the main ports of arrival were towns on the western side of Britain, and industrialized urban centres further inland.

For some, their journey to Liverpool was only a stepping stone for the longer journeys towards America and Australasia. Liverpool would be for many of those, later known as 'dhá bád' or 'two boat' people, their first stage. Given the danger of sea travel due to overcrowding, unsanitary conditions, inadequate food and water supplies, and the constant danger of illness and disease, many Irish migrants found that their journey ended while at sea.

Already in the 1841 census there were almost 50,000 Irish-born people living in Liverpool. For this Irish community, simply surviving was a daily struggle. Living conditions for the poor in Liverpool at that time were, as in so many cities, atrocious; overcrowding and disease were rife. The first public washhouse in Britain had been established in Liverpool in 1842 by a Derry woman called Kitty Wilkinson, who realized how vital good hygiene was for the prevention of the spread of disease during a cholera outbreak ten years earlier. Because of her crusade, the Baths and Washhouses Acts of 1846 and 1847 came into existence.

But the historical experience of the Irish in Liverpool is, of course, inextricably connected with the tragedy and the memory of the Famine of 1845 to 1847, which drove many more to Liverpool in search of escape.

In just three years during the Famine, almost 1.3 million Irish took the boat to Liverpool, sick, starving and seeking relief.

Often they left no surviving family behind to remember them. John Jackson in his *The Irish in Britain* (1963) wrote:

> More than 280,000 Irish people arrived in Liverpool in 1846 and less than half of them eventually embarked for destinations overseas. A further 300,000 entered Liverpool in 1847 and many of them, particularly the 'really poor', stayed on.

Many were Irish speakers. These waves of desperate Irish people seeking survival and speaking a foreign tongue were moving into urban spaces that had already experienced hostility and sectarianism. P. J. Waller, in his *Democracy and Sectarianism: A Political and Social History of Liverpool 1868–1939*, tells us how poverty, fever and Irishness came to be spoken of in the same breath in response to a wave of 'Famine Irish':

> In February 1847 Liverpool's fatalities from what was called "Irish fever" were 18 per cent, which was substantially above the national average.'

And as to poverty:

> Over 173,000 persons – probably 95 per cent of them Irish – were relieved in Liverpool from 18 to 26 January 1847.

One can easily imagine how a previously welcoming, warm environment could change as a tidal wave of arrivals replaced the previous streams, particularly when a sectarian demagoguery was available to whip up passions, with a compliant print media fuelling the flames.

During the crisis years of the Famine of 1845 to 1847, while it is estimated that over one million Irish perished at home, from hunger or, more commonly, from hunger-related diseases, in the decade following 1846 – when the floodgates of emigration opened to a population fleeing a stricken land – more than 1.8 million Irish emigrated. Over half of these fled during the Famine years of 1846–50.

Frank Neal's 'The Famine Irish in England and Wales', in Patrick O'Sullivan's *The Irish World Wide* series, has given us a valuable insight into the experience of flight from famine from the personal accounts of emigrants, including the story of the occupants of *The Wanderer*, a vessel with 200 'wretched' creatures from Skibbereen and the story of Jeremiah Sullivan, his wife and five children. Turned off his farm in Skibbereen, he sold his horse and cow for £3 and began the journey from Cork to Newport and started to walk to London. 'Death from Starvation' was the verdict of the coroner on the deaths of the three children, including the baby who had been kept alive on sugar and water as they begged their way to London.

We must never forget the suffering of the victims of the Famine, including those who perished en route to this city or shortly after arrival, as well as those who gave their lives helping the sick and dying. It is a testament to the people of Liverpool today that so much has been done to mark that dark period in our history, such as the Great Hunger Memorial, which was unveiled by my predecessor, Mary McAleese, in 1998, and where I laid a wreath earlier today.

What was the reaction to the arrival of this enormous wave of Irish fleeing famine? Graham Davis tells us of the fears it generated:

> It is no accident that the most heated reaction to Irish immigrants was found in the key reception points of Glasgow, Liverpool and Cardiff. The impression of being 'swamped' was real enough in Liverpool, the main point of entry, not only for the Irish settling in Britain, but also for the thousands of Irish who were on short-stay migration before embarking on the Atlantic voyage to North America. For a period in 1847, Liverpool was engaged in distributing famine relief to many

thousands of starving immigrants. Its institutions, already struggling to cope with its own resident population, were quite incapable of coping with the scale of an unprecedented emergency situation.

And, as Davis saw it:

> This crisis, already apparent before the famine influx, was exploited by local religious and political leaders, among whom Protestant Irishmen were prominent, whipping up anti-Catholic feeling as a means of gaining political control of the city council. This proved spectacularly successful, and as a consequence, religious hatred and sectarian violence found its most extreme and prolonged form in Liverpool. Religious riots blighted the Irish experience in other cities, Glasgow, Stockport, and Cardiff. The annual rituals of St Patrick's Day and Orange Day processions were rallying points for Catholics and Protestants which could spark off rioting and violence between the two communities. The establishment of the Catholic hierarchy in England in 1850 or the virulently anti-Catholic lectures of William Murphy and other Protestant zealots in the 1860s provoked rioting from indignant Protestants and Catholics. Yet, even in cities affected by the 'Murphy Riots', accompanying the anti-Catholic rhetoric aimed at the Irish, there was a pronounced revulsion among the majority of moderate Protestants, fearful that vulgar Catholic baiting only led to the destruction of property.

Graham Davis identifies a key feature at the source of the fears that led to anti-Irish feeling. In the chapter he contributed to Patrick O'Sullivan's *The Irish World*, he wrote:

> More influential in alarming the host community than the scale of immigration were the apparent levels of *concentration* of Irish

settlement… It was claimed that nearly one million poor Irish had
flooded into Liverpool in the first fourteen weeks of 1847; War-
rington and other towns around Liverpool were 'crowded with
them' by April.

At national level, the London *Times* had, together with *Punch* and others,
consistently developed a stereotypical version of the Irish as insatiable
in their demands, ungrateful and disloyal. They supported the British
Government's interpretation of Famine policy, and saw the Famine and
the response to it as a matter for local resolution, even going so far as to
suggest that the Famine was even providential in its causes. Time does
not allow, but the ownership structure of *The Times*, which defined its
editorial policy, is of the greatest importance in understanding official
attitudes and the ideological adherence to a non-interventionist strategy.
Trevelyan, who believed that fate should have its place in economic and
social policy, wrote editorials for *The Times*.

The later exodus of men, women and children meant that migrants
would carry an ongoing memory of hostility and culpable neglect at best,
and more usually an abiding communal recall of the consequences of
imperial degradation. That memory would live on beyond the seas, a fact
recognized decades after the Famine in *The Times*' own editorials. The
London paper was quoted in *The Nation*, May 1860, as follows:

> If this goes on as it is likely to go on… The United States will become
> very Irish… So an Ireland there will still be, but on a colossal scale,
> and in a new world. We shall only have pushed the Celt westwards.
> Then, no longer cooped between the Liffey and the Shannon, he will
> spread from New York to San Francisco, and keep up the ancient feud
> at an unforeseen advantage… We must gird our loins to encoun-
> ter the nemesis of seven centuries' misgovernment. To the end of
> time a hundred million spread over the largest habitable area in

the world, and, confronting us everywhere by sea and land, will remember that their forefathers paid tithe to the Protestant clergy, rent to the absentee landlords, and a forced obedience to the laws which these had made.

In Liverpool itself the adjustment of the Irish community took place slowly and was assisted by the emergence of those who learned that one could be both Irish and British at the same time, and whose lives reflected a shared human response to poverty, unemployment and casual labour.

The story of Irish people in Liverpool was, and continued to be into the modern period, one of reinvention, both for those who travelled from Ireland to Liverpool and for those who grew up here as part of the Irish community, some of whom regularly returned to Ireland, in later years even coming back to Ireland as permanent residents.

Irish history of course owes a significant debt to Liverpool and its people. During his lifetime, the great trade union leader James Larkin was inclined to claim that he was born in Ireland and to have moved to Liverpool in his youth, but we now know that he was born in 1876 in Liverpool, in Toxteth, to parents from Armagh. Like many Irish people born and raised here to a working-class family, he found employment in the docks, where he was known as a strong and sober worker, before gaining a permanent position in his trade union.

Larkin was well aware of the use his political opponents would make of his being born outside Ireland. Their propaganda suggested that this in some way diminished his commitment to Ireland. He knew, and frequently spoke in public about the fact that to be Irish did not mean that the concerns and needs of those from other backgrounds were of less importance. He could state with conviction that he loved Ireland 'as I love no other land and no other people', while at the same time devoting his energy to the great questions of international politics.

Larkin's Liverpool background provided him with the key insight that a narrow form of national identity can, too often, be used to mask class expropriation, privilege and exploitation. However, the movement of ideas and political struggle, as much as the movement of people, is never solely in a single direction. While Larkin's career can be seen as an example of a Liverpool-born Irishman's influence on the Irish political landscape, one that was informed by the migrant experience, Irish politics itself has often been important as a divisive and at times dominant theme within British parliamentary politics: 'Britain's Irish problem'.

Earlier this year, we marked the centenary of the introduction of the Third Home Rule Bill, and the ensuing Ulster Crisis. It is sometimes difficult to appreciate the extent to which Irish political questions and political figures dominated Westminster in the years before the First World War.

Ireland's British problem and Britain's Irish problem have to be understood in the context of poverty and the social consequences of the Industrial Revolution and the new forms of capital and labour of an age of empire. Time allows me to refer to just one, but significant, parliamentary example. T. P. O'Connor, originally from Athlone, was MP for Liverpool for over thirty years, from 1885 to 1929. He was famously the only Irish nationalist MP ever elected to a constituency outside Ireland. In his time at Parliament, he saw the introduction of the three Home Rule Bills, as well as the Easter Rising, the First World War, partition and independence. His speeches show an ethical conviction combined with pragmatism. The language itself displays a familiarity with the writings of Engels on Manchester from the 1840s:

> The Tory Party still remains the party of the monopolists and the selfish, but it has learned that household suffrage means a con-siderable weapon in the hands of working men, and, accordingly, though it may put its tongue in its cheek, it keeps that tongue very civil whenever it begins to utter opinion. Furthermore, Liverpool

was not a manufacturing town with a spine of skilled workmen who could, ceteris paribus, command wages whatever their opinions. Liverpool's social structure was 'honeycombed' with purely commercial interests. No one knows where the influence of a single wealthy family may begin or end. The clerk is afraid of losing his situation, the shopkeeper a customer, and so on through the whole gamut from high to low.[2]

In his career, O'Connor demonstrates that strain of Irishness which ran and is still running through British politics, giving strength to the claim that Liverpool itself is perhaps the quintessentially Irish city in Britain, a city that was at the heart of an industrial revolution and open not only to trade, but to the human flotsam and jetsam that came from the sea, including the distressed Irish refugees.

This cosmopolitanism, the city's locus as a place of migration, in which the Irish experience has been central, is one of the key elements that made modern Liverpool such a dynamo of creative energy in the British cultural sphere. It very successfully celebrated a year as City of Culture in 2008.

The number of Irish-born in Britain grew steadily throughout the twentieth century, reaching a peak of almost one million in the 1960s. And it was in the 1960s that Liverpool became associated with the major cultural, social and political changes taking place across the world. The Irish in Liverpool were to experience and experiment with new sights and sounds as the town went through its own extraordinary cultural revolution.

Liverpool had the Beatles. Like Jim Larkin and others, John Lennon and Paul McCartney grew up in a city in the throes of great change, a dynamic place, a gateway to and from the rest of Britain. They became a global phenomenon, innovative and at the cutting edge of artistic

---

2   P. J. Waller, *Democracy and Sectarianism: A Political and Social History of Liverpool 1868–1939* (Liverpool University Press, 1981).

experimentation, while at the same time comfortable in their identities, and rooted in the city from which they emerged. In this, they typified the experience of later generations of migrant families.

Their first, and only, performances in Ireland, fifty years ago this month, were a revelation, something emancipatory, much more than an overseas tour – an invitation to those who were young in Ireland to a version of freedom that had been forbidden for more than a century, a suggestion that the presentation of the self could include rhythm, the body, longing and love, and all without guilt. And Liverpool would continue to give the world original and popular musical forms, music with an oblique Irish contribution.

The Beatles were certainly emblematic of their time, of that moment when popular culture and the creative avant garde were in sync, and when music, writing, art and performance played a key role in the struggles for new freedoms, for free speech and civil rights. And we should not forget that three of the four Beatles were of Irish extraction, nor that in their first television appearance in 1962 they were introduced by another Irishman, Gay Byrne, then working for Granada television.

We should remember too that the music travelled in both directions. Irish groups and artists were frequent and welcome performers in Liverpool, mixing and merging folk, ballads and rock and roll.

Within living memory are the stories of the second major wave of Irish emigration, after the Second World War – some of the 250,000 Irish people who came to Britain between 1950 and 1960. And it is to them and their descendants in particular that we owe thanks for the preservation, nurturing and promotion of Irish heritage and culture in Liverpool.

It was these generations, Irish-born and Liverpool-born, who supported and strengthened the traditional Irish organizations such as the GAA and established new ones, such as the Irish Centre, first at Mount Pleasant and now at St Michael's, and the Irish Community Care Merseyside, which continue to go from strength to strength.

Organizations in Liverpool and its surrounding areas were not limited by their geography. They recognized the importance of contact with and support for Irish organizations in other parts of Britain. The first national chairman of the Federation of Irish Societies was a Liverpool man, the late Tommy Walsh. He laid the foundation for what is now a vital advocacy organization for the Irish community throughout Britain.

It was their willingness to give so freely of their time, energy and imagination that ensured the survival and continued success of community and cultural organizations in Liverpool. They embodied the particular virtue of so many Irish people that we try to ensure, if I may use a celebrated phrase that Liverpool has made its own, that nobody will have to walk alone. As Tommy Walsh says in his book *Being Irish in Liverpool*, 'helping... came naturally'.[3] Without the volunteers, many Irish organizations simply could not deliver their valuable and essential services.

That spirit and those virtues are alive and well today. And the work of these organizations is still as vital as ever; though many in the Irish community have done exceedingly well here in Liverpool, there are still those, from student to pensioner, who are vulnerable, who need our support, comfort and care.

And of course, the historically strong connections between Liverpool and Ireland continue today. Liverpool and Dublin are twin cities; thousands of Irish people support Liverpool football teams and travel regularly for matches; Irish culture is celebrated every year by 'The Liverpool Irish Festival'; thousands of Irish students study here.

These reflections on our past, and on our many reinventions, our multiple modernizations, should also encourage us to look forward with confidence to a future of renewed and strengthened co-operation between our two countries.

Liverpool represents something unique in the Irish migrant imagination.

---

3   Tommy Walsh, *Being Irish in Liverpool* (St Michael's Irish Centre, 2011), p. 143.

It is both a home and a crossroads, a place where the Irish have moved to, and moved from. It occupies a special position in the British–Irish relationship, a place of exchange, economic, cultural and political, where identities and borders become fluid and blurred. It is both Irish and British, and also something very much more. It is cosmopolitan in the best, inclusive sense.

Those of us who live in Ireland should also, I suggest, remember those British neighbours who so often welcomed their new Irish friends and helped them to make a home in this country. Half of my own family worked, married and reared their families in Britain. Today a further generation moves easily between Ireland and Britain.

It is important to remember that the warm bilateral relationship that we enjoy today with Britain is founded to a large extent upon the lives and contributions of generations of Irish emigrants who settled in this country. Its strength is a testament to the generations of Irish people who did so much to make Britain what it is today while at the same time fostering understanding, tolerance and co-operation between our two countries.

The Queen's visit last year to the Garden of Remembrance to honour those who fought against Britain for Irish independence, and the ceremony at Islandbridge where the Queen and President McAleese together commemorated the thousands of Irishmen who gave their lives in British uniform in the Great War, underlined how far our two nations have come, how successfully we have left the shackles of the past behind us and emerged as confident partners on the world stage.

Of Migrants and Memory

I T IS AN honour to be asked to deliver the British Council Lecture and a particular pleasure to be asked to do so in Belfast and here at Queen's University.

I am glad to speak as part of a continuous reflection on identity and belonging, so well represented in the British Council's publications – the four volumes of *Lives Entwined* – to which my words are a response, in particular to Volume Three, with its beautiful essays on identity and memory, such as Olivia O'Leary's, and Volume Four, with its frank and impressively honest expressions by young people of their experiences of identity, their encounters with others and their wish to see the full flowering of a peace yet to be encountered at a wider community level. It is interesting to contrast the undeniable optimism of the reflections in Volume Three with the uncertainty that is at the heart of Volume Four.

Fiú sular tháinig na foilseacháin seo amach ba mhinic a bhain an British Council leas as an aidiacht 'entwined' le cur síos a dhéanamh ar na naisc dhaonna i gcroílár na gcomhcheangal sna hoileáin seo. Go dearbh,tugann an ceithre imleabhar sa tsraith Lives Entwined léargas iontach ar cé chomh casta is atá na naisc dhaonna seo agus an dóigh ina bhfuil siad ag athrú de shíor. (Even before these publications, the British Council has often used the adjective *entwined* to describe the human connections which lie at the heart of relationships on these islands. The four volumes in the *Lives Entwined* series do indeed illuminate wonderfully the complexity, and the ever-changing nature of these human connections.)

The word 'entwined' may seem particularly apt at first glance. It contains the notion of strength and also of a multiplicity of strands, not one source of connection but many, woven as much by custom and accident as by design. But 'entwined', as a concept, contains too a sense of entanglement, of knots tightly made and difficult to undo, and I wish, in this lecture, to consider the function of memory in the confrontation of stereotypes. The undoing of the difficult knots of memory, I suggest, requires a willingness to acknowledge old destructive assumptions if we are to share together an ethics of memory that will serve a still maturing peace in the present – one that may become, we all hope, an enduring peace.

That emerging dialogue about the past demands a reworking of memory. The project must not stop at that, of course. It must generate a process of inclusive suggestions and actions that will create a future that is imaginative, kind, non-judgemental, forgiving and that offers a truly human co-existence. To get there requires the letting-go of old stereotypes invented to serve power relationships, and sustained by myths reinforced in the wider culture.

When I spoke at Magee College last April on 'The Transforming Power of Culture' I drew on Richard Kearney's use of the late French philosopher Paul Ricoeur's work on the ethics of memory. Professor Kearney argued that we must acknowledge the conflict between narratives of the different sides to a conflicted history, and also proposed ways to assist in their exchange and ultimate revision. He suggested five steps, which I explained in more detail in that lecture: first, an ethic of narrative hospitality; second, an ethic of narrative flexibility; third, narrative plurality; fourth, a transfiguration of the past and, finally, pardon.

Thinking since I first read Professor Kearney's work as to how we might make, all of us on these islands, a journey that would release us for the future and all of its shared possibilities, I am struck by the importance of examining the stereotypes that affect our view of each other. In addition to rejecting a false, accommodating amnesia about events, we simply cannot ignore the consequences of the crippling versions of 'the other' that enabled us to speak in the past of what was essentially 'Irish' or essentially 'British'.

That we are, happily, in a new time of warm reciprocal relationships provides us with an opportunity to examine the sources of the stereotypes we have had of each other, and which have to be acknowledged in order to let go of them. It goes without saying that the revision which will bring the most benefit has to be one which both sides of our entangled relationship are called upon to undertake, if the knotted sleeve of history is to be unwound and remade – a commitment to a mutual self-interrogation in history.

None of this is to take away from the magnificence of generous gestures that have already been made. To choose an obvious example, Fintan O'Toole in his essay 'Chums' in Volume Four of *Lives Entwined* captures the importance of Her Majesty Queen Elizabeth's visit to the Garden of Remembrance and its powerful significance:

> The ceremony in the Garden of Remembrance transformed the visit by making it also about them, the English. It wasn't just the Irish who were being bravely mature: it was also the English. Generations of English superciliousness towards Ireland (the suave, upper-class, good-natured sort being the worst) was disavowed in that moment. The queen managed a dignified humility and simplicity that were the polar opposites of condescension. Her gesture was not, as some overexcited commentators and headline writers sought to insist, some kind of homage to the rebels who beat the Brits. It was more meaningful than that.
>
> It was a simple acknowledgement that Ireland is a different place,

with its own history and mythology, its own encoded meanings.
Different, that is, but equal.[4]

'Separate but equal' was the injunction Olivia O'Leary's mother gave to her daughter, as recorded in Olivia's very beautiful essay, and this phrase was used as a title for Volume Three of *Lives Entwined*. It is a good phrase to remember.

The task of undoing stereotypes can never be achieved unless it involves a revision that includes all of the entwining ideas and memories with which we have bound ourselves. To exclude or evade awkward moments is to create an opportunity for a malignant future.

I find it useful to begin our interrogation of stereotypes with the experience of migration. The late Edward Said commented that everything that is really interesting happens in the interstices of narratives. And it is perhaps in the area of migrant lives that this is most clearly demonstrated. Our social sciences have, I suggest, been too sedentary in their assumptions about human migration. They have missed what literature has often caught: the human negotiation of the spaces between the place of origin and final destination.

Transience, after all, is the defining feature of the migratory experience all over the world; and it is on migrants, migrant communities and particularly migrant children that the cruel anti-immigrant stereotype falls most heavily.

At certain stages of human migration populations mingle and change takes place. When the disabling stereotype is not given free play, so much is possible. Yet the context for its emergence has to be recognized. For example, Ireland and Scotland share a mythology, a number of languages, a fine musical tradition and a great deal of history. Irish migrants in the fifth century – the Scoti – gave Scotland its name. The masterpiece

---

4   *Britain and Ireland: Lives Entwined*, Vol. 4, p. 38.

most readily associated with Ireland – the Book of Kells – was made on the island of Iona. A Gaelic political culture survived in the Scottish Highlands long after it had been brought to an end in Ireland.

These connections also contain paradoxes that have value for us today. The strong Protestantism in the Scots Gaelic tradition, for example, gives us access to new ways of thinking about language and identity in our own nationalist and unionist traditions.

Much of the pattern is made up of more specific local connections, such as the seasonal migration from Donegal and Achill Island for 'tattie-hoking' on potato farms in Scotland between June and October each year. There are traces of these links even today, for example in the Scottish tunes brought home by Donegal fiddlers. Such benign residual consequences, which we must cherish, nevertheless occurred in the context of an economic relationship between two economies, one of them powerful, the other relatively powerless. Celebrating the music and the literature does not require any amnesia about the economic or the human consequences of such power relations.

Yet much of the migrant experience is lost to sight in Scotland. In contrast to the Irish in America, Irish emigrants to Scotland remained locked in relative disadvantage, educationally and socially, until well into the last century. It was not until the mid-century that their story was told – and then largely by others. The circumstances of their exclusion, imposed or chosen, is deserving of our attention.

The migrant is better represented in literature than in the social sciences. Patrick McGill, Dónall Mac Amhlaigh and others writing in their diaries, and a later generation of writers such as Tom Murphy and Edna O'Brien, would give voice to that experience in the novel and in the theatre. They wrote of the immigrant caught between two worlds but belonging fully to neither.

The way migrants present themselves is complicated. Not only do the colonized and the colonizer take images of each other into their personae, but they see also the value of a mask; and so many of our relationships on these islands have been conducted from behind masks.

James C. Scott's work *Domination and the Arts of Resistance*, which dealt with strategies of defence, effectively overturned, at a theoretical level, the notion of false consciousness as applied to peasant behaviour. Far from being in the grip of false consciousness, what seems to be cunning peasant deceit to one participant in an exchange (the landlord, the policeman or the magistrate) is a survival strategy for the other. This defensive strategy evokes, in turn, a particular stereotypical response. The encounter is staged behind masks that are culturally crafted and painted by both sides.

There is an old example of this masked exchange in English theatre. Helen Burke wrote of Sir Robert Howard's *The Committee*, produced in 1662, which sets a discussion taking place in a London street between two Cavaliers – Colonel Careless and Colonel Blunt, both hoping for a reversal of the confiscation of their estates by the Puritans – and their encounter with a blanket-clad figure who, when asked his identity, states:

> *A poor Irishman, and Christ*
> *Save me and save you all,*
> *I prithee give me sixpence*
> *good mastero*

Such an exchange, Burke tells us, went on to become one of those set pieces that audiences used to assess the skills of those performers who were engaged to perform the stage Irishman 'line of business'.[5]

In her essay, Burke argues not only for the significance of this stereotype for the following centuries, but suggests that we in contemporary Ireland have much to learn from an examination of such images of 'the other'

---

5   For a discussion of 'lines of business' see Lisa Freeman, *Character's Theater: Genre and Identity on the Eighteenth-Century English Stage* (University of Pennsylvania Press, 2001), pp. 32–3.

when we in our turn are dealing with immigration in a way that is perhaps tolerant but stops far short of the recognition of equals. She puts it thus:

> Howard's blanket-clad beggarly figure acquired its cultural currency because it provided a comforting fiction of immigrant management and control for the expansionist, market-driven nation that came into being in the post-Restoration period and of the prehistory and afterlife of this fetishized subject/object also helps to explain the entrenched nature of the resistance that Irish immigrants faced as they sought to advance socially or economically in Britain in the centuries that followed. Recent scholarship on the treatment of the non-Irish immigrant in contemporary Ireland also provides a useful point of entry into this analysis. Present-day Ireland prides itself on having become more cosmopolitan and more multicultural in recent years, a self-congratulatory image that, as Gavan Titley points out, is reflected in advertisements and in the media in 'stylised and aestheticised tableaux of difference and diversity'.
>
> This celebratory depiction of a multicultural Ireland, however, as he and others have noted, functions rather to manage diversity than to fully engage with its challenges and complexities; and in the context of what is actually happening on the ground in Ireland, it acquires something of the status of a soothing mystification.[6]

Centuries after the first production of *The Committee*, in Edna O'Brien's story *Shovel Kings* one immigrant says of another that he 'doesn't belong in England and ditto in Ireland'.

But there have been welcome changes. During the summer, I was

---

6 Gavan Titley, 'Celtic, Christian and Cosmopolitan: "Migrants" and the Mediation of Exceptional Globalization', in Debbie Ging, Michael Cronin and Peadar Kirby (eds), *Transforming Ireland: Challenges, Critiques, Resources* (Manchester University Press, 2009), p. 166.

privileged to attend the Druid Theatre's staging of a trilogy of Tom Murphy's plays in London: two of them dealt with the Irish emigrant experience in all of its rawness and complexity, and the other with the searing tragedy of the Great Famine. They were rapturously received by the theatre critics.

Drawing on my son John Higgins's work on violence in the early plays of Tom Murphy, I was moved to read again the reviews of Kenneth Tynan and Harold Hobson, critics I had held in awe when I was a student of English literature. Reacting to the first London production in the 1960s of *A Whistle in the Dark*, one of them suggested that the Home Secretary should deport not only the playwright but all 'Irishmen'. One said, 'This is arguably the most uninhibited display of brutality London theatre has ever witnessed'. The other suggested that, while never afraid of meeting an Irishman, 'he would not like to meet Mr Murphy after dark'. Huge progress has been made in the intervening years in changing what was once a collision of stereotypes.

Because so much of our migrant experience was invisible – and the voice of the migrant was rarely captured – we easily overlook it and its distinctive concerns and cadences can often be lost to us. So many in both of our nations are, as a result of migration, neither fully British nor fully Irish.

There were also, of course, frozen images of the English in Ireland. Somerville and Ross's *Experiences of an Irish R.M.* had an ironic view of obtuse English visitors and officials. George Bernard Shaw was rather more blunt about them. Today, the English language does not exist in Ireland as the memory of an imposed vernacular. It is the language not only of Shakespeare and Shelley and Blake, but also of Yeats, Joyce, Beckett and Heaney and all those of us who use it and love it, including those who honour the writers who have been such a great force in the cause of our borderless humanity. Many of our contemporary poets write in Gaelic and English, and some in several other languages, including the minority languages of Europe.

Imirce – an mórshruth leanúnach de dhaoine soir siar, ó thuaidh agus ó dheas,chuig na hoileáin seo agus uathu – ar chuid dár stair agus dár neart í. Éilíonn an imirce gníomh daonna na hathnuachana – ní hamháin sa duine aonair ach i ngach sochaí dár gcuid, ag cothú ár ndearctha agus ár modh machnaimh agus bíonn sé ár dtástáil maidir le meas ar éagsúlacht lena chinntiú nach mbeimid sásta go deo le caoinfhulaingt uireasach.
(Migration – the great and constant flow of people east and west, north and south, to and from these islands – constitutes both our history and our strength. It is in itself a great call for a human act of renewal – not only of the individual but of our societies, and it demands that we respect difference, and never be satisfied with an inadequate tolerance.)

Historically, to leave one place for another has always involved a loss of certainty. But the journey into the unknown can also be a beginning of self-discovery and of growth. For example, the English language was changed by Caribbean and African poets who, as Derek Walcott put it, 'cannot curse the circumstance of the encounter without remembering that it gave to me the tongue of Shakespeare'.

To migrate voluntarily or involuntarily is to break a connection, lose a comforting intimacy of thought and being. Philip Larkin, who spent some years as sub-librarian at this University, wrote at that time that 'to start in a new place is always to feel incompetent and unwanted'.

The literature of the Irish in Britain does not reflect any single experience of Irishness there but rather multiple experiences, many neglected. In his *The Literature of the Irish in Britain 1725–2001*, Dr Liam Harte describes the significance and limitations of this body of literary work:

> The best are powerful acts of imagination in their own terms, meditations on how journeys 'across the water' breed strange and unexpected dichotomies, produce new patterns of seeing, living and remembering, prompt different stories about who we are and where

we belong. Even the middling formulaic works, with their peculiarly vivid reflections of personality and experience, deserve better than to be airily consigned to the midden of literary history. In offering us intimate glimpses of interior worlds, these variegated acts of self-portraiture help us to understand better the role that migrant imagination and its witness have played in shaping those fluid, contrapuntal concepts – home, place, belonging – that are themselves cognates of that most labile and vexing of abstractions: Irishness.

Dr Harte's intention is clearly to demolish through the witness of literature the myth of a homogeneous Irish migratory experience. He describes his book as:

> a contribution to the ongoing project of purging any lingering traces of the myth of homogeneity that clings to the diffuse entity 'the Irish in Britain', and the related task of dispelling assumptions that the experience of immigrants was the same throughout England, Scotland and Wales. Autobiography, as many scholars have argued, is uniquely poised to capture the complex, multi-dimensional nature of historical reality... even though the writing self remains elusive.

He issues a caveat as to method and theory:

> I regard much of this material as a form of resistance writing through which culturally disempowered and displaced subjects seek to become known autobiographical agents taking charge of their own representation – a case of the written-off attempting to write themselves back into social and cultural history, if you will.

Linked to this struggle of the migrant in a new and strange place is a sense of invisibility. Joseph O'Connor, writing of the Irish in another great immigrant city, has spoken of the windows of tenements in New York behind which 'life was made, losses endured and hope nurtured while out in the street the whole world went past never looking up at the windows'.

This, however, is not quite right. Let us not forget what we owe to the rich exilic tradition in literature. The late Josephine Hart, echoing Frank O'Connor's comment that 'an Irishman's private life begins at Holyhead', spoke of 'the great gift of exile', of the liberation that it can bring.

Migration has broken down barriers to understanding, made modernizers of us, taught us to maintain poise in the face of change; to live in two, or even more, worlds at once; to adapt and to move between those milieux in a continual process of change as we strive towards the realization of the human possibilities we share with others. Migration has created regional and local connections far more complex and profound than conventional political relationships.

We in this island are involved in a new kind of symbolic migration – from peace to true reconciliation. In the peace process, we have been engaged in one of the most ambitious and far-reaching political projects of our times.

The results, and we must say this with all due caution, realizing that much has still to be secured and that so much has yet to be even begun, show that lives have been transformed beyond what might have been imagined when we began that journey. We remember the great moments of public reconciliation. But there are quiet moments also, the stuff by which the ordinary is made divine. Harry Clifton in his poem 'Deep Ulster' has reminded us of what it is to live in the ordinary curiosity that the absence of fear, the assurance of peace, makes possible:

> To dream, just potter,
> In the yard, to fiddle with local stations
> In the kitchen, where news that is no news
> Finally, at last, fills up the years
> With pure existence.

The sense of entanglement and horrific memory is most vividly present in the lives of those who lost loved ones during the Troubles, who live with terrible injuries and the legacy of violence. More than any other group, they have been asked – and are asked daily – to make a most difficult accommodation for peace. No group has done more to bring about the benefits we have all gained than they have, and I salute them. Theirs is a huge moral gift. The bereaved are asked to 'do what must be done' every day that they are forced to live with loss. Those who have not lost can talk more easily – even, at times it must seem to the wounded, glibly – of 'moving on', but that is not easily done. The challenge of reconciling with those who caused that loss is a dreadful one.

But those of us who are more fortunate face a challenge also: to make sure that we do not allow new divisions to arise between those who suffered and those who did not, between those who live every day with what happened to them and those who are intent on 'moving on'.

Part of that challenge is to root out hatred from our midst. Hatred is a word that has almost dropped out of our public discourse. We have become accustomed to talking of sectarianism, but is that not hatred by another name? It is bred by intolerance and indeed by an inability to change. It is not unique to any one group or place. It operates in two directions, one act of disregard feeding off another. Jack McConnell has described it as a secret shame. Yet if we fail to name it and discuss it, we blind ourselves to the harm it can do.

The great benefits that flow from such open horizons are well illustrated here in Belfast's thriving arts scene. The Belfast Festival kept open lines of communication and of inspiration across the world during some of the most difficult days of the Troubles. During the 1970s, the Festival brought Joseph Beuys and the Royal Swedish Ballet to Belfast, among many other international artists.

We know how important these events are at times of great stress. Dubliners still remember, for example, the day in 1973 that the England rugby team defied IRA death threats to travel to Ireland and play to a standing ovation at Lansdowne Road – all stereotypes suspended for the enjoyment of a game that knew no borders and was simply a graceful human event.

The points of connection that I described earlier are addressing some of the most important challenges of peace, because ultimately these are not issues of politics or legislation or policing. The solution lies not just with government – though government bears a heavy responsibility – but with countless individuals who take a journey into the unknown, animated by a generosity of spirit, and who are willing to review the narratives they know, are willing to listen to the narrative of the other, to pause, review, forgive, allow or pardon.

The next stage of the peace process may lead us to the peaceful enjoyment of the complex ways in which our lives are intertwined.

It was George Bernard Shaw who first used the words made famous by John F. Kennedy: 'Some men see things as they are and ask "why?" Others dream things that never were and ask "why not?"' For the past twenty years, as if making up for lost time, we have been asking 'why not?,' and the answers have brought us to unexpected places.

There are more things that we are doing together every month, areas where we are not disabled by any stereotypes, old or new. Over 1,000 flights connect Britain and Ireland every week. The flow of trade between our countries amounts to €1 billion per week. Britain is our largest market for tourism and the largest market for our indigenous exports, and the benefits flow in both directions: Britain exports more to Ireland than to all of the major emerging economies combined. Forty-five thousand Irish people sit on the boards of British companies.

But some areas are taken for granted, to the extent that their importance might be overlooked. The first is culture, and by this I mean sport and entertainment as much as theatre and literature. The most vivid reminder of this came during the London Olympics at the first ever women's boxing finals, when Team GB's Nicola Adams from Leeds fought for gold in the first bout and Ireland's Katie Taylor from Bray fought for gold in the second. The ExCel arena was filled with Irish and British fans who cheered as one, first for Nicola Adams and then for Katie Taylor. It was a unique moment when a stadium full of Irish fans sang 'Olé Olé' for a British athlete from Leeds. Perhaps this is what Joseph O'Connor means when he writes of the 'shared citizenship of affection' or, as others might put it, 'being neighbourly'. But perhaps this should be no cause for surprise. Over 20,000 Irish people live in Leeds, which has particularly strong links to Co. Mayo. For its part, Bray has its Royal Hotel and has been the location for two of the best-known films dealing with English and Scottish mythology – *Excalibur* and *Braveheart*.

These are manifestations of lives entwined.

As to what is formally recalled, what should be remembered, what should not be forgotten: in a decade of centenaries we are able to include, and honour, all those Irish who died for the ideal they thought was important, both those who helped create the Irish State and those who shaped the United Kingdom, and all the lives lost, including the 200,000 Irishmen who fought in the British Army in the First World War.

When the children and grandchildren of migrants take pride and inspiration in their past, that can help unlock new potential in society – as the United States has learnt to its great benefit. The growing pride felt by those of Irish ancestry in Britain and those of British ancestry in Ireland will be a source of energy, inspiration and vigour for society.

We can certainly take pride in what Irish emigrants and their descendants have contributed to British culture – to popular music, for example, where the Irish influence extends from the Beatles to the Pogues, Dexy's Midnight Runners, Oasis and The Smiths, John Lydon of the Sex Pistols and many others. These are examples not just of lives entwined but of very creative human connections.

There are, of course, challenges we still face together, in Europe, in Northern Ireland, Britain and Ireland. Foremost among these is the necessity of providing jobs for a talented new generation emerging from our schools and colleges.

Our common future needs the creativity of our young people, and we must ask how we can avoid new divisions between those with good prospects of finding a job and those with poor prospects – or no prospect at all. For society in general, that absence of hope can only lead, in the words of a poet and teacher here at Queen's University, Sinéad Morrissey, to

> *A delicate unravelling of wishes*
> *That leaves the future unspoken*

To conclude, then, no matter how effective the political and economic solutions we find to these challenges, circular migration will continue to be a fact of life – within and between our societies and further afield. It can already be seen in the vibrant young Irish community in London and in the growing numbers of British citizens working in Ireland. This has always been the basis of our shared citizenship of affection.

So if today the number-five batsman on England's cricket team and the out-half on their rugby team bear Irish names, and if many of Ireland's international soccer players are born in England, I predict that this trend will only continue.

And just as these connections can help make us more resilient, more creative and in some cases, perhaps, more sensitive and reconciled, they can also bring surprise results, endless possibilities, *féidireachtaí gan teórainn*.

As I have said on other occasions, no matter how rooted and sedentary our lives, we are all migrants – if not in space, then certainly in time. We are all the richer for the interconnectedness that migration brings with it, facing a shared future beyond the hubris of false certainties. We go where our intertwined lives take us.

May I illustrate the point by using one of the languages that enrich our societies and our thinking. This is Nuala Ní Dhomhnaill's account of a journey begun in hope and apprehension that concluded with undreamt-of rewards – Moses's journey in a basket woven of reeds. I will read it first in Irish and then in its translation into English by Paul Muldoon:

Cuirim mo dhóchas ar snámh
i mbáidín teangan
faoi mar a leagta naíonán
i geliabhán
a bheadh fite fuaite
de dhuilleoga feileastraim
is bitiúman agus picbheith cuimilte lena thóin.

ansan é a leagadh síos
i measc na ngioicach
is coigeal na mban sí
le taobh na habhann,
féachaint n'fheadaráis
a dtabharfaidh an sruth é,
féachaint, dála Mhaoise,
an bhfóirfidh iníon Phorain?

(I place my hope on the water
in this little boat
of the language,
the way a body might put
an infant
in a basket of intertwined
iris leaves,
its underside proofed
with bitumen and pitch,

then set the whole thing down amidst

the sedge

and the bulrushes by the edge

of a river

only to have it borne hither and thither,

not knowing where it might end up;

in the lap, perhaps,

of some Pharaoh's daughter.)

Reflecting on the Gorta Mór: The Great Famine of Ireland

Some narratives and their legacy

FANUEIL HALL, BOSTON

5 MAY 2012

T HIS IS NOT my first time in Boston, but it is my first time here as President of Ireland and I cannot think of a more appropriate place to visit given the deep historical connections between this city and Ireland. I know there are few sites in this great country which have been more historically significant than Faneuil Hall, and it is truly humbling to be speaking in the same spot where George Washington, Daniel Webster, Susan B. Anthony and Frederick Douglass addressed some of the great questions of American history – independence, women's equality and liberation from slavery.

There is no single narrative of the Great Irish Famine. We are compelled to acknowledge the many different elements that make up the story of Ireland's greatest disaster. Whether it is the trauma of the Famine itself, the clearances of families before and after the catastrophe, the emigrations for seasonal work across the Irish Sea that bled life from our ancestors as they sought to pay the rent, the tyranny of landlordism and the emergence, after the Famine, of a grazier class – native predators as acquisitive and cruel as any absentee landlord – from all this we have many narratives that have to be revisited, kept open, revised and made more inclusive of much that was forgotten or perhaps deliberately avoided in a great silence amongst the survivors at home and abroad.

The inherited narratives can never be fully complete. We must, given the scale of the event itself and the enormity, rapidity and devastating effect of the forces at work, be open to amending what we have taken as the iconic event – the master narrative – and add in missing pieces, drawing on new scholarship, so much of it carried out by scholars in the United States who have admirably and patiently explored the complexity of the *Gorta Mór* – the Great Famine of 1845–50. It is when we acknowledge what has been omitted, and speculate on why, that we are best prepared to use our own Famine experience in such a way as to generate an appropriate ethical response to the obscenity of recurring famines in our own time.

The Irish Famine of 1845–50 was the greatest social disaster – in terms of mortality and suffering – that Ireland has ever experienced. It was also the worst social calamity based on crop failure ever experienced in Europe, indeed, in the 'developed' world, in modern times. The very terms in which it is described, the struggle for an adequate term, hint at its complexity, and at the different ways in which historians and the people at large have sought to describe the disaster. It has been called 'the Great Irish Famine', the 'Great Hunger', the 'Irish potato famine', *an Gorta Mór* and, in some Irish-language communities, *blianta an droch-shaoil*: the years of the bad life.

The salient facts of the calamity are not in dispute. From late summer 1845 a hitherto unknown fungus, to which there was no known antidote, attacked and partially destroyed the potato crop in Ireland. In 1846 the blight was more severe and destroyed virtually the entire potato crop. The ravages of starvation and various diseases in 1847 earned for that year the grim description 'the Black 47'. Though the actual blight was less severe in 1847, the potato harvest was poor, as seed potatoes had either been consumed during the scarcity in 1846 or had simply not been set, due to panic and the disruption of normal life. The blight was again very bad in 1848, especially in the areas of greatest poverty and population pressure in the south and west. The partial failure of the potato in 1849 and 1850 prolonged the crisis and the suffering into the early 1850s.

During the crisis years it is estimated that over one million Irish perished from hunger or, more commonly, from hunger-related diseases. In the decade following 1846 – when the floodgates of emigration opened to a population fleeing a stricken land – more than 1.8 million emigrated, more than half of these fleeing (more as refugees than as emigrants, as the historian Peter Gray has remarked) during the famine years of 1846–50. The population of Ireland, which was close to 8.5 million in 1845, had fallen to 6.6 million by 1851. It would continue to fall – due to the relentless drain of emigration – for many decades to come.

One missing piece of the narrative is perhaps our insufficient recognition of the fact that the famine and the emigration it caused had different effects on different classes among the Irish population. When the potato failed in 1845, huge numbers were 'at risk', but some much more than others. Perhaps a million and a half landless labourers were almost totally dependent on the potato, while it was a major component of the diet of a further three million (mostly cottiers and smallholders) of the rural poor.

The recently established workhouse system was overwhelmed by the tsunami of desperate and starving applicants. The voluntary sector of charitable organizations – churches, local relief committees, contributions from overseas – was likewise swamped during the famine years.

What of the government response? There has been bitter controversy and recrimination – at the time of the famine itself and since – regarding the state's response to the crisis generated by the failure of the potato. This past experience of state failure, policy blindness, perhaps driven by ideology, should lead us to reflect on the general issue, in our contemporary conditions, of the appropriate response of state and state-led institutions to the regular and scandalous famines of our own times. The failure of an economic policy at global level to take account of our interdependency, of sustainability or the diversity of paths to development underlies the repetition of contemporary famines. For governments and the institutions in which people place their trust, it remains one of the great unresolved ethical challenges of our time – the daily and unnecessary loss of life to hunger and preventable diseases.

While the context of the Great Famine is hard to grasp, so also are its consequences. We must remember that while the Great Famine unleashed a great tide of emigration of the poor and the desperate, particularly from the west of Ireland, emigration from Ireland did not begin with the Great Famine. Emigration, in different forms, had already established itself. It was overwhelmingly seasonal in the western regions of the country. This seasonal migration was integrated into the agricultural economy of Britain, and while migration to North America was heaviest from the north of Ireland, it was not confined to those areas.

While the emigrants to America after the Famine were fleeing famine and seeking to survive, we should not forget earlier involuntary migrations – the fact that in earlier centuries Irish indentured servants, vagrants and felons had formed a substantial part of the labour force of the Caribbean. In the late 1660s, for example, there were 12,000 Irish in the West Indies of whom 8,000 were settled in Barbados. Three hundred and fifty thousand people left Ireland in the three-quarters of a century before the American Revolution. While some scholars pinpoint the early decades of the eighteenth century as the beginning of significant emigration, Kerby Miller puts it a full generation earlier.

Seasonal migration, which linked both cottiers and smallholders through the rent they paid to landlords to the agricultural economy of the neighbouring island, drew up to 100,000 seasonal migrants from Ireland each year. Of course, their labours did not necessarily change their objective economic status, as the rents demanded of them were adjusted to take account of their earnings.

While the Famine did not initiate emigration, neither did evictions commence with it. The clearances of smallholders had begun decades before, when the economic yields of the long war against revolutionary France, which required intense production, began to fall, and arable cultivation gave way to pasture.

It is worth remembering, too, that different streams of migration contained different types of migrants with different capacities. The 1.5 million who had emigrated from Ireland between 1815 and 1845 were mostly, as Gearóid Ó Tuathaigh puts it, 'Protestant and prudential'. While the emigrants drew strongly from the northern half of the country, and did indeed include a sizeable Protestant element, towards the end of the period the numbers of Catholics were increasing. Donald Akenson has asked us too to bear in mind that while the flood of emigrants after the Famine would be towards cities, Irish people were still ending up in rural settlements right through to 1870. But the urban experience was crucial. Alan Munslow, in his study of the Boston Irish, tells us:

> Of the forty-three most populous cities in America in 1870 the Irish were the largest first generation immigrant group in twenty-seven and second in the rest.

Standing behind our Famine experience and the adjustment to it is the issue of land. The massive expansion in Ireland's population between 1780 and 1821 was assisted by the phenomenon of 'partible inheritance'. That is, with a low life expectancy, unions were formed and children born on tiny parcels of land. As historian Joe Lee put it, fields gave way to families. In the post-Famine adjustment the families would give way to fields, with one male inheriting all the land, one female marrying out and the rest of the females having to travel abroad for work. Land hunger would dominate Irish society after the famine and it profoundly influenced Irish politics for the remainder of the nineteenth century and the early decades of the twentieth.

The late-nineteenth-century Ireland of conservative smallholders was made possible, and assisted, by emigrants' remittances. Land would often push other issues, social questions and questions of national independence into a secondary place. The late nineteenth century would, for example, close in a confrontation between smallholders – the agricultural labourers and the cottiers had been virtually eliminated by the Famine and emigration – and a class of large-scale graziers who had come to hold land in greater volumes than the erstwhile English landlords. These new native proprietors, however, enjoyed a formidable form of protection. They could claim to share a religion with their victims, and espouse the nationalist cause of separatism, Home Rule or national independence with those they excluded from a living on the land.

The long-established seasonal migration to Britain had not been without difficulty. Not only because of their willingness to work for lower wages but for a whole set of religious and ethnic reasons, Irish migrants to Britain were faced with hostility, often by those on the margins themselves. Rivulets of seasonal migration gave way to a new flood of Famine migrants and led to increased animosity. In their flight from hunger they were at different times depicted as disease carriers, at best inferior and perhaps the victims of the just judgment of God. In latter decades attitudes towards the Irish were influenced by political events of the day, such as concessions by the English Government in response to agitation for Home Rule.

Frances Finnegan's study of York is a valuable regional analysis of this process. In 1846, during the Famine, the news-reading public in York had been treated to regular recitals of suggested Irish characteristics which were hardening into permanent – racial – features. Stereotyped as violent, lazy and dirty, the Irishman was presented as a menacing contrast to his 'Saxon benefactors': 'Englishmen have the reputation throughout civilized Europe of being the most enlightened, plodding, charitable nation on the face of the earth... Show us a case of apparent distress and do not our purse strings as if by instinct loosen themselves?' Sometimes too the Irish were accused of a lamentable ingratitude. Referring to the suspension of public works in Ireland, the *Gazette* commented: 'The Irish people are literally Irish in everything they do. Every act of their lives denotes their peculiarity.' It was this characteristic 'difference' in the Irish race which, it was suggested, justified the suspension of the public works aimed at relieving poverty.

After the crisis of 1847 the British Government, which altogether spent £10 million on the Irish Famine in the entire period 1845–51, decided that famine relief should be funded from within Ireland. Christine Kinealy Rogers refers to a *Times* editorial headlined: *Why should the United Kingdom pay for the extravaganza of Ireland?* As Kinealy puts it: 'The *Times* again marshalled a vitriolic campaign against further assistance to Ireland pointing out to its readers the "total absence of gratitude" shown by the Irish people and adding that this money "had broken the back of English benevolence".'

The London *Times* had, together with *Punch* and other journals, developed a stereotypical version of the Irish as insatiable in their demands, ungrateful and disloyal. These papers supported the British Government's interpretation of the famine as a matter for local resolution or even providential in its cause. Yet the post-famine exodus of men women and children created a memory of culpable neglect at best and, more usually, an abiding communal recollection of imperial degradation, a response that would now live on beyond the seas.

Frances Finnegan gives us a wonderful insight into the mind of the regional press and its attitude to the Irish in York. For example, in relation to the cutting of relief in 1848:

> ... in consequence of the infatuated and wicked conduct of the
> peasantry, who have obstructed the operation of those means of

employment intended for their relief, and by a system of insubordination and outrage have endangered the lives of the officers and overseers appointed to superintend the works… Where is the people except in Ireland, who would by brutal force and violence assail the very parties who are engaged in laudable efforts to save a nation from famine and death?

Racial and religious prejudice are combined in the *Gazette*'s extraordinary editorial of 10 July 1847, in the very eye of the Famine hurricane, regarding the 'fearful visitations to which Ireland has been subjected during the past two years':

> Famine and pestilence have, we trust, taught wisdom and English benevolence conquered in some degree the prejudices of the Celt. The Irish people are not so stolid as not to perceive that the acts of the Saxons give the lie to the ravings of the lay and clerical agitators, and that in the hour of need, when tens of thousands were falling victims to famine, the exciters of turbulence even if they were willing, were powerless to check its ravages until Saxon energy and Christian philanthropy stepped between the living and the dead.

The *Yorkshireman* refers to the unfortunate 'difference' in the Irish race to which I have already referred. In April 1847 it stated: 'The Irish are a strange and unfathomable people. Their ways are not such as other men – their motives are often past finding out. They will neither profit by exhortation nor learn wisdom by the science which teaches by example.'

Irish ingratitude is referred to again and again. In an editorial entitled 'The Irish Begging Box Again', the *Yorkshireman* commented in 1848:

> Our readers will recollect that during the last two years this country, while labouring under the deepest depression of trade and a

declining revenue, came magnanimously forward... to arrest... the famine and plague in its sister country. Englishmen did this in the front of the deepest ingratitude. They gave upwards of 3 million in money, the recipients all the while thanking them with a gibe and menacingly shouldering a pike. England, however, laughed this mockery of rebellion to scorn and continued to pour golden gifts into the lap of the disaffected and miserable people. We had thought that there would be an end to this; and that Ireland newly emerged from the rebel field would scarcely have the hardihood to again appeal to the extraordinary charity and benevolence of the English Parliament. Irish beggary is importunate and its objurations and solicitations stereotyped. The inhabitants will take no refusal. Shut the door in their faces and ten to one a musket is levelled at the door. Remind them of the hundreds of thousands already distributed amongst them, and they will reply that they got no more than their own... The cry hitherto has been 'Ireland for the Irish'. Let it be so. England will be the gainer by the bargain.

This was the kind of prejudice to be found in two York newspapers even before the main influx of the post-Famine immigrants, and it was more virulent after their arrival. Frances Finnegan says of those stereotypes:

Their influence, of course, cannot be measured and would in any case have been confined to the comparatively limited newspaper readership of the well-to-do classes in York and the surrounding countryside. However, if such attitudes were not merely reflections of the public's views, but also instrumental in forming them, then their influence could have been considerable – within that very group which was to be responsible not only for administering to and governing the Irish, but in the form of Reports, Minutes, letters etc., of leaving a legacy of descriptions and impressions concerning them. That those in authority – magistrates, Poor Law Guardians, sanitary officials and governors of the Ragged Schools – were prejudiced against the Irish is illustrated throughout this study. The extent to which this prejudice led them to make stereotyped, misleading judgements about them however, and even worse official reports containing evidence apparently, but not always in reality, based on facts, has rarely been considered.

On the other hand, Finnegan also tells us of some of the exceptional behaviour of concern and solidarity that came, even at the cost of life itself, from such as the Quaker Samuel Tuke. Tuke voiced his enlightened but unorthodox, and no doubt unpopular, views in public as well as in private: views that were in sharp contrast to those in authority in York. Addressing a meeting of Friends at Devonshire House in June 1847, for example:

> He entered into an animated apology for the Irish people, against the wholesale condemnation in which they are commonly involved. They are stigmatized, he said, as lazy, reckless, and regardless of human life. But the charge of laziness is disproved by the multitudes of those who come over to reap our harvests, and those who labour at the heaviest employments. They have been most thankful for work; they have undertaken it even in a state of destitution and depression of animal powers which might well have excused them from the task… It is said the Irish are reckless, yet a most interesting evidence of their thrift, their patriotism and their natural affection is to be seen in the remittances of the poor emigrants in America to their relations at home.

Tuke died of an illness contracted helping Irish people in the direst of circumstances. His daughter's diary entry is quoted by Frances Finnegan and is itself very moving:

During this summer, my father's heart has been full of the wrongs and sufferings of Ireland, and his head busy devising schemes for the temporary relief of the starving people. Many have flocked to York, as to other places, to escape the horrors of famine; and to find employment and food for these was my father's unwearied care. They are dying of fever around us. One morning, a poor Irishman died of fever in a ditch. He and his wife and child had been travelling about for weeks, and at last being taken ill, had begged a lodging, but no one would take them in, so they sought shelter under a hedge. James took them a blanket and some old carpet, and William [Hargraves] some straw for the night; but in the morning the man died. My father and James attended the inquest. The former said it was most affecting (and I remember well how much he was affected in narrating it) to see the child – a girl about ten – saying she would never leave her bonny father and holding a large clasp-knife, kissing it, and saying it was her father's knife. 'A child full of sentiment', my father called her; and the poor woman said the man had been 'a beautiful husband' to her. My father went to the Fever Hospital next day, to see the poor Irishwoman and her child. He found the woman living, but expecting to die. The child looked up at him so sweetly, he said, and he intends to take care of her if the mother dies.

But I am speaking here in Boston, the city towards which many of the Irish directed their hopes, some straight from Ireland and others who hoped to get to America from Liverpool. Their entry into Boston was not without difficulty. There had already been established a version of Boston life that reflected the values of earlier migrations – ones that were often hostile to the circumstances and beliefs of a new wave of impoverished Irish, different in beliefs and often in language.

We are here today, of course, not only to commemorate the victims of the Great Irish Famine, but also to celebrate the lives that those who emigrated forged in this city out of adversity, and their achievements in creating enduring links between our countries. While those who arrived in Boston after the Famine might have had the assistance of these contact networks, they also collided with – in a cultural, economic, social and religious sense – settled Irish American migrants of the pre-Famine period.

Neither were the media of their time universally favourable. The *Punch* cartoons, after all, crossed the Atlantic. In America, most Irish became city dwellers and, since they had little money for onward passage, settled in their cities of disembarkation. By 1850, the Irish made up a quarter of the population in Boston, New York City, Philadelphia, Pennsylvania and Baltimore.

Although there had been Irish men and women in Boston since this city's earliest days, it is in the aftermath of the dark days of the 1840s that emigration to the United States took place on a much larger and continuous scale. In April 1847 over 1,000 Irish emigrants landed in Boston on just one day, and over 37,000 arrived in that year alone to a city whose population was then only 115,000.

The Boston evidence shows the determination of the 'famine Irish' to overcome poverty and prejudice, to empower their children, who, in their turn, were dedicated to further advancement and social mobility. They made a sustained commitment to serving the public good and contributing to the prosperity of their 'new world'. This is evident everywhere in this country, in the state of Massachusetts and in the proud city of Boston: in the police and fire services; in education; in business, industry and finance; in health, welfare and philanthropy; in all aspects of religious life; in politics and public administration; in science, technology and innovation; in all branches of the arts, creativity and cultural expression.

Alun Munslow, in his article 'A "Bigger, Better and Busier Boston". The pursuit of political legitimacy in America: the Boston Irish, 1890–1920', tells us: 'For the Irish Catholics urban politics was the primary means of negotiating the contracts of cultural dominance and subordination in the New World. Municipal politics became the key discourse that in Boston indicated the dominant Yankee Protestant and the subordinate Irish Catholic relationship.'

Boston was the second largest entry port (after New York) in the USA for famine emigrants. By 1840 Boston, still no great 'melting pot', was strongly Anglo-Saxon and Protestant in its culture. It saw itself as a confident, orderly cultural and social centre. The heavy influx of famine-Irish 'refugees' aroused fear (and loathing) among many of the city's settled population. As one historian has written of the city:

> Boston, which had prided itself on being a clean, healthy city and had not had a major epidemic of smallpox since 1793, suddenly found itself with slums where the pox flourished, along with... other diseases... The city was frightened by this horde of Irishmen loosed in its midst. Before the arrival of the Irish Boston had been a community composed largely of tradesmen, artisans and merchants. Now it harboured a seemingly inexhaustible supply of men and women who accepted... working conditions that local labour scorned. In 1850, of the city's boasted 136,831 citizens, c. 30,000 were newly settled Irish immigrants, who brought with them a religion that was antipathetic to the religious convictions of the original English settlers.[7]

Remarkably, among these famished emigrants there were those who held a deep regard for the learning, lore and history recorded in the large corpus of manuscripts written in the Irish language, the language of a large percentage of the famine emigrants from the rural countryside. This material was copied regularly and circulated among the Irish peasantry, and significantly shaped their historical consciousness. They treasured

7   Brett Howard, *Boston: A Social History* (Hawthorn Books, 1976), pp. 57–8.

these well-worn manuscripts. The Boston Athenaeum (an independent research library) in this city holds several of these manuscripts, gifted to it by Thomas Graves Cary, President of the Athenaeum from 1846 to 1859, and, it seems, acquired by him from famine emigrants.[8]

Among the most poignant evidence of the trauma of dislocation are the letters written by some of those emigrants (or by 'scribes' – literate agents – acting on their behalf) to the *Boston Pilot* newspaper, seeking information on their 'missing' relatives and friends. These letters have been collected, edited and published by Ruth-Ann Harris, Donald Jacobs and Emer O'Keefe.[9] There were, of course, other casualties: those who vanished into the vastness of America. The *Boston Pilot* maintained a 'Missing Persons' column – as a service to readers in America and in Ireland – from 1831 to 1916. In the period 1831–50, some 5,655 'missing persons' from Ireland were sought in these columns. Here are some examples:

MAY 1846 – INFORMATION WANTED

Of James Hurley, formerly of Waterford, Ireland, who left Boston on the 13th of May 1845, and has not been heard from since. Any information respecting him will be thankfully received by his brother, Michael Hurley, addressed to him care of Mr. Nicholas Power, No. 20 Atkinson Street, Boston, MS.

28 NOVEMBER 1846 – INFORMATION WANTED

Of Patrick Curtis, who emigrated from county Clare, parish of Ogoneloe, last spring, and left his parents and family in Cabotville,

---

8   Cf. article by Dr Cornelius Buttimer in Pádraig de Brún et al. (eds), *Folia Gadelica* (Central Books Ltd. 1983).
9   Ruth-Ann Harris, Donald M. Jacobs and Emer O'Keefe (eds), *The Search for Missing Friends: Irish Immigrant Advertisements Placed in the Boston Pilot*, Vol. 1, 1831–1850 (Boston: New England Historic Genealogical Society, 1989. Frontispiece; extensive index of names. Published in co-operation with the Irish Studies Program and the Department of History at Northeastern University, lxii, 684 pages; First Edition (1989).

MS, 11th of September last, and has since been seen in Boston. He is 17 years old, of a robust form, slightly pockpitted, sandy-coloured hair and curled locks; wore a grey frock coat of Irish frieze, with a velvet cape. Any person who finds him out will perform a charitable act by writing to his disconsolate father, Patrick Curtis, Cabotville, MS.

The legacy of the Famine to contemporary Ireland includes a strong appreciation among Irish people of issues such as food security and a strong commitment to humanitarian aid and relief. It also resulted in the formation of many diaspora communities who never forgot their origins.

The emigration tide in the decade following 1846 deeply embedded a culture of 'exit' from Ireland, and as the generation of the famine emigrants settled in their new countries, they created networks of Irish communities overseas to receive, assist and sustain the chain migration of Irish people, following their family and neighbours to start a new life and find new opportunities. It is hard to fully recover how those leaving Irish shores during the famine felt – their sense of loss, displacement and anxiety must have been intense, but also their hope for new beginnings and a new life. We celebrate those emigrants today for their courage, resilience and perseverance. We also pay tribute to those who started their voyage during the famine but who perished on that journey. These memories are an ethical wellspring for our response to the migrants and famines of our own times. We are challenged to place ourselves in the circumstances of others by such memories.

During the worst of the Famine, around 250,000 left Ireland in a single year, and I know that far more emigrants left the West of Ireland than any other region of the country. Families did not migrate *en masse*; younger members were often the first to leave. Emigration almost became a rite of passage, and the evidence shows that, unlike in similar emigrations throughout world history, women emigrated just as often, just as early, and in the same numbers as men. Roy Foster has explained: 'The emigrant started a new life in a new land, sent remittances [reaching] £1,404,000 by 1851 back to his/her family in Ireland which, in turn, allowed another member of the family to emigrate.'

The journey for our emigrants was no doubt treacherous and difficult, but the instinct for survival, the will to live, which had seen the famine emigrants survive the calamity and the ocean crossing, must have been extraordinarily strong. It must have been one of the main factors that enabled them, and in time their children, to put down firm roots in their new countries. This determination to survive and to succeed was passed on to later generations of Irish in the diaspora community, and must have inspired them as they made their mark in every area of the new societies in which they settled.

As I have said, the effects of the Irish Famine on Ireland, culturally, economically, socially and politically, cannot be overestimated. For a significant number of the Irish abroad, the Famine has been an important part of their self-awareness. Some retained a close interest in their homeland. They brought out family members. They helped build churches in the devotional Catholic surge that followed the Famine. They helped clear their relatives' shop debts. They sought to contribute to their mother country's progress and development. This would mean, in some instances, support for movements dedicated to achieving an independent Irish state, or for strengthening the various strands of Irish cultural identity: the Gaelic League, the Literary Revival, the Gaelic Athletic Association and so on. In more recent times they have encouraged economic co-operation and investment, philanthropic work and, of course, support for and consolidation of the peace process in Northern Ireland. All of these commitments have marked the continuing interest of Irish-Americans in maintaining links with their ancestral homeland.

In recounting the terrible story of the Famine I should mention, in particular, the assistance that came to Ireland from Boston in those difficult times, especially the remarkable career of Captain Robert Bennet Forbes.

Robert and his brother John Forbes were instrumental in petitioning Congress for the release of two naval ships that eventually took aid to Ireland in the spring and summer of 1847. They promoted this idea after attending a public meeting here at Faneuil Hall on 18 February 1847, a few weeks after the news came that Ireland was indeed facing the prospect of massive starvation. It was at that meeting that the New England Relief Committee was formed under the Mayor of Boston, Josiah Quincy, and only a couple of days later that the petition to Congress was made to turn over the USS *Jamestown*, which was in Charlestown Navy Yard, and the USS *Macedonian* in New York to private hands so that food and aid could be sent to Ireland. The loading of the *Jamestown* began appropriately enough on St Patrick's Day, 17 March 1847, was carried out by the mostly Irish Boston Labourers' Society as unpaid labour, and was finished within nine days. Forbes and the other ship's officers undertook this voyage pro bono, as did many of the crew, and the others had their wages paid by contributions from the public.

Upon arrival at Cobh on 12 April 1847, the cargo unloaded 800 tons of provisions and supplies. The New England Relief Committee funded a total of $151,000 out of the approximately $300,000 of recorded aid that went from Boston to Ireland in 1847. While in Cobh, Forbes met the local dignitaries, but seems to have been most impressed by the famous temperance crusader Father Theobald Mathew, who took him on a tour of the poorest areas of Cork city. A local committee was appointed to oversee distribution of the cargo to Cork city, Cobh, Kinsale and Skibbereen. This is one of the very first examples of a United States naval vessel being turned over to civilian control so that humanitarian relief could be given to desperate people facing hunger and disease – a good and early instance of turning swords into ploughshares.

Captain Forbes's efforts were greatly appreciated in Ireland, and he received testimonials from the Corporations of Dublin and Cork as well as a beautiful engraved silver salver which is now at the Forbes Museum in Milton. As we recall this act of humanity and generosity, I am delighted that there are descendants of Captain Forbes here with us this morning.

.This was not the only effort that was made here in Boston. The Charitable Irish Society, the oldest Irish organization in the western hemisphere, of which Captain Forbes was a member, was also instrumental in sending aid, even to the extent of cancelling their annual dinner and donating the cost instead. On 7 February 1847 the city's newly appointed Catholic bishop devoted his first pastoral letter to the plight of the Irish: 'A voice comes to us from across the ocean; the loud cry of her anguish has gone through the world...' He urged his parishioners to give unstintingly: 'Apathy and indifference, on an occasion like this,' he said, 'are inseparable from crime!'

His words remain equally powerful today. The bishop and his relief committee quickly raised $20,000. Christine Kinealy's 'Potatoes, Providence and Philanthropy: The Role of Private Charity during the Irish Famine', published in volume six of the *Irish World Wide* series, gives an illuminating account of those who sprang to the assistance of the Irish people, ranging from the young Sultan of Turkey, Abdülmecid, who sought to give £10,000, to the Choctaw Indians and the seventeen shillings collected in pence and halfpence from prisoners of the *Warrior*, a prison hulk moored in Woolwich.

Hunger has a deep resonance with the Irish people. Our experience of famine has echoed through the generations and has shaped the values and principles that are embedded in us and also in our development programme today. Ireland's aid programme, known as Irish Aid, is based on a partnership with the developing world. It is clearly focused on poverty in sub-Saharan Africa. The programme pays attention to the poorest and most vulnerable communities, building self-respect, dignity and hope. One of its major priorities is to support global efforts to reduce hunger. In addition to attending to the immediate needs of those who are victims of natural and man-made disasters, Ireland is also working to address the root causes of starvation.

I am proud to say that Ireland has become a leading global advocate in the fight against hunger and has committed to spending 20 per cent of its overseas aid budget in support of activities that can improve access to food and reduce undernutrition in the world's poorest countries. In addition to Government efforts, Irish non-governmental organizations try to lead the way in ensuring that the issues of hunger and undernutrition are placed high on the global agenda. We do this not only because we are urged by historical memory to act in this way, but because it is right. It is an example of the Irishness we wish to be known by, ethically taking our share of global responsibility.

Building on, and learning from, our shared experience of famine, Ireland and the US are working in partnership to lead efforts to combat undernutrition around the world. Since September 2010, Ireland and the US have been pioneering the 1,000 Days of Action to Scale Up Nutrition. This movement aims to prevent the irreversible effects of undernutrition on children during the critical 1,000 days between pregnancy and age two.

As I have already said, the effects of the Irish Famine were profound. The large-scale emigration during the famine in Ireland has of course resulted in strong and enduring links between Boston and Ireland: President Kennedy when he was in Ireland on his famous 1963 visit, the first ever by a sitting US President, said in Eyre Square that 'nearly everyone in Boston is from Galway'. Far be it from me as a former Mayor and national parliamentary representative for Galway to deny the truth of that statement, and certainly the ties that bind Boston and Ireland are especially strong in Galway and the west coast of my homeland.

I would like to thank the community in Boston for honouring the Irish Famine victims here today in such a dignified and respectful way. The links between our countries, although forged out of tragic circumstances, have endured and I know will continue to deepen and prosper, through the strength of our shared experiences and vibrant diaspora communities.

CULTURE

Patrick Kavanagh and the Migratory Experience

INNISKEEN, CO. MONAGHAN

26 SEPTEMBER 2014

E ARLIER THIS YEAR Kieran Duffy, a very dear friend from Monaghan, from 'Blaney', as he would put it, died at a very young age. He was a brilliant pianist who often played at Áras an Uachtaráin. He was also a former student of mine but, much more importantly, he was an outstanding teacher of English literature. He loved poetry and his favourite poet was Patrick Kavanagh. As he recited Kavanagh's work, and talked about the setting of the early poems, he always made a connection for me with the landscape of Monaghan.

Among the courses I taught in UCG, now NUIG, and which were taken by Kieran were one on the sociology of migration and another on the sociology of literature. In teaching these there was an obvious temptation to use the work of novelists and poets simply as evidence. But even respecting such cautions, it was a fact that if you wanted insight into the truth of Irish existence, you had to turn to literature. The sociological theory then in vogue was heavily structural-functionalist, empirical in method, and incapable of handling material that captured the way people actually lived and how they felt in conditions of transience. This was a sociology that described structures, identified roles, and the persons who constituted society simply fitted neatly and without conflict into their allotted functions.

What interested me, by way of contrast, was the centrality of the migratory experience in the work of Irish writers – in novels, short stories and poems. It seemed to me that there was a richness of Irish experience that was available to us in writing of a literary kind and that was missing from the social sciences of the time. An exception might have been *The Limerick Rural Survey* of Jeremiah Newman and Patrick McNabb, in which I see, for example, people like Kavanagh's Maguire, the unmarried farmer of his magnificent long poem *The Great Hunger*. As my students and I discussed the emigrant stories of Patrick MacGill, Dónal Mac Amhlaigh and many others, we came to the conclusion that the migratory experience was also of special significance in the poetry and prose of Patrick Kavanagh.

It is for another day to reflect on why such a central experience as migration, which affected millions of Irish people, did not feature very strongly in the Irish curriculum. Migration dominates every period of Irish history and, sadly, the sense of loss associated with it has returned as many of our young people are again compelled to seek work abroad.

I believe that it would be possible to sustain the suggestion that the most important characters in global literature have been migrants. But in my suggestion that the migratory experience can help us understand the work of Patrick Kavanagh, I am referring in a more limited way to the relationship between the poet, his sense of place and the forms of intimacy sought, discarded and pursued in a new place, or recovered in memory.

There have been many very fine studies on the work of Patrick Kavanagh, including those of Dr Antoinette Quinn and of Kavanagh's brother, Peter, whom I met in 1996 at the unveiling of a plaque in St Mary's Church in Haddington Road. What I have to say today is but a modest reflection on one facet of the poet's life.

I suggest that Kavanagh's journey between the rural world of Monaghan and the city reveals some important features of the migratory experience. He was, in my view, a particularly vulnerable migrant, ultimately unsuccessful both in his departure from his home place and in his engagement with the city, a migrant who perhaps left it too late to leave his rural world and too late to enter a new and complex urban one. Kavanagh had also to negotiate a way into, and to perform within, a literary community that often resisted him, and which he often excoriated with vitriolic abuse, as in his satirical poem 'The Paddiad', a blast against his fellow poets published in Cyril Connolly's *Horizon* in August 1949.

The experience of migration can never be understood simply by describing the place of origin or the place of arrival. Migration is, above all else, about transience and all the uncertainties that go with it. In the act of migration itself, imagination is infinite and the circumstances of the migratory move finite – creating a world of contradictions. Given securities are surrendered, and the search for personal significance is negotiated in strange conditions, and with strangers, something for which there can only ever be partial preparation.

Neither is the act of migration a linear or simple experience. The urge to leave is not determined solely by the inadequacy of the place of origin, and, on the contrary a sense of place may endure in the memory long after the connection with it has been broken. Then again, destination is rehearsed in the imagination long before the act of leaving itself. Leaving is thus never simply a rejection of rural life. It is the balance between the rehearsed alternative of the city of the imagination and the familiar environment that has become less loved.

The flux that is at the heart of transience strikes at many of the taken-for-granted versions of Irish life. After all, the sedentary life is not our common experience. Yet so much Irish scholarship assumes a kind of life associated with property, the security of ownership, and a neat allocation of roles in the community. When I was first reading Patrick Kavanagh,

I had just encountered *Family and Community in Ireland* by Conrad Arensberg and Solon Kimball which was an extended version of their work on rural Ireland in the 1930s, published as *The Irish Countryman*. That work depends on a neat allocation of roles between farmers, their wives and their children. The participants move in a structurally determined way through an existence of defined roles, and mostly in silence. Women stir the coals in the fire as they prepare food for a morning when men would leave for farm work and the women themselves would set about the domestic tasks of farmhouse and farmyard. These men and women have always struck me as the ghostly players in a dangerously over-determined fantasy.

I mention this because Patrick Kavanagh was writing his early poems, as a young man in his twenties, at the same time as this highly abstract model of Irish existence was becoming, among US scholars in particular, the most influential version of Irish rural life. It is in this early work by Kavanagh that we find the fullness of rural experience, with all the beauty that proximity to a nature renewing itself offers to the innocent imagination, an imagination still open to the spiritual dimension of life. Indeed I have been struck by the recurrence of 'soul' as a theme in Kavanagh's poems.

'Free Soul'

Yesterday I saw the Earth beautiful
Through the frosted glass of November's tree
I peered into an April country
Where love was day-dream free.

And in the steam rising from the dung-heap
Another firmament was blown
Dotted over with fairy worlds
And lamped with silver stone.

Over the bleak grey-bearded bogs
I looked and beheld the last Atlantis
And surely it was not November
But a time the freed souls grant us.

The 'spiritual', too, shifts in meaning, at some times identifying the divine in nature's renewal, at others in the awe of clerical pomp and the rituals of the church calendar, and even in a form of moral scrupulosity.

There is, I believe, more than one self crafted in Patrick Kavanagh's work. There is a self of the spirit that requires sensual expression and is repressed by grinding rural economic circumstance; there is a poetic self that is seeking endorsement from his peers in the community of the arts; and there is a social self communicating with the public. All of these versions of Kavanagh are interconnected and mediated through the migratory experience.

The Ireland of Patrick Kavanagh, especially of the early poems, was an Ireland made safe within bounded fields that defined one's status. On to that status were layered all the requirements of respectability, with its necessary restraint and the consignment of feelings to a silence that could not be broken without serious consequences for one's personal reputation. Yet none of this was sufficient to suppress entirely the imagination of a close encounter with nature.

The spiritual hunger is reflected, for example, in 'To a Blackbird':

O pagan poet you
And I are one
In this – we lose our god
At set of sun.

And we are kindred when
The hill wind shakes

Sweet song like blossoms on
The calm green lakes.

We dream while Earth's sad children
Go slowly by
Pleading for our conversation
With the Most High.

The politics of publication, the post-colonial circumstances of judging what was acceptable literature in the metropolitan centre are also important to an understanding of Kavanagh. Antoinette Quinn made a valuable point in her *Patrick Kavanagh: Born Again Romantic*, when she referred to Kavanagh's attempts to seek to publish his neo-Georgian pastoral poetry in England in the 1930s, and to restrict his more direct poetry of Irish rural life to Irish publications.

This, I believe, illustrates a more general aspect of Irish writing in English in the early decades of the twentieth century. The assumption was that if one's work was to be treated as serious literature it had to be published in London. We only have to look at the correspondence between Liam O'Flaherty and his English mentor David Garnett for an example of how the pressure to produce work that would satisfy a wider international readership might lead to the devaluing of what was close to one's experience, because it was seen as unacceptably limited and local.

The experience of migration is, of course, an inevitable departure from the warmth of local certainties. Yet this departure is never complete, and literary expressions of migration very often recount a cycle of return and redemption. I do not suggest that this happens in the case of Patrick Kavanagh, but I was moved by Antoinette Quinn's quotation of a friend recalling Kavanagh saying on his deathbed: 'In God I believe.' It is as if no early version of the self that sought even temporary certainties is ever truly discarded.

In between the points of origin and destination is the most complex and dangerous phase of the migrant's existence. Seeing ourselves as migrants in time, it is in the middle period, when anxiety about the finitude of existence is unavoidable, that the greatest changes take place.

In Patrick Kavanagh's case engaging with the city begins with a note of optimism, but that optimism will fade. Migrants frequently rehearse their return, as John Berger showed in *A Seventh Man*. Migrants go to railway stations not only to encounter people from their own region who are new arrivals but to subconsciously enact the journey they themselves hope to make when they return. Patrick Kavanagh's experience of transience, in the city, with all of its insecurities and uncertainties, made that return impossible for him. The negotiation of his different selves required an urban setting, an engagement with what might have been a piranha tank of rivalry and backbiting, but a milieu within which he tried to function.

The urge to belong is a feature of migratory transience. The migrant is attempting to enter a world that is not only strange to him or her, but in which the accommodation of the stranger is not guaranteed by any tradition of hospitality. An artistic community in the throes of conflict – in an atmosphere of authoritarian philistinism, like Dublin in the 1930s – no doubt presented special challenges to Kavanagh. The migrant writer may find it useful to discard his or her previous identity in the effort to enter this new world, and he or she may adopt a persona that fits the expected version of the stranger: in Kavanagh's case, he plays up to the caricature of the rural poet.

If the migration, as in Kavanagh's case, is a constant state of flux of moving from one location to another, within and between cities like Dublin and London, the prospect of intimate relationships and the possibilities of imagination are changed. The search for recognition in a new world of critics, reviewers and rival poets is a very different experience from the disconsolate personal adjustment to the wet drills of the Monaghan field.

For the migrant who has left with the intention of never returning, the heady experience of urban sociability is very attractive, a world where day and night are blurred – with a sense that you must absorb it all to make up for the experience of a life deferred, of all that you have missed. This experience is, of course, full of danger, leading to a cruel sense of disappointment and disillusion. I believe it occurred early in Patrick Kavanagh's experience.

'PEGASUS'

My soul was an old horse
Offered for sale in twenty fairs.
I offered him to the Church – the buyers
Were little men who feared his unusual airs.
One said: 'Let him remain unbid
In the wind and rain and hunger
Of sin and we will get him –
With the winkers thrown in – for nothing.'

Then the men of State looked at
What I'd brought for sale.
One minister, wondering if
Another horse-body would fit the tail
That he'd kept for sentiment –
The relic of his own soul –
Said, 'I will graze him in lieu of his labour.'
I lent him for a week or more
And he came back a hurdle of bones,
Starved, overworked, in despair.
I nursed him on the roadside grass
To shape him for another fair.

I lowered my price. I stood him where
The broken-winded, spavined stand
And crooked shopkeepers said that he
Might do a season on the land –
But not for high-paid work in towns.
He'd do a tinker, possibly.
I begged, 'O make some offer now,
A soul is a poor man's tragedy.
He'll draw your dungiest cart,' I said,
'Show you short cuts to Mass,
Teach weather lore, at night collect
Bad debts from poor men's grass.'
         And they would not.

   Where the
Tinkers quarrel I went down
With my horse, my soul.
I cried, 'Who will bid me half a crown?'
From their rowdy bargaining
Not one turned. 'Soul,' I prayed,
'I have hawked you through the world
Of Church and State and meanest trade.
But this evening, halter off,
Never again will it go on.
On the south side of ditches
There is grazing of the sun.
No more haggling with the world . . .'

As I said these words he grew
Wings upon his back. Now I may ride him
Every land my imagination knew.

Patrick Kavanagh's work has a strong sense of the intimacy of place, of the personal, and of the unstable flux of life. I was very moved by Peter Kavanagh's *Patrick Kavanagh: 1904–1967, A Life Chronicle*, an extraordinary testament to a relationship between brothers. That book catches, too, the atmosphere of the time – the heady, abandoned, bohemian, if also precarious, and often impecunious existence of writers in an Irish state that had exalted respectability and property as higher goals than the aesthetic values to which the disparate community of poets, that drank with such abandon in Dublin pubs, aspired.

Peter Kavanagh's book is valuable, among other reasons, for allowing us to relive the story of *Kavanagh's Weekly*, the poet's short-lived attempt to have a public voice on cultural and social issues. He evokes the struggle to publish the journal, and his own role in it, often without the co-operation of his brother Patrick. Peter also describes the scrabble to find employment in an inhospitable environment, made more difficult by a diminishing willingness on Patrick's part to make any concession to the mores of the time.

I began my reflection on the experience of Patrick Kavanagh as a migrant by saying that literature should never be reduced to evidence for a sociological model. This is not to say that it is not richly suggestive of a truth that illuminates social experience. *The Green Fool*, *The Great Hunger*, *Tarry Flynn* and Kavanagh's other works do have an importance of a social, anthropological kind. Even with all the later self-critical reservations of their author piled upon them, they have a life of their own. This is a life that even the author cannot take from them. They have had a major influence. The importance that Antoinette Quinn attaches to Kavanagh's precisely realized 'Shancoduff' is something with which I very much agree:

> In Kavanagh's country verse, familiarity breeds affection and in 'Shancoduff', where he achieves a perfect marriage between the roles of farmer and poet, his insider's knowledge of small-farm life

gives substance and specificity to his customary reflectiveness. Not a single abstraction intrudes into the poem. Yet his apprehension that critical reaction to his local poetry would be unfriendly proved correct. 'Inniskeen Road: July Evening' was ignored by most contemporary critics and Donagh MacDonagh noticed it only to lament its unfortunate conclusion. John Gawsworth and Maurice Wollman both passed up the opportunity to anthologise 'Shancoduff'. Published in the *Dublin Magazine* in 1937, it was not collected until 1960.

'Shancoduff' is radically innovative not only in its blend of agricultural realism and an unobtrusively Catholic ethos (Armagh, Glassdrummond Chapel), but, more fundamentally, in its fashioning of a distinctively new poetic personality, affectionate, playful, vulnerable. This is not descriptive or symbolic verse; it is entirely self-creating, using others to distinguish the self.

If I may read 'Shancoduff':

My black hills have never seen the sun rising,
Eternally they look north towards Armagh.
Lot's wife would not be salt if she had been
Incurious as my black hills that are happy
When dawn whitens Glassdrummond chapel.

My hills hoard the bright shillings of March
While the sun searches in every pocket.
They are my Alps and I have climbed the Matterhorn
With a sheaf of hay for three perishing calves
In the field under the Big Forth of Rocksavage.

The sleety winds fondle the rushy beards of Shancoduff
While the cattle-drovers sheltering in the Featherna Bush

Look up and say: 'Who owns them hungry hills
That the water-hen and snipe must have forsaken?
A poet? Then by heavens he must be poor.'
I hear, and is my heart not badly shaken?

Perhaps in this there is redemption.

With his refined instinct, his craft, the struggle of it all, Patrick Kavanagh made not only his place of origin and his experience of migration worthy subjects of poetry; he also brought the Ireland of his times, its beauty and its savagery, indelibly into our consciousness. That is probably why so many people have their favourite Kavanagh poem. It simply rhymes with their existence. Long may it continue to be so.

Remembering and Imagining Irishness

THIRD THOMAS FLANAGAN LECTURE,
AMERICAN IRISH HISTORICAL SOCIETY, NEW YORK

1 MAY 2012

T HOMAS FLANAGAN WAS a pioneering historical novelist, critic and great friend of Ireland and Irish scholarship. His critical work on Irish writers and fiction included the Irish American contribution such as that of Eugene O'Neill.

I should begin with a note of thanks and appreciation. It was customary in the Gaelic tradition to offer a praise poem to a generous host and benefactor. As our subject tonight was not a poet but a great writer of prose, let me praise – in prose – Dr Kevin Cahill, who has led this Society for many years.

John McGahern once remarked that Ireland is composed not of one but of thousands of tiny republics, each with their own manners and rules. I realized the truth of this when I was told that Dr Cahill, among his many accomplishments, is also Uachtarán of Sliabh Luachra, and that as far as the people of that part of Kerry are concerned, he bore the title of President many years before I did.

I want to extend our heartfelt appreciation to you, Kevin, not only as the embodiment of the spirit of this Society, the man who has done more than any other to secure its future and that of its beautiful home, but also as a great teacher, physician and humanitarian who has generously given of his skills, both in the United States and Ireland and globally. *Tréaslaím leat as ucht d'obair agus gabhaim buíochas leat.*

I have given the title 'Remembering and Imagining Irishness' to my remarks as I believe that, poised as we are in Ireland on the threshold of a decade of commemorations, some reflection on the ethics of memory and how we might see our complex history is a necessary preliminary to envisaging our future with courage and confidence.

Ireland has been, and must now again be, renewed through memory and imagination. Renewing Ireland, and with it our sense of what it means to be Irish, is one of the most urgent challenges facing us. It is a challenge that is partly about economic renewal but which also goes well beyond it. It is about constructing an ethical relationship with others and it can free us from models of economy and society which are disastrous in their social consequences.

This is not a new challenge for Irish people. I suggest that the Irish have repeatedly mined the past to meet the needs of their present crises. We have done so not as sentimentalists but as modernizers. Contrary to the caricature often drawn of us, we are among the greatest of modernizers – innovative and adaptive to a rare degree. This is an insight which is perhaps better preserved among the Irish diaspora than in Ireland itself.

What remembering and imagining have in common is myth-making: remembering is often initiated so as to achieve a healing; to find a rationalization; construe an event in such a way as to be both a warm cloak for the self and a dagger for the threatening other. The act of imagining needs some element of myth to retain belief, and as a mechanism for the retention of hope in the unrealized possibilities of being human and truly free, in joyous co-existence with others on this vulnerable planet of ours.

Myth-making is hardly confined to the Irish. Yet I think we can immodestly claim to have excelled at it in our different ways, in different times, and from different outposts, and very often the consequences of inventing mythical instruments for defence were destructive not only for those we opposed but for ourselves. But it is in literature that we Irish have perhaps laid bare the full creative potential of myth-making.

That achievement is not divorced, however, from historical context. It carries the burden of history but flies from it, making something new.

James Joyce, for example, drew on so much of the memory baggage of his people, yet he did not surrender it to what he inherited as the form of the novel. After his early stories, he did not adhere to the craft of imitation that was available to him in the prevailing genre of social realism. In his great novel *Ulysses* he brought something entirely new into the world.

An ancient myth stemming from an oral tradition, shop-soiled, reworked and reworn, became a frame for something entirely contemporary and mould-breaking. It became a vehicle for what silences had sought to cover, for intimacies forbidden, racisms thinly disguised and faiths no longer trusted but not easily discarded and never forgotten.

In their myth-making, Irish people have had to be modernizers again and again in different circumstances of adversity at home and abroad, in transcending the challenges of exile and the transience of the migrant experience.

The Irish people had an oral tradition that demanded the celebration of both victory and the horror of defeat in verse that could defeat the passing of time. The people had to suffer dispossession and the regular experience of famine culminating in the *Gorta Mór* of 1845–47. The emigration of almost two million people in the decades that followed the Great Famine demanded a new rendering of the inherited myths, including the myth of exile.

Well before the Famine, Irish people had in large numbers substituted the state language of the colonizer, English, for their own ancient language, which was often the language of the poor. Survival, whether in a precarious existence at home or as a migrant in America, demanded a new language in order to enter the new society. English was the vernacular required for law, for school, for church, and even the precious letter home from the emigrant.

Irish people would take that adopted language, adapt it, distort it ironically and make something entirely new of it, and, as a final flourish, use its new form to invoke both ancient versions of independence and new forms of republican existence. In this they would be assisted again and again by Irish Americans.

We are now in a time that needs new myth-making, a new vision of Irishness, and I believe that this involves both an ethical form of memory and the courage of imagination. What should we remember, and how, what might we come to know, to imagine, dare to hope and offer to an Irishness for new times?

There is no better starting point for a discussion on how Ireland might be remembered and imagined than with a consideration of Thomas Flanagan and his work. He defies all attempts at categorization.

He was a great American writer who wrote a trilogy of great Irish novels, the grandson of Irish immigrants who, by his own account, was only pale-green 'to the point of translucency' as a young man, and yet who devoted much of his life and writing to recovering the Irish historical experience through his fiction. As a literary critic he was balanced, wise and understated. He was as much at home discussing Yeats and Joyce as he was discussing Ernest Hemingway and William Kennedy. A great rescuer, he recovered from neglect and restored the reputations of Maria Edgeworth, Lady Morgan and William Carleton. Most of all, Tom Flanagan was the teacher who warned against any simplification of Irishness. 'My Irish American identity', he said, 'is typical only in the sense that there is no such typical experience.' Identity, he added, is a personal matter, complex, slanted and convoluted.

If identity is always elusive, the issue for immigrants – and the choices required of them – are even more so. For many, it was easier to put on and wear the mask expected of them than to shape a new identity. Shaping that new identity took time and was itself fraught with difficulty. Thomas Flanagan notes that the experience of many immigrant communities was that of the ghetto for the first two generations, and that this was often succeeeded by a self-ghettoization, a refusal of mainstream and official culture that was seen as unwelcoming or elitist.

William Kennedy has painstakingly recorded a lost and wholly Irish American world where, as Tom Flanagan shrewdly observes: 'Protestants, rarely glimpsed, are like unicorns, comely and delicate of bone.' Irish Americans felt themselves caught in a double bind: if they entered the establishment culture they cut off their roots and the source of much of their vitality. If they refrained from doing so, they remained trapped in a cultural province.

At the same time as they were refashioning the societies they had entered, Irish immigrant communities were also refashioning what it meant to be Irish, feeding the sources of emergent nationalism. The impact of the Irish immigrant experience on Ireland itself was creative, profound and lasting. Modern Ireland was constructed as much in Edinburgh and New York as in Galway or Dublin.

Though the immigrant mask at its point of destination may have been seen as conservative and backward-looking, in reality the Irish proved to be great modernizers, many having already chosen, as I have said, to learn English in Ireland. Some did this so as to prepare their children to survive and succeed, either overseas or in an Ireland where English was the key to literacy. The value that they set on education in their new land can be traced in bricks and mortar in countless high schools in all of New York's boroughs and in the colleges of Fordham and St John's, Manhattan. By the 1890s the Irish language was spoken in Ireland as a main language by less than 5 per cent of children under ten. For older children and adults the proportion was higher, but the Irish language was in decline. The great task of saving the language was undertaken by the Gaelic League led by my predecessor Dubhglás de hÍde.

Yet it was English that became the language of Irish separatism. Gradually, writers took control of our own story through journalism and creative writing. Stephen Dedalus's determination 'to forge in the smithy of my soul the uncreated conscience of my race' was shared in a different medium by journalists such as John Boyle O'Reilly, John Devoy and Finley Peter Dunne.

Emigration taught the Irish a further skill – the ability to maintain poise in the face of change, to live in two or even more worlds at once, to adapt and to broker. This is the migratory experience, the marginalization of consciousness, caught in literature but so often missed in the social sciences. 'To be an American conscious of his Irish identity', Flanagan once wrote, 'is to exist within complexities, paradoxes, contraries, ambiguities, ironies, and, perhaps, a few pitfalls.'

The use of memory as both solace and resentful dagger is at the heart of some of the finest writing in Irish America. Eugene O'Neill mined his family's immigrant experience and in the process revolutionized American theatre. 'The thing that explains more than anything about me', he once told his son, 'is the fact that I'm Irish.'

It is 100 years since the first Abbey Theatre performances in New York. Those performances transfixed O'Neill, then a twenty-three-year-old part-time sailor living in a boarding house and recovering from a failing marriage. So a theatre company that had revolutionized Irish theatre exerted a profound influence on a writer who in turn revolutionized American theatre. Great things happen when cultures converge and influence each other.

We often think of innovation as a matter only of the literary sphere, for example Joyce revolutionizing the English language from within. But John Scottus Eriugena stands unique among Western thinkers of the early Middle Ages in the linguistic ability and intellectual daring that enabled him to synthesize strands of thought from West and East into a coherent system that is probably without comparison in the eight centuries between Augustine and Aquinas.

We are rightly proud of Shaw, Yeats, Beckett and Heaney. Yet when Irish Nobel laureates are invoked, Ernest Walton, born in Dungarvan and joint developer of the first particle accelerator that split the atom in 1931, is often overlooked. It is easier to appreciate a poem by Yeats than to consider the disintegration of lithium; but William Rowan Hamilton in mathematics, Robert Boyle in chemisty, astronomer Agnes Mary Clerke and John Tyndall in the physics of light are also expressions of the Irish mind, as are so many Irish scientists and technologists, so many of whom teach and research in the United States. Creativity can have many manifestations – a poem or a painting, but also a new business model, medical treatment or nano-plastic composite.

But I want to return briefly to an earlier example, both principled and pragmatic, of the role that memory plays in imagination and renewal. On a snowy January night in Boston in 1897 some fifty men gathered to found the American Irish Historical Society. Their purpose was to challenge the monolithic view of American history that diminished the role played by emigrant groups in favour of an Anglocentric narrative. They included Catholics and Protestants, some born in Ireland, others from families long established in this country.

Henry Stoddard Ruggles claimed descent from an Irishman who had come to America in 1657. Theodore Roosevelt – who became President of the United States in 1901 – claimed descent from the Barnwall family, associated with Drimnagh Castle in Dublin. Augustus St-Gaudens, the great sculptor of the Parnell monument in O'Connell Street and the magnificent relief on Boston Common commemorating Colonel Shaw and the first black combat regiment in the US Army, was born in Dublin to a French father and an Irish mother. John Boyle O'Reilly, born in Dowth, County Meath, had been a trooper in the 10th Hussars before he was a Fenian, convict, fierce patriot and, later, newspaper editor. Thomas Flanagan described John Devoy, another participant, as that 'fierce and splendid old Fenian rebel'.

The AIHS was as much about the future of America as about the history of the Irish in America. Like Pearse and Joyce in the decades that followed, its founders were exercising choices over what was remembered, over what was retrieved from the brutal editing of history, mining the emigrant experience to replenish this country while also contributing to an emerging Irish identity. Their intent was to create a United States that valued and welcomed diversity and that built its narrative on genuine historical integrity, on what Tom Flanagan described as 'the enriching actualities of the American cultural experience'. They initiated their work in the same year that Yeats and Lady Gregory began the partnership that later led to the foundation of the Irish National Theatre.

The foundation of this Society was no isolated phenomenon, but part of a wider appreciation that something very precious was disappearing and would soon be irretrievable. It was also part of a process aimed at bringing the immigrant experience into the mainstream of American memory.

In another area, in a different city, a valuable act of cultural retrieval was under way. By the time the founders of the AIHS had come together in Boston, an Irish-born Chicago police officer, Francis O'Neill, had set about retrieving a different heritage, recording the work of some of the innumerable traditional Irish musicians who had emigrated to that city but whose repertoire was fast disappearing.

Music may be the most portable of art forms. While depending for its survival on appreciative listeners, among emigrant communities the audience for the music diminishes as new generations busy themselves with the task of integrating into the host culture. But the permeability of music to other forms of composition and performance may also mean, as happened in the Irish case, that it comes back home enriched and renewed. The link between music and place also renders it fragile. Eavan

Boland, herself no stranger to displacement, has described how song, sea, weather and home become one in the singers of the West of Ireland,

> *Every night their mouths filled with*
> *Atlantic storms and clouded-over stars*
> *And exhausted birds.*

We should all be grateful to Francis O'Neill for initiating one of the greatest works of cultural retrieval, saving for posterity countless melodies that would otherwise have been lost.

We should remember too that the Famine emigrants to Boston brought valuable fragments in their bundles of possessions, manuscripts copied and shared, some of which are now in the Athenaeum in Boston. What was retrieved, by O'Neill and others, is probably only a small fraction of what was lost in the decades following the Famine when New York resonated to the sound of Irish – both spoken and sung. Graffiti in Irish, etched in plaster on a wall of what is now the South Street Seaport Museum in Lower Manhattan, are among the few physical remains of a chapter in the history of Ireland and New York now largely lost to time.

Much of the oral tradition was entirely lost to posterity. Eavan Boland puts it well when she speculates that Atlantis is less a place than a metaphor for what has vanished irretrievably:

> *Maybe*
> *what really happened is*
> *this: the old fable-makers searched hard for a word*
> *to convey that what is gone is gone forever and*
> *never found it. And so, in the best traditions of*
>
> *where we come from, they gave their sorrow a name*
> *and drowned it.*

This preoccupation with memory and retrieval is also common to many Irish-American writers. William Kennedy's painstaking reconstruction of Albany in the late nineteenth and early twentieth centuries is comparable in its own way to Joyce's reconstruction of Dublin.

But the traces of lost lives go back far beyond the Famine, and can be located in the most unexpected places and recovered in the most surprising ways. Perhaps a serendipitous finding might illustrate this process. Deep in the Rappahannock Valley in the tidewaters of Virginia a cabinetmaker in the eighteenth century used a distinctive design known as the trifid foot. It is virtually unknown in Virginia outside the Rappahannock Valley, and unknown in England, but is a common form in Irish furniture. It is the signature only recently identified of an Irish craftsman who arrived in the valley sometime in the 1760s or 1770s, and reminds us that the Irish emigrant experience is rich and various. Fifty years before the Famine, New York's most vigorous trading community hailed from the northern counties of Ireland and occupied itself largely with the trade in flax seed from the Hudson Valley.

I want, however, to invoke this evening the act of remembering, not just as an act of retrieval but as a forward-looking act, as an exercise of will and of conscious choice, an essential part of the process of renewal, an illumination of the unrealized possibilities of a future Irishness – *na féidireachtaí gan teorainn.*

The impulse that drove Finian to a rock eight miles from the coast of Kerry, and 1,500 years ago drove Columbanus to what is today France and Italy, required a vision of the future, a vision that laid strong cultural foundations across Europe. The same impulse in 1632 drove Mícheál Ó Cléirigh and his collaborators to collect and transcribe manuscripts from the disappearing bardic culture; they had an eye to the future and made possible the imaginative reinvention of Ireland in succeeding centuries.

The Gaelic Revival was likewise concerned more with what Ireland might be rather than what it had once been. If we wish then to pass from failed paradigms, embark on the new and necessary reflections and policies that will serve to secure our future, we must realize that an amnesia about what Irishness was, at home or abroad, will not serve us well.

One clear thread connects the foundation of the AIHS: the work of Tom Flanagan and our circumstances today.

The AIHS came into being as Irish people around the world began to prepare for the centenary of 1798. Some of the material in your archives relates to the United Irishmen, to Robert Emmet and Wolfe Tone. That centenary, it has often been remarked, had more to do with Ireland as it was in 1898 than as it had been in 1798. The celebrations marked a turning point in the political campaign for self-determination after a decade of relative inactivity.

The Irish Parliamentary Party used it to build momentum towards Home Rule, overlooking the ambiguity inherent in what had been a bloody popular uprising. The Church recalled it as the struggle of a catholic people for religious emancipation, and tried to ignore the strong strain of secular republicanism in the uprising.

Eighty years later Thomas Flanagan again retrieved this period in Irish history for a wider audience. Writing at the height of the Troubles, the episode he chose was not the rebellion in Ulster or in Leinster which, he felt, were too burdened with 'a kind of sentimental nationalist cult' but the lesser-known uprising in Co. Mayo.

Now we are again on the threshold of centenaries of events that shaped Ireland for much of the past 100 years. Recent weeks have seen the centenaries of the first Unionist Rally against Home Rule, the introduction of the Third Home Rule Bill into Parliament and the sinking of the *Titanic*. In September we will mark the centenary of the Ulster Covenant and in coming years we will mark the birth of the Labour Party, the Great Lockout of 1913, the start of the First World War and the events that led to the Easter Rising, the War of Independence and the Civil War.

These anniversaries are also an opportunity to reflect on the American dimension of Irishness, to consider the close connections between the Labour movements in both countries, links that brought James Connolly to New Jersey and New York as a labour organizer, and Jim Larkin to Bute, Montana.

The anniversaries are also an opportunity to make peace with our complex identities. It seems to me that as the twentieth century progressed we became less comfortable with our variegated identities. The polarizing events of 100 years ago had the effect of fixing and freezing national and religious identities for the decades that followed in a way that was exclusive and confrontational, narrowing our horizons. It is the recovery of and respect for complexity that will set us free.

The sense of Irishness, as a common identity across national boundaries, could also benefit from renewal. We have too often fallen into the trap of uncritically allowing shallow differences to define us. That cannot change fast enough.

The Irishness that I believe is now emerging, but the possibilities of which have not yet been fully realized, is one that will be informed by the experience of the Irish abroad as much, or even to a greater extent than it will be by those of us who live in Ireland. Distance grants perspective, and it is not accidental that so many of our most perceptive scholars choose the lens of temporary exile, and are people of Ireland at home and abroad.

It is an Irishness that will be assessed in a global context and I believe that its ethical content will be one of the measures by which it will be tested. It is an ethical content that has to draw on the well of memory, from the richest depths of such periods as the seventh century when for the good not only of the widest conception of Europe, but for all humanity and the beauty and wonder of scholarship, those Irish scholars such as Columbanus set out from Ireland to Bobbio in Italy.

It is not only from memory that the Irishness of a new departure will come, but from what is imagined as possibility, and is capable of being brought to fruition. This, I repeat, will not be a new task for Irish people. Ireland is not a society that has simply moved out of tradition into modernity. As scholars such as Declan Kiberd have pointed out, Irish people have again and again been required to modernize, to adapt, and to learn, in order to deal with what was initially strange.

To learn a new language; to arrive in a new society and culture; to negotiate all the demands that migrants faced required a flexibility of mind that today's Irish people possess, and it is a possession enhanced by high levels of education, higher than most cohorts of the same age in any European country. That is why I believe that the new Irishness, built on an ethical base and full of creativity, will usher in a new and exciting period in Irish history.

Derek Mahon, Tom Flanagan's close friend, has recently written about the need to renew values in an Ireland that has seen such materialist excess:

> *It's time now to go back at last*
> *Beyond irony and slick depreciation*
> *Past hedge and fencing to a clearer vision*
> *Time to create a future from the past.*

We are at such a point of renewal. It is a great challenge – renewing Ireland and also renewing the sense of what it means to be Irish after the events of recent years. Those outside Ireland who share a sense of Irishness are vital to that process.

That process of renewal is one to which we must give our best efforts at home and abroad. That, after all, is simply consistent with the spirit of our constitution, acknowledging Ireland's 'special affinity with people of Irish ancestry living abroad who share its cultural identity and heritage'.

Just as the founders of this Society helped bring the Irish immigrant experience into the American mainstream, I hope that we, working together, can bring the wider global Irish experience, its ideas and innovative talent, back into the Irish mainstream.

The Global Irish Network, which was given new momentum by the gathering for the Global Irish Economic Forum at Dublin Castle last October, is one element in that process. The Certificate of Irish Heritage offers a formal recognition of Irishness that extends beyond the first two generations currently entitled to Irish citizenship. This year will see the first awards of a new Presidential Distinguished Service Award for the Irish abroad. These are small but important steps in a new attentiveness to the vital contribution that all those who belong to the Irish family can make to the process of renewal.

To return, and to finish, *mar fhocal scoir*, memory abounds in Seamus Heaney's uncollected tribute, 'A Night Piece for Tom Flanagan'. In it Heaney conjures the shades of Wolfe Tone, Maria Edgeworth, John Mitchel, George Moore and William Carleton. Then, blinking into daylight on the steps of his house overlooking Sandymount Strand, more figures from the ever-present past pause to pay tribute to the writer who so honoured and attended to our past:

> *Think of one out walking there*
> *With his ash-plant,*
> *Headed from Night-town to the Tower,*
> *By Sandymount.*
>
> *Our genius loci, fount of inwit,*
> *Our conscience-forger lifts his hat,*
> *And tips you an old world salute*
> *As if to say*
> *'Yes, yes' to you and all you write,*
> *Your mastery.*
>
> *And now a bat flits from the trees*
> *To grow a form I recognize,*

The silent flap of W. B.'s
Great soul in flight,
He circles thrice to greet you, flies
Into the night.

George Steiner wrote that 'without the true fiction of history, without the unbroken animation of a chosen past, we become flat shadows'.

Thomas Flanagan gave us not flat shadows but the 'true fiction' of history. He did so with an eye fixed firmly on the present and the future. In the last lines of his greatest novel, memory and imagination are harnessed to present purpose, and I am delighted to let him have the last word: 'It is in the brightness of the morning air, as the poet tells us, that hope and memory walk towards us across meadows, radiant as a girl in her first beauty.'

'When we hold to our ears the convoluted shell of the past,' he once noted, 'what we hear are our own voices. But... the voices... have been instructed by all that we know about the past, all the contradictory things that we feel about it, all that we have imagined about it. Those voices make possible for us imaginary selves, imaginary opposites, imaginary others.'

John Hewitt
Summer School

||||||||||||||||||||||||||||||||||||||||||||||||||||||||||||||||||||||||||||||||||||||

MARKET PLACE THEATRE, ARMAGH

28 JULY 2014

*I*S Í SEO *an chéad deis a bhí agam teacht go hArd Mhacha mar Uachtarán na hÉireann. Táim, dar ndóigh, ar an eolas maidir leis an mbreithiúnas machnamhach a thug Aodh de Blácam, iriseoir Éire-annach sna 1930idí, ar Ard Mhacha, nuair a thug sé cathair gheanúil air agus a dúirt: 'fair in its site, its sacred buildings and homes of learning, its air of quietude, culture and ease'.*

(This is my first opportunity to come to Armagh as President of Ireland. I am of course very aware of the reflective assessment given to it in the 1930s by Aodh de Blácam, an Irish journalist who called Armagh a lovable city, 'fair in its site, its sacred buildings and homes of learning, its air of quietude, culture and ease'.)[10]

I approach the subject of John Hewitt, his life, work and legacy with some trepidation. This is a region that is so leavened by the poetic instinct that humility is more than usually necessary.

As I am speaking in tribute to a writer who was so well aware of the

---

10   Aodh de Blácam, 'The Black North' (1938), in Patricia Craig (ed.), *The Ulster Anthology* (Blackstaff Press, 2006), p. 379.

appalling waste of life that is war, and a writer of conscience who often reflected on the ethics of internationalism, I am also conscious that the violent loss of life going on as I speak would not only break his heart, as it is now breaking the hearts of many people, but also force his pen.

Allow me, then, just a few words on those present circumstances. I believe that the enormous increase in instability and conflict at the present time is a great challenge to the international community. It also represents a great failure. It surely must be a matter of profound concern to citizens across the globe that in so many conflicts – in Gaza, Syria, Iraq, Ukraine and elsewhere – loss of life is increasing daily, security is decreasing and refugee numbers are escalating relentlessly, with horrific consequences for the most vulnerable. It is a time when we are challenged to come up with new solutions in the search for peace, realizing that a diplomacy of narrow interests, compounded by the consequences of diplomatic failure, is threatening all of our human achievements.

The appalling loss of life in Gaza is a tragic example of the failure of diplomacy. There is an acute awareness among our Irish citizens, especially, of the importance of building and securing peaceful resolution to such conflicts. In recent weeks I have received a great volume of correspondence from members of the public expressing their horror at what is happening in Gaza, and I share their horror at the perceived failure of language itself in describing a solution to this intractable conflict. In celebrating the life of John Hewitt – one who cared so deeply about peace and the relations between peoples – it is appropriate that we reflect on the relevance of Hewitt's work in the atmosphere of today's violent confrontations.

In preparation for my speech today I read, inter alia, Peter McDonald's assessment of John Hewitt in the *Oxford Handbook of Modern Irish Poetry*,[11] in which he remarks that Hewitt dead has been far more influential than Hewitt the living writer. This view is no doubt influenced by the fact that

11   Fran Brearton (ed.), *The Oxford Handbook of Modern Irish Poetry* (Oxford University Press, 2012), pp. 479–80.

he is now a subject of that most potent form of Irish commemoration – the literary summer school – and I wish to acknowledge my debt to Frank Ormsby's magnificent introduction to the *Collected Poems of John Hewitt*, and to Patricia Craig's fine piece in a recent edition of that incomparable journal *Irish Pages*.

What an excellent programme you have for this week, with one of Ireland's leading poets, a dazzling prose writer and memoirist, John Montague, as one of the speakers at this Summer School. I will be reflecting briefly on some of the connections John Hewitt made with John Montague and how these connections have given us greater insight into the meaning of Hewitt's work.

When I visited Coventry as part of my State Visit to the United Kingdom earlier this year, I met many Irish emigrants who were amongst the half a million Irish men and women who travelled to England in the 1950s to work on the construction sites, in the hospitals and schools. I was able to celebrate the fact that there is virtually no aspect of British civic or political life that has not been enriched by the Irish community. I was pleased to bear witness to their contribution to British culture, and to their continuing contribution to the renewal of our own Irish identity.

Of course, Coventry received a very special emigrant from these shores in the 1950s when John Hewitt left Northern Ireland to take up the position of Director of the Herbert Art Gallery and Museum. It was in that bittersweet exile that he wrote many of his most thoughtful and resonant poems, including 'An Irishman in Coventry' (1958), which he composed the year after he moved to that city. It ends with the words:

> Yet like Lir's children, banished to the waters,
> Our hearts still listen for the landward bells.

It is interesting to reflect on how Hewitt's sense of identity seems to have been changed by his move to Coventry. He was an Ulsterman in Northern

Ireland but an Irishman in England. Hewitt, of course, reflected a great deal on the issues of identity and memory. In an article in the *Belfast Telegraph* in November 1958 he wrote:

> In the heart of the English midlands looking back from the fulcrum of middle age on my personal adventures among those books which were a significant part of my Irish past, I sometimes wonder if time and distance have given me a perspective and objectivity or if sentiment and the ordinary wear and tear of memory may not have distorted details and proportion.

Hewitt's vision of Ulster included a multitude of identities competing for space. His 'Ulsterman'[12] was part

> *Kelt, Briton, Saxon, Dane, and Scot,*
> *Time and this island tied a crazy knot.*

But categories and their naming should not obscure from us the gift of a father's egalitarian thought that would endure as a permanent legacy in his son's life, one that might, as Frank Ormsby tells us, have led to the young John Hewitt borrowing ten shillings from his mother to buy a second-hand five-volume set of William Morris's *The Earthly Paradise*.

Hewitt said of his poem 'The Colony' (1953) that it was the definitive statement of his realization that he was an Ulsterman.[13] In this poem, Hewitt evoked the point of view of a Roman colonizer in England in the period when the Roman Empire itself was in decline. Edna Longley has described this poem as a 'sophisticated poetic model of Ulster politics'.[14]

12   'An Ulsterman' (1938).
13   Quoted by Frank Ormsby, *Introduction to the Collected Poems of John Hewitt* (Blackstaff Press, 1991).
14   Edna Longley, *The Living Stream: Literature and Revisionism in Ireland* (Bloodaxe Books, 1994), p. 126.

The Irish Times[15] used the poem's closing line, 'we shall not be outcast on the world', for the title of an editorial responding to an initiative of British Prime Minister Edward Heath in 1973 that would result in the Sunningdale Agreement – for a power-sharing government in Northern Ireland involving Catholic Nationalists and Protestant Unionists – later that year. The editor argued that the majority in Northern Ireland now had a chance to prove that they were in their right place and wrote, 'In the words of their own poet, John Hewitt, the Northern majority will be able to say: "We would be strangers in the Capitol; /This is our country also, no-where else; /And we shall not be outcast on the world".'

Hewitt was very forthright in invoking and declaring his Planter identity and heritage. Indeed, as part of a literary tour in 1970 he jointly published with John Montague *The Planter and the Gael*,[16] with both poets contributing work from their respective viewpoints and being very aware of their representative status.

In his introduction to that collection, Michael Longley wrote that 'each poet explores his experience of Ulster, the background in which he grew up and the tradition which has shaped his work. John Montague defines the culture of the Gael, John Hewitt that of the Planter. The two bodies of work complement each other and provide illuminating insight into the cultural complexities of the Province.' The integrity of both poets, Hewitt and Montague, and Longley too, is reflected in their rejection of any convenient amnesia about the complex past.

John Wilson Foster, in a study published in the 1970s, showed how the land itself is evoked in *The Planter and the Gael* through the different backgrounds of Montague and Hewitt. Montague's poems reflect loss, decay, absence and exile, whereas Hewitt views the land through a Planter's sensibility, invoking the human labour expended on it, the memory of

---

15 Editorial, 25 March 1972.
16 John Hewitt and John Montague, *The Planter and the Gael: An Anthology of Poems* (Arts Council of Northern Ireland, 1970).

harnessing its fertility, husbanding it and taming it for productive use. This legacy is also an invocation of a particular kind of Irishness. For Hewitt, his identity was bound up in place and a land shaped by work. Another example of Hewitt's connection to the landscape can be seen in his poem 'Townland of Peace' (1944), in which he traces his sense of himself, of his family and of the landscape from his grandfather's time to the present. There is here, I believe, a claim for a sovereignty of sensory intimacy, an intimacy with land.

Perhaps the most resonant example of Hewitt's understanding of the complex identity of those who live in Northern Ireland is contained in his essay 'Planter's Gothic: An Essay in Discursive Autobiography'.[17] In this work, Hewitt discussed his reaction to a Gothic tower built by a colonist on the remains of a much older round tower. Discussing its impact on him,[18] he said:

> It is the best symbol I have found for the strange textures of my response to this island of which I am a native. It may appear Planter's Gothic, but there is a round tower somewhere inside, and needled through every sentence I utter.

He had, then, a multifaceted understanding of identity in Northern Ireland, but Hewitt was also very aware of the connection of the region he called home to a wider Europe. In an introduction to a catalogue for an art exhibition in Belfast, he wrote:

> At the beginning of the last century Belfast was in full contact with the flow of European events. But in the intervening period, mainly

---

17   John Hewitt, 'Planter's Gothic: An Essay in Discursive Autobiography', in *The Bell* (1953).
18   Quoted by Frank Ormsby, *Introduction to the Collected Poems of John Hewitt* (Blackstaff Press, 1991).

for political-economic reasons, the scope of wit and culture suffered a time-lag of increasing proportions. Our province became provincial. However, since the Great War and partly consequent upon it, the acceleration of social change has narrowed the gap between Ulster and Europe. Once again our best aesthetic thought is coloured by contemporary tendencies.[19]

Hewitt himself spent a lot of time in Europe. The Public Record Office of Northern Ireland holds his notebooks with their detailed accounts of his educational holidays in Europe.[20] As they, the diaries, wryly note, because of his egalitarian sympathies he was naturally attracted to Russia and countries such as Czechoslovakia, East Germany, Hungary, Poland and Yugoslavia. Consideration of the materialist and statist excesses of these regimes, and how this affected Hewitt, is a subject for another day.

Hewitt was always very insistent that the location of his home region into the wider European context was vital and that leaving out any element of the broader picture would lead to profound misunderstandings. In a letter to John Montague he stated:

I always maintained that our loyalties had an order: to Ulster, to Ireland, to the British Archipelago, to Europe; and that anyone who skipped a step or missed a link falsified the total. The Unionists missed out Ireland: the Northern Nationalists (The Green Tories) couldn't see the Ulster under their feet; the Republicans missed out both Ulster and the Archipelago; and none gave any heed to Europe at all. Now, perhaps, willy nilly bundled in the European rump of the Common Market, clearer ideas of our regional and

---

19   John Hewitt (1934), Preface to Ulster Unit, exhibition catalogue, as quoted by Riann Coulter, 'John Hewitt: Creating a Canon of Ulster Art', *Journal of Art Historiography*, 1934.

20   'Introduction to Hewitt Papers' (2007), Public Record Office of Northern Ireland, Ref D3838.

national allegiances and responsibilities may emerge, or our whole sad stubborn conglomeration of nations may founder and disappear for ever.[21]

Hewitt's views on the opportunity that Europe presented to Northern Ireland were very close to the thinking of the Swiss philosopher Denis de Rougemont.

Rougemont was a committed European federalist who saw that Europe, after the Second World War, needed a new concept of unity. He looked to the regional model, to the principle of subsidiarity, and also to the origins of the continent and its founding myths.[22] For him, Homer's *Iliad* and *Odyssey* were more relevant than the nation state for understanding the future of Europe. Indeed, for Rougemont *the ultimate foundation of our European identity is not the national state, but the European unity represented by our shared cultural roots.* The ancient myths that we, along with the other peoples of Europe, have absorbed as the foundations of our literatures provide us not only with a shared vision but also a respect for cultural diversity. Our founding myths are universal and their traces can be found in the diverse wisdoms of the world, in all of our faith systems.

I think that Rougemont was very perceptive in his insights that a shared influence of myths and cultural memory intangibly links us all together in Europe. The categories of both memory and imagination must always remain open.

An open sensibility of this kind can also be seen in the work of Michael Longley, a poet who was a contemporary of Hewitt in the Belfast Group.[23] On the eve of the IRA's ceasefire in 1994, Longley had been working on a poem, 'Ceasefire' (1994), based on the *Iliad*. He sent a copy of the

---

21 John Hewitt, Extract from a letter to John Montague, 1964, John Hewitt Collection, University of Ulster, Coleraine.
22 Denis de Rougemont, *The Idea of Europe* (Macmillan, 1966).
23 Mark Carruthers, *Alternative Ulsters* (Liberties Press, 2013), pp. 195–205.

finished work to John Banville, then Literary Editor of the *Irish Times*. Recognizing the quality and importance of the work, Banville 'stopped the presses' and ensured its inclusion in the paper in the same week as the ceasefire was declared. The poem is based on the episode in the *Iliad* which tells the story of Priam, the King of Troy, and Achilles, the Greek warrior who killed his son Hector. Priam, the distraught father, comes to the Greek camp to plead for the return of his son's body. Achilles, moved by the old king's grief, grants his request and agrees to a truce to allow the Trojans time to hold a proper funeral. I have more than once quoted the words Michael Longley gave to Priam:

> *I get down on my knees and do what must be done*
> *And kiss Achilles' hand, the killer of my son.*

One cannot but be struck by the generosity, empathy and remorse that are reflected in these words, rooted as they are in a poem that has its origins 3,000 years ago. Longley's words echo back through the millennia to Homer, and forward to today, with great immediacy and power. Troy was not saved by the gesture; the war resumed after Hector's funeral. The moral intention in the action and the words, however, has its own sustaining power. It is appropriate for us to remember Hannah Arendt's suggestion that in order to have authentic meaning, forgiveness must be aimed at either preventing or enabling future events.

Denis de Rougemont coined the phrase 'a Europe of the regions'.[24] He suggested that it was necessary to leave behind arid concepts of territorial division and instead consider the interdependent relationships that all communities experience. For him, the key thing was to allow human communities to co-operate in very practical ways, and he was particularly interested in border regions which, he felt, would be in the vanguard in

---

24   Denis de Rougemont, *The Idea of Europe* (Macmillan, 1966).

teaching the rest of Europe how to order itself. He believed that it was only by overcoming divisions that we would preserve our diversity.

Hewitt engaged with similar concepts through his prose work and his poetry. His vision of regionalism began with a revival of the poetry of peace. He worked throughout his life to promote the regional culture of Ulster as a distinct identity. In his poem 'Townland of Peace' he wrote:

> *But these small rights require a smaller stage*
> *than the vast forum of the nations' rage*
> *for they imply a well-compacted space*
> *where every voice recalls its nation's place,*
> *townland, townquarter, county at its most...*

Hewitt was of the view that:

> Ulster considered as a Region and not as a symbol of any particu-
> lar creed, can command the loyalty of every one of its inhabitants.
> For regional identity does not preclude, rather it requires, mem-
> bership of a larger association. And whatever that association may
> be... there should emerge a culture and an attitude individual and
> distinctive... and no mere echo of the thought and imagination of
> another people or another land.[25]

This is both a suggestion and a recognition of the importance of a rooted imagination – an uninhibited, generous imagination.

Culture can play an enormous role in reinvigorating the wider society. I had the opportunity when I was Minister for Culture during Ireland's Presidency of the EU in 1996 to oversee a key piece of legislation that focused on the integration of cultural considerations into community

---

25   John Hewitt, 'Essay on Regionalism: The Last Chance', published in *The Northman*, 1947.

actions.[26] It affirmed that access to culture and the expression of cultural identity were essential conditions for the full participation of citizens in society. In this period of high unemployment, with its related insecurities and poverty, as we pursue a sustainable economic recovery we must not lose sight of what culture offers in helping us reclaim a flourishing role in the wider global community.

Hewitt's views on regionalism also bring to mind the ideas of the French philosopher Paul Ricoeur. In his work, Ricoeur posed the question as to how one might be modern and yet sustain tradition, how we might revive an old dormant civilization as part of universal civilization.[27] He understood that it was not easy to remain authentically personal and at the same time practise tolerance towards other civilizations. As he saw it, the discovery of the plurality of cultures is never a harmless experience. So how is an encounter with different cultures possible when understanding the other can seem like a dangerous venture that could result in the loss of your own cultural heritage? Ricoeur's own answer to this question was that a culture had to engage with what had preceded it, what is occurring around it and what flows from it.

In considering what Ulster regionalism means, Seamus Heaney also had a perceptive insight: 'Each person in Ulster lives first in the Ulster of the actual present, and then in one or other Ulster of the mind.'[28]

Hewitt saw the different traditions as interrelated, and he felt the best way to recognize the reconciling implications of this was at the regional level. For Hewitt, the region was small enough to win the kind of loyalty that is needed to transcend differences. The region could also act as a counterweight to what he saw as the prevailing forces of over-centralization. He was convinced that we must, as social beings, facing the

---

26   Meeting of the Council AUDIOVISUAL/CULTURAL AFFAIRS, Brussels, 16 December 1996 – European Council – PRES/96/381, 16/12/1996.
27   Paul Ricoeur, *History and Truth* (Northwestern University Press, 1965), pp. 271–84.
28   Seamus Heaney, *Place and Displacement* (Trustees of Dove Cottage, 1984).

enormously complicated structure that is the modern nation state, find some smaller unit to which to give our loyalty. He saw this as a necessary precondition to the invigoration of regional agriculture and industry.

John Hewitt's views on the importance of developing a regional outlook can also be seen as his reaction to the impact of partition on Northern Ireland. His hopes for an inclusive regional loyalty were, of course, stymied by the Troubles. But now that we have emerged from that dark period, there is an opportunity to revisit and draw inspiration from Hewitt's ideas.

I am struck particularly by the recent analysis of the 2011 census results by the Northern Ireland Statistics and Research Agency.[29] For the first time, the census has included questions about national identity. Particularly notable was that, when asked how they viewed their national identity, 29 per cent of people included 'Northern Irish' rather than 'British' or 'Irish' as a part of that identity: something new is emerging here.

Hewitt's understanding of these questions of regionalism and identity are relevant in grasping how people see themselves in the context of their wider allegiances to Ireland and the UK. People are perhaps now more comfortable endorsing multiple identities that suit the shifting way in which we, as individuals, relate to a world that is increasingly fluid and porous, one that we must struggle beyond boundaries and states to make accountable and sustainable.

We must also consider the new community of immigrants in Northern Ireland. More than 120,000 arrived between 2000 and 2010. To quote a Northern Irish Assembly paper, 'there is little doubt that the inflow of new residents from countries as far apart as Poland, Brazil and East Timor, has enriched the culture and society of Northern Ireland'.[30] It will be fascinating to hear from those migrants how their own identities change

---

29 *Census 2011: Key statistics for Northern Ireland*, December 2012, Northern Ireland Statistics and Research Agency.
30 Raymond Russell, 'Migration in Northern Ireland, Research and Information Service of the Northern Ireland Assembly' (Paper 31/12, 2012).

as they respond to what they are making of their new home region, and to see what their responses will be to the national identity question at the next census in 2021.

May I, to conclude, repeat how Hewitt was a man who understood that we all are the bearers of multiple allegiances, multiple identities, and are empowered by hopes and ideas yet to be realized. John Hewitt understood that to find peace, he needed to know his own place in the world. His lifelong effort was to understand himself and his place – his identity, his culture, his region – and to achieve an understanding of the self and the world; and his search was informed by an inherited respect for the potential of an emancipatory egalitarianism. There is in his work a moral utopian instinct that remains as valuable now as it was when Hewitt first fashioned it for himself.

It is with gratitude and respect that I grant him the final word from 'Townland of Peace':

> *Now and for ever through the change-rocked years,*
> *I know my corner in the universe;*
> *my corner, this small region limited*
> *in space by sea, in the time by my own dead…*

Culture and Transformation

I AM DELIGHTED TO be here today in Magee College. In a little over six months, I have had the opportunity to visit this wonderful city twice – during the Presidential Election campaign, and, two days after taking up office, when Sabina and I were in the Millennium Centre to enjoy some wonderful performances at the All-Island School Choir competition.

Next year the Maiden City will become Derry-Londonderry, the City of Culture. I look forward to the sights and sounds of a wonderful chapter in the history of this great city. The year of celebration will give us an opportunity to affirm culture and creativity in a way that brings together all communities that share the city, its wider hinterland and both parts of this island.

Derry was a city of culture well before it acquired this new and deserved recognition. Some of Ireland's finest living creative minds have been nurtured here, finding words, music and inspiration to reflect the wonder and greatness within and without these walls. This is a Derry which lives in literature and song, parallel to the living city.

Seamus Heaney was born in rural County Derry and spent his formative years here in this city, whose people and places have been an enduring presence in his poetry and prose. Derry takes on an almost mythical quality in his work: 'The Landscape was sacramental, instinct with signs, implying a system of reality beyond the visible realities.'[31]

Jennifer Johnston captured in her work a city going through its darkest times but still vibrant and possessing a wild beauty – a trouble-stained city pushed up against the wide expanse of Lough Foyle, the city streets giving way to country lanes. Seamus Deane, a distinguished son of Derry, also finds beauty in the ordinary, the everyday life of people and place, memorably describing a homecoming to his native city:

> *Crusts of light lie pulsing*
> *Diamanté with the rain*
> *At the track's end. Amazing!*
> *I am in Derry once again.*
> *Once more I turn to greet*
> *Ground that flees from my feet.*[32]

Ní hamháin go bhfuil áit ag Doire san fhocal scríofa, ach tá an cumadóir Phil Coulter tar éis ómós a thabhairt dá bhaile dúchais ina chuid ceoil agus amhrán mar atá déanta ag mórán daoine eile leis. Tá sé suntasach go bhfuil an áit seo i ndon go leor ealaíontóirí a spreagadh agus go bhfuil sé i gcónaí mar áit a spreagann a leithéid de chruthaitheacht.

(It is not only the written word that is inspired by Derry. The composer Phil Coulter has honoured his native place with music and song as so many others have done. It is invaluable that this place can elicit such creativity.)

Creativity is not, of course, limited to the artistic sphere alone. In my inaugural speech, I spoke of creative communities where people can give

---

31   Seamus Heaney, from 'The Sense of Place' (1977), in *Preoccupations: Selected Prose 1968–1978* (Faber and Faber, 1980).
32   Seamus Deane, *Gradual Wars* (Irish University Press, 1972).

expression to new ideas, where people can effect positive changes at local level. Creativity is a powerful resource that has to be nurtured in our communities and lays the foundation for social, cultural and economic transformation.

That positive change can occur through creative thinking is shown by John Hume's hugely important contribution to Northern Ireland's recent history. He is an inspirational figure and we owe him a huge debt of gratitude for his courage in bringing peace to this place and the whole of the island. John Hume had a vision of the future – one where violence was no longer the currency of politics, where, as alternative, people engaged in dialogue to find a fair and balanced accommodation between equally legitimate aspirations. Even during the darkest days, when many people despaired, John had the courage to imagine a Northern Ireland at peace – what it might look like and what the route map to get there should be. It was that moral imagination, that intellectual creativity – endlessly articulated and restated – that became the template for the Good Friday Agreement and the basis for the partnership politics that Northern Ireland enjoys today.

The city of Derry and its people have, in many ways, been the most creative influences on the peace process and have led the process of trans-formational change, in many cases, before it was embraced in other parts of Northern Ireland.

Mark Durkan and Martin McGuinness have both occupied the office of Deputy First Minister and discharged their duties with great integrity, effectiveness and generosity. Speaker William Hay, a proud representative of the city of Londonderry, has nurtured and promoted good working relationships between all the parties in the Northern Ireland Assembly.

The community in Derry has also played its part. As the first Vice Chairman of the Policing Board, Denis Bradley courageously pioneered the implementation of the new policing structures in Northern Ireland. On the sometimes contentious issue of parades, the loyal orders and the city traders in Derry showed what can be achieved when people engage with each other with mutual respect rather than staying frozen in a sterile impasse. The families of the Bloody Sunday campaign showed too that their very long struggle for justice did not bring with it a hardening of the heart; that the truth, eventually acknowledged, liberated us all; and that vindication was not followed by recrimination but by a healing dignity and generosity.

It is difficult to believe that thirty-two years have elapsed since the establishment of the 'Field Day' project. Its first production was, of course, Brian Friel's *Translations*, which premiered in the Guildhall in Derry on 23 September 1980. The founders of 'Field Day' wanted to establish an open space – a conceptual 'fifth province' that transcended the sterile divisions of politics and allowed issues of culture and identity to be constructively explored. They saw how art and culture could combat prejudice and narrow the chasms of mutual misunderstanding between the two political traditions in Northern Ireland.

Art and culture have the same potential to play that transformative role today and they are needed more than ever. The powerful dominance of the neo-liberal economic model over the last thirty years has had a very negative impact, not just on an economy where speculative investments and deregulated markets have wreaked financial havoc, but also on how we interact with each other. The tendency of recent decades to regard the individual as primarily a consumer, to whom one sells more and more goods and services, rather than as a citizen who actively participates in society, has had an impoverishing effect on all our lives.

Culture can prevent and treat some of these negative effects. It can build an understanding of the many facets of sustainability, promote a sense of solidarity, positively inspire a model of economy that values fairness and is ethically robust, and be the bedrock from which, self-confident about the integrity of our own culture, we can reach out to understand and respect other cultures. Culture is therefore a matter of public policy that needs to be brought in from the margins. It is not a residual issue tangential to the needs of the real economy.

Creativity and culture are also firmly rooted in a sense of place, a sense of belonging. This feeling of belonging somewhere is fundamental to our sense of community. I know that the people of Derry identify very strongly with their own corner of the city and county. They want to preserve and protect their home place. They feel proud of 'their' area – whether it is on the City side or in the Waterside, in the Bogside or in the Fountain. This community feeling is a valuable asset to the city, if it can be harnessed to bring people together. It can also be abused, however, and used to forge rivalries and notions of 'them' and 'us'. A sense of community and love of place should be unifying factors, not ones that create division and separation.

The Irish Government's Reconciliation and Anti-Sectarianism Fund has for many years supported initiatives in Derry that aim to overcome the burden of the past and to build cultural and economic connections at a community level that will transcend historical differences. Last summer, for instance, the Fund supported the InterAct Festival, which enabled young people from all over Derry and surrounding areas to express themselves through the creative arts. The Fund has also provided support to the Junction, in its promotion of 'ethical and shared remembering' – an inclusive and sensitive approach to the city where cultural differences can be respected.

History can also be used to unify or divide. Over the coming decade, we will be marking a series of anniversaries of momentous events – from the introduction of the Third Home Rule Bill and the signing of the Ulster Covenant in 1912, through the Great War and the Easter Rising, to the signing of the Anglo-Irish Treaty, the Partition of Ireland and the advent of Civil War. These events and the way in which they were communicated have had a defining impact on political structures and national identities on both sides of the border. How we choose to commemorate these centenaries now, what events we decide to prioritize and what versions of the varying historical narrative we listen to, will have a major impact on the process of reconciliation and mutual understanding on this island. In short, how do we address the inevitable question of conflicting narratives? I am conscious of the work of contemporary Irish philosopher, Richard Kearney, in addressing this challenge and I am happy to extend our gratitude to him for his public engagement on the issue.

Richard Kearney, following the French philosopher Paul Ricoeur, has suggested five ways of dealing with conflicting narratives.

First, an ethic of narrative hospitality; as Ricoeur puts it, this means: 'Taking responsibility in imagination and in sympathy for the story of the other through the narratives that concern the other.'

Second, an ethic of narrative flexibility – being open to showing, and being shown, how each event can be interpreted differently in different generations and by different narrators.

Third, narrative plurality; or, as Ricoeur says: 'The ability to recount the founding events of our national history in different ways is reinforced by the exchange of cultural memories.'

Fourth, transfiguration of the past – by this is meant, as Kearney puts it, 'a creative retrieval of the betrayed promises of the past'. This allows the unfulfilled future of the past – with all its emancipatory promise – to be made available as an instrument for our present and future.

Finally, pardon – this involves moving beyond a narrative of openness to the act of forgiveness. This recognizes the difference between a form of amnesia, which would be false and even amoral, and an amnesty that will open the window for the time when, as Kearney writes, 'an ethics of reciprocity is touched by a politics of pardon'.

I have drawn on this work in a number of engagements North and South and I have combined it with the writing of Hannah Arendt on the issue of forgiveness.

Bearing in mind these reflections, we should seize the opportunity the various centenaries provide to deepen mutual understanding of our shared histories, North and South. While recognizing that different people can adhere to differing interpretations of the same events, it will be important that the commemoration of these anniversaries is carried out in a spirit of tolerance. Historical accuracy, too, will be a cornerstone of commemoration, and historians will have a vital role to play in ensuring that intellectual rigour prevails over any polemical distortion of past events.

However, our exploration of the past will not be simply an academic exercise. It must also be a deliberate act of imaginative engagement. Our artists surely have a key role in shaping the ways in which we, as members of overlapping communities, gain a deeper insight into the events of the past. Such an approach will provide us with not just a better understanding of our history, but also of who we are today, and how important it is to remain focused on reaching the destination of a shared society and reconciled island.

I am, of course, very conscious that this decade of centenaries may not be at the top of the agenda for some people. Many Irish men and women are much more preoccupied by the struggle of coping with the severe impact of the current recession. In these difficult times, when the economy faces many difficulties, it is easy to fall into the trap of despair and despondency. People are naturally concerned and worried about the future, especially about the employment prospects for the younger generation. I know that both administrations on the island are working very hard, separately and together, to put in place policies and measures that promote economic growth and boost employment. As part of these efforts, it makes eminent sense to broaden and deepen North–South co-operation with a view to improving the quality of services to citizens on both sides of the border and to optimize the economies of scale that come from a shared approach to providing those services.

In this region, the implementation of the North West Gateway Initiative is an important priority. Other practical examples of the value of North–South co-operation include the shared provision of cancer services in Altnagelvin Hospital and of international broadband links via Project Kelvin. I also look forward to closer links between our higher education institutions – including the involvement of this wonderful institution. North–South engagement has been a feature of life at Magee College almost from its inception, when a Dublin architect called Gribben designed the college building in the late nineteenth century.

Co-operation, mutual understanding and respect are themes to which we must return time and time again. As we learn to live together on this island, we must also look forward and plan for a shared future; one which includes all people regardless of their social class, community affiliation or ethnic identity; and one in which our citizens do not live segregated lives. The legacy of history means that there are undeniable differences between our two main traditions. We should not seek to ignore the existence of these differences. We can and should, however, acknowledge these differences with mutual respect, whilst making the conscious decision to work together, live together and celebrate our common history in a way that enhances the quality of our shared society.

As I mentioned earlier, one of my first official engagements after becoming President was here in Derry. The occasion was the All-Ireland Choirs competition, where secondary school children from all over the island gathered to make music and sing together. Seeing those young people enjoying themselves together, both on and off stage, showed me clearly what the future can and should look like for the people of Ireland. Many other organizations bring young people from both parts of the island together through culture and sport. I rejoice in the fact that such events have become commonplace, and are increasingly regarded as remarkable only for the talent and skills on display.

Ladies and gentlemen, I am full of hope for a great future for this island and this city. We have come so far and through such dark times, with the people of Derry leading the way out of conflict; showing how a society can transform itself, and the positive role that a rich culture can play in that transformation.

Derry's Peace Bridge is in many ways the physical embodiment of the transformation I have been talking about. In admiring the Bridge, I was struck by its almost sinuous quality: it reminded me of Alice Oswald's description of Westminster Bridge in London as 'the stone wing-bone of the city'.[33] It is not just a bridge bringing people together; it is not just a bridge bringing communities together; it is not just a bridge bringing North and South together; it is a set of wings by which our people, our communities and our cultures can rise up and fly to a new future together, leaving behind the wasteful burdens of the past.

33   Alice Oswald, 'Another Westminster Bridge' in *Woods* etc. (Faber and Faber, 2008).

TOWARDS AN ETHICAL
FOREIGN POLICY

Of Memory and Testimony

The Importance of Paying Tribute to the Emancipators

LA UNIVERSIDAD CENTROAMERICANA, SAN SALVADOR, EL SALVADOR

24 OCTOBER 2013

I AM PROFOUNDLY MOVED to be here today at the Universidad Centroamericana. It means so much to me and to my wife Sabina to have the opportunity of remembering those who died and suffered in El Salvador during the 1980s as they stood up for the defence of human rights. Theirs was a struggle for greater social justice that included emancipation from poverty, access to land and the basic means of livelihood for the poorest Salvadorans.

This is my third visit to El Salvador. When I first came to your country in January 1982, the atmosphere was very different from the one which now happily offers such opportunity and hope. El Salvador was then a place where every day people were being tortured, raped, killed and 'disappeared'; a place where countless others were being displaced and forced to become refugees. Families were broken up. The country's social fabric was being torn apart as a result of the violence exerted by the state on the insurgent forces and the non-combatant population alike, but also because of the reckless impunity which accompanied that violence.

Indeed it was under the protection of state bodies, but outside the law, that crimes of the gravest sort were being committed. Opposition political leaders, trade unionists, churchmen, human rights activists, educators, co-operative leaders and beneficiaries of the agrarian reform – that is, all those who were perceived as 'subversives' by certain elements of the privileged establishment and their supporters within the government and army – became the target of systematic acts of terror. In an effort to deprive the guerrillas of their means of survival, entire communities were destroyed by members of the armed forces and their paramilitary adjuncts. This was notably the case in rural areas, where violence was indiscriminate in the extreme.

Violence breeds violence. State violence was the greater part of the violence often in alliance with the paramilitary forces of the Right such as the Arena Party, but human rights were also being violated by members of the guerrilla forces, particularly through the forcible recruitment of combatants, hostage-taking and the murder of mayors, government officials, judges and those designated as traitors or *orejas* (informers). Five per cent of the complaints registered in the early 1990s by the UN Commission on the Truth for El Salvador thus concern the Farabundo Martí National Liberation Front (FMLN).

With the end of the war and the signature of the Chapultepec Peace Agreement on 16 January 1992, Salvadorans embarked on the difficult task of confronting the causes and results of such devastating violence, as well as – to quote the words of the UN Truth Commission – 'the issue of the widespread, institutionalized impunity which had struck at its very heart'.

So let me express my admiration for the Salvadoran people, for the courage they have shown throughout the terrible conflict, for the outstanding spirit which they have generously demonstrated in the peace process, and for the ways in which they are now tackling the memory of the dark times.

Memory, indeed, is one of the greatest forms of interrogation bequeathed to us by the twentieth century, with its cortège of mass crimes and experiments with totalitarianism. How and what are we to remember? How are individual and collective memory to be articulated? In what ways does the 'duty of memory' summon us to do justice to the dead? What is the relationship between memory and history? These are first-order moral questions. They are central to the work of important thinkers such as Maurice Halbwachs, Hannah Arendt or Paul Ricoeur – work that I find myself returning to again and again as I attempt an answer to such questions, not only in the case of El Salvador but in so many places where conflict and suffering have occurred, including Northern Ireland.

According to the Argentine human rights activist Juan E. Méndez, while it is the case that each society coming out of a war attempts to confront its past in the way it deems most appropriate to its specific situation, the role of 'truth' in building durable peace must be recognized, and its pursuit is essential. As he puts it: 'the question of how to address a legacy of human rights violations occupies a central place in most transition processes to democracy because it says something of the quality of the nascent regime'.[34]

It is therefore encouraging to acknowledge, in the wider Latin American region, the important cathartic role played by institutions such as the Museum of Memory and Human Rights in Santiago de Chile, or the Space for Memory and the Promotion and Defence of Human Rights in Buenos Aires, which I had the privilege to visit last year. The creation of such spaces allows those who experienced abuse of human rights and direct personal loss during an armed conflict to tell their stories and to see the histories of their loved ones reinserted into the communal memory.

---

34 My translation. Quoted from J. E. Méndez, 'El derecho humano a la verdad. Lecciones de las experiencias latinoamericana de relato de la verdad', text published in 2007 as a contribution to the project *Historizar el pasado vivo en America Latina*.

The struggle against impunity is also important. That struggle is not only endorsed by dedicated institutions, but it is also, we must never forget, made possible by the courage of so many remarkable individuals, who continue to battle against the obscuring of the past and seek to salvage from the grim oblivion of death and torture the spirit of their loved ones.

Last year in Chile I met with Joan Turner Jara, the widow of the great singer and songwriter Víctor Jara, who was tortured and executed in the early days of the Chilean military dictatorship. In Argentina I was asked to speak in remembrance of Patrick Rice, an Irishman and human rights advocate who, as a young priest in the 1970s, had been imprisoned and tortured under the military junta, and who went on to be the driving force behind the UN International Convention for the Protection of All Persons from Enforced Disappearance. I met Fatima Cabrera, who was seventeen when she was kidnapped, tortured in a cell adjacent to Patrick's and imprisoned for three years, and who, years later, became Patrick's wife. She was accompanied by one of their daughters. Talking with these women, I could sense the determination that animates the families and friends of those who have suffered at the hands of an iniquitous regime, and their commitment to the cause of human rights everywhere.

Similarly, here in El Salvador it is heartening to see the positive role played by institutions such as the Centro Monseñor Romero, hosted by this university, and dedicated not only to sustaining the memory of Archbishop Óscar Arnulfo Romero and numerous others whose lives were cut short by violence, but also – through its pastoral activities – to nurturing the values of social change, and a spirit of hope in the Salvadoran people.

When it is difficult for families to access information about the fate of their loved ones, the work performed by this university's Instituto de Derechos Humanos (IDHUCA), which, for the past few years, has conducted a restorative justice tribunal, is most valuable. And so is the project 'History, Memory and Justice in El Salvador', launched in 2011, which has seen the IDHUCA coming together with students and faculty of the University of Washington's Center for Human Rights, who are working on declassified documents from the CIA and various US government departments, such as the Department of Defense and the Department of State, in order to seek justice for the victims of the Salvadoran war.

I also find inspiring the project of creating a definitive register of those who died. I am pleased to note that Ireland's development assistance programme contributes, in some small way, to this project of remembering through the support granted to the Sisters of Chigwell's work with the survivors and their families in El Mozote.

'Why care?' some could be tempted to ask; 'it is a thirty-year-old conflict.' But for those who have lost a loved one, it does not matter how many years have passed. The questions and pain are always present, for there is no greater object of sorrow than a human life not being allowed to bloom to its full potential. The naming of each and every one of those who died or was made to 'disappear' is of the utmost importance. This is something I personally feel strongly about.

Only through the restoration of the integrity of individual histories, through the work of memory, can solid foundations for a shared, peaceful future take shape. Thus to celebrate the fifteenth anniversary of our own peace process in Ireland, marked by the endorsement through referendum, in 1998, of the Good Friday Agreement by the people of both parts of the island, we organized – last April in Dublin – a reading of the names of all those who died in the conflict. It was a very moving ceremony. The act of naming summons up the person's singularity. The calling of the name is a means by which to rebut the reduction of a loved one, neighbour or fellow citizen to the indifferent category of the 'subversive', the 'enemy', and to refuse the subsuming of the loss in the all-encompassing denomination of 'the war', 'the conflict', 'the Troubles'.

I look forward to visiting, tomorrow, the Memorial to Memory and Truth in Cuscatlan Park, where – thanks to the dedication of the Committee of the Mothers of the Disappeared and Assassinated of El Salvador – the names of 30,000 of those who died in the recent war are inscribed. Among the thousands of names engraved on that wall is that of Óscar Arnulfo Romero. It is of course impossible to consider the Salvadoran collective memory without reflecting on the place which Monsignor Romero occupies in it, and it is worthwhile to evoke here the remarkable trajectory of this extraordinary man.

In the chapter they dedicate to him in their book entitled *Cultural Memory*, Jeanette Rodriguez and Ted Fortier explain how, at the same time as Romero began his Episcopal leadership, the Salvadoran Jesuits 'underwent a conversion that led them to publicly side with the poor'.[35] By 1973 the Jesuits had implemented their 'preferential option for the poor' by enrolling students from the poorest areas into the Universidad Centroamericana, and developing – in El Salvador as in other Latin American countries – 'Christian base communities', in which people were enabled to discuss the realities of their lives in light of the Scriptures, and the various means at their disposal to address the injustices that surrounded them.

Archbishop Romero may have, at the outset, criticized the Jesuits' 'political theology' as he tried to remain neutral in the face of the conflict that was tearing apart El Salvador. Of course silence and privileged friendship with those in power could be construed as political statements in themselves. According to Fortier and Rodriguez, it was Romero's friendship with Father Rutilio Grande, a Jesuit priest who was openly in favour of radical land reform, which 'planted the seeds of his later conversion'.[36]

On 12 March 1977, a few short weeks after Romero had been installed as

---

35 T. Fortier and J. Rodriguez, *Cultural Memory: Resistance, Faith, and Identity* (University of Texas Press, 2007), p. 58.

36 Ibid., p. 59.

Archbishop of San Salvador – a safe choice in the eyes of the Salvadoran establishment – his friend Rutilio Grande was murdered, along with a young boy and an elderly farmer. One hundred thousand people attended Grande's funeral, which, according to the same authors, was a 'church demonstration unprecedented in Salvadoran history'. The sermon that Archbishop Romero preached on that day, in which he defended Grande's liberating work, his solidarity with the poor and his pleas for justice, stunned everybody.

As Fortier and Rodriguez put it, ever after that funeral Mass, 'Romero dined with the poor, spoke out against institutional violence and encouraged people to reform their social structures in light of the Gospel'. According to them, the crucial element in the way Romero is remembered by the Salvadorans is that 'he is viewed as one who walked with the people, not one who changed the people's direction'.[37] He was '*el Obispo que anda con los pobres*'.

Monsignor Romero's commitment, not only as a witness but also as bearer of a vision of an emancipatory *realidad*, is reflected in the words of an address which he gave at the Catholic University of Louvain in 1980:

> As in other places in Latin America, after many years and per-
> haps centuries, the words of Exodus have resounded in our ears: So
> indeed the cry of the Israelites reached me, and I have truly noted
> that the Egyptians are oppressing them. By recognizing that these
> realities exist and then letting their impact reach us, we have been
> returned to the world of the poor, and have found it to be our right-
> ful place... In this world we have found the real faces of the poor
> of which Puebla speaks.[38] There we found peasants without land

37 Ibid., p. 60.
38 After the Second Vatican Council, the Latin American Episcopal Conference, which played an essential role in the formation of liberation theology, held two important conferences: the first in Medellín, Colombia, in 1968, and the second in Puebla, Mexico, in January 1979.

or steady work, without water or electricity in their poor dwellings, without medical assistance when the women give birth, and
without schools when the children begin to grow. There we found
workers with no labor rights, workers at the mercy of the economy's cold calculations. There we found mothers and wives of the
'disappeared' and political prisoners. There we met the people who
live in hovels where misery exceeds the imagination, a permanent
insult of the nearby mansions.

By using such words, by the example he was setting, the hope he
was enabling, Óscar Romero became dangerous for the Salvadoran
establishment, because he called into question the entire system of
oppression and the process by which, in his words, 'wealth is made a
god, private property is absolutized… [and] national security is made the
highest good by the political powers who institutionalize the insecurity of
the individual'. He denounced what he labelled a 'structure of sin' in his
country: 'It is sinful,' he said, 'because it produces fruits of sin: the death
of Salvadorans – the rapid death of repression or the slow death (but no
less real) of structural oppression.'

On 23 March 1980, at the end of his radio homily, Romero addressed
the ordinary soldiers of the army. This episode is related by one of the
Irish witnesses of those dark times in Latin America, Luke Waldron, in
his book *A Dawn Unforeseen: A Journey from the West of Ireland to the
Barrios of Peru*: 'Brothers,' Romero began, 'you are from the same people,
you kill your fellow peasants… No soldier is obliged to obey an order
that is contrary to the will of God.'[39] Then his voice grew louder: 'In the
name of God, in the name of this suffering people, I ask you, I beg you,
I command you, in the name of God, to stop the repression.' The next
day the Archbishop was shot dead by a sniper as he celebrated Mass in

---

39   L. Waldron, *A Dawn Unforeseen: A Journey from the West of Ireland to the Barrios of
Peru* (The Liffey Press, 2013), pp. 91–2.

the Chapel of the Hospital Divina Providencia. During the funeral, a bomb went off outside the cathedral and the panic-stricken mourners were machine-gunned, leaving an estimated thirty to forty people dead and several hundred wounded.

Monsignor Óscar Romero's life and death have been an inspiration to a generation of advocates for human rights and social justice all over the world. It is in his name and on the anniversary of his death, 24 March, that the United Nations now hosts the International Day for the Right to the Truth Concerning Gross Human Rights Violations and for the Dignity of Victims. Just as importantly, the Archbishop is regularly conjured up in the dances, songs, poems and theatre performances of the Salvadoran people, and on the murals and posters that cover the walls of their cities. The strength of his words continues to galvanize their faith, and to crystallize their aspirations for a more just society.

Óscar Romero has become an illuminating icon, not only for the Church but for the oppressed of the world and those in solidarity with them. We, in Ireland, can recognize the moment of his death as a founding event in what would become a widening of interest in, and support for, human rights by the Irish people. I would like to share with you my own brief reflection on my connection with these events in the 1980s. What is one to make of one's involvement with another people's struggle? What is the appropriate role of the witness, and what is the role of testimony in the complex passage from experience to memory, to history?

I wrote in 1991 that, if one has witnessed the bodies of the assassinated, the mutilations, the victims of death and torture, as I have, then not only must the gaze not be averted but the life of the observer must be allowed to change. An obligatory commitment to bear witness is called into being.[40]

Through my engagement with the Central American peasant struggles of the 1970s and 1980s, confronted with the evidence provided by the Irish

---

40 M. D. Higgins, 'The Gaze Not Averted', in *Selected Poems* (Liberties Press, 2011), p. 123.

NGO Trócaire and other NGOs, by the Irish missionaries and by Bishop
Eamon Casey – who gave evidence not only to us in Ireland, but also to
the American bishops – I felt encouraged to testify, to report on these
violations of human rights and to do my best to raise my fellow citizens'
awareness of what was going on in Central America and elsewhere.

Many of you in this room are first-hand witnesses, and some of you are
the survivors of the events to which I make reference. As Paul Ricoeur put
it, your testimonies are where the making of history begins. They matter
greatly. I quote Ricoeur: 'We must not forget that everything starts, not
from the archives, but from testimony, and that, whatever may be our lack
of confidence in principle in such testimony, we have nothing better than
testimony, in the final analysis, to assure ourselves that something did
happen in the past, which someone attests having witnessed in person.'[41]

The act of witness thus lies at the root of every historical archive and
documentary proof. 'Indeed,' wrote Ricoeur,

> it is the force of testimony that presents itself at the very heart of
> the documentary proof. And I do not see that we can go beyond
> the witness's triple declaration: (1) 'I was there;' (2) 'believe me;'[42]
> (3) 'if you don't believe me, ask someone else'... we have nothing
> better than testimony and the critique of testimony to give credi-
> bility to the historian's representation of the past.[43]

I would like to recall for you just some of the names of the people I met
in El Salvador in the early 1980s, and the circumstances through which

---

41 P. Ricoeur, *Memory, History, Forgetting* (University of Chicago Press, 2006), p. 147.
42 According to Ricoeur, the self-designation of the testifying subject gets inscribed in
    an exchange that sets up a dialogical situation. It is before someone that the witness
    testifies to the reality of some scene of which he was part. This dialogical structure
    immediately makes clear the dimension of trust involved. The witness does not limit
    himself to saying 'I was there'; he adds 'believe me'. When the receiver of the testimony
    receives it, the testimony is not just certified, it is accredited.
43 Ibid., p. 278.

I became acquainted with them. I do so as a means of paying tribute to these men and women who maintained hope during dark times. Doing so will also allow me to evoke the long-standing bonds of friendship and solidarity between Ireland and El Salvador.

My first encounter with El Salvador and its people occurred in October 1978, when I met Marianella García Villas. As the President of the Human Rights Commission of El Salvador and the first woman elected to the Salvadoran Parliament, Marianella visited Ireland at the invitation of Trócaire and met members of the Irish Parliament to discuss the intensifying war in her country.

I met Marianella again in January 1982, in Mexico City, where she was then living in exile following two arrests by the Salvadoran Army. Marianella visited Ireland on a second occasion in 1982, when she was elected Vice-President of the International Federation for Human Rights. This was a year before her torture and death at the hands of the Salvadoran Army in March 1983.

Around the same time as I met Marianella, I was contacted by a group of Irish Franciscan priests who were based in the city of Gotera in the Salvadoran department of Morazán – an area that suffered tremendously during the war. These priests provided extensive evidence of major atrocities in their area and also the first information about the role of the US military in arming and training Salvadoran soldiers located in the nearby parishes. In mid-1979 the families of two of these Franciscans, along with staff from Trócaire, set up the 'Irish El Salvador Support Committee', with whom I maintained close contact for over two decades. This contact with the Franciscans was to prove crucial in relation to the 1981 El Mozote massacre, to which I will refer later.

In September 1980 I was contacted by Jean Donovan, an American lay missionary who was working in La Libertad. In 1977 Jean had studied for a year in the University of Cork in Ireland, and she was aware from the media of the position I had taken on El Salvador. During our

1980 meeting she described the killings in her area and the number of community leaders assassinated by the infamous death squads.

Three weeks later Jean Donovan returned to her community. On 2 December 1980, together with an Ursuline sister named Dorothy Kazel, she drove to the airport in San Salvador to meet two Maryknoll sisters, Ita Ford and Maura Clarke, who were returning from Managua. The four women were last seen alive driving from the airport down the main road and being stopped by the National Police at a roadblock. Two days later their bodies were discovered in a makeshift grave about fifteen miles away. Jean was twenty-seven years old. In 1982 I had the privilege of giving the keynote address at the Irish launch of the film *Roses in December*, which documented Jean's life and death.

On 26 December 1981, shortly after I had organized an inter-parliamentary hearing on El Salvador in Ireland, I got a telephone call from Salvador Samayoa, a former Minister of Education and Professor of Philosophy at the Universidad Centroamericana (UCA), who was acting at that time as a member of the political commission of the FMLN. Samayoa described a massacre which had taken place on 11 December in the community of El Mozote, Morazán, leaving several hundred people dead. *On 10 December, units of the Atlacatl Battalion had detained all the people living in the village. Having locked them up in their homes overnight, the following day they systematically executed in groups first the men, then the women and lastly the children.* Salvador Samayoa asked me to try to bring a parliamentary delegation from Ireland to investigate these horrific killings.

Our delegation spent three days in Mexico, where we met with Marianella García Villas and other exiles, before travelling to San Salvador. On arrival at the airport in El Salvador we were arrested, questioned and deported to Nicaragua on the basis of an exclusion order signed by General García, the Minister of Defence. This expulsion received wide publicity in Central America and in Ireland, and four days later

President José Napoleón Duarte issued a press release saying that it was a 'misunderstanding' and granting us the right to travel freely within El Salvador to assess for ourselves the human rights situation there. We returned a week after our 'mistaken exclusion'.

The Archdiocese of San Salvador and the Jesuits having offered to provide security for us, we travelled to the war zones in Morazán, Chalatenango and Cabañas, and met with survivors of rural massacres, human rights activists, Members of Parliament, the head of the armed forces, priests and Irish missionaries, notably the Gotera Franciscans and the Poor Clare sisters, who were also working in the Morazán department. We did not get to El Mozote, as the road was blocked by the armed forces. But we did meet with Rufina Amaya, one of the few survivors from the massacre, whose husband and four children had been murdered there.

Upon our return to San Salvador I was interviewed by Raymond Bonner of the *New York Times* and Alma Guillermoprieto of the *Washington Post*, who subsequently visited the area and whose reports shook international public opinion at the end of January 1982. Irish missionaries had managed to obtain photographs of the murder site, and our delegation was able to take this evidence back to Ireland.

Back home, we set to the task of challenging official reports denying that a mass execution had taken place in El Mozote. A conscious campaign to refute our testimonies got under way in the US and internationally and attempts were made to rebut the evidence and impugn the integrity of Bonner and Guillermoprieto.

Yet years later, and despite these campaigns of denial, the UN Truth Commission found that the El Mozote survivors' accounts were 'fully corroborated by the results of the 1992 exhumation of the remains'. And in December 2012 the Inter-American Court of Human Rights (CIDH) found the Salvadoran state to be responsible for the deliberate and targeted killings of over 800 people, more than half of whom were children, and stated that 'the killings in and around El Mozote were part of a "systematic plan of repression" by the military during the civil war'.

I was, as you can understand, extremely pleased to hear about President Funes's historic apology on behalf of the Salvadoran state in January 2012, in which he referred to El Mozote as the worst massacre of civilians in recent Latin American history. This was a truly significant moment in the journey towards truth, and it is something all Salvadorans can be very proud of, as can they be of the protection of the village as a Cultural Heritage site, with its poignant monument to the dead and its Garden of the Innocents, where the names of all the children are inscribed. These are moral gestures of immense significance.

I would like, finally, to evoke the memory of the six Jesuits who were brutally murdered on this campus on 16 November 1989 – namely Ignacio Ellacuría, Rector of the UCA and an internationally known philosopher and theologian; Segundo Montes, head of the university's Sociology Department and Human Rights Institute; Ignacio Martin-Baro, a pioneering social psychologist; Juan Ramón Moreno Pardo and Armando López, theology professors; and Joaquín Lopez y Lopez, founder of the *Fe y Alegría* network of schools for the poor. Julia Elba Ramos, a cook and the wife of a caretaker at the UCA, and their sixteen-year-old daughter Celina were also killed to ensure that there would be no witnesses.

I had met Ignacio Ellacuría and Segundo Montes in January 1982 in San Salvador, together with another of their colleagues, Jon Sobrino, also one of Central America's best-known theologians.[44] The UCA's monthly reports and statistics on the war were at that time widely recognized as the most credible source of independent information.

The Jesuits had close links with Ireland; they valued Irish support for peace in their country. Father Ellacuría had undertaken his Tertianship in Ireland, and Armando López had studied theology in Miltown Park

44 Jon Sobrino, who also lived on the campus, survived the killing as he had been invited to a theology conference in Thailand.

in Dublin. Both were passionately interested in Irish affairs and had attracted Irish Jesuits to work in El Salvador. In 1984 and 1986 Ignacio Ellacuría and Jon Sobrino visited Ireland and gave us a detailed account of the human rights and political situation in El Salvador.

I am deeply honoured today, as President of Ireland, to pay tribute to these six men, their cook and her daughter. I am touched to see how they are so vividly remembered in this university, where they lived and died, and where the Jesuits worked for a more equal and just society. Indeed the UCA Jesuits will be remembered, not only for their tragic deaths, but also for their passionately argued philosophy which contributed so much to the development of new paradigms for Latin America's poor. In doing so, I assure you, they were always at risk. I recall the remarks of a high-ranking but ill-informed foreign observer who was based in San Salvador in 1981 and who, jabbing at a map in front of us, said: 'With the Jesuits, it begins with literacy, then it's co-operatives, but we all know it all ends up with Marxism!'

Let me share with you the wiser and more humane consideration of a poet: 'Even if the hopes you started out with are dashed, hope has to be maintained.' These are the words of my friend, the recently deceased Irish poet and Literature Nobel Prize Laureate Seamus Heaney. Indeed the long account I have given, of people whose lives were ended in the most brutal manner, would be dispiriting if we did not also acknowledge the transformational power that these lives have had for all of us. The emancipatory promise encapsulated in the lives of the UCA's Jesuit martyrs, in that of Marianella García, of Jean Donovan and of so many others who bore the torch of hope at the darkest of times – that emancipatory promise is available and will remain available for us as an instrument for our future betterment.

Today, when we speak of human rights, we must do so in the fullest sense, paying attention not just to the crucial concepts of civil and political rights, of that most fundamental right to life and liberty, but also to economic, social and cultural rights – in essence, to the right to human flourishing. As Pope Francis put it in his letter to British Prime Minister, David Cameron, ahead of the G8 meeting convened last June 2013 in Northern Ireland:

> Every economic and political theory or action must set about pro-viding each inhabitant of the planet with the minimum wherewithal to live in dignity and freedom, with the possibility of supporting a family, educating children, praising God and developing one's own human potential. This is the main thing; in the absence of such a vision, all economic activity is meaningless.

Pope Francis is speaking a similar language to those who gave their lives for a new reality in Central America and those who continue in solidarity with their sacrifice.

Let me, to conclude, say once more that I am so happy to be back in El Salvador, where peace is now being made and sustained.

Remembering
Kader Asmal

I T IS A great honour to be with you today in Soweto, a place and a name which was, for so much of my lifetime, shorthand for the gross unfairness and inequality of the old South Africa. It is truly wonderful to be here at the Soweto Campus of the University of Johannesburg.

The great novelist V. S. Naipaul, as the grandson of an Indian immigrant born in Trinidad, is an astute observer of the wider post-colonial conversation to which Ireland, like South Africa, has contributed a distinctive voice. Here is the first sentence of his powerful novel, *A Bend in the River*: 'The world is what it is; men who are nothing, who allow themselves to become nothing, have no place in it.'

This is a bleak and challenging statement, written in the late 1970s, when there was much to feel bleak about here on this continent and especially in South Africa. At one level Naipaul is of course right: the world is what it is. But perhaps the key point – and I can think of nowhere better than Soweto to make this observation – is that people can change this: we can change our world; we can shape it and make it better.

Men and women, here in Soweto and in towns and villages all over this country, many of which like Sharpeville are burnt into our memory, fought for a fairer, a more equitable, a more just South Africa. They did not allow themselves to be treated as nothing; they stood up for their personal worth, their rights and their dignity, often paying a heavy price.

It is appropriate here in this historic place, which has borne witness to some of the most challenging events in recent South African history, to reflect on twenty years of democracy and freedom and the decades of struggle that preceded it. Such reflection also has great significance for Ireland, as we observe a decade of commemoration, of events that included the First World War – a war which brought death and destruction to Europe and Africa – and our own struggle for self-determination, leading to the emergence of an independent Ireland.

The story of the Irish and their contribution to South Africa is as rich as it is complex; it is a human story of sacrifice and contradiction. Today, there are more than 30,000 Irish citizens living in South Africa, some of them recent arrivals. There are many more who can trace their ancestry back much further. It is a story of colonized and colonizer, of those seeking riches and those providing succour and education. It is a story of struggle and of the fight for freedom in Ireland and South Africa.

In 1814, the Cape Colony was ceded by the Dutch to the British and this period saw the earliest Irish arrivals, as part either of the colonial administration or the British Army. Ireland itself had been formally joined to the United Kingdom in 1801, though in effect had been ruled, at least in part, as a colony since the twelfth century.

The history of the Irish in South Africa might well have been different had *The Neptune* been allowed to disembark in Table Bay in 1849. The ship was carrying some 300 prisoners, many of them Irish political prisoners who had taken part in a failed rebellion against British rule the previous year. The intention had been to establish a penal colony in the Cape. However, following a furious campaign by residents of the

Cape, the plan was abandoned and instead *The Neptune* sailed on to Van Diemen's Land, or Tasmania.

A rather different cohort of Irish men and women were to make their mark in this country. It has often been said that our missionaries have been ambassadors for Ireland long before Ireland became an independent state. This is especially true in Africa. Wherever they have been, in addition to providing for spiritual needs, they have built schools and clinics in some of the most difficult circumstances.

The first Irish missionary in South Africa who has been documented was Bishop Patrick Griffith, a Jesuit originally from Limerick, the county of my birth, who arrived in Cape Town in 1838. The following year he purchased the site on which St Mary's Cathedral now stands. From there, Irish missionaries moved to other parts of the Western Cape and to Grahamstown in the Eastern Cape. With the discovery of gold and diamonds there was further expansion to Johannesburg and Kimberley.

Today there are still large numbers of Irish priests and nuns all over South Africa. Most were here throughout the years of struggle, when they continued to provide healthcare and education in some of the most disadvantaged and oppressed communities. Descendants of Irish immigrants have also played a significant role in the religious life of South Africa and in the struggle against apartheid, among them the late Archbishop of Durban, Denis Hurley, who in another connection lived on Robben Island as a young boy, where his father was stationed as lighthouse keeper.

The discovery of gold and diamonds saw a new wave of immigration to South Africa, and it should be no surprise that some 6,000 Irish came to seek their fortunes here. That number included many who would go on to campaign for Irish independence from Britain, including Arthur Griffith and John MacBride.

During the Anglo-Boer wars there was much sympathy from Irish nationalists for the Boer cause, with many seeing it as a proxy for their own struggle for Home Rule for Ireland. Two units of an Irish Brigade, numbering about 600 men, fought with the Boer armies. At the same time a much greater number of Irish – some 30,000 – were fighting in the British Army.

Later, in the first half of the twentieth century, relations between our nations were friendly. The iniquities of the apartheid system introduced in 1948 did not have an immediate impact on Irish attitudes towards South Africa. But opinion began to harden, especially after the Sharpeville Massacre in 1960. The Rivonia Trial in 1963 and 1964 led to a campaign in Ireland for the release of political prisoners in South Africa. The shift in attitudes took on real momentum in 1964, with the foundation of the Irish Anti-Apartheid Movement by my good friend, the late Kader Asmal.

Professor Asmal made a huge contribution to human rights in Ireland, North and South. He played an important part in the formation of the Civil Rights Movement in Northern Ireland and he was one of the founders of the Irish Council for Civil Liberties in 1976. He was a professor of law for twenty-seven years at Trinity College in Dublin, specializing in human rights, international law and labour law.

Kader, with his wife Louise, was at the heart of the struggle against apartheid and he galvanized Irish attitudes. He and Louise garnered support from across the political spectrum and beyond. It was often a struggle managed out of the Asmal household, and underpinned by dedicated volunteers who campaigned to isolate apartheid South Africa at all levels, including sport and cultural links. For example, a succession of Irish playwrights refused to allow their work to be performed in South Africa.

The Springbok rugby tour to Ireland in 1970 was a pivotal event, building huge momentum in our country and intersecting with our own new awareness of the lack of civil rights in Northern Ireland. While the matches did go ahead, the tour was marked by huge protests against the Springbok (and indeed Irish) teams for taking part, and against the apartheid regime. The struggle against apartheid around the world was often epitomized by protests against tours by Springbok teams in defiance of the international community's efforts to isolate South Africa. Since the end of apartheid, rugby has become a great connection between our two countries, with the mighty Springboks being very welcome and indeed formidable visitors to Ireland. Though not, perhaps, as formidable to us as they once were!

For people of my generation, the struggle against apartheid was *the* great defining moral argument of the second half the twentieth century, an issue which united people from Dublin to Durban. Having seen peace return to Europe and the birth of what we know today as the European Union, apartheid seemed to us one of the great obscenities. The utterly repugnant idea that one's race should predetermine one's prospects in life needed to be fought.

I want to tell one short story to illustrate just what impact this injustice had in my own country on one small group of people in Ireland. In July 1984 a group of workers, mainly young women, in an Irish supermarket refused to handle produce imported from South Africa. For this refusal they were suspended, thus marking the beginning of what would be a three-year battle by twelve determined and brave workers. Their principled stance eventually led our government to ban South African goods from being sold in Ireland, and this ban remained in place until the end of the apartheid regime.

By their action, these ordinary working people highlighted the injustice of life in South Africa for the great majority of our nation and forced the government to act. They illustrated a point perhaps most eloquently made by the famous Irish statesman and philosopher Edmund Burke over 200 years ago: 'Nobody made a greater mistake than he or she who did nothing because they could only do a little.'

This is the point that those striking supermarket workers were making. The actions of millions more people around the world in confronting the moral outrage that was apartheid, those who marched, or boycotted rugby games, or refused to buy South African goods, all in their own way contributed to the wave of change and transformation that eventually helped South Africans to liberate themselves.

Kader Asmal's contribution went beyond fighting the good fight in Ireland. He was also preparing to build a new South Africa. As a member of the ANC's Constitutional Committee, he and Albie Sachs drafted the Bill of Rights in the kitchen of his home in Foxrock, Dublin, in 1988. The Bill of Rights, which was subsequently incorporated into the new South African Constitution, was a truly seminal document and an essential element in the transition to democracy.

Kader was not finished yet, however, and on returning home to South Africa he became Minister for Water Affairs in its first democratic government, and later Minister for Education. Among his initiatives was the launching in 2001 of the South African History Project, 'to promote and enhance the conditions and status of the learning and teaching of history in the South African schooling system, with the goal of restoring its material position and intellectual purchase in the classroom'. Archbishop Desmond Tutu has remarked that 'what we learn from history is that we don't learn from history'. Despite this justified scepticism, Professor Asmal rightly ensured the central role of history in the school curriculum.

I am delighted that the Irish Government has honoured the contribution that Kader made to Ireland and South Africa by establishing the Kader Asmal Fellowship Programme. Each year, we intend to send ten students to Ireland to pursue Master's level studies in the areas of business management, food science, agriculture and nutrition, international development and public administration. As part of this programme, and in particular recognition of Kader's contribution to law, we have, in co-operation with the Council for the Advancement of the South African Constitution, reserved one fellowship in international law at Kader Asmal's old university, Trinity College Dublin.

I am of course in South Africa for the second time in twelve months.

The last visit was to honour Nelson Mandela, a man whose personal story of sacrifice and statesmanship remains one of the most powerful and moving of the twentieth century. I was privileged, along with those brave workers who risked their livelihoods to strike against apartheid, to attend Nelson Mandela's funeral here last year in the company of many world leaders and to pay tribute to the outstanding international statesman of our generation. Nelson Mandela belongs to South Africa but also to the world, to all people fighting against injustice.

Mandela and those who fought apartheid and created your new state also helped us end the violent sectarian conflict in Northern Ireland. All sides learnt lessons from your experience, often in private, unannounced visits to your country, where enemies could talk and begin to explore pathways to peace and justice.

In 2000 Cyril Ramaphosa, former Secretary General of the ANC and now Deputy President, together with Martti Ahtisaari, former President of Finland, were appointed to work on weapons decommissioning in Northern Ireland. This process was crucial to building trust between the two communities there. It was an important step on the path to the decommissioning of the Provisional IRA's weapons and the establishment of the devolved power-sharing institutions in Northern Ireland, which continue to provide peace and stability. We remain extremely grateful for Mr Ramaphosa's personal contribution to the Northern Ireland Peace Process – but also to the powerful example of reconciliation provided by your leaders and your people.

This year marks the twentieth anniversary of the first democratic elections in South Africa and the establishment of its first freely elected government under President Mandela. Since the advent of democracy in South Africa, Ireland has been a strong supporter of the process of transformation. In 1994 Irish Aid, the overseas development agency of the Government of Ireland, began a programme of support to South Africa that continues to this day.

In those twenty years since democracy was established in your country, Ireland has provided support to South Africa's democratic institutions, to the social sectors and to sustainable rural livelihoods through local economic development. In partnership with you, we have assisted in the areas of education, the elimination of gender-based violence, health, water and sanitation and HIV and AIDS. We are currently also supporting economic growth through the Department of Trade and Industry's strategy to develop special economic zones, through the training of nurses and schooling in commercial law.

We are committed to continuing that support and to working with you in the challenge – a challenge we face ourselves – to build inclusive and sustainable economic growth. As we reflect on the achievements of twenty years of democracy in South Africa, we find ourselves asking a very basic question: how can individual nations achieve such social and economic goals in an increasingly globalized and interdependent world?

The impact of climate change and the depletion of the natural resources on which current economic growth is based are already leading to changes in the way that economies are evolving. Over the next decades we are going to see a process of economic transformation which will affect the value of basic assets such as land, water and forests. The prices and markets for many commodities will alter radically as new, more efficient technologies become available, and as cleaner renewable sources of energy replace traditional fossil fuels.

It is universally accepted that poor people and poor countries are most at risk, and already suffer most, from the impacts of climate change. This, however, does not mean that efforts to slow, halt and reverse climate change will necessarily benefit them. We must acknowledge, then, that the very necessary move to more environmentally sustainable economic models involves both risks and opportunities for poor people.

Proponents of Green Growth see the transformation to sustainability as an opportunity to renew and accelerate economic growth. Undoubtedly, private corporations and countries are already moving to become market leaders in new technologies and to secure control over the markets and assets that will be critical to sustainability.

However, in the processes of economic transformation, the greatest benefits may accrue to those who are best positioned to take advantage of them – those who already have control over assets, wealth and political processes. It does not have to be so. The shift to sustainability, if managed ethically and fairly, offers the possibility of making economies more inclusive and of directing new economic opportunities to people who are currently excluded from progress and prosperity. This, however, will not just happen by itself. Poverty reduction will not blindly follow the growth of markets. Across Africa we have seen, over more than a decade, some of the highest growth rates in the world, and yet the numbers of hungry people remain persistently high and some of the most basic millennium development goals are still out of reach.

If, then, economic growth alone does not necessarily improve the position of the poor, we must not make the same mistake of assuming that what is good for the environment is *automatically* good for poor people. To do so would risk developing policies that might achieve greater environmental sustainability while failing to reduce poverty.

In the forthcoming debates about the UN's sustainable development goals, we must instead bring together sustainability and poverty reduction as overarching aims. This will require concerted political will to put in place active policies to ensure that the transition to sustainability prioritizes benefits for the poorest and most vulnerable people. This means taking choices such as:

- ensuring poor people's rights over land – instead of facilitating acquisition by external investors;
- opting for hundreds, or thousands, of small-scale energy systems, which can provide energy in the most remote communities – rather

than investing in a few big-ticket hydro or clean-coal power stations that will serve only those already connected;

- guiding investments and regulating markets in areas such as biofuels and carbon sequestration so that they provide livelihoods for poor people – rather than increasing competition for the assets they depend on;
- investing in the livelihood technologies of poor households to increase resilience to climate change – rather than seeing sustainability as a technological import from industrialized countries;
- managing natural resources to prioritize jobs, reinvestment of profits and sustainable public finances – rather than just going for growth and ending up with an underpriced and overexploited extractive industry sector;
- directing climate change finance to the poorest and most vulnerable households.

These are not simple policy options; they are significant political decisions. Taking these decisions requires strong and visionary leadership – the kind of leadership provided by Nelson Mandela, for example – but they also depend on the ability of marginalized communities to exert influence over policymaking.

Empowerment of those living in poverty is a critical means of reducing poverty. The right investments in economic and social infrastructure, combined with legislative measures supporting basic rights – to decent work, to gender equality, to ownership and control over individual and collective assets – are important building blocks of economic empowerment. They will improve the terms on which poor people engage in markets and will make economic growth more inclusive and more effective in reducing poverty.

Such measures cannot be an add-on to a sustainable economic development agenda. Climate scientists warn us about tipping points, beyond which climate change becomes catastrophic. Who is to say that there are not social tipping points beyond which governance failures become self-perpetuating?

The rise in inequality is a direct consequence of poorly regulated markets; but inequality is not inevitable. I have said on many occasions that we need to revitalize public policy. We must reinvest governments and the political process with the responsibility to define social objectives for the economy. This is the only way in which states and governments can have the ability to make a real social contract with their citizens and deliver on it. Those countries that have made most progress on the millennium development goals are countries where governments have taken on this role. We must recognize this as a fundamental task for all governments.

You, the young educated people of South Africa, represent a precious resource. To you and your generation will fall the role of sustaining and leading the new South Africa as it moves forward. I want to wish you well on your own journey in this wonderful country, blessed with so much potential and with a great future ahead of it.

Thank you again for the opportunity to meet with you and talk with you here today. You have inspired me and convinced me that the links between South Africa and Ireland are not the result of history alone. They matter to both our peoples now, and as we face common challenges in the years to come.

The Future of Diplomacy in
Conditions of Global Change

RECEPTION FOR THE IRISH HEADS OF MISSION,
ÁRAS AN UACHTARÁIN

14 JANUARY 2015

F OREIGN POLICY IS an essential part of the identity of any state; it reflects both the way in which we, as a national community, construct our view of the world and the complex and diverse manner in which we are affected by and must respond to the dynamics at play in this wider world.

We Irish have faced colonization, the struggle for liberation and the consequences of not only hunger but famine and migration. These experiences are at the heart of our collective awareness. It is important, I believe, for members of Ireland's diplomatic service, and for all of us concerned with Irish foreign policy, to consider the contemporary significance of this legacy and of the legacy handed down to us by previous generations of foreign policymakers and diplomats. Indeed, the early architects of Ireland's foreign policy had a sense that Ireland's history and political traditions had given our country a specific ethical, and emancipatory, perspective on world affairs.

Such a vision was manifested, for example, in their defence of the voice, and right to independence, of small nations in multinational fora such as the League of Nations, the Council of Europe and, from 1955 onwards, the UN. It was not without its contradictions, of course, as the plea for the freedom of other peoples was accompanied by a strident anti-Communism, in particular at a time when the Council of Europe was preoccupied by the threat of the extension of Communism in Europe.

That Ireland was particularly qualified to advocate the cause of other nations pressing for self-determination was powerfully expressed by Frank Aiken in the speech he gave to the UN General Assembly in October 1960. In his address, Aiken referred to Ireland as a state whose people retained 'a historical memory' of domination by a foreign power:

> A memory... which gives us a sense of brotherhood with the newly emerging peoples of today, a memory which makes it impossible for any representative of Ireland to withhold support for racial, religious, national or economic rights in any part of the world, in South Africa, or Tibet, or Hungary. We stand unequivocally for the swift and orderly ending of colonial rule and other forms of foreign domination.

Another founding figure of Irish international diplomacy, Seán Mac Bride, documented in his writings the significance of the Irish liberation movement in international relations throughout the first half of the twentieth century. In his *Message to the Irish People*,[45] Mac Bride recalls the meetings his mother had in Paris with revolutionary leaders from Egypt, Morocco and India, such as Bhikaiji Cama, known as the 'Mother of the Indian Revolution'. He also relates his own encounters with Ho Chi Minh at international summits during the 1920s, and his friendship with Nehru, tracing the links between the Irish Constitution of 1937 and the 1948 Indian Constitution.

---

45 Seán Mac Bride, *A Message to the Irish People* (Mercier Press, 1985), pp. 38–40.

During my recent visits to Africa and China, I was struck very strongly by how much actions taken by Irish diplomats in regard to decolonization, to human rights, to the struggle against apartheid, to disarmament and nuclear non-proliferation, to peacekeeping were appreciated – how all these initiatives have contributed to forging Ireland's good name on the world stage, and how they continue to inform the sympathy our nation enjoys among developing countries. This is a moral heritage we must cherish: one that is valuable both in itself, and as an asset in our relationships with other nations.

At its best, diplomacy is a practice that strives to creatively balance the pursuit of national interests with an open, enlarged, ethical consciousness, one that is grounded in a recognition of our solidarity as human beings sharing a fragile planet. Preferably, such a project should stem from a shared European public sphere, but it also has to be sought at global level.

The narrow pursuit of material gains and the so-called 'realist' conception of international relations, which portrays the state as 'the coldest of all cold monsters',[46] one that knows no moral code, are, in my view, but two avatars of a narrowly utilitarian and impoverished version of diplomacy.

Things have changed, of course, since the days of the Cold War, an era when prudence was the primary virtue required in the exercise of international relations. Morality has made a comeback in foreign policy debates; the citizens of pluralist democracies exert greater demand for continuity between domestic and international policy principles. Yet the depiction of 'professional' diplomatic activity and *raison d'état* as being in conflict with 'emotional' and 'moralist' public opinion still holds in some foreign policy circles – and indeed it is an opposition as ancient and enduring as the deadly confrontation between Antigone and Creon.

This evening, then, I would like to invite all of you, Ambassadors,

---

46   Friedrich Nietzsche, *Thus Spoke Zarathustra.*

Heads of Mission and foreign policymakers, to uphold those values of peace, solidarity and global justice that have inspired the actions of your distinguished predecessors. You are the recipients of a long and admirable tradition – one that runs from the human rights work of Roger Casement to that of Mary Robinson and that includes, for example, the lead taken by Ireland in recent years on the control and abolition of cluster munitions and the protection of human rights defenders.

This tradition can, and must, continue to shape our country's response to the great challenges of our age. The rise of nations belonging to what used to be called the 'Third World' is one such defining shift of our times – a shift that Ireland must welcome and support.

We are now presented with both a challenge and a test: to exercise Ireland's credit in creating a new atmosphere in global South–North relations. We must not waste the real opportunities that exist, for example, to build a new North–South dialogue in which we must achieve real, binding and transparent commitment to actions against climate change. Old divisions have to be healed, or at least managed, and Ireland as a 'middle power' is presented with challenges and opportunities of a diplomatic kind.

No less importantly, Ireland's appointment, together with Kenya, as one of two co-facilitators of the UN negotiations on the post-2015 Sustainable Development Goals is a critical opportunity for our country to contribute to a strong global agenda that will seek to eradicate extreme poverty and food insecurity in the next generation, through a process that gives voice to those most affected by global inequalities. Ireland can be an important voice, too, in revising our definitions of development.

For this to happen, however, a radical change of approach is necessary in the way the North relates to the South. The nations of the South must be free to imagine and implement new models of social, economic and cultural development, rather than submit to a hegemonic, and already failed, paradigm of growth.

We are in new circumstances, facing new challenges but also old issues that have been neglected or evaded and must now be addressed for the sake of global survival itself and the peaceful co-existence of future generations – issues such as global poverty, global debt and the reduction of food production to a commodity at the mercy of speculation by hedge funds. And I very much welcome the fact that, after many decades, the role of the state is again being recognized as essential in responding both to global challenges and to the destructive operation of unregulated financial markets.

For the reasons I have stated earlier – Ireland's unique historical experience as a Western European country without an imperialist legacy, and the capital of sympathy we enjoy amongst many Southern nations – I believe that our country can play an important mediating role in achieving the necessary shift in vision and discourse. We cannot afford such confrontations as were experienced in relation to the United Nations Conference on Trade and Development, for example – opposed from its foundation by those seeking an unrestrained role for international markets. We cannot afford to abuse the concept of reform as an attempt to undermine our shared multilateral institutions.

There is a new, multipolar world in the throes of emergence; let us be attentive to the diversity of voices that resound across the globe. And let us endeavour to craft truly collective solutions for our shared challenges. Of course, as you are aware, multipolarity does not necessarily chime with multilateralism; and, yes, there are reasons to fear the formation of some new regional balances of power instead of the co-operative international system for which so many are calling.

When writing these remarks I thought of Julius Nyerere's comments after the G7 Toronto Summit on Debt in 1988:

> The Toronto Agreement, like other plans for other groups of debtors, was a menu of technical proposals. But the solution to this tragedy

cannot be found at a technical level. It has to be the outcome of bold political action... how can there be peace without justice.

Yet, however complex the task may be of building a new architecture of legitimate and well-resourced multilateral institutions – based on genuine representativeness, an ability to translate agreed principles into action and a recognition of the intergenerational nature of our responsibility towards the planet – it is a task worth undertaking. And I believe that it is also a task Irish diplomats have the necessary skills to undertake successfully. Indeed, our diplomats' dexterity as negotiators, their ability at cultivating good relations with their foreign counterparts and at building flexible alliances in order to broker deals are qualities widely recognized among our partners.

When reflecting on the skills required of diplomats in the current state of international relations, it seems to me that a good diplomat remains, at a basic level, someone who has genuine empathy for the foreign society in which he or she lives and works. That he or she is, in other words, a translator, or a 'knowledge broker', able to read cultural and ideological complexity as context, and to empathize with the point of view of the local people so as to better communicate the message and positions of the country he or she represents, and, vice versa, to convey to this country the local people's views and values within the frame of their own circumstances. To be an ambassador from the North will require an ability to understand, and recommend, movement in response to, and often in concert with, changes originating in the South.

We are seeing, around the world, a weakening of state institutions and the emergence of new actors. This has led many foreign policy practitioners to push the boundaries of traditional diplomatic tools and channels. After the Arab uprisings in particular (which very few had foreseen), there was widespread recognition among Western embassies of the need to enlarge and diversify their networks beyond dialogue with other diplomats and official functions held in the capital city, in order to explore the margins, both social and geographical, establish contacts with non-governmental actors and track the emergence of new social movements.

In doing so, creative use can be made of the new social media. The ability to select the best sources and to discern who has real authority or legitimacy in the public debate – be it a young rural blogger or a representative of a religious minority – can add real value to any diplomat's information mission. Of similar importance is the courage to convey to one's Department even those dissident voices that are not part of the status quo of the day. The economist Raúl Prebisch was one of those who warned against assumptions, such as those used in monetary theory, being taken as universal truths for consumption by the South.

Of course, one must avoid the temptation to regard the civil society of any country uncritically, in an atmosphere where the state has, as I have said, too often been portrayed negatively, usually as the most fundamental obstacle to unregulated market forces. A movement for ethical globalization has quite a long way to go, and it will not necessarily be assisted by the substitution of celebrities on platforms in place of elected politicians.

If I may mention an old concern of mine, I would add accountability and openness to the characteristics of any good foreign policy. Three decades ago, in an era when there was no Oireachtas Foreign Policy Committee, I advocated, in Seanad Éireann, in favour of increased public participation in foreign policy debates, and for the need to make accountable what was said and done, or not said and done, in the name of Irish citizens. My arguments were outlined in a 1988 article published in the journal *Studies*.[47] Reading that article, or the Seanad debates which it recalls, one can see that the discussion was centred on whether

---

47   Michael D. Higgins, 'The Case for an Oireachtas Foreign Policy Committee', in *Studies: An Irish Quarterly Review*, Vol. 77, No. 305 (1988), pp. 63–7.

foreign policy was an executive function or whether it could and should accommodate democratic accountability.

Leading the opposition to my proposal in the Seanad was a former and very fine Foreign Minister for Ireland in the early 1980s, Professor James Dooge. He quoted at the debate in Seanad Éireann on 10 December 1986 a version of the minutes of a seminar he had attended organized by the European Centre for Parliamentary Research and Documentation under the title of 'Foreign Policy and Parliamentary Democracy'. He quoted the speech of the President of the First Chamber of The Netherlands, Dr. P. A. J. M. Stemkamp, who had addressed the issue of the role of executives and publics in relation to foreign policy. This was the classic realist position: 'Undeniably a contrast began to emerge between the emotional approach of part of public opinion (often fed by pacifism and moralism) and the businesslike approach of the government aiming at the feasible.'

So we are faced with a choice of diplomatic strategies. I want to emphasize how important it is that we give ourselves the means and time to decipher the intricate and confusing trends at play in the world today. Engagement with the wider intellectual debate and with research in the social sciences and humanities takes on a greater importance in such an uncertain world. The three days you have spent discussing the foreign policy challenges of our times are a milestone on that path. May I commend the Department of Foreign Affairs and Trade for undertaking such a wide-ranging reflection, and wish you all the very best in your future endeavours.

The importance of the craft of diplomacy is surely underlined by the events of last week in France and Nigeria, which have exposed the horrific consequences of violence grounded in fanaticism. Terrorism, but also novel uses of technology and science, such as cyber attacks and remote, extra-judicial executions performed by machines, blur the boundaries between war and peace and risk instilling generalized suspicion between and within our societies.

The work of those who seek to build friendships between peoples, to construct peaceful, collective resolutions to the root causes of conflicts – this work is of immense importance and should be celebrated.

I have no doubt that each and every one of you here tonight will help to craft a new voice for Ireland in this new world – a voice of creativity and freedom; but also a voice of fidelity to our rich history and traditions, a voice of generosity and solidarity with the struggles of the emerging nations.

To Members of the 47th Infantry Group, United Nations Interim Force in Lebanon (UNIFIL)

MAY I THANK you, Lieutenant-Colonel McCarthy, and all of the personnel from the 47th Infantry Group for your warm welcome to South Lebanon. This is my first visit, as President, to an Irish peacekeeping contingent abroad, and as President of Ireland and Supreme Commander of the Defence Forces I very much welcome this opportunity to acknowledge the professionalism, the bravery and the commitment to peace and humanitarianism that lie at the core of your engagement as peacekeepers.

Ní hé seo an chéad uair dom bualadh leis an daichead is a seachtú (47ú) Cathlán Coisithe. B'fhéidir gur cuimhin libh gur thug mé féin agus Saidhbhín cuairt oraibh ar lá níos fuaire agus níos fliucha i nGleann Uí Mháil mí na Samhna seo chaite, agus sibh ag tabhairt faoin chéim dheiridh de bhur dtraenáil agus ullmhúchán sular fhág sibh don Liobáin. Tá an-áthas orm bualadh libh arís inniu agus an lá a chaitheamh libh ar an dtalamh anseo sa Liobáin Theas.

(This is not, however, my first meeting with the 47th Infantry Group. You may recall a very overcast and wet day in the Glen of Imaal last November, when Sabina and I visited you as you were entering the final phase of your training and preparation for this deployment to Lebanon. I am very pleased to meet you all again, to share the day with you and to have this occasion to meet with your commanding officers as well as with representatives of the local community here in South Lebanon.)

I am looking forward to seeing the Irish camp and to hearing of your experiences as you come to the end of your present posting.

On behalf of the Irish people, I wish to thank each and every one of you for the part you have played, through your service here, in continuing the proud tradition of Irish peacekeeping. This tradition is an essential component of Ireland's foreign policy, driven as it is by the values and principles that have guided the actions of our state on the international stage ever since independence – a commitment to multilateralism and to the values of peace, international security and global justice.

We Irish, as a nation, have colonization, liberation, hunger and migration at the heart of our historical experience. Such an experience has made us particularly sensitive to the plight of the oppressed and the struggles of those nations who are blighted by war or food insecurity.

During my visits abroad as President of Ireland, and most recently during my official visits to Africa and China, I felt how Ireland's stance on decolonization in Africa, on human rights, on the struggle against apartheid, on disarmament and nuclear non-proliferation and, of course, on peacekeeping, are recognized and appreciated by our foreign friends. All of these initiatives have contributed to giving Ireland a good name on the world stage, and they continue to inform the sympathy our nation enjoys. This is a moral heritage we must cherish and build upon; it is valuable both in itself, and as an asset in our relationships with other peoples.

The high regard in which Irish peacekeepers are held is often mentioned in discussions with my foreign counterparts, and indeed it was a theme that featured prominently in the conversations I had with various government officials in Beirut yesterday.

Ireland's commitment to peacekeeping is predicated upon our wider commitment to multilateralism, that is, the conviction that peaceful and negotiated collective solutions can be found to most of the challenges arising on our shared planet. The history of Irish peacekeeping is bound up, therefore, with the wider United Nations' peacekeeping mission. As we commemorate, this year, the seventieth anniversary of the establishment of the United Nations and the sixtieth anniversary of Ireland's membership, it is my hope that the Secretary General's Review of Peace Operations will reinvigorate the international community's support for the UN as an essential provider of peace and security.

As you know, it is here in Lebanon that Ireland's peacekeeping story began, in 1958, when fifty members of the Permanent Defence Force were deployed as military observers with the UN Observer Group. When the UN then went on to launch its first large-scale peacekeeping mission, in the Congo, the Irish Defence Forces sent their first overseas contingent to that country, and there they also learnt their first bitter lessons and suffered their first casualties. Over the following decades, as the UN peacekeeping footprint has expanded, so too has the Irish contribution to UN missions. Few nations in the world can say that their peacekeepers have stood every day for over five decades at so many UN posts across Europe, Asia, Latin America, Africa and the Middle East.

This extensive operational experience means that peacekeeping is second nature to Irish troops: it is deeply embedded in the culture and spirit of the Force. This has enabled Ireland to consistently provide the UN with highly trained, well-equipped peacekeepers who unwaveringly perform to the highest standards in often difficult circumstances. Today, over 370 Irish peacekeepers, mainly from Óglaigh na hÉireann, are bringing this experience to seven UN missions, including three in this part of the world.

This particular mission – UNIFIL, or to give it its formal name the United Nations Interim Force in Lebanon – embodies the spirit of the United Nations: its troops are drawn from thirty-eight countries, and all are working together, and with the local community, to bring peace and stability to South Lebanon. Within this group, Ireland is once again closely co-operating with Finland, a country with whom we share a long history of peacekeeping.

UNIFIL played a key role, back in the 1980s, in monitoring the cessation of hostilities in this region, notably through its chairing of tripartite talks with the Lebanese Armed Forces and the Israeli Defence Force; indeed it was for a while the only forum for such exchanges. Of course, UNIFIL's mandate has evolved significantly since Irish troops were first deployed here in 1978. I know that many of you in the current mission are involved in a variety of tasks, ranging from counter-improvised explosive device detection to civilian–military co-operation and humanitarian assistance.

Equally important is the commitment of the mission to building good relations with the Lebanese authorities and local communities. Some of you, for example, are involved in developing micro-projects in partnership with municipal authorities and community groups. I understand that a range of initiatives have been completed, including a women's agricultural co-operative, the provision of support for community centres and local schools and, more recently, the development of community sports facilities.

These interactions with the surrounding population and your contribution to their economic and social development are an essential component of any stabilization process. I am sure that the time, effort and skills you invest in these projects are deeply appreciated and contribute to the warm regard in which Irish peacekeepers are held here in Lebanon.

May I also avail of this occasion to commend the Permanent Defence Force on their implementation of the UN Security Council Resolution on

'Women, Peace and Security', which aims to enable women to participate more fully in conflict resolution and post-war recovery. The contribution of the Irish contingent here to making this resolution a reality has been rightly acknowledged, and I want, in turn, to congratulate you on your achievements in this field. Your engagement on issues such as this forms an important part of Ireland's commitment to tackling gender inequality and promoting human rights.

Ours are particularly challenging times, and this is a particularly challenging region, for global peace and security. The UN's peacekeeping force has more than tripled during the past fifteen years: resourcing and managing this rapid expansion is a tremendous test for the Organization. So is the task of responding to the novel threats that have emerged in recent years, and to new types of conflict that have resulted in the largest displacement of human populations in global history.

We are all acutely conscious of the fact that, more often than not, UN peacekeepers are now deployed to countries and regions where there is unfortunately no peace to keep and where reconciliation processes are fragile or absent. The nature of war has evolved dramatically over the past few decades, from the inter-state conflicts that marked the early days of UN peacekeeping missions, to civil wars within states and, more recently, new forms of violence – appalling mass killings, kidnappings and disappearances – perpetrated by groups who do not owe allegiance to any state. These groups often invoke a distorted interpretation of religious texts that were previously taken as sacred and revelatory in their invitation to peace.

Thus the role of peacekeepers has never been so necessary, and it has never been as complex. It now entails tasks such as the building-up of potentially democratic institutions; reform of the security sector; human rights monitoring; and the protection of civilians. I am confident that the training you have received, including those days you spent in the Glen of Imaal, has prepared you well for such difficult mandates, and that, however harsh the realities around you may be, you always find the necessary strength and stamina in the conviction that this world would be less safe without the United Nations as its peace custodian.

We stand in a small country which, in previous times, managed to successfully organize relations between its constituent communities, but which, over several decades now, has suffered greatly from the confrontations between these communities as well as with its Israeli and Syrian neighbours. This small country now has to cope with the disastrous consequences of the brutal war raging in Syria.

The displacement of almost four million Syrians, so many of whom have fled to the safety of Lebanon, places intolerable stresses on the fabric of Lebanese society and its delicate tapestry of religions, clans and political forces, as the Palestinian refugee crisis did forty years ago.

I salute the tireless efforts of so many volunteers from across the world who are doing what they can to ease the plight of refugees. The remarkable work of these volunteers and NGOs, and your own work as peacekeepers, should not, however, become a substitute for diplomatic action in the search for a resolution to the horrific violence causing so much suffering in this region. Nor should the refugee crisis be seen as a problem only for Lebanon and other neighbouring countries: it is a matter of concern and of moral responsibility for Ireland and all members of the international community. *A Óglacha na hÉireann.*

I am aware that the consequences of this war in Syria have been experienced in different ways by each of the three UN missions in this area. I am delighted to note that, when the UN Disengagement Observer Force came under threat in 2013, the UN immediately looked to Ireland as a credible and experienced peacekeeping provider to reinforce the mission. As a nation, we took great pride in the swift and courageous support offered by your colleagues in the Mobile Force Reserve to their fellow peacekeepers on the Golan Heights in August of last year.

Sadly, UNIFIL has recently lost one of its men. May I extend my sincere condolences to all of you, and more particularly to your colleagues in the Spanish contingent, on the tragic death of one of your comrades last January.

Que descanse en paz el espíritu de su compañero español. (May the spirit of your Spanish comrade rest in peace.)

Over the decades of our participation in this mission, Ireland too has suffered painful losses. Later today I will have the opportunity to pay my respects, at the memorial in Tibnin, to the forty-seven Irish personnel who lost their lives while serving with UNIFIL. Thankfully, many years have passed without any loss of life among our Irish peacekeepers, but you can rest assured that the sacrifice made by your former colleagues during their service and the tragedy borne by their families are duly remembered. *Ar dheis Dé go raibh a n-anamacha.*

You are experiencing separation from your families and friends while serving in the field. I know that there are many UNIFIL veterans among you today, but for fifty-one of you it is the first time you have served overseas and spent such an extended period of time apart from your loved ones. On behalf of the Irish people may I, once again, thank each and every one of you for your service, your sense of duty and your dedication to the cause of peace.

Preparing for the Global Humanitarian Summit

O'REILLY HALL,
UNIVERSITY COLLEGE DUBLIN

2 JULY 2015

*I*S MIAN LIOM *comhgháirdeas a dhéanamh leis an tOllamh Deeks agus leis An Coláiste Ollscoile, Baile Átha Cliath as ócáid an lae inniú i Halla Uí Raghallaigh a eagrú. Bhí áthas orm glacadh leis an cuireadh óráid a thabhairt ag Cruinniú Mullaigh Dhaonnúil na hÉireann, a thugann le chéile daoine aonair agus ceannairí ó réimse leathan eagraíochtaí a bhfuil baint acu le gníomh daonnúil in Éirinn agus thar lear.*

(May I congratulate Professor Deeks and University College Dublin for hosting today's event in O'Reilly Hall. I was delighted to accept the invitation to speak at this Irish Humanitarian Summit, bringing together as it does leaders from the wide variety of actors involved in humanitarian action in Ireland and abroad. That community of concern includes academics, non-governmental organizations, UN agencies, public- and private-sector representatives, and, very importantly, members of the diaspora communities here in Ireland.)

Ireland has a lengthy history of humanitarian engagement, and that record has become strongly linked to the positive aspects of Irish national identity. The experiences of famine and of emigration are of course influences on Ireland's foreign policy in general and its approach to overseas aid in particular. The early architects of Ireland's foreign policy had a sense of our country's history providing us with an ethical, and emancipatory, perspective on world affairs, and this view was widely shared by the Irish people. Whether it was in response to the war in Biafra in the 1960s, the famines in Bangladesh and Ethiopia in the 1970s and 1980s or the tsunami and Haiti earthquake in more recent times, Irish people have shown time and again an eagerness to offer their help to the suffering and most vulnerable.

In making such a response Irish people are embracing their responsibilities as global citizens. The Irish State delivers these values through our foreign policy and the work of Irish Aid, and through the work of the Irish NGOs present in the room today. The efforts of Irish humanitarian workers in the field are in turn highly respected within the humanitarian sector for their commitment and professionalism. Irish Aid's much-commended Rapid Response Initiative harnesses the expertise of Irish humanitarian professionals from across a wide range of professions, deploying them to crises across the globe at short notice when needed.

As President, and previously as a member of the Dáil and Seanad Foreign Affairs Committee, I have had the privilege of visiting many of the projects supported or administered by Irish humanitarians in difficult circumstances around the world. I have witnessed the work of Irish Aid during my visits to Lebanon this year, and to Ethiopia in 2014. In Ethiopia I visited camps for South Sudanese refugees fleeing the conflict which has engulfed the world's newest state. Hundreds of thousands of people have sought shelter in Gambella in Ethiopia, while one and a half million more are internally displaced within South Sudan's own borders.

While our humanitarian action may have been shaped by our national cultural and political identity, Ireland's humanitarian work is also grounded on the contemporary values of solidarity, democracy, justice, freedom and respect for human rights and equality. In addressing the present humanitarian crisis, I believe we must invoke those values, not as a form of predictable rhetoric but as guidance to our future direction.

We are at a critical moment in world history, facing a series of tests and choices that will determine not only the fate of millions of our fellow global citizens now, but which will define the future of our planet. I spoke in January, at the launch of the European Year of Development, of my belief that 2015 is on a par with 1945 in terms of the potential that it has to reshape how humanity deals with the challenges we face. By the end of this year, the post-2015 development agenda will have to be finalized and the new Sustainable Development Goals will be called upon to provide a road map for the future.

Ireland has had the great honour, and great responsibility, of co-chairing with Kenya the negotiation process for finalizing the Sustainable Development Goals. In addition, a new climate change agreement will have been signed in Paris. I have recently been invited by President Hollande to address a preliminary conference in Paris later this month on the theme of 'Summit of Consciences for the Climate'. The two processes of sustainable development and responding to climate change are profoundly interconnected.

In each area – development, climate change and displacement – we will be required to undertake work that should inform good policy, work that will allow us to recognize the underlying causes of our current situation. It is a matter of concern as to whether the will for such engaged scholarship exists at the present time. Certainly it seems missing from current discourse at the political and institutional level.

We will need political and moral leadership that is courageous and far-sighted and grounded in the founding values of human rights. In the spheres of law, policy and diplomacy we must accept our obligations and duties in an interdependent world – obligations that may indeed be grounded in international law, but that run deeper and are also moral obligations.

I wish to focus in particular today on the dramatic increase in humanitarian need we are currently witnessing as a result of specific wars and political collapses in Africa and Asia.

Let us first be unequivocal that this present crisis of displacement is not an issue that can be compartmentalized in a silo that we might label 'security', or seen simply as a regional concern for some. It is a global issue which is directly concerned with the protection of human rights. In approaching this issue, we must, I will argue, make a fresh commitment to the universality of human rights and to the common humanity of all and we must also understand the current humanitarian crisis in proper historical context. The alternative is to choose short-sighted responses based on a narrow sense of national self-interest – a choice that would be nothing short of disastrous.

Let us begin by considering the true nature of what we are witnessing at present. As recently confirmed by the UN High Commission for Refugees, the number of refugees and displaced persons is now at its highest level since figures were first recorded in the 1950s. Global forced displacement accelerated in 2014, once again reaching record levels. By the end of that year, 59.5 million people were forcibly displaced worldwide as a result of persecution, conflict, generalized violence or human rights violations. This constitutes 8.3 million persons more than the previous year (51.2 million) and is the highest recorded annual increase. To date, the response to the humanitarian reality behind these population numbers and the root causes driving people to move has been wholly inadequate.

In recent months, we in Europe have seen these great humanitarian challenges become manifest in the Mediterranean, where this year alone almost 2,000 people have already died in attempting to make the perilous journey across the sea while fleeing conflict and grinding poverty.

Ireland's LÉ Eithne, in its first weeks of deployment in the Mediterranean, has rescued more than 2,700 desperate migrants from unseaworthy craft of various shapes and sizes. While retaining the integrity of the distinction between aid and military action – a crucial distinction which I recognize and support – the scale of drowning we have witnessed in the first months of this year demands emergency action and, as Supreme Commander of the Defence Forces, I suggest I speak for all of the Irish people when I say how proud we are that our naval forces can make this contribution.

The numbers of lives which have been lost on Europe's southern and eastern borders have been truly shocking, and we must recognize that this is a human and not a natural phenomenon. This increased level of displacement has specific causes. In Africa and in the Middle East, too, we are seeing great levels of displacement, prompted by war and conflict and by catastrophic failures of politics and of development strategies.

The conflict in Libya and neighbouring African countries continues to crowd migrants into boats on the Mediterranean, while that in Syria continues to push refugees across the borders into Turkey, Lebanon and Jordan. More than half (53 per cent) of all refugees worldwide, as recognized by the UNHCR, came from just three countries: Syria (3.88 million), Afghanistan (2.59 million) and Somalia (1.11 million).[48]

This is not solely a European problem. Many of those displaced will go on to seek protection in Europe, but most will stay in neighbouring states where, we must never forget, the great majority of the world's refugees are to be found. The leading host countries for refugees are not the most developed states but those neighbours who receive grossly inadequate support. At the end of 2014, Turkey hosted 1.59 million refugees, Pakistan 1.51 million, Lebanon (a country with a total population of less than 4.5 million) 1.15 million, Iran 982,000, Ethiopia 659,500 and Jordan 654,100.

Given this reality, we must ask why so much of our discourse has focused on questions of security and border control, on alleged 'pull factors', to the neglect of the conditions from which people are fleeing and those they find themselves in when they reach another country.

---

48   These figures are all taken from the UNHCR report for 2014. Figures exclude Palestinian refugees, who are dealt with under a separate legal regime.

Analysing the UNHCR figures, we are confronted with the many contradictions in how developed countries approach the movements of people from areas of conflict. As the UN High Commissioner for Refugees has noted: 'We cannot ask these countries to keep their borders open and to close other borders.' The High Commissioner has correctly identified this as an untenable position. Worse, we are failing to support these countries which are hosting so many refugees, with the inevitable consequence that the global situation will deteriorate further for them and for us. As the High Commissioner has described the receiving states: 'They are the first line of defense for global collective security and they are pillars, essential pillars, for regional security. If they fall, the consequences will be dramatic for the whole world.'

We know that much of this migration catastrophe flows from political and diplomatic failures and, too frequently, from neglect of indicators that a conflict is looming. In 2014, Ireland provided almost €15 million in funding to address the Syria crisis. So far in 2015, €3.3 million has been allocated to UN agencies (€1.5m for the World Food Programme, €1 million for UNICEF and €800,000 for UNHCR Jordan) for Syria. On 31 March 2015, at the third International Humanitarian Pledging Conference for Syria in Kuwait ('Kuwait III'), Minister of State Sherlock announced a pledge of €12 million on behalf of the Irish Government. The total value of Ireland's contribution to the Syria crisis with these additional amounts comes to €41 million.

Internationally, however, as recently reported by Amnesty International, only 23 per cent of the UN humanitarian appeal for Syria's refugees has been funded. As a result of this shortage, aid agencies have repeatedly had to reduce financial assistance to refugees. The immediate consequence of this failure to fund or resettle refugees from the war is that the neighbouring states are unable to cope and are increasingly imposing restrictions on people fleeing from the fighting.

Most of those arriving in Italy by boat are leaving from Libya, a country facing great political difficulties which has no functioning asylum system. Libyan authorities have little capacity to prevent migrants leaving their shores, and there is no indication that the numbers coming to Libya from other states will decrease.

Little is being done to support the authorities in Libya and European states have been slow to agree a response that would remove the impulse for desperate people to get into the boats in the first place or provide safe pathways to protection or resettlement in front-line states. Again and again we encounter not just a reluctance, but a resistance to acknowledge the consequences of diplomatic failure, to learn from that failure or to take responsibility for it.

The response, such as it has been so far, has focused heavily on border controls, security and targeting those who are smuggling migrants across frontiers. These steps are of course necessary as part of a comprehensive strategy, but the emphasis to date has been misplaced. Any suggestion that the current situation can be resolved with such measures alone is misguided, and may lead to security consequences that are far more dangerous to Europe in the longer term.

I believe that the reality of the present situation, including its historical origins, has become obscured, as have the moral and ethical issues at stake for institutions, international organizations and national governments and their populations. The dangers that we face include the risk that we might lose sight of the universality of human rights and human dignity, on which our international order is based. At stake is the moral force and authority of the international system itself.

The principle of universality of rights and human dignity, as expressed in the Universal Declaration of Human Rights, is the very foundation of the United Nations and this principle must be our starting point.

I met with the Secretary-General of the United Nations, Ban Ki-Moon, at Áras an Uachtaráin just a few weeks ago and we discussed the challenges associated with the global crisis of migration and refugees. To mark

World Refugee Day just two weeks ago, the Secretary-General has said: 'Refugees are people like anyone else, like you and me. They led ordinary lives before becoming displaced, and their biggest dream is to be able to live normally again... let us recall our common humanity, celebrate tolerance and diversity and open our hearts to refugees everywhere.' When we consider the obligations and responsibilities that flow from our common humanity, the position of civilians fleeing war should not be alien to any nation, including those that currently enjoy prosperity and peace.

I have spoken elsewhere about the 'ethics of memory'; about the importance of how we apply our memory of the past to the challenge of building better futures. One of the great dangers of forgetting our own past is that we can have a false sense of security about the present, or come to view differences between us and others as essential rather than stemming from contingent events or unaccountable forces. We have all shared a troubled history, and our systems and standards of protection were put in place at the mid-point of a troubled century when many European nations witnessed enormous destruction and displacement.

If compassion is to be grounded in empathy, then we would all do well to remember ethically the experiences of our own forebears. For Ireland, we remember that, among the more than one million who fled famine and disease during a few short years in the mid-nineteenth century, who set out to cross the Atlantic in search of a new life, many were driven to make perilous journeys in inadequate vessels to harbours or where local populations at times treated them with hostility; but there were also those who accepted them and gave them the opportunity to begin new lives.

For all European nations, the memory of the refugee experience should be within the reach of one or two generations. The level of displacement across this continent both during and after the Second World War left few regions untouched; for example, well over ten million ethnic Germans were expelled from eastern and central Europe or left voluntarily between

1945 and 1950. The refugee camps established at the end of the war did not finally close in Europe until 1960.

Even in more recent times, Europe has faced large refugee movements. In the 1990s in the Balkans 2.7 million were displaced and 700,000 sought asylum in Western Europe. At the global level, too, the world has met such challenges before, and the international response to the wars in Vietnam, Cambodia and Laos in the 1970s ultimately saw millions of civilians resettled in North America, Europe and Australasia.

We must reject, then, any idea that the current crisis is unprecedented or beyond our capacity. Our human rights obligations, under UN treaties and under the European Convention, are universal and non-derogable – they cannot be ignored or violated under any circumstances. They are also unquestionably to be applied without discrimination on the grounds of legal status, race, religion or nationality.

As to the extent of these obligations, in the first instance there are those to protect the right to life of those we encounter at sea. In the case of the Mediterranean, the European Union must do more to expand search-and-rescue operations, and these missions must be prioritized over concerns about border controls. Yes, comprehensive long-term solutions must be found to reduce current flows of people across the Mediterranean, but in the interim we cannot accept that deterrence ever justifies the loss of life.

There is also the right to freedom from non-refoulement, in other words the legal principle that should prevent returning a persecuted refugee to the state that has persecuted them, which is being blatantly violated in South-east Asia and elsewhere. Again the need for regional co-operation and co-ordinated action cannot justify tactical responses that risk the loss of life.

At the level of national governments we need to have in place robust domestic refugee systems that are fair, equitable and efficient. In the Irish context, I welcome the publication this week of the report of the

Working Group on improvements to the protection process, including direct provision and support to asylum seekers.

We must recognize that the scale of the numbers needing protection will require substantive and generous action. Beyond the immediate issue of search-and-rescue and receiving refugees, and that of supporting institutions in the front-line countries, we must also look at resettlement. In framing its response to this great challenge, the international community has a moral as well as a legal obligation, not merely to rescue those crammed into often makeshift and extremely dangerous vessels, but also to provide long-term solutions afterwards.

UNHCR estimated in 2014 that 378,684 Syrian refugees in the five main host countries were in need of resettlement. However, to date the number of places offered to these most vulnerable of Syria's refugees, who are unlikely to return safely to Syria in any foreseeable future, stands at just 87,442. At the global level, Amnesty International has called for 300,000 refugees per year to be resettled.

Even within Europe itself, we might also ask what does solidarity mean in relation to migration and asylum policy? Italy, Malta and Greece cannot be abandoned or expected to fulfil Europe's duties on their own, simply by virtue of geography.

Taken together, the universal and non-derogable rights – the right to life and the right to freedom from torture, and to non-refoulement – represent the core values of the institutional framework we put in place after the Second World War to promote peace in the world. If Europe is to recapture the vision of its founding fathers, then it must be a Europe built on respect for basic human rights, including economic and social rights and respect for the rights of migrants and refugees. If we allow these rights to be diluted by the rhetoric of prejudice and fear, we risk undermining the moral legitimacy of our various positions on the world stage. This in turn will weaken, and perhaps is already weakening, our influence and capacity to act in response to the very real threats to these values.

Fundamentalism and extremism are at the heart of the conflicts that are driving most of those who are displaced, often accompanied by a rhetoric of hate about the purported conflict between faith-based values and the values of an allegedly decadent West. A rise of extremism in one corner of the world has the potential to affect us all. While technological advances offer great innovation in our ability to communicate with each other, they can also be harnessed for ill and in the malign use of digital media, and the threat of such extremism can spread and flourish faster than ever before. We cannot hope to succeed in defeating extremism by deepening systems of 'othering' those who arrive in Europe seeking our protection.

This is a moment for leadership that is courageous, grounded in an unqualified commitment to human rights and informed by a long-sighted understanding of the gravity of the present situation. This is a moment for European leaders to engage with their parliaments and with their electorates and, rather than yielding to new populisms based on fear, to make the case for solidarity and protection. Are we to be limited in our actions by the narrow self-interest of the present, or are we to fulfil the duties bestowed on us by the principles of universal human rights, by our debt to history, and by our obligations to the future? These are the questions we must answer.

While it is appropriate that 'Serving the Needs of People in Conflict' has been chosen as a core theme of the World Humanitarian Summit, responding to the consequences of conflict is not enough. The international community must also consider how to take such preventative action as will best enable them to engage actively in advance of conflicts. More and more, the international community is reacting inadequately to the worst events after they have happened.

The current crisis is the product of failed diplomacy, a failure that the whole of the international community shares, and the powerful share more than most. We are witnessing the sapping of the authority and influence of a genuine internationalism.

At the same time I want to recognize those who continue to act for sustainable peace and security. They must be supported, and it is the responsibility of us all to work through multilateral institutions and diplomatic channels to promote peace where it is absent, and to sustain it where it is fragile.

Alongside our aid programme and policy engagement, Ireland plays an important role through the international peacekeeping operations that it supports. Within three years of joining the United Nations, the first contingent of Irish peacekeepers was deployed as part of an observer mission to Lebanon in 1958. Since then, Ireland's commitment to blue-helmet peacekeeping remains unbroken, and it is probably the most visible expression of Ireland's support to the United Nations.

When I visited the Irish contingent of peacekeepers which forms part of the UNIFIL mission in Lebanon earlier this year, I was struck by the quiet, sustained and sensitively delivered professionalism of Irish soldiers and members of *an Garda Síochána*, who make incredible sacrifices to bring peace and stability in places where it is fragile or threatened.

Other factors that are contributing to global instability must also be addressed. The effects of climate change make international borders appear even more irrelevant. Humanity's interdependence across borders, oceans and continents is apparent in the face of typhoon, flood or drought. And those most affected by these events are those who are already the poorest and the most vulnerable. Global inequality is most strikingly illustrated by the way in which climate change most affects those who have least contributed to it.

The interlinked and recurrent emergencies that climate change causes require interlinked, global solutions. We must recognize the solidarity that binds us together as human beings, and acknowledge that we all share a responsibility for this fragile planet, and a duty of hospitality towards all those who live on it.

We must never simply reduce a human experience to a nameless quantification. I am pleased to note that the overarching theme of the Irish Humanitarian Summit is 'Putting Affected People at the Centre of Humanitarian Response'. The first responders in any emergency, whether natural or man-made, are the people who are themselves directly affected. Neighbours share food with those who are hungry, relatives shelter families forced to evacuate their homes. These responders are the most effective in addressing the immediate needs of the victims.

By focusing on those who are most affected and treating them as key agents in their own recovery and development, with all of the respect and dignity that it entails for their cultures, the global humanitarian community can begin to make real progress in saving lives and enabling communities to improve their position, even to flourish.

In order to help communities reduce their vulnerability to disasters before they strike, humanitarian agencies need to learn from the communities themselves what the risks are, and incorporate the community's existing coping mechanisms, with their instinctive intelligence and indigenous wisdom, into their work. Similarly, building 'resilience' and helping communities' own abilities to mitigate the effect of disasters can only be achieved by harnessing local knowledge. It is this harnessing of local knowledge, coupled with external expertise, which will help communities to withstand shocks and transform their societies by 'building back' from disaster better than before.

It is also essential to take into account the position of women in both development and humanitarian practice. We must recognize that women are disproportionately and uniquely affected by disasters and armed conflict. Ireland's Second National Action Plan on Women, Peace and Security recognizes both the particularly adverse effect of conflict on women and girls, and their critical role in conflict prevention, peace negotiations, peace-building and governance.

It was with enormous pleasure that in March this year I accepted the invitation of Mlambo-Ngcuka, UN Under-Secretary-General and the

Executive Director of UNWOMEN, to become one of ten World Leader Global Champions for the UN Women's *HeforShe* campaign. This global movement has at its core the principle of solidarity; it is a movement that seeks to bring one half of humanity together in support of the other half. I look forward to making my own modest contribution in carrying out this role with passion and energy in the months ahead.

In conclusion, as we take up this important work of preparation for these summits on development, climate change and the humanitarian crisis, my hope is that world leaders will make wise, brave and, yes, the necessary radical decisions. The European Union, and other international institutions and member states, must commit to addressing the protracted conflicts or cyclical food crises which drive so many of our global fellow citizens to such desperate measures. We must propose solutions that acknowledge co-operation, interdependence and solidarity, and not individual and national self-interest – positions that are apparent to a worrying degree in the current European discourse.

Thar na spriocanna agus na gealltanais, na ráitis bheartais agus na fógartha, tá sé riachtanach go gcoimeádfadh oibrithe cabhrach, parlaiminteoirí, lucht léinn agus gníomhaígh, ar aon dul le go leor agaibh sa chomhluadar seo, cuntas as ceannairí domhanda chun cinntiú go gcoinníonn siad na gealltanais a rinne siad.
(Beyond the goals and commitments, the policy statements and the declarations, it is essential that aid workers, parliamentarians, academics and activists, like many of you in the room today, hold world leaders to account and ensure that they deliver on the promises made.)

The most vulnerable people on our fragile planet require your intervention, your solidarity. They are entitled to no less if we are to hope together for a better and more secure world.

On Receiving an Award from the Republic of Chile

TRINITY COLLEGE, DUBLIN

14 JANUARY 2016

I T IS A great honour to welcome Foreign Minister Muñoz to Ireland. I am particularly delighted to have the opportunity to reflect with him on one of the most moving events of my political life, the opportunity of engaging with the Chilean people in conditions of dictatorship. I clearly, and with the greatest affection, recall the arrival of those Chilean families fleeing persecution and death. I recall with special affection Hugo and Resa Ramirez, and those other families in Shannon and Galway. With other concerned parliamentarians, travelling at our own initiative, without state support, I took part in an international election observation mission to Chile in 1988, and wished to pay tribute to the people of Chile and to their commitment to democracy and human rights.

It was my immense privilege to bear witness to the momentous vote of the Chilean people on 5 October 1988. I, along with my then political colleagues – TD Pat McCartan, Senators Shane Ross and Joe O'Toole – were among hundreds of International Election Observers invited by the Association of International Parliamentarians for Democracy in Chile, whose Secretary-General, Ricardo Lagos, would later become President of Chile.

I travelled out a week in advance, and as I was the first International Observer to arrive, on 22 September, I became known as *Observador Uno*. I remember holding a press conference which was widely attended, though some papers ran headlines such as '*El Retorno de O'Higgins*' and editorialized on the terrible things a person such as myself might be expected to write about Chile.

As the map for allocations of International Observers was blank I volunteered for one of the more remote areas in the south of the country, Punta Arenas. I stayed at the house of Roberto Lara and his wife Liliana Soucarret Romer and during my stay visited Bishop Tomás Gonzalez, an opponent of the dictatorship, and in whose church a bomb had been placed by supporters of the dictatorship. He, a friend of the poor, brought me to visit opponents of the regime, including the Secretary of the *No* Campaign who had lost his job after thirty years' service with the National Petroleum Company because he supported the Campaign.

Under the slogan '*Chile, La Alegria ya viene*' the people of Chile, in enormous numbers, affirmed in full voice their deeply held commitment to political freedom and brought about the beginning of the end of over fifteen years of military dictatorship. In Punta Arenas, where one in four of those employed worked for the military, the vote was delivered at 6.50 a.m. – *Sí* 3,879, *No* 4,892. Nationally, of over seven million votes cast, almost four million voted *No* (54.7 per cent). I had the privilege of witnessing a people choosing a path based on an old respect for values of decency, democracy and human rights and the future possibilities it created.

If I may recall a short extract from my diary of that time, here is what I wrote of these events in 1988:

> At the entrance to the town of La Hermida is a little shrine to a fifteen-year-old boy whose nickname was Pete. There had been a confrontation here on the day Pinochet was named by the military as their candidate, and Pete had been killed.

His mother, Rebecca, a small woman with striking brown eyes, sits in her neat house under a wall-hanging of Salvador Allende. Every second word she speaks is of oppression. At the edge of the *población* there is a circus of the North American variety. It is a Pinochet initiative directed against the 'subversiveness' of native or popular culture such as that championed by Violeta Parra and the tortured and executed Victor Jara.

Outside the tent a bear is being fed, but most people are watching a condor with a rope around its neck.

The condor is the mystical black eagle of the Andes. An Andean ceremony involves the ritual tying of a condor to a bull's back; when it has gorged itself on the hapless beast, the bird is released and soars to a height of four thousand metres. It is a horrific image, but I cannot get out of mind the parallel with the role of the military in Latin American society – an elite whose prestige and power has been sucked from the life-blood of the people. They are worse than vultures.

As the day of the plebiscite nears, there are more demonstrations. Near the Plaza de Armas, the mothers and wives of the tortured and disappeared – Madres de los Desaparecidos – are placing posters on the wall. When the army arrives, the soldiers pull down the posters.

The women continue to protest. Some are dragged away by the hair. The literature asks: *Me tortiraron, me asesinaron, me despaeciron, me olvidastea?* ('Should the tortured, the disappeared, the assassinated be forgotten?') One of the women becomes involved in an argument with two female office workers – *Momias* – who talk of discipline.

The television cameras are first to arrive on the scene, followed by the tank housing the water cannon, which sprays contaminated water mixed with chemicals and acid on the demonstrators. This is how Pinochet deals with the opposition.

At the Cárcel Pública – the public prison – there is talk of a hunger strike. It is just past midday when the gas is released; we all run into the doorway of a block of flats. An old woman, her daughter and two young children are handing out salt and slices of lemon. The gas is being used indiscriminately, and it gets into everyone's eyes, even those who are some distance away from the main protest.

In the doorway, the photo press are coughing, except for those who have come prepared with World War II-style gas masks. An old woman weeps softly: 'For fifteen years it's the same.' The water tank approaches, the soldiers alight from the truck, and the children are almost knocked down. His mother grabs Jorge, and I carry Lionel up to the landing and out of immediate danger.

Later in the week, I revisit La Hermida to talk at greater length with Rebecca, and to visit Olla Commones: the communal cooking places, like soup kitchens, from which the poorer families are fed. Last night I heard Pinochet say, 'I am middle class, Lucia [his wife] is middle class. The middle class is the biggest class.' I had heard this one before: has Mrs Thatcher, the General's greatest fan, not said something similar? In Rebecca's case, everybody is poor.

Rebecca talks of her son Pedro Mariquo, known as 'Pelluco'. On 1 May 1984, he went to Park O'Higgins, where a demonstration was taking place. He was in good spirits, she tells me. He came home and, after eating, was playing football. Some local youths had lit a fire. A police patrol car came. Four men got out, and one fired three shots. The first bullet lodged in Pelluco's back and the second in his neck; the third grazed his head.

By 10.30 p.m. he was dead.

She relates the events, and her attempts to get justice, without emotion, and also describes the subsequent harassment of her daughter Antoinetta and her son José Christian. She ends firmly with the statement: 'They will never break me.' She is wearing a 'No' badge. I leave her to her work.

The final 'Rally for the No' takes place on the Saturday before the vote. At one point two million people fill the streets. La Alegría is coming close. On Sunday, the 'Sí' campaign has its final rally – more a cavalcade of cars. The rich, and those who aspire to be rich, are on the side of Pinochet. Against them are the poor and those who value democracy.

Let me say, in the presence of distinguished diplomats, how I can still not understand how the dictatorship was supported, overtly and covertly, by so many governments, how its opponents were allowed to be abused, even murdered. Then too, we should reflect on the role of Professor Friedman and Los Muchachos de Chicago in supporting the economic model of the dictatorship, of using the Chilean people and their children as a laboratory for a mechanistic and extreme version of market theory.

Mr Foreign Minister, during the years which have passed since that momentous day in 1988 we in Ireland have followed, with interest and admiration, your country's progress as a truly democratic republic grounded in a true respect for human rights and a set of political choices that place the common good at their heart.

I am honoured to be among the international recipients of this recognition from the Government of Chile. I would like to pay tribute to those humane, courageous men and women of the international community in Santiago who in 1973 opened their embassies to Chilean refugees, people like the then Swedish Ambassador to Chile, Harald Edelstam, who was consequently declared persona non grata by the junta and expelled from the country.

I commend Chile for honouring the memory, in a most practical way, of its refugees by its current policy of welcoming Syrian refugees. Who among us can afford to forget our humanity, to forget the open doors that were ours to walk through to sanctuary when we or those of our people needed it?

I recall too the extraordinary work carried out by Irish missionaries in

Chile during the darkest years of the dictatorship, and I am delighted that they have been also honoured with this award. Throughout the seventeen years of military dictatorship, the Columban Fathers co-ordinated their efforts with the Vicariate of Solidarity which was set up by the then Cardinal Archbishop of Santiago, Raúl Silva Henríquez, to offer refuge and support to victims of human rights violations. They also participated actively in the anti-torture movement named after Sebastián Acevedo, the man who burnt himself alive to protest the torture of his son by secret police.

Tragically, the Columban Fathers suffered terrorism themselves, and very directly, when their house was stormed in 1975, resulting in the murder of their housekeeper, Henriquetta Reyes, and the detention and torture of Dr Sheila Cassidy. Two Irish Columban priests, Fr Brendan Ford and Fr Desmond McGillicuddy, were expelled by the junta in 1983 – among other things for running a 'politically oriented soup kitchen', as it was reportedly described by police at the time.

The actions of those courageous Irish priests in Chile are emblematic of the selfless work of Irish missionaries around the world as they seek to protect the dispossessed and underprivileged. *Beir Beannacht orthu go deo.*

I had the happy opportunity to return to Chile in 2012 as President of Ireland twenty-four years after the plebiscite of 1988. I was welcomed by President Piñera, and had the privilege of meeting Patricio Aylwin. While there I visited the Museum of Memory and Human Rights as well as the home of Pablo Neruda on Isla Negra. I reflected in those hallowed places on the tragedy of the lives lost and shattered, 3,000 murdered, 3,000 disappeared, tens of thousands tortured, raped and abused. I recalled the dignity, energy and hope I encountered when I first visited in 1988. It was wonderful to see in 2012 that the dignity, hope and energy of 1988 continued to pulse through the country.

I was also privileged to meet, once again, Joan Jara, widow of the singer Victor Jara who so generously put his great artistic gifts and, ultimately, his life at the service of our common humanity. I spoke, on that occasion, of how passion for justice cannot be halted by torture, or censure, or even murder. It is that passion that must remain at the heart of any society that claims to be about the task of building a real republic.

As with all true democracies, Chile continues to face the challenges of deepening democracy in new global conditions. Each generation is charged with the ethical remembrance of past struggles as it continues to build and develop a democracy which began life as a courageous vision. That is something we are deeply aware of here in Ireland in this year of important commemorations, as we reflect on the inspiring words of our Proclamation of Independence and remember the men and women who fought for a free Irish State and a democratic Republic.

Chile's defence and development of democracy is important for its own people, but it also has a resonance beyond its borders. In that spirit I express my gratitude to Chile for the example it gives to the world of respect for human rights, promotion of sustainable human development and a socially inclusive model of economic governance.

DEFENDING
AND RENEWING
DEMOCRACY

The Future of Parliaments

Parliamentary Assembly of the Council of Europe

PALAIS DE L'EUROPE, STRASBOURG

27 JANUARY 2015

I T IS, FOR me, both an honour and a great pleasure to be in this Chamber, in this distinguished institution, the Council of Europe, which recalls the first steps of Europe's moral and cultural reconstruction after the devastation of the Second World War. I am animated, too, by a particular sense of urgency as all of us, elected representatives of the peoples of Europe, are seeking to make our way through what can truly be described as a 'fragile moment' for democracy.

Ours are times when, again, we acutely need the opportunities offered by the Council of Europe as a unique pan-European body – and these are times, too, that require us to rekindle the values of human dignity and democratic pluralism that the Council upholds.

As one of the ten founding members, Ireland is keenly aware of the important role the Council of Europe has played in shaping our own path in European co-operation. The young Irish State had remained neutral throughout the Second World War; it was, in the late 1940s, a poor country, geographically peripheral, whose foreign policy was coloured by unresolved issues with its powerful neighbour and former colonizer, the

United Kingdom. Thus Irish participation in the Hague Congress and in the negotiations in London, culminating in the Council of Europe Statute in 1949, represented an important early engagement with the ideas then coalescing about the shape of post-war co-operation.

Over the years, our membership in the Council and our implementation of the European Convention on Human Rights have been fundamental in consolidating the rule of law and supporting positive social change in Ireland.

Today, in the face of the new challenges that overshadow Europe, it is important to start by reaffirming my country's solid commitment to multilateralism, and to the goals and principles that have guided the Council of Europe's endeavours throughout the sixty-five years of its existence.

Indeed, ever since its foundation, and with a renewed sense of purpose after the end of the Cold War, the Council of Europe has provided an essential catalyst for:

- First, highlighting the fundamental principles of pluralist democracy, respect for human rights, and the rule of law;
- Second, the setting of standards in the human rights area through the European Convention on Human Rights system and other legal mechanisms;
- And third, confirming the common goal of a freer, more tolerant and just society in Europe.

This is a framework for which we must consciously care as an indispensable component of the architecture of stability, peace and trust we have been building on this continent over the decades. It is a legacy of profound ethical significance, one that is admired and emulated across the globe, which we must be mindful not to unravel. Rather, we must extend and strengthen it.

Before I come to those damaging currents which, in my view, threaten the destruction of our European systems of cohesion and co-operation, may I acknowledge more specifically the Council of Europe's immense contribution to the vindication of human rights, in the fullness and indivisibility of their application.

Of course, the European Convention on Human Rights and its Protocol, which my country signed in 1950 and ratified in 1953, and the activities of the European Court of Human Rights lie at the centre of the Council's work. I am delighted that I will be visiting the Court this afternoon, an institution which is so fundamental to European democracy in the broad sense.

Ireland's deep regard for the activities of the Court and for its role in strengthening democratic debate is reflected in our support for the Court's webcasting programme. Since 2006, Ireland has voluntarily funded the webcasting of Grand Chamber hearings before the Court. By allowing free access to some of the most important proceedings taking place here in Strasbourg, this project not only enables citizens to better understand the Court's operations and the rights that flow from the Convention itself; it also makes citizens aware of the way in which the vindication of human rights can invigorate democratic life and social change in their own country.

In the area of socio-economic rights, the adoption of the European Social Charter was a milestone in suggesting that human flourishing entails the effective enjoyment of social, as well as civil and political rights. I am glad to say that Ireland has been a supporter of both the original and the revised Charter, and that it has accepted the collective complaints mechanism presided over by the European Committee of Social Rights.

A further strength of the Council of Europe has been its emphasis on the role of culture in nurturing democracy. For the Irish, a nation that wishes to preserve its ancient Gaelic language, the adoption of the Convention for the Protection of National Minorities, to give but one example, was an important step towards the recognition of cultural rights throughout Europe.

Taken together, the human rights structures of the Council are a model in the protection of rights and liberties, and they also demonstrate a firm commitment to the fundamental principle of the indivisibility of human rights in their civil, political, economic, social and cultural dimensions.

This is not to say that Ireland is blind to the possibilities that might enhance the efficiency of the Court and the Council at large. My country is supportive of the reform process undertaken by the Court, and we of course welcome its achievements in reducing the enormous case backlog which, at one point, threatened its very functioning.

More broadly, Ireland endorsed the decision of the 2005 Warsaw Summit to refocus on the Council of Europe's primary mission to promote human rights, the rule of law and democracy in Europe, and it has been a long-standing supporter of Secretary General Jagland's efforts in that regard.

Yet, while recognizing the need for qualified, informed and positive reform, I wish to express my disquiet at the attempts to undermine the very legitimacy of both the Court and the Convention on Human Rights. Some of the criticisms addressed to the Court are part of a wider political argument about Europe, and given Ireland's particular historical, political and territorial situation, the terms of this debate are for us a very serious matter for concern.

Let me state things very clearly: the European Convention on Human Rights must remain the cornerstone of human rights protection in Europe. And to those who might suggest that there is a tension between the principles of parliamentary democracy and the international protection of human rights, let us respond unequivocally that parliaments flourish in an atmosphere where rights are vindicated.

These two propositions must be the basis for our collective discussions at a crucial juncture in our history. European co-operation currently faces a range of serious difficulties that are of concern to all European citizens, but in a particular way to their elected representatives. Indeed it is in your capacity as delegates of the national parliaments of Europe that I address you today; and it is by appealing to your experience and sense of responsibility as parliamentarians that I now turn to the alarming trends – some of a new kind, others the recrudescence of old evils – that imperil democracy, social cohesion and our shared future.

As a former parliamentarian myself, honoured to have spent over three decades serving in the Irish National Parliament, including some years as a member of this Assembly (from 2001 to 2003), I have the greatest respect for the work parliamentarians do to fulfil the needs and aspirations of the citizens who elect them, and for debating, differing, and yet reaching accommodation on the important issues that shape our world.

The suggestion I wish to put before you today is that, however grave the challenges we face, they also offer parliamentarians an opportunity to reassert the relevance of parliamentary democracy and discourse, their ability to represent citizens and their capacity to revitalize the project of European co-operation.

The first challenge we are facing, as the Members of this Assembly are acutely aware, is the disquieting return to our continent of grave geopolitical fractures, which have disastrous human consequences. As we meet here this morning, armed conflict is continuing on the territory of a member state of the Council, Ukraine, with catastrophic repercussions for its citizens.

Putting an end to military violence so as to enable people from all sides to return to their homes and communities and rebuild their lives is a pressing task. Longer-term and deeply rooted differences have to be tackled in a spirit of dialogue and co-operation, founded on justice and a respect for fundamental rights. This is a test and a challenge for diplomacy. And it is here that the Council of Europe has a clear, and indeed imperative, contribution to make, beyond the important initiatives that have already been undertaken by Members of this Assembly.

A second, profound challenge to democracy and social cohesion arises from new forms of fanaticism and conflict whose ramifications reach out to the heart of our European cities. These threats were brought home to us most recently in Paris, where – within the space of three days – we saw freedom of expression assaulted in the most direct and dreadful of ways, through the murder of a satirical paper's entire editorial team, and a further four men coldly assassinated in an act of pure anti-Semitism.

The task of responding to the root causes of such threats is of immense complexity. This is not just because these new forms of violence arise at the obscure intersection of global geopolitical tensions, individual trajectories and beliefs, and deeply rooted social inequalities, but also because there are great risks inherent in the responses that might emerge from fear and anger among our citizens, and in the political exploitation of these passions.

I know that the Ambassadors of the Council of Europe's forty-seven member states have agreed, last week, on a decision to step up action against terrorism. The challenge, of course, is not confined to reactive responses; it entails understanding and addressing the motivations of those young people who are drawn to extremism and political violence. The challenge also extends, I believe, to those novel uses of technology and science, such as cyber attacks and extra-judicial executions performed by unmanned machines, that blur the boundaries between war and peace, and risk stoking generalized suspicion between and within our societies.

I sincerely believe that the Council of Europe, and this Assembly in particular, must continue to play an important role in upholding the rule of law in the face of destructive forms of extremism, as well as state hubris. The Council of Europe has shown in the past that it had the ability not to lose sight of fundamental human rights, for instance when the general atmosphere in the West had overtones of a new crusade. One example was the 2006 report by Senator Dick Marty documenting the participation – both active and passive – of some of the Council's member states in CIA detentions and transfers, so-called 'renditions'. Senator Marty's report was of great international significance in recasting debates on the balance between counter-terrorism and the protection of human rights. I myself referred to this report during debates in Dáil Éireann, our Lower Chamber. I could clearly see the great benefits derived from linking discussions taking place in national parliaments and those in European venues.

More broadly, I believe that parliaments offer an important channel to increase public participation in and awareness of foreign policy debates. The conception of 'professional' diplomatic activity as being in conflict with 'emotional' and 'moralistic' public opinion is, in my view, a flawed one. Parliaments can and must hold governments accountable for what is said and done in the wider world in the name of their citizens.

This debate on whether foreign policy is an essentially executive function or whether it can accommodate democratic accountability is by no means new. Among the issues reported back during the first years of Ireland's membership of the Council of Europe was that of the relative powers in this organization of the Assembly and of the Council of Ministers. In 1949, Irish delegate Seán Mac Bride remarked to the Dáil: 'To a large extent the Statute which is presented to the House is designed to shackle the members of the Assembly but I feel that, with the passage of time, the Members of the Assembly themselves will take things into their own hands.'

Foreign policy is not the only domain where parliaments should reassert their relevance. Economic and fiscal policy is, I suggest, another essential area for active parliamentary activity. Indeed a third, perhaps less directly confrontational but no less undermining, threat to the future of European democracy is revealed in the largely unquestioned leeching of power and authority from parliaments to the apostles of a narrow version of fiscal orthodoxy. Today, global financial markets are assumed to be self-regulating, and unaccountable bodies such as rating agencies are given greater attention in the media than parliaments debating the fears and welfare of their citizens.

What has happened, we must ask ourselves, to the field of public economics and its decision-making structures, previously located in representative institutions, where differences based on declared assumptions were respected? It has conceded so much ground to a single version of expert knowledge about the so-called 'laws' governing the economy. And how have we let rating agencies, which act as a modern panopticon, not bound by any democratic requirement, gain such influence over the lives and prospects of our citizens. What can be done?

Parliaments, at both national and European level, must urgently claim back competence and legitimacy on economic and fiscal matters. In saying this, I am not denying the limitations that severe fiscal constraints, combined with intense global competition, impose on our elected representatives' ability to craft policy options. What I am saying is that no single economic paradigm can ever be adequate to address the complexity of our world's varying contingencies. The current status quo – whereby decisions which are the legitimate object of political debate have been abandoned to an automatic set of rigid fiscal rules, even as economists themselves disagree over the theoretical soundness of such rules – is a highly perilous one for the future of our polities.

Parliaments matter. Centuries of effort have been invested by European citizens in securing the vote. It is to their elected representatives that citizens look for accountability; for opening up new collective possibilities in the creation of new policies; and for connecting them to wider horizons through their work in international organizations such as this Assembly. We cannot let go of these hard-won advances.

It is my profound conviction that a strong case can be made for the centrality of ethics to our deliberations on economic matters. Indeed questions of political economy can never be purely technical ones. They have an intrinsic normative dimension and should, therefore, always be open to political discussion and dissension.

My message is not a pessimistic one: national parliaments, and supranational parliamentary bodies such as this one, can reclaim a central role in preserving the public world that lies at the heart of European democracy, that essential space shared by citizens who must be free to debate openly, whose children must have access to a pluralist scholarship and be enabled to imagine alternatives to the ideas that govern their present circumstances.

The Council of Europe has shown the lead in addressing the fiscal questions of our time from an ethical perspective, as is demonstrated by the recent initiative of the Commissioner for Human Rights on the theme of 'Safeguarding Human Rights in Times of Economic Crisis'. If we are to respond to this crisis of democracy in a holistic manner, parliamentarians obviously have a most valuable perspective to offer. Every day, on the streets, in their clinics, they encounter unemployment, poverty and feelings of alienation and insecurity.

'The need to let suffering speak is the condition of all truth', Theodor Adorno once said. This is, I believe, also profoundly valid for political truth. And the suffering all of us elected representatives should endeavour to voice is not just the distress we encounter in our parishes. We must also address contemporary issues of global significance, such as climate change and the sustainable development goals currently being negotiated in the United Nations.

These decisions will have a real impact, not just on the peoples of 'the South' but for all of us. We should revise simplistic, binary definitions of development, not just because elements of 'the South' are now in 'the North' and, vice versa, some features of 'the North' have migrated to 'the South', but also because global environmental and social issues, such as the scale of the refugee crisis in Europe's own neighbourhood, demand a complete shift in consciousness and language.

These great global challenges require all of us to take part in a conversation about our humanity. And they also present our parliaments – should they seize the opportunity, assert their legitimacy and design clever institutional strategies – with a unique chance to reassert their relevance.

Let us not be daunted by the magnitude of the task. Let us, rather, bring as much energy and competence to the project as we can. Let us build such bridges as will secure the trust and confidence of our people by showing ourselves to be responsive on the fiscal and economic crises that concern so many of those we represent. Let those who have the experience of parliament show that we can negotiate the pathways from national arenas to the complex, supranational structures of decision-making and power now facing us. You have the mandate to do so on behalf of your electorates. I wish you well in seizing back the terms of debate about the defining economic and social choices of our time.

This is an essential imperative if we truly wish to preserve the democratic system created for Europe after the Second World War, which held firm as the division of the continent ended twenty-five years ago. We have to engage in a cultural and ethical refounding of the kind that was completed by the architects of European co-operation at the terrible mid-point of the twentieth century.[49]

Today, again, we are invited to reach back to a fertile tradition, to the scholarship, moral instincts and generous impulses of European thought. And, drawing on the work of utopian and ethical visionaries, we are also

---

49 Not only did the Hague Congress (1949) bring together representatives from across a broad political spectrum – such as Altiero Spinelli, Winston Churchill, Konrad Adenauer, Paul-Henri Spaak, Józef Retinger and Hendrik Brugmans, among many others – but also philosophers, writers, intellectuals, scientists and scientists such as Bertrand Russell, Denis de Rougemont, Alexandre Marc, Salvador de Madariaga, etc. Three years before, in 1946, Unesco had been created, and in that same year the Rencontres internationales de Genève had sparked a vivid debate on 'Europe as culture' between such figures as Julien Benda, Karl Jaspers, Georg Lukacs, Francesco Flora and Maurice Merleau Ponty.

urged to develop a realistic strategy for sustaining a culture of peace, democracy and human rights in Europe. We are required to be bold as we work together, in co-operation, open to the world, caring for it, in an inter-generationally responsible way – and all of this is possible.

The European Court of Human Rights has been described as 'the Conscience of Europe'. Extending with poetic licence that term of honour to the Council of Europe as a whole, we might regard all of you here as citizens of the 'Republic of Conscience' described by Seamus Heaney in the famous poem he wrote to celebrate International Human Rights Day. This poem closes with the following lines:

> *The old man rose and gazed into my face*
> *and said that was official recognition*
> *that I was now a dual citizen.*
>
> *He therefore desired me when I got home*
> *to consider myself a representative*
> *and to speak on their behalf in my own tongue.*
>
> *Their embassies, he said, were everywhere*
> *but operated independently*
> *and no ambassador would ever be relieved.*

The Challenge of Human Rights for Contemporary Law, Politics and Economics

2015 Daniel O'Connell Memorial Lecture

THE BAR OF IRELAND

19 NOVEMBER 2015

T HIS ANNUAL EVENT has come to serve an important function in the protection of human rights in Ireland and in ensuring that those who defend human rights are recognized with an important place in the diary of the Irish Bar and of all those concerned with Irish law.

Previous lectures have emphasized Daniel O'Connell's own remarkable achievements in so many spheres, and his unfulfilled attempts to advance human rights in his time – not only in relation to equality and civil liberties for Catholics, but also in support of such causes as Jewish emancipation and the abolition of slavery.

Born at a time when Catholics could not enter the Bar (an exclusion only lifted in 1793), under his uncle's patronage O'Connell had the rare privilege of a full university and legal education in France, in London and at the King's Inns. He went on to enjoy a hugely successful legal career as a circuit barrister; and as a prosecutor, legislator, defendant (a victim of a shamefully unfair trial, during which it seems the Attorney-General challenged O'Connell's defence counsel to a duel!) and prisoner, O'Connell participated at every level of the judicial system save that of the bench – an aspiration that remained unfulfilled, though perhaps considering his temperament that may have been for the best.

The cases and campaigns in which 'the Counsellor' – as he was known among his peers at the Bar – was involved still resonate today, as do his feats of intellectual and oratorical skill as an advocate, his strategic political genius and his unfailing, stubborn commitment to the ideal of justice.

However, rather than simply retrace his fascinating life – and all of its ambiguities – in the space of a memorial lecture, the theme I have chosen looks briefly at the contemporary challenge of human rights – the challenge, and the promise, that human rights continue to present for law, for politics and for economics. In addressing these current issues, I believe that the legacy of O'Connell remains relevant to the work before us in our time and that his life and achievements can continue to inspire us.

Human rights are essential if a society is to allow its citizens as individuals to live with freedom and dignity and enable them to form a cohesive democratic polity. Human rights are never merely an aspiration: they remain an urgent requirement of law and of our democracy. They are universal, not confined by space or time, not confined to certain parts of society, or indeed to those we feel are deserving of rights. As the words of the Preamble of the United Nations Universal Declaration of Human Rights put it, 'recognition of the inherent dignity and of the equal and inalienable rights of all members of the human family is the foundation of freedom, justice and peace in the world'.

May I suggest, however, that despite the achievements already made in advancing human rights in Ireland and in Europe, the demands now being presented to us will define us in the eyes of future historians. The demands of which I speak are of a social, economic, legal and environmental kind and they will determine the circumstances of the coming generations.

We need not look far for persistent denials of rights in our time, which require of us the same passionate and forceful advocacy that was needed in O'Connell's era. We need political leadership on many of the great human rights issues. In the spirit of O'Connell, efforts in the legal sphere aimed at meeting the state's human rights obligations should be seen as complementing rather than conflicting, enhancing rather than diminishing, political and administrative measures.

I would also like to mention the challenge of imagining new rights structures and mechanisms of enforcement in the area of economic and social rights. The legal protection of these rights offers us an opportunity to make practical progress in addressing the underlying inequalities in our world. Moreover, legal protection of such rights can help us address the great crisis of political legitimacy which threatens to undermine and destabilize the institutions of our democratic system.

But there is a danger, when we consider the extensive range of legal instruments developed over the past century, that we might think the project of human rights is much more developed than it really is.

That legal protections and equality legislation at the national and international levels have expanded since the period of O'Connell is undeniable. Certainly, in the last century the establishment of the United Nations, the Council of Europe and Strasbourg Court and the proliferation of treaty law and human rights institutions have marked a new stage in human history. Landmark achievements at the national level such as the abolition of the death penalty, legal guarantees of gender equality and the provision of legal recognition to the equal status of all children, are also rightly celebrated. Looking back, these reforms may seem to be the outcome of an evolutionary process, one that was inevitable.

We must guard against any such assumption that the narrative of human rights in Ireland or globally is linear, or that it is a project near completion. Progress has been made, and this must be acknowledged, but – as you know well – the demands of universal rights and human dignity continue to be tested every day in our courts.

In the sphere of the criminal trial, for example, the evolution of the rights of defendants does not flow only in one direction: technological innovations, and changes in the forms of crime itself and the response to it, or changing social conditions, may bring new arguments for exceptionalism and derogation of rights. In this as in other areas, the work of the human rights lawyer is far from settled.

The human rights discourse is not helped by removing it from a more general consideration of the distribution of power. Rights can even be used as a defence of the status quo or of the interests of powerful companies or individuals. Baroness Onora O'Neill, philosopher and politician, speaking at one of the public events held last year under the President of Ireland's Ethics Initiative, suggested 'that we should look at rights not as our rights, but as someone else's, which we have a duty to protect, guarantee and realize'.

Human rights are the tools by which, in undemocratic times, unthinkable aspirations can become an irresistible case for equality – as we have recently seen in Ireland in the case of same-sex marriage. What is required of us is not simply that we protect and enforce established rights, but also that we look for new possibilities to use rights to enhance citizenship, dignity and equality.

The challenge for the human rights lawyer is to seek out violations of human dignity beyond those that are popular or obvious; to identify violations of rights and dignity not previously understood as such; and to conceive of new realities where, through imaginative and creative application of the law, human dignity can be vindicated, and find greater and freer expression.

The role of the human rights lawyer should not be confined to the courtroom. An adequate definition of the role requires him or her to do more than act for those in need; it calls on him or her to empower and facilitate. In taking up this work, you are drawn inevitably to the margins of our society. We should recognize that there remain communities among us that are, in their everyday experience, denied their rights and require the principled and energetic advocacy of lawyers – for example people with disabilities, prisoners, undocumented migrants and members of minorities who suffer racism and discrimination, including members of the Traveller and Roma communities.

We hear echoes of the great tasks undertaken by previous advocates when we consider, for example, contemporary forms of slavery. O'Connell in his time confronted explicit and legally sanctioned forms of dehumanization by fighting to end slavery in the Americas – indeed, he refused to set foot in the United States as long as slavery was legal. He refused to recognize a US ambassador to Britain because he was a slave owner. He was criticized by sections of Irish-American opinion for his refusal to moderate his condemnation of slavery in his lecture tours. Today, we are confronted by more insidious forms of forced labour that must be exposed and ended.

In Ireland, as in other developed countries, men, women and children continue to be exploited, and I commend the work of organizations such as the Migrants Rights Centre Ireland who have been involved in recent cases in this area.

Sa chaoi chéanna, is mian liom comhaltaí an Bharra agus Barra na hÉire-ann a mholadh as bhur gcuid oibre, lá i ndiaidh laé, chun tabhairt faoi na ceisteanna seo trí bhur gcuid oibre fairsing 'pro bono', tríd an Scéim Cabhrach Deonach agus go háirithe tríd an tacaíocht a chuireann sibh ar fáil d' Eagraíochtaí Neamhrialtasach agus d'eagraíochtaí phobail.
(In the same vein, I commend the members of the Bar for the work that you continue to do to address these issues on a daily basis – through the extensive pro bono work done by your members, through the Voluntary Assistance Scheme, particularly in your support for NGOs and community organizations.)

Creating and maintaining a space for civil society is intrinsic to this process of breathing life into legal rights. It is imperative that states maintain a safe environment in which civil society can operate effectively. Given its critical role in holding governments to account, it is of great concern that the effective functioning of civil society is becoming increasingly restricted in many countries around the world.

I am particularly concerned at the reprisals carried out against human rights defenders, including those who seek to co-operate with UN Special Rapporteurs and those who participate in the work of the UN Human Rights Council. I will always remember when I was witnessing the trial of the Citizens of Fatsa in Turkey in the time of General Evren, a prisoner telling me how he and his fellow prisoners were forced to watch the beaten body of their lawyer being paraded before their cells in Diyarbakir.

Internationalism was a key theme of O'Connell's own work, not just in relation to slavery and Jewish emancipation, but also in his support for the liberation movements in South America and elsewhere. We are all members of the human family, and a commitment to internationalism has informed the best expressions of Irish national identity from that time onward and should always be central to our foreign policy as an independent nation.

In this spirit, I was glad to see Ireland take the lead on drafting and negotiating two Human Rights Council resolutions affirming the importance of creating a proper space for civil society. For the first time at the Council, this issue was recognized as a human rights concern. In its role on the Human Rights Council, among the other issues given priority by Ireland were freedom of religion and belief, the rights of LGBT persons, the rights of the child, and internet freedom. Ireland's exemplary role in these issues must be matched by its vigour in seeking compliance with human rights from new actors of great power, such as transnational corporations.

The project of achieving human rights and equality does not end with codification and legislation at a formal level. O'Connell was committed not only to achieving legal change but to leading the change in popular consciousness and opinion that could underpin and guarantee the reform of laws.

He was acutely aware of the importance of an informed public opinion in supporting reform. Crucially, he did not use regressive sentiment as an excuse for inaction or compromise; rather he set about the hard and dogged work of engaging with the public. He embraced the most difficult and politically inconvenient issues of his time from a perspective of first principles, even when to do so risked damaging his own immediate political objectives. He made many decisions on principle, including of course his fateful decision to call off the great Clontarf meeting for the repeal of the Union in 1843, in order to avoid bloodshed after the government had banned the gathering.

We in our time are challenged, for example, by the terrible problem of refugees and migrants arriving in Europe, which is both a great human rights issue and also a great test of political leadership. We are living through the largest population displacement since World War Two, with some sixty million people forced from their homes by war or its consequences. We see the results of this in the tumultuous movement of people across the Middle East and the tragic deaths in the Mediterranean Sea of refugees trying to reach Europe.

The General Secretary of the United Nations, Ban Ki-Moon, who came to visit me recently, said on International Migrants Day: 'Let us reaffirm our commitment to shape diverse and open societies that provide opportunities and lives of dignity for all migrants.'

As a matter of law, when states are unable or unwilling, for whatever reason, to protect their citizens' fundamental human rights, the international community must act to ensure their safety and protection. For that reason, the 1951 UN Refugee Convention and its 1967 Protocol – based on the principle of not returning refugees to states that have persecuted them – remains the cornerstone of refugee protection, and is as relevant now as when it was first drafted. The legal position is clear, but the implementation of these obligations tests the capacity and resolve of national states.

This is an international challenge demanding an urgent and effective international response. Solidarity often appears to be fragile, and the danger of regression to prejudice and suspicion is real. I am concerned that, in the absence of co-ordinated and comprehensive agreements between EU states, the goodwill of the European people may dissipate or even turn from compassion to fear: we are seeing some worrying signs of this, and some would seek to use the terrible terrorist attacks in Paris as a justification for exclusion and the denial of rights. We must challenge xenophobia by building cohesion and sympathy.

We must not let our failures in confronting global poverty and deepening exclusion define this moment in history as 'pitiless times', as Vijay Prashad of the World Forum for Democracy put it. And I was moved today to read Vijay Prashad's description of the liberal leader of Mali, Alpha Oumar Konaré, and his desperate plea for relief from crushing debt so as to save the cohesion of his society. This plea fell on deaf ears, and al-Qaeda took over Timbuktu in April 2012, with terrible consequences for its people and the city's ancient libraries.

If we are to gather the best fruits of the tradition of human rights it must be observable in all our policies, including international debt and development. Human rights should never be a residual consideration.

Much of the response to the global challenges we now face has been reactive at best, and nearly always in response to emergencies. In such a critical moment there is a grave danger that we may lose sight of the more fundamental issues of rights that are at stake. For example, we can anticipate now, given the intense conflicts in Syria and Afghanistan, that the large-scale movement of refugees into Europe is likely to continue for some time. What is required is a positive European response to this situation, grounded in the core values of human rights on which the idea of a peaceful Europe was constructed, and an energetic attempt at the construction of a global institutional architecture that can deal with this massive migration.

Closer to home, we must recall that the Convention on Human Rights is not some externally imposed restriction on states' rights within Europe; it is a founding document and statement of values of a peaceful and just Europe. The Convention and its values are not something to be sacrificed in times of conflict or when confronted by extremism – these are the very values that we must defend and assert at such times, and we turn to these documents now as we frame our response to the terrible events of the past week in Paris and Beirut.

The identity of post-war Europe is, at its better moments, defined by the rule of law and the protection of democratic freedoms. However, a false dichotomy is sometimes postulated between law and democratic government, with some suggesting that the legal protection and judicial enforcement of rights can lead to a diminution of democratic institutions.

Remembering O'Connell, we might recall that the argument that legal human rights protections are inimical to democracy was one also made by those powerful institutions which resisted the emancipation of religious minorities, of slaves and of women in the nineteenth century, and that these forces had to be defeated and replaced.

Human rights, democratically defined in law and agreed by sovereign governments, should be central to our political and economic thinking and to our policymaking, not just as an academic exercise, not just in the courtroom, but in all aspects of public life.

Indeed, less time might be spent arguing in courtrooms if a human-rights-centred approach informed the drafting, development and implementation of all public policy. The difficulty lies not in any deficiencies in those rights' standards, but in the failure of agencies, both public and private, to commit themselves to meeting their legal obligations under human rights law. Dialogue between the judicial and the executive branches of government on issues of rights can not only be healthy but also achieve much-needed reforms.

A significant innovation in the legislation which established the Irish Human Rights and Equality Commission, for example, was the introduction of a positive duty on public bodies to place human rights at the heart of public decision-making, thus ensuring that these tenets are an integral part of an organization's daily work. This mechanism should not be seen as an impediment, but serve to assist public bodies in meeting their legal obligations. Creating a positive atmosphere, in language, procedures and care, can enhance the experience of those who deliver the guarantees of the state as well as those who receive them.

The engagement between law and government and administration can be productive and enriching; but none of the institutions can succeed without the legitimacy of popular support. O'Connell's own career was marked by great legal and political triumphs, but it was to end in a kind of failure and rejection. In his attempts to move from Catholic Emancipation to Repeal of the Union, his strategy of holding peaceful mass meetings was criminalized from above, by government, while disillusionment grew from below.

O'Connell asked the people to place their faith in reform that might be achieved from within and through a corrupt and asymmetric political system – a system which proved to be incapable of those reforms that would have given it legitimacy in Ireland, and a legal system that proved incapable of meeting the greatest and most urgent needs of its subjects. Repeal of the Union would come in the end through force, many decades after his death.

Our position today as a free and democratic republic is wholly different from that of the mid-nineteenth century. Yet there is a danger that the economic and social strains being felt across Europe will have a detrimental effect on cohesion within our society. This is all the more reason why we must defend our fundamental democratic values and why our laws must continue to give effective protection to the weak and the vulnerable.

At an international level the capacity of poorer nations to forge cohesion and democracy is not facilitated by an unfair structure of trade, debt and asymmetric participation in global institutions.

The crisis of democratic legitimacy in Europe – alarmingly obvious in falling electoral turnouts across the continent – stems from a growing sense that European and national institutions are not meeting the needs of their citizens, that politics is not sufficiently relevant or does not respond adequately to the lived experience of the people.

This brings me to my final point: the need for new institutional structures and instruments. I have made the case, on many occasions over recent years, for a new, reintegrated approach to economics and politics: one that will renew a connection between economics, ecology and ethics; one in which the essential needs of citizens are given priority, and in which the operation of the market can be regulated. This is, surely, an approach that can distinguish between essential needs and insatiable wants.

I believe that human rights law, widely and generously understood, can give us some of the tools with which to achieve the new approach that is needed. The vast inequalities of our time will require profound changes to our democracy and our economic policy. What can help, I believe, is the installation of a kind of floor of essential social goods that should form the agreed foundation of economy and society. These social goods, meeting need and allowing citizens to participate fully in the democratic republic, should be matters of human rights. The legal protection of these rights is the great challenge of our time.

Connecting human rights to these questions of economics and social policy is an opportunity to close the legitimacy gap in Europe between the institutions and the needs of the people. Nothing alien or novel is required. In existing treaty law, the framework is already there to reground the European Union and its institutions. Surely the Charter of Fundamental Rights, which sets out a broad range of economic and social as well as civil and political rights, should at last be taken seriously.

Following the Lisbon Treaty in 2009, the Charter of Fundamental Rights now has the same legal value as the fundamental Treaties of the European Union themselves. Indeed, in the short time since the Lisbon Treaty came into force, the Charter has been referred to on many occasions by the European Court of Justice, and now operates as the primary source of human rights in the EU.

Interest in the potential of the Charter is high, but it is also fair to say that the Charter is not widely understood by European citizens, and this includes many lawyers. National administrations and the EU have an important role to play by ensuring access to practical information for the citizen on the judicial and non-judicial remedies open to them. We need to breathe life and purpose into the Charter.

The European Convention on Human Rights, as interpreted by the Strasbourg Court, has also been applied in a wider way by engaging with some of the most pressing economic and social issues facing European people. When the European Union eventually becomes a party to the Convention, as provided for in the Lisbon Treaty, this will help to underpin the Union with a stronger body of human rights law. But all of this requires our articulate support, and a determination to make these aspirations a reality.

I salute all of you who have been activists in this great work. The role of the lawyer is a privileged one: your skills and training provide you with the capacity to make a huge contribution to human rights in our society, not just by applying existing legal norms, but by extending them and bringing the protection of human rights to those who are in most need.

In conclusion, I would like to leave you with a quote from Eleanor Roosevelt: 'If you want a world ruled by law and not by force you must build up, from the very grassroots, a respect for law.'

The corollary, I suggest, is that the law must gain the respect of the people, through its relevance to their most essential needs – and that work is a project that remains to be completed.

The Human Rights Discourse:
Its Importance and Its Challenges

The Human Rights Commission's Annual Lecture

PILLAR ROOM, ROTUNDA HOSPITAL, DUBLIN

10 DECEMBER 2012

*I*S MIAN LIOM *mo bhuíochas a gabháil le Maurice Manning agus an Coimisiún um Chearta an Duine as ucht an chuireadh léacht bliantúil an Coimisiún a thúirt. Is onóir dom í a thúirt. Ba mhaith liom i dtús báire an deis seo a thapú le toghadh na hÉireann ar Chomhairle na Náisiún Aontaithe um Chearta an Duine a thréaslú leis an Tánaiste agus Aire Gnóthaí Eachtracha, Éamon Gilmore. Mar a dhúirt an tAire é féin ag am an tofa, is tacú láidir é sin dár gcáil idirnáisiúnta. Is léiriú iontaoibhe é sin, ag na Náisiúin Aontaithe, as ár n-infrastruchtúr maidir le Cearta an Duine anseo sa bhaile agus as ár ról taitheanta i gcearta an duine sa réimse idirnáisiúnta araon.*

(I wish to offer my thanks to Maurice Manning and the Commission for Human Rights for an invitation to give the Commission's annual lecture. It is an honour for me to deliver it. I would like naturally to take the opportunity to congratulate the Tánaiste and Minister for Foreign Affairs on the election of Ireland to the United Nations' Commission for Human Rights. As the Minister himself said at the time of the election, this is a strong endorsement of our international profile. It is a mark of the trust of the United Nations in our institutional protection of the rights of the individual at home and in our recognized role in their protection in international affairs.)

Firstly I would like to take this opportunity to congratulate the Irish Government through the Minister for Foreign Affairs, Eamon Gilmore, on Ireland's election to the United Nations Human Rights Council. As the Minister himself said at the time of the election, this is a strong endorsement of Ireland's reputation internationally. It is a show of faith, by the UN, both in our commitment to human rights here at home and our role in the area of international human rights advocacy.

Membership is both an honour and a responsibility which I am confident Ireland will embrace fully. It will allow Ireland to play an even more active role in the promotion and protection of human rights worldwide. Given our own complex history, we have a long tradition in the field of human rights protection. Last night I attended a presentation by Front Line Defenders of the lives of those who defend human rights and who must have our solidarity if we are to be serious about delivering human rights.

When Seamus Heaney gave this lecture in 2009 under the title 'Writer and Righter', he made reference to the power of language, the dignity of the individual and the powerful moral and philosophical thought that lay behind the first principle of the United Nations Universal Declaration of Human Rights. Of those who have taken the Universal Declaration as the guiding principles of their interventions as human rights workers he wrote:

> The great web that unites those local, national and international endeavours has thirty meshes and each of those meshes is woven into and woven out of the document which we celebrate... the United Nations Universal Declaration of Human Rights ... this promulgation

made an immense difference to the work of each and every person and indeed nation striving for justice and equality, and each and every person and nation suffering injustice and inequality. In ratifying the principles articulated in the Declaration, the governments of the world gave epoch-making sanction to the human need for fairness and natural justice, and in doing so they strengthened the moral standing of international law. Even if the articles of the Declaration are not legally binding, there is immense potency in the cogent, simple language in which they are framed, as is evident in the all-encompassing first Article: *All human beings are born free and equal in dignity and rights. They are endowed with reason and conscience and should act towards one another in a spirit of brotherhood.*

Referring to that first Article of the Convention, Seamus Heaney went on to illustrate the importance of its basis in the foundational texts of the European tradition:

> Behind the primary words and sentiments of that first article, of course, you can hear the echoes of many of the great foundational texts of Western civilization, from Sophocles' paean to the wonders of man in the famous Chorus in his Antigone, through Christ's Sermon on the Mount, right on up to the American Declaration of Independence and the French Declaration of the Rights of Man.

Seamus Heaney has, of course, himself contributed to the discourse and reality of human rights, most memorably in his poem 'From the Republic of Conscience'.

I share the view that Seamus Heaney and so many others hold as to the moral significance of the Universal Declaration of Human Rights. It draws on a strong philosophical tradition, and one that is not simply idealistic, but empowering in its promise and emancipatory in its effect.

In the minds of so many its goals are achievable, and we must all welcome the fact that it has been a real contribution to peace and reconciliation in societies that have suffered war and conflict, as we ourselves know.

Human Rights are enshrined in the 1948 Universal Declaration of Human Rights and the 1966 International Covenants on Civil and Political Rights and on Economic, Cultural and Social Rights, as well as the subsequent conventions covering specific rights issues, namely racial discrimination, discrimination against women, torture, the rights of the child and the rights of those with a disability.

Bhí ballraíocht an-éagsúil ar fad ag na Náisiúin Aontaithe a ghlac leis an Dearbhú níos mó ná seasca bliain ó shin seachas mar atá ag na Náisiúin Aontaithe sa lá atá inniu ann. De thoradh ar thaithí an díchoilínithe as féin, tháinig na dosaein ball nua chuig na Náisiúin Aontaithe, baill a raibh cuimhne acu ar an gcos ar bolg agus ar an streachailt agus a raibh dóchas agus ardmhianta acu. Arís, i ngan fhios dóibh féin, tugadh cuireadh dóibh nó b'éigean dóibh rogha a dhéanamh idir údair iomaíocha cumhachta domhanda, leaganacha nua den impiriúlachas gan seilbh fhisiciúil ach le hidé-eolaíocht thiarnasach, faoi spreagadh an mhíleatachais, in atmais-féar an Chogaidh Fhuair.

(The United Nations that adopted the Declaration more than sixty years ago had a very different membership from the United Nations of today. In succeeding decades the experience of decolonization alone brought dozens of new members to the United Nations, members with memories of oppression and struggle, hopes and aspirations. In the years that followed such new members found themselves invited, or forced, to exercise a choice between competing sources of global power, new imperialisms that did not involve physical occupation but were ideologically authoritarian and militaristic in the atmosphere of the Cold War.)

The dream of empire, with its insatiable appetite, devouring the rich diversity of what was indigenous and different, was succeeded by a materialist dream of modernization, built on an earlier myth of progress. This led to shallow, ideologically driven definitions of the developed and modern on the one hand and, on the other, the forces of restricting tradition.

Of equal importance, to a fractured world, was the fact that a narrow scholarship was brought into existence. Ethics, philosophy in all its forms and disciplines, and political theory were split away from what were perceived to be the new management crafts appropriate to a public world based on a globalized market: a public world best served by defining an economic space that could in some circumstances replace an accountable state. The competing alternative was a statism that suppressed personal freedom and curtailed civil society. The non-quantifiable material of inherited and contemporary culture, and the life wisdom of minorities and indigenous peoples, were pushed to the margin. In what was regarded as developed society, culture was offered a peripheral existence as a tolerated form of recuperative recreation in the productive life of consumption.

In our contemporary condition, the shattered mosaic of our common existence cannot be remade, nor perhaps should it be reconstituted from any single shard of what lies at our feet. In making something new we need to draw on the ethics of human rights; to privilege such essentials as the recognition of dignity in the social milieu as much as in the person. Such a dignity as is appropriate for the human rights-centred world which we wish to achieve, a world with the stamp of humanity on it.

Lenár linn féin, ní dhearnadh a dhóthain machnaimh i gcónaí ar an mball-raíocht athraithe sin sna Náisiúin Aontaithe. Tá domhan nua á chruthú faoi láthair ina bhfeictear an cumhacht á bhogadh ar ais chucu sin ónar baineadh é ar an gcéad dul síos. Ina theannta sin, má léiríonn cuimhne lucht na cumhachta coilíniúcháin go bhfuiltear áiseach agus toilteanach maidir le díchuimhne ar a ngaolmhaireacht stairiúil leis an impiriúlachas agus a iarmhairtí, tá an fhianaise ann, ar an taobh eile, go bhfuil cuimhne shoiléir ag an dream a bhí coilínithe roimhe seo ar an taithí agus an stádas a bhí acu san am a caitheadh agus ar an difríocht idir é sin agus na féidearthachtaí nua atá rompu.

(In our own times the fact that the membership at the United Nations has radically changed seems not always to have been given sufficient thought. A new world is emerging at the present moment, a moment which is seeing a shift of power back towards those from whom ethical, social, cultural and productive capacity was originally taken. That contemporary shift, however, is to states rather than peoples, with all of the consequences and new problems that this creates when some administrations deny human rights in the name of security and are often supported from abroad.)

It is worth bearing in mind that while the memory of the colonizing powers may prefer a willed amnesia over empire and its consequences, the previously colonized peoples have a clear memory of their past experience, their past status and the difference between it and their potentialities now and in the future.

Securing an appropriate accommodation for each other's narratives in the contemporary world is not easy. The diversity and the different historical experiences of our global community remain a challenge that is not easily satisfied by an appeal to the mutual benefits of shared economic interests in the future.

Human rights discourse has a particular history. It is worthwhile to reflect on the circumstances in which the Universal Declaration of Human Rights came to be drafted. Mark Goodale in his *Surrendering to Utopia* points to the curious background to the crafting of what came to be the 1948 Universal Declaration of Human Rights:

> In 1947 the United Nations Commission on Human Rights, which was chaired by Eleanor Roosevelt, sought statements on the draft version of what would become the 1948 Universal Declaration of

Human Rights. These statements were solicited in a variety of ways and through a variety of institutional channels, but perhaps the most important were the efforts of the United Nations Educational, Scientific, and Cultural Organization (UNESCO). UNESCO solicited statements on a proposed declaration of universal human rights from different academic, cultural, and artistic institutions and individuals. Although the essentially colonialist milieu within which the United Nations emerged after World War II rendered any attempt to achieve universal consensus through its working bodies utopian at best, the outreach efforts by UNESCO prior to the adoption of the UDHR were intended to gauge the diversity of world opinion about what Johannes Morsink describes as the 'aggressive' push to forge an 'international consensus about human rights'.

The diversity of world opinion was defined at the time within a rather narrow frame – moral, political and cultural – but it also seems to have ignored a source close to home, one that had specialized in threatened cultural systems and their survival. I refer to the work of the American Anthropological Association. It is not my suggestion that an anthropological approach alone should define human rights; simply that it was, and is, a valuable tool for understanding the context of the implementation of what might become a universal right.

Mark Goodale suggests that the conventional wisdom that the AAA was consulted is wrong:

> According to documents in the US National Anthropological Archives, there is no record of UNESCO making a request to the AAA for an advisory opinion on a declaration of human rights. Instead, it appears that one anthropologist, Melville Herskovits, was approached by UNESCO in his capacity as Chairman of the

Committee for International Cooperation in Anthropology of the National Research Council (NRC), a post that he assumed in 1945.

There were many reasons why culture as a concept and as a policy area was perceived as something of a malign force. The world was very close to the experience of culture having been abused within a racist philosophy, one that had led to the concentration camps to which the world was now trying to respond. The survival of such a view, in part perhaps, explains the slowness in the European Union in the modern period to allow a prominent space to culture in treaty discussions. The consideration given to culture in the Universal Declaration itself is limited, and cultural rights had to wait decades before they entered the human rights discourse in a meaningful way.

One can see today in the early neglect of these issues the seeds of the problems that would confront the human rights discourse right into present times. Many unresolved questions remain: is it possible to have a single source for a universalism that might prevail across all the members of the United Nations? Was it ever possible? Or must we accept that it is perhaps more fruitful to recognize and build on the slow emergence of a trans-national assemblage of impulses to universalism; to speak of what might be gathered from different cultural sources and systems as essential for the implementation of universal human rights? While doing so it is important not to lose the legal and social protections we have gained. In other words: can cultural differences be taken into account in such a way as not to strip human rights of their essential protections?

There are even more fundamental questions. Do human rights seek their origin in the gradual extension of rationalism? Can codes for their implementation be derived, and even imposed, from within a rationalist tradition, one that is solely drawn from within the Western canon?

Human rights scholars are divided as to how we should advance. There are those, such as Jack Donnelly, who go so far as to say: 'If people are uncomfortable with that [human rights] tradition, because they are afraid of seeming Western-centered, neglectful of local and traditional modes of governance, or accusatory, then that is their problem.' Others have sought to strike a middle position, one that is more nuanced. This is the position of Peter Uvin, and is also clear in the philosophical approach of John Rawls, Martha Nussbaum and Amartya Sen, the work of the latter stressing capacities, capabilities and choices.

There are those such as Abdullahi Abdullah Ahmed An-Na'Im who argue for the acceptance of cultural difference but who do not take an absolutist position. A decade ago he wrote:

> The cross-cultural approach, however, is not an all-or-nothing prop-
> osition. While total agreement on the standard and mechanisms for
> its implementation is unrealistic, in some cases, significant agree-
> ment can be achieved and ought to be pursued as much as possible...
> Provided such agreement is sought with sufficient sensitivity, the
> general status of human rights will be improved, and wider agree-
> ment can be achieved in relation to other human rights.

If we are to recognize and seek the impulse for human rights in the full range of cultures through which people live, we must accept that some of our fellow world citizens locate the source of their human rights in, for example, revealed systems of faith. That cannot be ignored. The dialogue we need for a global consideration of universalism is defined by how we answer these questions.

Going back to the founding moment of the Universal Declaration and the evidence that anthropology never had any real prospect of influencing the Drafting Commission of the Declaration chaired by Eleanor Roosevelt, Mark Goodale quotes Johannes Morsink's account of the stages through which the drafting process of the Declaration went and includes a succinct pen picture of the six key drafters:

The seventeen members of the Commission for Human Rights were exclusively member-nations; a drafting committee of eight members was then created from within this group of seventeen. Morsink divides the individuals who played a key role in actually drafting the document into two groups, which he calls the 'inner core' and the 'second tier drafters'. There were only six members of this first group: John P. Humphrey, a law professor from Canada and the UN Secretariat's first human rights director; René Cassin, an international lawyer and diplomat from France; Peng-chun Chang, a Chinese scholar (with a PhD in Education from Columbia University); Charles Habib Malik, a philosophy professor at the American University in Beirut (with a PhD from Harvard); Hernán Santa Cruz, a military judge from Chile and a former professor of what could perhaps be called 'military science'; Alexie P. Pavlov, a lawyer from the Soviet Union who was the USSR's ambassador to Belgium during the time the UDHR was being drafted; and finally, Eleanor Roosevelt, former first lady of the United States and chair of both the commission and the drafting committee. And among this small group, Humphrey was the person who produced the crucial first draft of the declaration.

If we look at the composition of this group of key drafters, therefore, we begin to understand a little more about how the eventual declaration of universal human rights took the shape it did: three jurists, professors of philosophy and education (both trained at US institutions), and a saintly daughter of an American dynasty. And given that Humphrey, the 'primus inter pares' of this inner core of drafters, was the Gale Professor of Roman Law at McGill University at the time of his appointment to the UN, it is not surprising that the NRC/AAA Statement on Human Rights… which expresses an understanding of the world that is almost diametrically opposed to the one reflected in the UDHR, is never mentioned among the

sources that Humphrey (or anyone else) drew from (even if simply
to negate its claims) during the drafting of the Universal Declaration of Human Rights.

To suggest that some key issues, such as the problems that arise in locating
human rights in differing cultures, and the possibility or impossibility of
universalism, were glossed over in the founding moments is not for a
second to detract from the contribution that the human rights discourse
and those who draw on it have made in the decades that followed the
ratification of the Universal Declaration of Human Rights. It is simply a
fact that the Declaration has served as both model and inspiration, and
we must never let go of what has been achieved through the instruments
of international law.

Again it is easy to understand how – with the memory of war so fresh,
and particularly the horror and the bathos of human cruelty to which
humanity had sunk, and which was revealed when the concentration
camps were opened – there was at the end of the 1940s such a wave of
ethical revulsion that it tried to sweep away all differences of heritage
and the detritus of old conflicts. The nature of humanity itself became
a matter for reflection, and Western thought sought to save itself from
ever again sinking to such a level. We must never take from that moment.

These concerns were authentic, and the new language of the Universal
Declaration was perceived as necessary and was widely welcomed. The
endorsement of states that followed seemed to be a great moral moment
for leaders from different continents. Minorities took hope, and even
if the great changes in consciousness, of education in thinking about
human rights, were yet to take place, a symbolic step of great significance
had been taken.

It goes without saying that it is important that the human rights
discourse not be devalued as mere rhetoric at an international political
level, as it is by some critics. Neither should principles be reduced to the

pursuit of aspirations. Both of these challenges arise now as the period of the World Millennium Development Goals comes to a conclusion and there are calls for a succeeding set of commitments that may emerge as either aspirations or undelivered rights.

There is an opportunity to move the human rights discourse to centre-stage. May I suggest that it would be best if this were done in a spirit of appropriate humility and by giving attention to what were previously neglected difficulties, by freeing the discourse not only from its founding constraints but from the taint of power relations that were the legacy of empire; freeing it, too, from the hubris of a model of economics that lays claim to the status of science, or makes the moral claim to be a source of inevitable progress.

Human rights practitioners should not be disheartened by the call for a critical debate on the subject. These advocates for rights can point to the rich harvest of their efforts in terms of protection of the most vulnerable, in so many parts of our shared world, and this is a task that continues. Nevertheless if a global consciousness is to be created, the policy issues have to be reconciled with actual practice at home and abroad. The discourse of human rights atrophies, and political spokespersons have recourse to using the human rights language as sticks with which to beat each other in periodic reports on each other's records.

Within national boundaries, the coming into existence of National Human Rights Institutions was an important development. It served as a reminder that a vindication of human rights had to take place at home, as well as being a commitment solemnly announced from time to time at international bodies and used to call for actions from other governments.

In their valuable paper 'Equality and Human Rights Commissions in the UK and Ireland: Challenges and Opportunities Compared', Colin Harvey and Sarah Spencer address the role and remit of equality and human rights commissions, their duties and powers, how independence and accountability can be achieved, and indeed how issues of resourcing can affect the possibilities of achieving a sustainable defence of minorities. They describe the emergence of an international code of practice – the so-called Paris Principles:

> Concerned that the authority of such bodies could be undermined if some were seen to lack independence from government or the powers to be effective, the UN General Assembly endorsed a baseline standard covering the competence, responsibilities, composition and independence of national human rights institutions, the Paris Principles, in 1993. The Principles allow states some latitude in deciding what kind of institution is appropriate but carry authority in requiring that a broad mandate and sphere of competence should be set down in the country's Constitution or statute; and that the responsibilities of the institution should include the right, acting on its own initiative or by request 'to freely consider any questions falling within its competence', to submit proposals, reports and recommendations to Parliament, government and other competent authorities on any human rights issue, and to make public its views through the press including 'expressing an opinion on the positions and reactions of the government'. It should be able to examine existing and proposed legislation for conformity to international human rights principles, to contribute to reports that states submit to the UN supervisory bodies, to recommend new legislation and to have the power to hear any person and obtain any information or documentation necessary for assessing situations within its competence.

The Paris Principles state that national human rights institutions may also be authorised to hear and resolve complaints and should be able to carry out research and contribute to teaching and to promoting awareness of human rights, including discrimination. They should be composed of people broadly representative of civil society (in which unions, lawyers, professionals, academics and NGOs are specifically mentioned); and have their own staff and premises in order to be independent of government. Nor should they be subject to financial controls which might affect that independence. There is much, nevertheless, that is not specified in the Principles, including key matters such as enforcement powers, the precise nature of the commission's independence from government, or need for transparency in their operation.

This is a very valuable summary of agreed principles and the issues raised are worthy of the widest public discussion.

In the same year, 1993, as the Paris Principles dealing with international practice by National Human Rights Commissions were announced, another important component of the human rights discourse was being addressed: the connection between human rights and development. It was at the World Conference on Human Rights in Vienna in June 1993 that human rights became linked to the task of development. As my son Michael Higgins has written in his consideration of the prospects for a human rights perspective being afforded an appropriate place in development theory and policy:

> In the declaration and programme of action that emerged from the conference, the principles of universality, indivisibility, interdependence and the interrelationship of all human rights were accepted. Article 8 of the Declaration stated explicitly that 'democracy, development and respect for human rights and fundamental freedoms are interdependent and mutually reinforcing'. Article 10 stated that 'the World Conference on Human Rights reaffirms the right to development, as established in the Declaration on the Right to Development, in 1986, as a universal and inalienable right and an integral part of fundamental human rights'.

Had we arrived, then, at a new departure point in the human rights discourse? Scholars differed, Michael Higgins tells us, in their estimates of the Vienna meeting. Peter Uvin is representative of those who were sceptical as to what had been achieved. As to the Declaration on the Right to Development, he wrote:

> From its inception onwards, it was politically very weak. It was politically engineered as bad law: vague, internally contradictory, duplicative of already clearly codified rights and devoid of identifiable parties bearing clear obligations. It has been devoid of any real impact, it was perhaps the very last product of the NIEO years, and suffered from the political weakness of its promoters. In 1986, as in 1993, it was so watered down as to become meaningless. Affirming that all people have the right to development, and that such development consists of, and is realised through, the realisation of every existing category of human rights adds nothing to our knowledge, it adds only verbiage.

Peter Uvin's words and work are worthy of note. As a scholar with impressive experience in the field he was reacting to what he perceived to be the blindness of those who, while being concerned with the practical tasks of development, refused to see the violence of the economic and social structures which embodied the distress to which their efforts were turned.

Varun Gauri of the World Bank takes a different view. Gauri writes, for example, of what is achievable, of the practical results that would flow from an advocacy that requires states to publish and implement policies that worked within the language of Article 2 of the International Convention on Economic, Social and Cultural Rights. Gauri believes that progress can be made on concrete rights that could be specified in the short and medium term, even while the requirement to have general healthcare, for example, remained as an abstract right even if it was not fully fulfilled.

In such a discussion as to what is aspirational, and what is justifiable, we should remind ourselves too of Amartya Sen's distinction between a right that is not recognized and a right that is not being implemented. The recognition of the existence of a right, even if it is an aspiration is, in Sen's view, important.

Ireland's recent election to the United Nations Human Rights Council for the first time for a three-year term, having secured 124 votes at the UN General Assembly, is as I have said a tribute to its foreign policy. It is also a significant opportunity to advance a meaningful discourse on human rights at international level, to return to some basic considerations of issues that have been neglected and to make human rights firmly part of the development debate. In the much overdue reform of the multilateral institutions and the debate surrounding it, Ireland has a mandate for the assertion of a human rights perspective.

Sa bhaile, is féidir leis an gCoimisiún um Cheart an Duine tabhairt le fios go bhfuil rudaí nithiúla bainte amach aige i rith an dá bhliain déag atá faoi thuairisc aige ina thuarascáil den bhliain 2012. Agus é bunaithe mar thoradh ar Chomhaontú Aoine an Chéasta/Bhéal Feirsde, tá obair fhíorluachmhar curtha i gcrích ag an gCoimisiún san iliomad réimsí. I dtuarascáil na bliana 2012 déanann Uachtarán an Choimisiúin tagairt do na hathruithe go léir atá tarlaithe ag leibhéal an Stáit i réimse na gceart. Tá obair luachmhar déanta ag Comhchoiste Coimisiún Thuaisceart Éireann um Chearta an Duine agus ag Coimisiún um Cheart an Duine in Éirinn, mar a fhoráiltear faoi Chomhaontú Aoine an Chéasta/Bhéal Feirsde agus a ndéantar tagairt dó sa tuarascáil, chun comhthéacs a chur ar fáil inar féidir an obair thógála ar thodhchaí shíochánta a bhunú.

(At home, An Coimisiún um Chearta an Duine [The Commission on Human Rights] can point to real achievements over the twelve years which

it has covered in its 2012 Report. Established as a result of the Belfast
Good Friday Agreement, An Coimisiún has completed invaluable work
in so many areas. In the 2012 Report the President of the Commission
refers to the many changes in the rights area that have taken place at state
level. The work of the Joint Committee of the Northern Ireland Human
Rights Commission and the Irish Human Rights Commission, which was
provided for in the Belfast Good Friday Agreement to which the Report
refers, has been of great value in delivering a context in which the work
of building a peaceful future can be grounded.)

Beyond the issue of the resources needed for an effective and independent
Human Rights Commission there are fruitful prospects for future
discussion in a number of spheres, not only in the form of extension of
human rights practice to new areas, but also within some established
ones. For example, regarding mental health there is already room for
debate on the distinction between the right to health as a human right
and a code of professional practice that accepts a patient's human rights
in treatment after diagnosis. We must presume that one's right to health
should take precedence over the more limited right.

A strong Human Rights and Equality Commission will always have
much unfinished business – including issues of equality of participation
for different genders and members of minorities. The task of advocating
human rights compliance at its drafting stages as well as in its legal
implementation is an important democratic function. A society's
commitment to human rights is judged by its importance to decision-
makers as much as by decisions taken in its parliament. It has to
be accepted as part of our public decision-making that the quest for,
agreement on and vindication of basic rights are never made conditional
on gender, race, ethnicity, capacity or circumstances.

I do not underestimate the moral courage that is required to sustain
serious attention to human rights. It is also inevitable that those who

serve on the Human Rights Commission may often, either through experience or training, be in advance of popular opinion or that of legislators. That is the nature of the challenge: to provide leadership in increasing consciousness, education and persuasion.

The concluding paragraph of the 2012 Report of the Irish Human Rights Commission states:

> During its twelve years, the IHRC's work has touched on practically all aspects of the life of the nation. Although under-resourced for much of that time, we have tried to focus on the significant human rights issues facing Ireland. Few of the successes on promoting and protecting human rights are achieved alone but are the culmination of the endeavours of many people and organisations. Often the work may remain hidden; the prevention of a bad law being passed in the Oireachtas or of a questionable practice being struck down in one case before the courts can have significant implications for many of us. Human rights as a concept is an evolving one: it must be if it is to meet the challenges of a changing society. As the IHRC moves into a new phase with its planned merger with the Equality Authority, it looks forward to continuing to work for the protection and promotion of human rights and equality for all, acting independently of Government, and achieving recognition through the quality and authority of its work.

Is ráiteas macánta atá anseo ar dhea-obair atá déanta agus tiomantas cróga ar fiú é a mholadh go hard. Mar Uachtarán na hÉireann, molaim iad sin go léir a d'oibrigh i réimse na gceart daonna agus ba mhaith liom críochnú trí gach rath a ghuí ar lucht déanta beartas agus cleachtóirí sa bhaile agus thar lear agus iad ag cuidiú le leagan dár n-Éireannachas a chruthú a bhféadfaimis a bheith bródúil as agus a bhfuil cearta an duine ina chroílár.

(This is an honest statement of good work done and a brave commitment worthy of the highest commendation. As President of Ireland I commend all those who have worked in the area of human rights and I conclude by wishing policymakers and practitioners every success at home and abroad in contributing to a version of our Irishness of which we might be proud and which has human rights at its centre.)

I want to end tonight by recalling the words of Václav Havel in 1994:

> The idea of human rights and freedoms must be an integral part of any meaningful world order. Yet I think it must be anchored in a different place, and in a different way, than has been the case so far. If it is to be more than just a slogan mocked by half the world, it cannot be expressed in the language of a departing era, and it must not be mere froth floating on the subsiding waters of faith in a purely scientific relationship to the world.

Nearly twenty years on, these words still ring true. I thank you for your attention and company tonight.

Defining Europe in the Year of the European Citizen

PARIS-SORBONNE UNIVERSITY

18TH FEBRUARY, 2013

I T IS DEEPLY moving to be speaking in Paris and in an institution that has contributed so much to our attempts, over the ages, at putting the stamp of humanity on our shared existence. It was in Paris and its university lecture halls that so many of the concepts that put the stamp of reason on the ways we live together in society were first introduced.

Sometimes these ideas were welcomed and eagerly sought out. More often they were feared, they were derided, or became the target of sanctions and censorship from those who held power, and by the beneficiaries of authoritarian systems that were under threat from the emerging democratic movements in Paris. These movements were often fashioned by intellectual migrants.

Paris has always been specially hospitable to the migrant mind, and in our present circumstances in Europe, we have much to gain from such minds. While James Joyce and Samuel Beckett may be the best known examples of the Irish migrant intellectual in the modern period, Ireland has an even older connection with Europe and France.

James Joyce's call in his Trieste lecture to 'Hibernicise Europe and Europeanise Ireland' was, we must remember, anticipated many centuries earlier by such figures as Columbanus and Gallus, who brought precious scriptures and treatises from Bangor, through France in the early seventh century; John Scotus Eriugena, who brought Greek back into Europe after the dark ages and travelled all the way to the French King in the ninth century to translate Pseudo-Dionysius from Greek into Latin; Peter of Ireland, who taught Aquinas philosophy; and later George Berkeley, the 'Irish Cartesian', who engaged with French thinkers like Malebranche in the eighteenth century – and since I am advocating a rethinking of economics, may I mention the Franco-Hibernian thinker Richard Cantillon, born in Kerry in 1680, whose *Essai sur la nature du commerce en general*, written in 1730, was described by William Stanley Jevons as 'the cradle of political economy', and influenced Adam Smith and Karl Marx.

We Irish have a long history of travelling with intellectual curiosity and subversive creativity, and Paris (and the Sorbonne in particular), has been both a staging post and a destination for us.

Described by James Joyce as 'the last of the human cities', Paris was, at the beginning of the twentieth century, one of the most appropriate locations for seeing one's own people through the lens of exile, and mould-breaking writers were not alone in utilizing the experience of exile, or the freedom and the stimulating company of fellow exiles in Paris. The city's diverse community of dissidents was far from limited to literature.

Paris was frequently both a source and inspiration of the radical ideas and deeds that led the Irish on their slow road to independence.

The city served as a laboratory for political ideas for groups like the Fenians, who drew on the radical ideas that were emerging from within the walls of universities and the radical suburbs.

The talk among the exiles in the cafés and in the bars, sought to define the meaning of a genuine Republic, to discuss how it might be achieved, and what independence might bring with its promises of freedom, of dignity, of creativity, of solidarity, of a more complete humanity.

Scholars all over the world associate Paris with the legacy of its intellectuals, their ideas, their books, their discourse, their reputation for intellectual confrontation and public denunciations of injustice. It is the work of Albert Camus, Jean Paul Sartre, Simone de Beauvoir, Michel Foucault, Roland Barthes, Paul Ricoeur, James Joyce, Samuel Beckett or, in more recent times, that of public intellectuals such as Julia Kristeva, that has made so many curious – even envious – of the space of thought, performance and discourse that is the essence of Parisian intellectual life.

At moments of great change Paris is a most appropriate place in which to reflect on the current changes taking place on a global level and their implications for the European Union, its future, and how it might be perceived by European citizens.

I would like to suggest, as a preliminary, that the anti-imperialist writers of the late eighteenth century, especially Denis Diderot, are of great relevance if we are to envision how a European Union of citizens, which will contribute to the challenges presented by our increasing interdependence on our frail planet, might be brought into being.

I mean by this a meaningful, shared citizenship, a truly social Europe based on dignity, equality, solidarity and human rights.

I feel, now more than ever, at a time of economic crisis and loss of trust in institutions and decision-makers, that if Europe is to have a vision informed with all the energy, concern and creativity that the times demand, then surely the lives, the conversations, the anguish, the hopes, the beliefs, and the commitment of those thinkers of previous centuries who believed, in their day, that a world with the stamp of humanity was not only necessary, but that it was possible, are relevant to us as examples of the moral courage we need in facing the contradictions of our times.

After all, Paris was one of the locations where the contradictions between morality and ethics on the one hand, and the crude extension of empire on the other, were so thoroughly contested, and over such a long period. While it is true that the holders of power were assisted by the majority of the leading intellectuals of the time, with rationalizations that supported the assumptions or the belief systems of the day, there was also a dissenting scholarship that confronted the project of empire – dissenting voices that found themselves frequently put outside the walls, silenced, or indeed, as in the case of some of the writers to whom I will refer, thrown into prison.

A recent and very welcome treatment of some of these leading dissenting voices from the heart of empire is that of Sankar Muthu. It was his work that brought most forcefully to my attention the contributions of the opponents of empire in the period of the European Enlightenment. His seminal study, *Enlightenment against Empire*, deals with the thought and writings of Denis Diderot, Immanuel Kant and Johann Gottfried Herder. In the case of Diderot, I was intrigued to read that it was while he was imprisoned for his views on religion, and on the occasion of his being visited by Rousseau, he encouraged his visitor to take courage and risk publishing his thoughts. We are so clearly reminded by such examples of the sacrifices made by intellectuals who had real moral courage in the pursuit of truth, and saw the necessity of communicating it to the public.

These dissident scholars, in challenging the accommodating consensus of their day, were aware that imperial conquest was being rationalized by notions of a civilizing mission, by the idea of progress, by an accommodating theology that even denied souls to those who were culturally different, by a racism that refused to recognize the dignity of others of different skin colour. The dissident writers saw the need to challenge those scholars who sought preferment from the wielders of power.

Professor Muthu has done a great service in claiming a rightful place for such dissidents as scholars of immense moral insight and courage. They were not perfect of course. Kant, for example, never adequately resiled from his early statements on race, but his recognition of the corrosive effect of the very concept of empire and its legacy is of powerful moral significance.

That use of a counter-narrative raises issues for us today. We require a discourse in our times that allows us not only to make a new narrative for the defence of Europe, but which also enables us to contest the distorting narratives of the past that have been allowed to become hegemonic, and to challenge the accommodating amoral amnesia that offers us an existence in the present without a troublesome past.

Twenty-five years ago, in January 1988, President Mitterrand stood in this very chamber and addressed an issue of singular importance in the ethics of memory: how the French Nation was to engage with the bicentenary celebrations of the French Revolution the following year.

In his speech, President Mitterrand tackled the fundamental question of how to reconcile the contrasting aspects of the Revolution and its memory, its goals and animating principles, with the violence that it unleashed. He argued for a consideration of the Revolution *en bloc*, balancing all of its achievements with its excesses and avoiding the temptation to separate out the laudable and virtuous from the violence and the upheaval.

Here at the Sorbonne that January, and in a later speech in June 1988, President Mitterrand also argued that 'a people without memory is no longer a free people' and observed something that is universally true of the relationship between memory and freedom:

> dictators begin by wiping out the history of the facts that encumber them, by barring access to the past, and, believing themselves masters of the avenues to the future, muzzle any mutinous thoughts or words.

The year of the bicentenary, 1989, was itself one of revolution. It was a year when ordinary people across Central and Eastern Europe, including many who were inspired by Voltaire and Diderot, reached back to the unfinished Enlightenment principles of liberty and equality to reclaim their own freedom.

We are at a moment now, in Europe and in our shared vulnerable planet, when we must again turn to critical thought if we are to put an ethical stamp on our own societies and place our economics within a framework of ethical culture. We have to rework our past and present assumptions if we are to achieve a future which includes, for example, the achievement of intergenerational justice. We have to remember ethically if we are to understand the present with tolerance, and imagine the alternatives of the future with courage.

I suggest that in facing these challenges we are assisted in recent times by philosophical work such as that on the ethics of memory, so brilliantly accomplished by the late Professor Paul Ricoeur, a graduate and former Chair of Philosophy at the Sorbonne, whose ideas have, with great relevance, been applied by Irish philosopher Richard Kearney to our Northern Ireland conflict. This is work which speaks, for example, of steps towards an amnesty rather than an immoral amnesia in dealing with the legacy of conflict in Ireland and elsewhere. In the context of the European Union, the distinction between amnesia and amnesty has an under-utilized value in the recasting by some European nations of their past relations with the continents of the South, with peoples and nations that bear the marks of what Pankaj Mishra has called 'the Ruins of Empire'.

May I suggest, incidentally, that in relation to the matter of empire and its residues, even if an accommodating amnesia has rinsed the memory of empire from the minds of the descendants of some of the European imperial powers, no such amnesia is experienced by the descendants of those who have relatively recently emerged from the consequences of empire. They are very conscious of their history.

Let me briefly refer to Paul Ricoeur's work on the role of memory and the power of narrative as outlined in his *Time and Narrative* and *Memory, History, Forgetting*. Narrative, Ricoeur observed, 'provides us with a figure of something' that allows us to transcend the blind amnesia of the now. As Richard Kearney puts it, narrative enables us to resist the tendency to reduce history to a depthless present.

Thus narrative – combining ethics and poetics – and narrative memory have the important function of creating empathy, a way of identifying with as many humans as possible and participating in a common moral sense.

Narrative is a vital foundation stone of the social world, and we are challenged to make a narrative for a more just and social Europe with an ethical memory and an imagination freed from failure, one that is free to build an inclusive Europe.

This then is the task of memory. It is through narrating and re-narrating history, past, present and envisioned future, that we create through interaction a shared narratable world – one that can give us the capability of acting responsibly and in common.

We are, in contemporary Europe, confronted with uniquely difficult challenges. But the essential response lies in striving towards an open, politically engaged but questioning, socially and culturally aware, citizenship – a citizenship that develops and protects the institutions that protect individual rights and foster a sense of duty, responsibility and accountability. This is not the shallow contractual duty of consequentialism, a narrow ethics discharged from social obligation, but a duty founded on interpersonal encounter, respect and understanding. The university as a space for critical scholarship is central to this ambition. Universities must not be abandoned to a distorting neo-functionalism in the service of our failing economic models.

The moral issue of memory then cannot be avoided by Europeans. Facing the realities of an imperial past is required of us both morally and practically, at the level of international relations, if we are to have global peace; if we are to have a new discourse for a new Europe; if we are to achieve any movement towards universal human rights and if we are to build a transnational respect for the contribution of different cultures and belief systems.

What is the Europe we seek? How is it to be defined? How is it to remember itself? What does it wish to be – mere trading block or political community? In global terms, how is it to be engaged with or imagined by others? How does it wish to be remembered in the future? These questions are often avoided or sidelined as accommodation is sought for competing national interests, limited visions of narrow advantage which, at times under populist pressure, are used as part of an attempt to invoke a politics of fear, often delivered with a jingoistic rhetoric.

As to intellectual work – what price, we might ask, has been paid, including in our universities, for the rejection of normative theory, and its replacement by a deadly alliance of extreme individualism served by an irrational bureaucracy, and propagated as a substitute for the ideal that envisaged a society of equals as its project?

Now more than ever, we need open, critical and emancipatory scholarship that can accommodate a generous, humane version of Europe at home and in the global community. It would surely be a mistake not to draw on the powerful intellectual traditions within our different European discourses.

Would it not be tragic if we allowed others, through our silence or neglect, to abuse seminal European works of scholarship, such as has already happened, for example, in the distortion of Adam Smith's work by those who, ignoring his *Theory of Moral Sentiments*, misuse, by selective quotation, his *Wealth of Nations*? Through silence we collude with the ransacking and the distortion of the serious scholarship of previous ages.

Scholarship is at its best when it is emancipatory, when it enables and assists freedom. We need that scholarship now as we work towards a better future for the European Union.

Just as Diderot, Kant, Herder and others saw the flaws and consequences of empire at the heart of the European Enlightenment, many scholars around the world have seen the flaws and the consequences of a single hegemonic model of international economics, built on the myth of the efficiency of unregulated markets.

Such a model, arguing in its relatively liberal form for a limited state, or in its ordoliberal version, demanding the use of the State to impose arrangements for a de-peopled market economy, has been presented as the only acceptable alternative to the democratically-based models of social economy that emerged after the Second World War.

Jürgen Habermas puts it succinctly when, seeking to address the challenge of what we might do to save in a truly humane way a Europe he describes as 'our fragile project', he writes:

> My hope is that the neoliberal agenda will no longer be accepted at face value but will be open to challenge. The whole program of subordinating the life world to the imperatives of the market must be subjected to scrutiny... The agenda which recklessly prioritizes shareholder interests and is indifferent to increasing social inequality, to the emergence of an underclass, to child poverty, of a low wage sector, and so on has been discredited. With its mania for privatization, this agenda hollows out the core function of the state. It sells the remnants of a deliberative public sphere to profit maximising financial investors, and it subordinates culture and education to the interests and moods of sponsors who are dependent on market cycles.

I believe that what Jürgen Habermas is responding to is more than a fragile European project. It is a social crisis. It is the emergence and the acting out of what Habermas's great predecessor Max Weber saw as the 'bleak winter' that would replace 'the promise of Spring' when a perversion of rationality would become irrationality, as consciousness was numbed; when what is oppressive would come to be seen as inevitable and be received as natural.

The crisis to which the earlier work of Habermas pointed was a 'legitimation crisis'. The signs of this distorted rationality are there today in our European Union, as spectacle replaces discourse; as the length and content of communiqués become shorter and more banal; as managing the media replaces open and in-depth discussion. Alternative political options that might have generated a debate that would involve the citizens of Europe in being creative, in responding to global issues – be they issues of poverty, freedom, democracy or intergenerational environmental responsibility – are rejected, relegated to the past, ignored or dismissed.

The European Union was founded with the memory of war, with its vast loss of life, fresh in the minds of the founders. But to drift into 'unfreedom', because of democratic lethargy, as the Canadian philosopher Charles Taylor put it, is I suggest as much a loss as the imposition of unfreedom through force of arms or occupation. Indeed, as Montesquieu famously said:

> The tyranny of a prince in an oligarchy is not so dangerous to the public welfare as the apathy of a citizen in a democracy.

The present challenges at global level – be they those of freedom from hunger, the movement for universal human rights, the restructuring of economic theories of development, poverty, inequality or sustainability – need to be addressed, and become the recognizable defining marks of our new Europe, not only safe from war, but inviting others through open and respectful discourse to recast the global community itself in a robustly ethical way.

We need new and courageous scholarship; educational institutions that are committed to the sustenance and development of independent thought; an economic literacy that can take on board the demands of ethics and the insights of philosophy – a political economy for new times and new circumstances.

The challenges we now face are far more complex than those that prevailed, for example, at the time of the Cold War. Yet the intellectual energy seems so much less than that which prevailed in the decades following the Second World War.

Edward Said in his *Culture and Imperialism* suggests that we, in intellectual terms, may have experienced a type of collapse into our post-modernist condition:

> The deaths in the 1980s of Jean Paul Sartre, Roland Barthes, I. R. Stone, Michel Foucault, Raymond Williams, C. L. R. James, mark the passing of an old order; they had been figures of learning and authority whose general scope over many fields gave them more than professional competence; that is, a critical intellectual style. The technocrats in contrast, as Lyotard says in *The Postmodern Condition*, are principally competent to solve local problems, not to ask the big questions given by the grand narratives of emancipation and enlightenment, and there are also the carefully accredited policy experts, who serve the security mongers who have guided international affairs."

This passage expresses much more than a melancholy for the great decades of European intellectual work. It identifies the distance that has opened up between a privileged technocratic thinking in Europe that has, in so many respects, the character of the irrational bureaucracy that Max Weber forecast. It describes a continent that has recently tended to dismiss history, ignore its own rich intellectual legacy, and remain blind to other parts of the world where new thinking appropriate to a wider diverse world is developing.

There is, out there, a world that has moved on from the old order, and that is seeking to make itself felt, to bring new social models into existence – models that are very different from those that rely on the surviving vestiges of empire, and obviously very different too from the work of those scholars who fetishized the power of the centralized state at the cost of personal freedom. Cold War choices are no longer the alternatives being considered by the many countries previously forced to see them as the only path available to them.

In the wider world, change – welcome change in some places, threatening change in others – is underway. In the final chapter of *Culture and Imperialism*, Edward Said summarised the changes he saw at the beginning of the 1990s:

> The old invented histories and traditions and efforts to rule are giving way to newer, more elastic and relaxed theories of what is so discrepant and intense in the contemporary moment. In the West, *post-modernism* has seized upon the ahistorical weightlessness, consumerism, and spectacle of the new order. To it are affiliated other ideas like post-Marxism and post-structuralism, varieties of what the Italian philosopher Gianni Vatimo describes as 'weak thought' of 'the end of modernity'. Yet in the Arab and Islamic world many artists and intellectuals are still concerned with modernity itself, still far from exhausted. This is similarly the case in the Caribbean, Eastern Europe, Latin America, Africa and the Indian subcontinent; these movements intersect culturally in a fascinating cosmopolitan space animated by internationally prominent writers like Salman Rushdie, Carlos Fuentes, Gabriel García Márquez, Milan Kundera, who intervene forcefully not only as novelists but also as commentators and essayists. And their debate over what is modern or post-modern is joined by the anxious, urgent question of how we are to modernize, given the cataclysmic upheavals the world is experiencing as it moves into the *fin de siècle*, that is, how we are going to keep up life itself when the quotidian demands of the present threaten to outstrip the human presence?

When I first read that summary I was moved by the poignancy, the urgency, of such a statement. Today I see it as a rallying call, in times of uncertainty, for the defence of the public world, for public intellectuals and scholarship to re-engage.

How then might Europe present itself in these new circumstances? We must recognize that our problems are global. I believe that we must acknowledge the interdependent global nature of our lives together and their complexity, and accept the moral urgency of resolving conflicts that are planetary and have intergenerational consequences.

It must be a discourse that will include citizens from diverse settings, beliefs and cultures. It is perhaps an opportune time now, as we search for sources, to give the insights of not just the exilic but also the migratory experience their appropriate place as important sources of theoretical understanding. For uninhibited as it is by the burden of possessions, or by the authoritarianism of a respectability based on the sedentary and its unquestioned repressions and exclusions, the migratory experience has forged a morality out of the experience of transience whose richness we have neglected in the social sciences.

In a European Union where unemployment is our greatest problem and where youth unemployment is the most challenging feature, if we are to accept the need for intergenerational justice, we require as a beginning an acceptance that in an ever more interdependent world our global problems are not amenable to a merely technocratic response, nor are our challenges merely economic. They are social, political and cultural. We are, we must remind ourselves, social beings, not commodified consumers without a history, incapable of envisioning an alternative future.

Once more I turn to Paul Ricoeur and recall what he envisaged as the necessary steps towards a generous theory of citizenship. His developed Aristotelian view was that action be aimed at the good, be aimed at a good life with and for others in just institutions. If we are to attain that good life, we must work towards institutions that correspond to our sense of justice, both in the obligations that these institutions impose upon us and the privileges that they afford us. As Ricoeur put it:

It is as citizens that we become human. The wish to live within just institutions signifies nothing else.

The task for politics, therefore, is to establish what justice calls for, and to build the institutions that make justice effective. Power, held in common, must prevail over domination.

There is an abiding truth in Ricoeur's observation that

The wish to live in just institutions arises from the same level of morality as does the desire for personal fulfilment and the reciprocity of friendship.

Crucially, this desire to live well is not confined to living well with friends; it includes a desire to live well with others, with 'distant others', as Ricoeur put it. The desire to live well with others thus animates the 'life of institutions'. This is a vision of human living in a world that is a shared social existence of exchanged narratives; a vision of man that is not reducible to Homo Economicus. And this is not an invitation to abstraction. I agree with the late Richard Rorty's view that it is from our own circumstances and our own frailties that we must attempt to transform society.

It is political institutions, I believe, that must define the space and accountable character of the other institutions we need for a functioning state and economy. To live as conscious citizens means, as Raymond Williams might have put it, our becoming the arrow of our existence rather than the commodified target of the market and its agents.

It is the task of democratic politics to ensure that institutions are transparent and accountable. It is the task of politics to state its programme for the tasks of justice. It is upon that basis that politics seeks legitimacy and consent. It risks losing its legitimacy among citizens if it seeks to divert responsibility from the sphere of the accountable elected representatives, to an unaccountable technocracy or the mysterious marketplace.

The task of developing a consciousness of engaged and responsible citizenship in the member states of the European Union requires, for example, an educational system that allows space for critical awareness, allows democracy to educate, and which in turn democratises education.

Where are the ideas we need to come from, if not from the educational institutions and the open and free debate of public intellectuals? What are the prospects for that debate? How is it to happen in conditions of an ever more monopolized media, at a time when public service broadcasting in so many countries is in decline? It would be easy to sink into elitist pessimism in the consideration of such questions. But we must make the space, as others have done before us, and begin with confidence, and joy too, to craft our new European discourse. It is a time for public intellectuals to have moral courage, to break the silence, to reject false inevitabilities.

In our times, the connection in Europe between democratic discourse and emancipatory scholarship is dissolving rather than strengthening. However, we must take heart from the fact that already, in some other parts of the world, in other continents, that connecting discourse is producing a diversity of ideas for future living. Let us follow their example, and engage with their innovative thought as Irish migrant scholars did all those centuries ago at the Sorbonne and all over Europe.

Our universities must seek out new means of engaging with citizens about the possibilities of the long future of our lives together. Universities must break away from the quietude of that 'unfreedom' to which we are slowly drifting.

Scholarship is emancipatory when it offers ways of imagining the possibilities of a life lived to its fullest with sustainability and responsibility. We may have to consume to live, but it is not our destiny to live to consume.

In conclusion, let me salute again the rich intellectual legacy of Paris, the Sorbonne and the French people. Let me salute again the extraordinary courage of those earlier scholars such as Diderot, Rousseau, Kant and Herder who, in their time, confronted the populist accommodations with empire at the heart of the European Enlightenment, who took the risks.

Let us never forget that in making their commitment, they opened the space for others in distant places. C. L. R. James pointed to the space opened by Abbé Raynal, for instance, and the other Encyclopaedists, and the Revolution itself, for such revolutionaries as Toussaint L'Ouverture who was leading the struggle of his fellow Haitians, so recently emancipated from brutal slavery. As James puts it:

> ... in the hour of danger Toussaint, uninstructed as he was, could find the language and accent of Diderot, Rousseau and Raynal, of Mirabeau, Robespierre and Danton. And in one respect he excelled them all. For even these masters of the spoken and written word, owing to the class complications of their society, too often had to pause, to hesitate, to qualify. Toussaint could defend the freedom of the blacks without reservation, and this gave to his declaration a strength and a single-mindedness rare in the great documents of the time. The French bourgeoisie could not understand that elevated as was his tone Toussaint had written neither bombast nor rhetoric but the simple and sober truth."

We need public intellectuals now more than ever who will assist us in seeking a necessary, simple, generous and emancipatory strategy that adds to the flux of our fragile democracy.

Can the future of Europe be envisaged within a doctrine of narrow individual interests?

I suggest that it cannot. The disabling consequences of such a choice would not be confined to Europe but would be global. We must speak for our unrealised potential and humanity, address our realisable possibilities, rather than drearily serve in quietude as a blunt tool of discordant interests. That too was the conclusion and the suggestion of a great European, Václav Havel, as recorded in his diary following a visit to the institutions of the European Union some years ago.

What is this world that would bear the stamp of humanity? When Noam Chomsky gave the Bertrand Russell Memorial Lecture at Cambridge in 1971, he quoted Bertrand Russell's 'version of the world that we must seek' which was

> ... a world in which the creative spirit is alive, in which life is an adventure full of joy and hope, based rather upon the impulse to construct than upon the desire to retain what we possess or to seize what is possessed by others. It must be a world in which affection has free play, in which love is purged of the instinct for domination, in which cruelty and envy have been dispelled by happiness and the unfettered development of all the instincts that build up life and fill it with mental delights.

Such a vision not only still has relevance. It can have the force of inspiration. Let us have then a European project in this year of the European citizen that aims for an authenticity of life and language for all of our people and their institutions. May we move beyond a Europe of the arid spectacle, beyond the dead language, towards a genuine Europe of the citizens.

RENEWING ECONOMICS: TOWARDS A NEW POLITICAL ECONOMY

Public Intellectuals
and the Universities

LONDON SCHOOL OF ECONOMICS
AND POLITICAL SCIENCE

21 FEBRUARY 2012

I
T IS AN honour to be here at the London School of Economics and
Political Science.

I feel at home as an Irishman in an institution, and in a city, with
so many Irish connections. I feel at home in a country which is Ireland's
nearest neighbour and increasingly our close friend. And I feel at home
as an academic speaking to representatives of different cultures and to a
younger generation who are challenged by the changes taking place in
international economics, in politics and in the wider public world.

It is just nine months since Her Majesty Queen Elizabeth's State Visit
to Ireland, the first visit by a British monarch to an independent Ireland.
Her Majesty's visit, her perfectly judged words, her gesture of respect
for those who died in an Irish cause, her use of the Irish language, her
evident pleasure at being our honoured guest, symbolized the remarkable
transformation in relations between our countries and it was deeply
welcomed all over the island of Ireland.

When the LSE was founded in 1895 by four leading Fabians, Beatrice
and Sidney Webb, George Bernard Shaw and Graham Wallas, its founders

were convinced of the power of education not only to lift their fellow citizens out of poverty, but they were also convinced that citizens could understand, participate in and, in time, create an alternative form of society, one that would be egalitarian, democratic, tolerant and which would extend and deepen democracy in every aspect of life. Such an achievement would also, they felt, establish democratic socialism as an alternative to capitalism. The LSE would function as a mediating influence in radical change and offer an alternative to the violence of the class conflict which was widely advocated in a number of countries at that time and which seemed a real prospect in these islands too.

The century that was ending was one of immense change. The response to this change, as intellectual historians such as Henry Stuart Hughes have shown, gave us the great founding texts of sociology, of Marx, Weber, Durkheim, Croce and others. But it was not only philosophers and political theorists who responded to the turbulent new order that was emerging. Shaw and other creative writers engaged with the new social movements and the passionate debates around them, read the philosophical and political books and pamphlets and responded with essays, lectures and powerful literary works.

The writer as public intellectual, as analyst and campaigner for change, was a role that George Bernard Shaw and others assumed with vigour and dedication, and Shaw's involvement with the LSE was part of that public engagement, as was his sustained interest in the social change that he thought was necessary to transform Ireland, and the place of literature in fostering the consciousness that would demand and deliver that change.

Nelson O'Ceallaigh Ritschel in his recent excellent study *Shaw, Synge, Connolly and Socialist Provocation* shows how Shaw believed, like his fellow Fabians, that the conversion of the middle classes was essential for the democracy they sought to achieve. He was not joined in that opinion by his fellow playwright and Irishman John Millington Synge. Synge held an alternative radical view based on what he saw as the real suffering of the downtrodden, and thus he rejected as idealistic Shaw's project of converting the middle class. It was Synge's work that brought the nationalist Padraig Pearse closer to the revolutionary socialism of James Connolly, O'Ceallaigh Ritschel shows.

But for all their differences, these great dramatists had much in common. Shaw's influence in Ireland was mediated through the agency of Frederick Ryan, an Irish journalist who had attended Shaw's Fabian lectures in London and then went on to lecture in Dublin to Connolly's Irish Socialist Republican Party on democracy and drama, drawing on the works of both Ibsen and Shaw. The trade union leader William O'Brien attended these lectures and was influenced by them, as indeed was Connolly himself. This connection between London and Dublin, this flow of social-reformist ideas and arguments for the radical resolution of Ireland's relationship with Britain, knew no borders.

The Irish literary presence in London, in the figures of Shaw or Wilde or Yeats, inevitably meant that individual projects of achieving literary success and a wider audience were touched by the necessary irony of unresolved relationships between the two countries, by the question of their own Irishness. This would have a lasting effect on the consciousness of their audiences.

In so many ways the tragedy of modern Ireland's recent difficulties is that the new state did just what the founders of the LSE hoped. It was the first English-speaking country to decolonize, to walk in darkness down what would become a better-lit road – a road illuminated by teachers and students at the LSE. The problem for Ireland was the failure to achieve economic lift-off soon after independence. By the time the economic boom of the late 1990s began, leaders and people had all but lost any connection with the cultural and political traces of national revival which might, if they had been retained, have provided an ethical brake on, and ensured some degree of necessary regulation of, that rampant 'Celtic Tiger' economy.

The LSE at its foundation had an emancipatory purpose, and its early discussions about Ireland, through Shaw, had a direct effect on Irish realities and on Anglo-Irish relations. The practical orientation of the themes chosen by George Bernard Shaw in his lectures is perhaps insufficiently recognized in Ireland and Britain. He lectured on the working conditions of the labouring classes, but also on Ibsen and the morally informed social vision in the great Norwegian writer's plays.

Peter Gahan's *Shaw Shadows: Rereading the Texts of Bernard Shaw* is quoted in O'Ceallaigh Ritschel's book. Gahan insists that Shaw is explicit about the importance of mediating the violence inevitably flowing from the institutionalization of inequality and the denial, for example, of rights, even voting rights, to women:

> If Socialism be not made respectable and formidable by the support of our class – if it be left entirely to the poor then the proprietors will attempt to suppress it by such measures as they have already taken in Austria and Ireland. Dynamite will follow. Terror will follow dynamite. Cruelty will follow terror… If, on the other hand, the middle class will educate themselves to understand this question, they will be able to fortify whatever is just in Socialism and to crush whatever is dangerous in it.

Many students and thinkers around the world first encountered such teachers as Harold Laski in the early and middle decades of the twentieth century at the LSE. As a young student I recall Dr Labhrás O Nualláin, born in Manchester but Irish-speaking, who gave pioneering lectures at University College Galway speaking of the LSE and Laski's influence on those who had come to study there – students who aspired to lead their countries in what were to be the decades of decolonization and national independence. Through Laski and his writings such as *A Grammar of Politics* the LSE acquired a global reputation not only for sociological theory and research but for analyses of the role of the state and state-making.

I see such great achievements as the British welfare state, the National Health Service, pioneering work on equality, the need for solidarity with movements against colonialism and the recognition that an interdependent world needs responsible international institutions as a valuable legacy of the emancipatory scholarship of the LSE.

I remain in awe too of the moral content of the scholarship and the life of such giants of social policy as Professor Richard Titmuss. Professor Titmuss founded Social Policy as an academic subject and was the first occupant of the Chair of Social Administration at LSE in 1942. His work was drawn upon by all of us who would later lecture in social policy, poverty studies or equality. His was an engaged view of research and scholarship, and he did not avoid an engagement with competing models of government policy, whether in public health or pensions, poverty or social justice.

As a young university teacher appointed at the end of the 1960s, I had hopes for the emancipatory power of a humanistic social science. I could not have foreseen the second coming of the ideas of theorists such as Friedrich von Hayek or the influence they would have, not only on theory but on the policies they inspired. These policies would be privileged in the UK and the US in the 1980s and 1990s, not as policies chosen among various options but as a single, unchallengeable version of the connection between markets, economic policy and life itself.

This evening I would like to offer a brief reflection on public intellectuals, universities and the role of both in what I perceive to be an emerging democratic crisis, one that sets representative parliamentary accountability against unaccountable economic forces. It is a time when the credibility of parliamentary power has been called into question, when undemocratic alternatives to the state and civil society are being advanced and when, at institutional level – in Ireland, the United Kingdom, Europe and beyond – the legitimation crisis of which Jürgen Habermas wrote so many decades ago has begun to emerge. Having squandered credibility through light regulation and powerless regulatory authorities, the state itself has been made vulnerable to private forms of power.

There are, always, dominant myths that inform, even determine the discourse of the times. The myth of rational markets and infinite growth was the hegemonic fallacy of recent decades. Apart from some distinguished exceptions such as the Galbraiths, father and son, it was largely uncontested.

After the fall of the Berlin Wall and of state socialism – itself a distortion of the utopian impulse, indeed a dystopia – an extraordinary hubris emerged, which was little less than a utopian vision of the Right. Politics would now take second place to unregulated markets.

We have, as a consequence, been living through a period of extreme individualism in which the concept of society itself has been questioned. The public space in so many countries of the EU has been commodified, and it is as calculating rational-choice maximizers, rather than as citizens, that we have been invited to view our neighbours. That is the mark of our times, the paradigm by which, it is suggested, we should live our lives together. Our existence is assumed to be, is defined as, an ongoing competition between individual actors, at times neurotic in our insatiable anxieties for more goods and objects. As Zygmunt Bauman puts it in his book *Consuming Life*: 'Consumers become the promoters of the commodities they consume.' They become a commodified entity in their presentation of themselves.

These extraordinary changes depend on an intellectual rationalization. Writing in support of unregulated markets, of unaccountable capital flows, of virtual financial products, are scholars who frequently claim the legitimation provided by a university. The university is at times under pressure to demonstrate how useful it is as a supporter of the single prevailing model of society and economy.

I believe universities are challenged now, not only to recover the moral purpose of original thought and emancipatory scholarship, but also to recover the caring and concerned teaching that was offered by Harold Laski at LSE to students from abroad such as Krishna Menon. That university teaching was more than instruction: it was an encouragement to endure, to overcome the strangeness of exile and the loneliness of solitary study that came with the move from one culture to another.

The ethos of the LSE was also defined in its early days by significant public intellectuals such as Bertrand Russell, who taught German Social Democracy at the school between 1895 and 1896. After the publication of his tragically neglected book *Power* in 1934, he taught classes on the Science of Power in 1936. His 1934 book had outlined in detail how collective behaviour could be manipulated. 'If a crowd has gathered, particularly if music is playing, you can get them to believe in anything', Russell had written.

All this is a powerful legacy of teaching and research which had its beneficiaries far beyond the lecture halls of the LSE. The Irish in Britain, who were building and helping to shape the post-war contours of their host country, were also benefiting from the security of the welfare state and the National Health Service, which had the intellectual support of, among others, scholars at the LSE.

Now, in the second decade of a new century, it is not the LSE alone that is challenged to recover an ethos of emancipatory scholarship. All the universities in both our countries, indeed universities all over Europe and beyond, are challenged in similar ways. Much ground has been lost in terms of the public space, the public world, the shared essential space of an independent people free to participate and change their circumstances, to imagine their future.

The questions that are posed to universities now are questions that go far beyond narrow utilitarian issues.

Will universities seek to recover the space, the capacity, the community of scholarship, the quiet moments of reflection necessary to challenge, for example, failed paradigms of the connection between economy and society, and to intervene in the contest between democratic discourse and the authoritarian imposition of ideas? Drawing on their rich traditions, their best moments of disputation and discourse, will they seek to craft alternatives that offer a stable present and a democratic, liberating and sustainable future?

We are currently experiencing, I believe, an intellectual crisis that is far more serious than the economic one which fills the newspapers and television programmes. Such a crisis has arisen before at times of great or impending change and it has evoked a response from intellectuals who were forced to react to the collapse of prevailing assumptions and to engage with the need for a new paradigm of life and politics.

When Max Weber, the great social theorist, responded to the events of his time in the second half of the nineteenth century, he was not motivated by a sense of the end of empire in itself, but by his intuition that there was a change in the forms of empire, the response to which would be dominated by the technocratic thinking of the time. Weber proposed a commitment to rationality as the key building block of the future.

He was anxious to save as much as possible of the rationalist heritage of the previous century but at the same time to introduce something new, beyond logic, intuition and religious sentiment. He was therefore critical of the excesses of both positivism and idealism. Yet even then Weber saw the dangers of the potential abuse of that which could be claimed to be rational.

He spoke of the threat of a spring that would not beckon with its promise of new life, but would deliver instead a winter of icy cold. He prophesied an iron cage of bureaucracy within which conformity would be demanded to that which no longer recognized its original moral or reasonable purpose, a time when what was irrational would wear the mask of rationality, of a narrow technocratic kind.

A century earlier reason had been central to Adam Smith's *The Theory of Moral Sentiments*. Weber, of course, could not have envisaged the consequences of the journey that intellectual thought would make from reason to rationality, and then on to calculable rationality, and finally, in our own time, to the speculative gambling that is at the heart of so much global misery with its view of those humans who share our fragile planet not as citizens, but as consumers interested only in maximizing their choices.

We are in such a winter as Weber foretold. For example, we have arrived at the quite widespread acceptance by policymakers of a proposition rejected by the majority of serious economic historians – that markets are in fact rational. This, on occasion, leads to the suggestion, absurd as it may sound, that it is people who are irrational, and the markets rational. That the public, for whom Friedrich von Hayek once wrote that economics are too complex, requires, it is suggested, something other than the direction of elected governments.

They must be forced into a compliance with demands for which there is frequently scant scholarly support and, needless to say, no democratic mandate. This represents a challenge to democracy itself, and to the scholarship that supports it. The mediating institutions are losing authority and the prospect of raw conflict increases all over the world, as language – words without emancipatory force – gives ground to what is unaccountable but irresistibly global.

Nor is the intellectual crisis of our times simply a problem for the LSE or other universities. When Jürgen Habermas writes of the fragility of the European Union he is referring to the contest that is going on in Europe for the survival of the public world. Social Europe was born as a concept in response to the legacy of war and social misery. It was connected to a democratic discourse.

The project of that 'social Europe' is undermined by the commodification of ever more aspects of social life. European social capital, one of the strongest in the world, is being monetized, and it is clear we have now arrived at a crisis as great or greater than that faced by previous generations of political and social theorists. It is a challenge for all of us to craft our response to our crisis as they did to theirs in their time.

I believe that a university response that is critically open to originality in research, and is committed to humanistic values in teaching, has a great opportunity to make a European, even global, contribution of real substance; that such a university can be the hub of critical thought and promote its application through new models of connection between science, technology, administration and society. I believe Irish and British universities have a great opportunity to break this new ground.

Independent thought and scholarly engagement with our current circumstances are crucial. The fiction of rational markets needs, I humbly suggest, not only to be let go but replaced by a different kind of scholarship such as I have outlined.

Following Ernst Bloch, I believe that utopian alternatives must be accompanied by an actual practice that is realistic, and I suggest that it must be one that is applicable within institutions. I do not claim a space for abstract grand theory at the cost of middle-range theories or policies that have immediate relevance.

The concept of utopia has been recovered by writers like Ruth Levitas and others. And the insistence of Ernst Bloch that utopianism not only involves a rejection of what is, and a hope for an alternative, but also a strategy for its implementation, is central to the writing of the scholars in the Centre for Utopian Studies at the University of Limerick, to take just one example from my own country.

In recent times we have paid a heavy price for unfettered speculative accumulation, for light regulation, for the global consequences that followed the neutering of the Glass-Steagall Act in the US – an Act that had its origins in the great crash of 1929 and that sought to ensure it would never happen again by preventing commercial banks from engaging in speculative investments. The amendments to that Act released a flood of virtual financial products on the world. To that free-for-all many countries, including our own, added their own speculative property bubble.

The architects of these recent developments frequently invoked intellectuals willing to support them.

When I look back now at those subjects which I taught at NUIG and abroad – political science and sociology – subjects that emerged from the late-nineteenth-century work of Weber, Marx, Durkheim, Freud, Croce and others, I am struck by the urgency in the approach of such theorists to the social change of their times, and the effect that their writings had.

In response to the two world wars that followed the breakdown of Europe and the demand for new relations with a world it had previously dominated, Keynesian strategies emerged to address unemployment and poverty, and demanded that the importance of health and education be recognized.

The mid-twentieth century created a favourable atmosphere in which ideas of social capital emerged and in which social democracy mediated previously intractable class conflict. Those years also saw a public debate about the role of the state, the rights of the individual and social policy, and about the balance between these areas.

In succeeding decades political philosophy and social theory gave way to a narrower question of administrative analysis. The role of the state faded and applied studies of the state's actions held the field. A discourse based on solidarity, interdependency, shared vulnerability and community gave way to a discourse about lifestyle and individual consumption. The vision of a society of citizens gave way to a disaggregated mass of individual consumers.

I find Weber's nightmare of a rationality that in time would counter the original purposes of institutions, morphing into an irrational process, incapable of adjustment to change internally or externally, difficult to reject as an account of the modern period. As the Canadian philosopher Charles Taylor put it, we have been drifting towards unfreedom, and I suggest that for social cohesion there is nothing more irrational than unregulated markets.

Internationally, too, the context for universities has been changing. As parliaments were weakened at home, an ever more volatile global financial world has been emerging, unaccountable, at best amoral, in its demands and consequences.

New technology meant that speculative capital could move at tremendous speed in real time. At international level, while for a brief moment, around the birth of the United Nations, it seemed that international monetary and economic matters might be governed in an accountable way, such a moment quickly disappeared. Yet the need for such regulation remains, is urgent, and requires rearticulation.

For those of us who have had the privilege of being university teachers, the university is and will remain, I suggest, a space from which new futures have always emerged and must do so again. The ethos of independent scholarship is what delivers a previous generation's achievements into the present, and challenges that scholarship to renew itself.

I admire the singular dedication of individual researchers, the sacrifice they make, but I also value the importance of the teams that are necessary for co-operative achievements in the sciences. At the same time, I believe that the division between culture and the sciences is an unnecessary price that has been paid for a particular moment in the history of scholarship, a moment of hubris. It is time to recover the unity of scholarship. That, I suggest, might be our most valuable European contribution, one that will be valued by future generations.

As subjects are recast, unities can be restored, and we should consider Edward Said's suggestion that it is in the interstices between subjects that the most exciting intellectual work happens.

There is not, for example, any better future for economics as a subject and discipline than as political economy embedded within a system of culture. Would it not be an exciting initiative, I suggest with humility, for the LSE and an Irish university to establish an endowed Chair to explore the ways in which an ethico-cultural idea of Europe could be invoked to check the drift to unfreedom?

I suggest that the universities are crucial in the struggle for the recovery of the public world, for the emergence of truly democratic paradigms of policy and research. It is not merely a case of connecting the currency, the economy and the people; it is about recovering the right to pose important questions such as Immanuel Kant did in his time – what might we know, what should we do, what may we hope?

It is time to recover a proper consideration of the public world we share, the fragile planet for which we have responsibility, and lodge within it a concept of intergenerational justice. To achieve this, the state, civil society, communities and citizens are called to act in concert. These are issues and challenges that we, in Ireland, the United Kingdom and Europe all have in common. Happily, there has never been a better environment in which we might share our scholarship, our students and our concerns as we move together to acknowledge a new version of our interdependent lives.

We need to help forge a connection between the citizens of Europe and our shared European institutions, if the very idea of a democratic Europe is to survive. And we need to draw on debates within civil society to extend or deepen that democracy.

Those who would like a communitarian new beginning beyond our present institutions may have a powerful moral case, but I believe that to walk away from the state would be a tragic error on the part of those who seek an emancipatory transformation of our societies. Obviously, to rely entirely on advocacy directed at the state and to neglect the promise of alternatives within civil society would be a disastrous choice too. By their commitment to compassionate scholarship and teaching, public intellectuals can help bridge the space to that utopian impulse that we all need as vulnerable inhabitants of our fragile planet.

George Bernard Shaw would have encouraged us to save and reconstruct social democracy and to bring its refreshed promise to all the citizens of our shared Europe, a Europe committed to an ever-deepening democracy.

I wish the LSE the great future it deserves, built on the great founding principles to which we are all indebted, and to which George Bernard Shaw, as an Irishman moving between our two cultures, contributed so much – committed to justice and change, and recognizing, in his life and the work, no borders to intellect or moral purpose.

The Future of Work

The Edward Phelan Lecture 2015

I T IS A great honour to have been invited to deliver the second Edward Phelan lecture. I very much welcome this opportunity to pay homage to the achievements of Edward Joseph Phelan, a man who worked steadfastly to forge international labour standards that were grounded in a universalist vision of social justice; and who made his contribution through decades marked by war, a Great Depression and gross violations of human dignity.

It is essential that work, in all its facets as a shared human activity, be given a central place in the discussion on the values by which, we, as a community, wish to live. The question of 'good work' within the broader frame of 'the good life' is one of the defining issues of our times. Given Ireland's recent history, which has seen working conditions change dramatically in connection with wider European and global trends, it is most timely to reassess what is meant, today, by 'decent work'.

At the outset of this lecture, it is appropriate to recall Edward Phelan's role in building an international system of workers' rights. Edward Phelan – who was born in 1888 in Tramore, Co. Waterford – was a key figure in the small group of people who mapped out the basis for the International Labour Organization (ILO) during the Paris Peace Conference in 1919. As a staff member of the ILO for almost thirty years, and its fourth Director from 1941 to 1948, he was one of those inspirational and committed international public servants who, from the League of Nations period onwards, played a distinctive part in giving an ethical shape to world affairs.

The work of Edward Phelan also recalls a time when the discipline of political economy, for those of a progressive bent, was grounded in ethical reasoning and economic policy was geared to the objective of full employment. In 1931, for example, Phelan delivered one of the Harris Memorial Lectures at the University of Chicago, speaking with John Maynard Keynes on 'Unemployment as a World Problem'.[50]

As we are today again grappling with unacceptable levels of unemployment – ones that undermine social cohesion in Europe and beyond – it is worth reflecting on the significance of that impressive body of ideas and legal instruments bequeathed to us by a generation of men and women who were committed to promoting decent standards for human work.

Such reflection can valuably inform, I suggest, our understanding of the crucial issue currently facing labour – both organized and unorganized – namely that of the revival of labour rights after several decades of free market 'rule', or, more accurately, 'deregulation'. How can labour organize itself at national, European and world level, in a context where global financial capital is more speculative than productive? What form of work does contemporary global capitalism bring forth, allow and encourage? What form of internationalization can labour sustain in such a discouraging climate?

The passage from one form of internationalization to another – from that international normative framework built in the aftermath of the Second World War to the current institutional architecture organizing global trade – can be illustrated through the story of the official gift of the Irish government to the ILO: a huge mural entitled 'Irish Industrial

---

50   J. M. Keynes, K. Přibram and E. J. Phelan, *Unemployment as a World-Problem: Lectures of the Harris Foundation* (University of Chicago Press, 1931).

Development', commissioned from Seán Keating.[51] Gifted in 1961 by then Minister for Industry and Commerce Jack Lynch, Keating's work is hung opposite 'The Dignity of Labour', by the French artist Maurice Denis on the grand staircase of the William Rappard Centre.

The William Rappard Centre was built in the 1920s to house the ILO. It was the first building in Geneva designed to accommodate an organization of the League of Nations system, a 'Palace of Labour' adorned with many donations by trade unions and governments. When the ILO moved to Route des Morillons, in 1975, the General Agreement on Tariffs and Trade (GATT) secretariat moved in. The heads of the international trade body were not pleased with the atmosphere of the William Rappard Centre, so the works of art dedicated to the glory of work and the productive economy were concealed behind wooden screens and forgotten for a while.

It was not until recently, after the World Trade Organization (WTO), which succeeded the GATT, was authorized to expand within its current complex, that it was decided to uncover the two murals. But this gesture did not mark the reconciliation of global trade with 'the spirit of Philadelphia' – that emancipatory conception of labour which animated Edward Phelan and his colleagues. The alternative dogma spelt out in the first paragraph of the 1994 Marrakech Agreement, which established the WTO, defines competitiveness as the ultimate purpose of economic activity, and growth in output and trade as an end in itself: international relations in the field of trade should be conducted, this paragraph states, with a view to ensuring 'a large and steadily growing volume of real

---

51   Seán Keating's mural has a 'pre-history': in 1926, Harry Clarke had been commissioned to craft a stained-glass window to be gifted by the new Irish Free State to the ILO. The magnificent, so-called 'Geneva Window' was completed in 1930 but never made it to Geneva, because of the concern expressed by Irish officials at the 'subject matter of certain of the representations' (i.e. uncovered women and drunkards). The windows thus remained in Clarke's workshop after his death in a sanatorium in Davos in 1931, and were eventually bought to be displayed in the Wolfsonian Museum, Miami. It was not until 1957 that the idea of an official gift resurfaced in discussions between the Irish Government and the ILO, then represented by Michael O'Callaghan.

income and effective demand, and expanding the production of and trade in goods and services'.

These words are in stark contrast to the seminal Declaration of Philadelphia, adopted by the ILO in 1944 under the guidance of its then Director-General Edward Phelan, whose first paragraph affirms, in succinct and compelling wording:

'Labour is not a commodity'. (Declaration of Philadelphia, 1a)

Grounded in a philosophy of human emancipation, and seeing economic and financial policy as means of attaining social objectives, the Declaration states, in its second paragraph:

'All human beings, irrespective of race, creed or sex, have the right to pursue both their material well-being and their spiritual development in conditions of freedom and dignity, of economic security and equal opportunity'. (DP, 2a)

And then:

'All national and international policies and measures, in particular those of an economic and financial character, should be judged in this light and accepted only in so far as they may be held to promote and not to hinder the achievement of this fundamental objective'. (DP, 2c)

This hierarchy of purpose affirmed by the Declaration of 1944, whereby economic tools and measures are designed to serve the 'fundamental objective' of human development, not only guided the subsequent expansion of the ILO; it also inspired the early work of the United Nations in the social and economic fields.

We must ask ourselves why – and with what consequences – this order of priority has been overturned in the last three decades by what the legal scholar Alain Supiot, in his book *The Spirit of Philadelphia*,[52] described as 'the neoliberal utopia of the Total Market'.[53] More precisely, we must address the consequences this has had for the security of work for the mass of our citizens.

If it is the case that social justice, human freedom and dignity have been dropped from the list of political objectives, how might citizens respond to their new status as mere consumers within a socially unaccountable version of the economy? Are people a means to an end, and no longer the ultimate beneficiaries of economic activity?

Let me state very clearly that my questions are not aimed at disputing the market in itself, a social institution which long pre-dates contemporary capitalism. Rather, I am seeking to address the assumptions associated with a brand of economics that recasts the market as a general principle for regulating every aspect of the economy, treating labour, land and money as if they were pure commodities. Alain Supiot refers to Friedrich von Hayek's assertion that institutions based on the principle of solidarity derive from 'an atavistic call of distributive justice' that is doomed to wreck the 'spontaneous order' of the market.

The recent economic crisis has shown, on the contrary, that markets do require an institutional framework within which transactions between economic agents can be conducted, under the auspices of a third party that guarantees their fairness over the long term. Without such overarching regulatory authority, contractual relationships run the risk of becoming the expression of the will of those who are strongest and control the most resources.

---

52 A. Supiot, *The Spirit of Philadelphia: Social Justice vs. the Total Market* (Verso Books, 2012; French edn 2010).

53 The *International Labour Review* is the journal of the ILO. Cf. A. Supiot, 'A Legal Perspective on the Economic Crisis of 2008', *International Labour Review*, Vol. 149, No. 2 (2010).

My critique is directed at the fiction of the 'self-regulating market', an ideology which has underpinned the systematic deregulation of national systems of labour.

In what can be described as a form of regulatory Darwinism, democratically elected governments, and politics in general, have been portrayed as impeding the natural order of the market. As a consequence, the institutional foundations of markets have been gravely undermined, with legal systems themselves now being seen as just another product competing on the global market.

Indeed in the utopia of 'Total Market', not only services and goods, but also people can be mobilized in the cause of globalized competition: workers and the relationships they establish with their environment are reduced to tradable units of labour that 'can all be "liquidated" in the legal sense of this term'.[54] Supiot uses the term 'Total' in the sense given to that adjective by Ernst Jünger in the aftermath of the First World War, a crucial historical juncture in this conversion of people into usable energy fuelling the monotonous functioning of a war machine.

Jünger's chilling descriptions of work in *Der Arbeiter* (The Worker)[55] have uncanny resonance with some of the conceptions of labour that are prevalent today. I quote from *Der Arbeiter*:

> Our situation is peculiar in that our every movement is governed by pressure to set a record, while the minimum standard of performance we are required to meet is constantly broadening the scope of its expectations. This completely precludes the possibility that any sphere of life might ever stabilise on the basis of some secure and undisputed order. The resulting way of life is more like a deadly

---

54   Ibid., p. 153. Liquidation consists in making something fungible by converting it into cash.

55   E. Jünger, *Der Arbeiter, Herrschaft und Gestalt* (Klett-Cotta, 1932).

race in which all of one's energy is stretched to the limit lest one should fall by the wayside.

The emphasis on performance and output, the commodification of labour at the expense of a holistic conception of the worker's dignity, security and accomplishment, are all too familiar. Labour law has conceded much in the name of so-called 'economic realism' and a concept of 'flexicurity' which has yielded a great deal more flexibility than security.

The effects of the casualization of labour on the quality of work and on the morale of workers are of comparable importance to endemic unemployment in accounting for our fellow citizens' pervasive sense of alienation. We cannot be content with this state of affairs. The fact that this is the first systemic crisis without a compelling progressive vision on offer as a response should act as a wake-up call for all of us.

I would like to focus in particular on the fate of large swathes of the active population of European countries who find themselves trapped in chronic job insecurity. The term 'precariat'[56] is sometimes used to describe this new 'class' that has emerged from the most recent period of globalization. Unlike the proletariat – the industrial working class on which social democracy was built – the precariat is defined by partial involvement in labour combined with a growing array of unremunerated activities – often internships of various sorts – that are required to get access to remunerated jobs.

In his book *The Precariat: The New Dangerous Class*,[57] Guy Standing, of the University of London, defines the precariat as consisting of:

> a multitude of insecure people, living bits-and-pieces lives, in and out of short-term jobs, without a narrative of occupational development, including millions of frustrated educated youth... millions

---

56   From the contraction between 'precarious' and 'proletariat'.
57   G. Standing, *The Precariat: The New Dangerous Class* (Bloomsbury, 2014).

of women abused in oppressive labour... and migrants in their hundreds of millions around the world. They are denizens; they have
a more restricted range of social, cultural, political and economic
rights than citizens around them.

The rise of the precariat has been accelerated by the recent financial crisis, which ended an era during which Western workers' living standards were propped up by access to cheap credit and, in the Irish case, reliance on property inflation.

The turning point is to be located, perhaps, in the mid-1970s, those years when the GATT moved into the ILO's historic headquarters in Geneva, and when the financialization of the global economy really took off. Forty years later, economic inequalities have increased exponentially, splitting the world into 'a plutonomy and a precariat', to paraphrase the title of one of Noam Chomsky's articles on the subject.[58]

The shift towards precarious employment is not confined to low-skilled jobs. A case in point is what is happening in universities everywhere in Europe. In a recent piece entitled 'The Casualisation of Labour in Third Level Institutions', Micheal Flynn described[59] how in Ireland a considerable volume of teaching and research work is carried out by 'temporary lecturers', 'adjunct lecturers', and so-called 'teaching assistants' who have no job security at all and must repeatedly resume their elusive and exhausting hunt for the next short-term contract. As Flynn puts it: 'More academics now understand that researching the working poor does

---

58   Noam Chomsky, 2012, 'Plutonomy and the Precariat'. The term 'plutonomy' is taken
     from a brochure for investors published by Citigroup in 2005 entitled 'Plutonomy:
     Buying Luxury, Explaining Global Imbalances'. The concept was elaborated by a team
     of Citigroup analysts who argued that the share of the very wealthy in the national
     income of rich countries had become so large that the trends in these economies and
     their relation with other economies could not be understood any more with reference
     to the average consumer.
59   M. Flynn, 'The Casualisation of Labour in Third Level Institutions', *Irish Left Review*,
     12 September 2014.

not necessarily require field trips – that sometimes a glance towards the cluttered desks surrounding their own offices is sufficient.'

These questions were discussed last December during a seminar on the theme of 'Ethics in Higher Education' convened by UCD, the University of Limerick and UNITE, with the support of the President of Ireland's Ethics Initiative. The Irish Government has recently appointed a team from the University of Limerick to investigate the use of so-called 'zero-hour contracts', under which employees must make themselves available for work even though they do not have guaranteed hours of work.

In an article published in the *Irish Times*, Paul Sweeney, Chairman of the TASC's economists' network, showed that half of all of those in work in Ireland earn an annual salary of less than €28,500, while the top 1 per cent of income earners averaged €373,300.

If we are to learn from history, it is useful to remember that every progressive movement has been built on the needs and aspirations of the emerging 'class' of the day. Responding to the fears and the aspirations of those citizens among us who do not enjoy security of employment is a defining challenge for our times. It is a task not just for those who claim to represent the most vulnerable in society, but for all democrats, for trade unionists in all sectors, for workers' representatives on permanent contracts, and for tenured staff in our universities.

If no genuine alternative is articulated and translated into realistic policy options, populist politicians and religious preachers alike will find it easy to exploit the fears and insecurities of precarious workers.

This issue lies at the heart of the crisis of European democracy. We cannot afford to let social cohesion unravel under the combined effects of the dual movement I have described, the commodification of labour and the depoliticization of economic policy.

Karl Polanyi, the great Austrian historian and economist, warned in his time, the 1930s and 1940s, against the devastating consequences of both these trends. Arguing that labour, land and money are not mere commodities, Polanyi interpreted the insertion of these 'fictitious commodities' into the market in early-nineteenth-century England as a 'means to subordinate the substance of society itself to the laws of the market'. This, he believed, resulted in a counter-move by society to protect itself and reclaim social control of the economy, whether in benign form, as in the case of the American New Deal, or in the most destructive guise of Nazism and fascism.

In *The Great Transformation*, first published in 1944, Polanyi analysed the emergence of fascism in the 1930s as a perverted and opportunistic twisting of the social impulse to control the chaos of the self-regulating market. As he put it, commenting on the misguided attempts at restoring the gold standard after the First World War:

> the stubbornness with which economic liberals, for a critical decade, had, in the service of deflationary policies, supported authoritarian interventionism, merely resulted in a decisive weakening of the democratic forces which might otherwise have averted the fascist catastrophe. Great Britain and the United States – masters not servants of the currency – went off gold in time to escape this peril.[60]

Although the current chaos of the world economy may not be similar to that of the inter-war period, the lessons taught by Polanyi should not be lost for our generation. Distinguishing between populist manipulation of the masses and genuine empowerment of the citizenry through democratic debates on economic issues, it is important to affirm forcefully that no single economic paradigm can ever be adequate to address the complexity of our world's varying contingencies. Decisions in the economic and financial fields should always remain amenable to political debate; they should not be abandoned to rigid fiscal rules, even less so

---

60   K. Polanyi, *The Great Transformation* (Farrar & Rinehart, 1944).

as economists disagree over the theoretical soundness of such rules. We need to foster widespread economic literacy, supported by a pluralist scholarship and accountable policy options in a deliberative democracy.

There are some fundamental questions that we must face as honestly as possible: What if the moment for 'deliberative democracy', as advocated by Jürgen Habermas and others, is fading? What are the consequences of there being almost no space for discussing the ideological assumptions that lurk behind policy options?

As surely as modern democracy needed literacy in order to be established, today economic literacy is essential if we are to see through the illusions at play in the worlds of work, consumption, production and speculation.

It is therefore urgent for our elected representatives, trade union leaders and workers' representatives to claim back full competence and legitimacy on economic, fiscal and labour matters. Only through a comprehensive strategy enabling the mass of precarious workers to gain control over their professional lives, acquire social and economic security and a fairer share of the vital assets of our twenty-first-century society will populism and fundamentalism of all sorts be defeated.

The time has come to endorse the emancipatory promise of an economy interwoven with ethics, ecology and politics, so as to restore the order of ends and means between human needs and economic policies. The time has come, in other words, to revive 'the spirit of Philadelphia'.

As we work to end human subordination to a dubious notion of economic efficiency and to foster a rights-based approach to labour, we can with great benefit draw on the recent recommendations of the Commission for Human Rights of the Council of Europe. We can build, too, on the principles of the ILO's current Decent Work Agenda, which takes up many of the challenges the Organization faced at its inception.

This concept of 'decent work' is based on an understanding of work as a source of personal dignity and freedom, family stability, prosperity in the community and democratic participation. It also brings home to us a fundamental principle – one that is highly relevant to our historical moment: 'the conviction that social justice is essential to universal peace' (ILO Constitution).[61]

There are many encouraging signs that the fiction of the self-regulating market is breaking down. The recent global financial meltdown has made it plain that it is not sustainable to pretend that labour, land and money are unconnected to workers, the natural environment and the real economy.

Another telling illustration of the fact that the previous consensus around economic policy is unravelling is provided by the title of the World Bank's annual report, *Doing Business*, which this year bears the title: 'Going Beyond Efficiency'. In his foreword, the bank's new Senior Vice-President and Chief Economist, Kaushik Basu, goes so far as to write: 'Fortunately, market fundamentalism has, for the most part, been relegated to the margins of serious policy discourse… Economic efficiency is not the only measure by which we evaluate an economy's performance.'

It is important to recognize, however, that even though their flawed theoretical assumptions are exposed, some of the previous policy prescriptions endure, having taken on a life of their own in institutional thinking, within which trade unions can be trapped or ensnared.

Let us, nevertheless, rejoice in the small signs of hope that a new era is opening up for human work. It is essential that the ILO plays a leading role in shaping this new era. Ireland faces a historical opportunity to address these issues more actively as in 2017 our country will, for the first time, take up a 'titulaire' seat on the ILO's Governing Body.

It is my hope that all of us, in Ireland and in the ILO, will seize upon these possibilities and that we will craft, together, a new discourse on labour. I hope that today's event can be a spark to ignite this urgent debate on the future of work.

---

61   Principle embedded in the ILO's Constitution and reiterated in the Organization's 1998 Declaration on Fundamental Principles and Rights at Work.

An Adequate Economic Discourse for
the Europe of our Grandchildren

Some Thoughts on R. and E. Skidelsky's Book
How Much is Enough?'

THE INSTITUTE OF INTERNATIONAL AND
EUROPEAN AFFAIRS, DUBLIN

15 OCTOBER 2014

I WOULD LIKE TO welcome Robert and Edward Skidelsky to Dublin, and to thank them for agreeing to discuss the ideas in their thought-provoking book *How Much is Enough? Money and the Good Life* [62] from the perspective of the European project.

For those of you here who have not read the book, it might be useful to introduce very succinctly its core argument. Its starting point is a lecture entitled 'The Economic Possibilities for our Grandchildren' delivered by John Maynard Keynes in 1928 and published as an essay in 1930. Keynes argued that by the year 2030, the economies of developed countries would have 'lifted mankind to a state of sufficiency' whereby their people would be five to eight times better off and, therefore, would not have to work more than about fifteen hours a week. Keynes was right on the former prediction – growth of real income per capita in

---

62 Robert and Edward Skidelsky, *How Much is Enough? Money and the Good Life* (Penguin Books, 2013; first published by Allen Lane, 2012).

industrialized Western countries has been in line with his forecast – but he was proved wrong on the latter. According to Robert and Edward Skidelsky, Keynes's expectation that future generations would work only enough to live 'wisely, agreeably, and well' – that is, to enjoy what the Skidelskys call 'the good life' – was based on a confusion between 'wants' and 'needs'. They argue that in a capitalist economy, there is a satiability of basic needs but an insatiability of wants: 'capitalism, especially in its modern "turbo" form, has released the expression of insatiability from its previous restraints',[63] so that the demand for free time has not increased proportionately with income, but well-off people instead tend to work much more than they 'need' to in order to satisfy their reasonable needs.

How Much is Enough? offers a concept of 'the good life' that might fetter such insatiable wants. In Robert and Edward Skidelsky's view, the problem has two dimensions. The first is intellectual: we must, they contend, recover a sense of what money is *for* rather than pursue it as if it were an end in itself. Money is desirable insofar as it allows one to lead 'the good life', which is made up of seven basic constituents: health, security, respect, personality, harmony with nature, friendship and leisure.

The second dimension is political. We need to organize our collective existence to enable people to live the good life. The Skidelskys thus refute the notion that our visions of the good are essentially subjective, a mere matter of individual preferences, and they see the state not as a neutral arbiter, but as an ethically engaged party.

One might, and indeed many of us will, take a different view of the account of the good life put forward in the book. We are also likely to have diverging takes on the relative roles of the individual, the market and the state in delivering the adequate conditions for this good life.

Of greater relevance to my introductory remarks this afternoon is the fact that, as a conversation between a political economist and a

---

63 Ibid., p. xi.

philosopher – and a dialogue between a father and a son – *How Much is Enough?* offers a stimulating starting point for any discussion of the great challenges that face contemporary Europe.

Indeed the reading of Keynes proposed by Robert and Edward Skidelsky reminds us of a time when Western political economy was grounded in philosophical and ethical thought, and economic policy was framed primarily in relation to social objectives – in particular, in Keynes's case, the objective of full employment.

I was struck by the sense of fragmentation that characterizes the way we now talk about the future of our European Union. Many of the issues addressed by our distinguished visitors reveal this problem with language itself. There is in fact a problem with every one of these three words – 'our European Union'. The words 'our' and 'Union' have become difficult to grasp when distinctions between the strong and the weak, between debtor and creditor members, between Northern and Mediterranean economies, trip so easily off the tongue. And the word 'European' prompts questions as to whether we are speaking of the Eurozone, the wider Union or the European geographical space with its proximity to so many conflicts, some of which have been exacerbated by the absence of any common position that might have helped reduce panic and fear.

The European project, we must remember, was a promise that sprang from a desire for an alternative to conflicts that began more than 100 years ago in the ambitions of imperial powers. The European Community was a pragmatic attempt at co-operation, and in its best expression it was an invitation to the peoples of Europe to weave a tapestry of varying colours, textures and images that might have made the Europe of the twenty-first century a Union of peace, prosperity and solidarity.

Europe has had its visionaries. Jacques Delors, whose portrait occupies a place of honour on the walls of this Institute, was among them. He spoke of a 'Europe of the Citizens' and we must reflect on what happened to that vision. Have we lost it? Is the disconnect between the shards of our broken vision revealing a deeper malaise at the centre of our intellectual and moral lives? Is citizenship still attainable in a form that might be shared in a Europe that once valued its diverse cultures? The 'Europe of the Citizens', if it is to be achieved, requires more than a revision of thinking by those who are privileged to be given the space for intellectual work. The new thinking has to be informed by the experience of an empowered citizenry who have been given the scope, not just to exist within the economy, but to decide on what, for them, is a sufficient, secure, fulfilling and ethical life. If they are to have that opportunity, then ensuring the basic household's capacity to participate in society, with all the implications for housing, health and education, must be the vital issue.

The idea of a Social Europe is a project that held together the aspirations of so many potential citizens – but much has changed. The founders' hopes were crafted before the pressure for a minimal state held sway; before the endless pressure towards the commodification of existence itself, as Zygmunt Bauman put it; and certainly before the current form of globalization defined by high-speed financial transactions rather than trade between real economies. It was also before a Nobel Prize winner in economics could declare open war on welfare economics and theories of distribution, as Thomas Robert Lucas, a distinguished macro-economist, stated in 2004: 'Of the tendencies that are harmful to sound economics, the most seductive and, in my opinion, the most poisonous, is to focus on questions of distribution.'

It is my conviction that the cutting-off of mainstream economic theory from ethical reasoning undermines our capacity to address the 'crisis of legitimation' which has been facing the European Union for several decades now. Citizens do not feel represented by, and do not trust, the European institutions or even their national parliaments. Responding to this 'democratic deficit', as it is sometimes called, is made all the more pressing by the destructive forces unleashed by the financial meltdown of 2008 and the vulnerabilities it exposed in the Eurozone.

The consequences of recent events have been succinctly stated by Jürgen Habermas in his reply to a question in an interview that was published as the final chapter of his *Europe: The Faltering Project*.

> What worries me most is the scandalous social injustice that the most vulnerable social groups will have to bear the brunt of the socialised costs for the market failure. The mass of those who, in any case, are not among the winners of globalisation now have to pick up the tab for the impacts of predictable dysfunction of the financial system on the real economy! Unlike the shareholders, they will not pay in money values but in the hard currency of their daily existence. Viewed in global terms, this avenging fate is also afflicting the economically weakest countries. That is the political scandal. Yet pointing the finger at scapegoats strikes me as hypocritical. The speculators, too, were acting consistently within the established legal framework, according to the socially recognised logic of profit maximisation. Politics turns itself into a laughing stock when it resorts to moralising instead of relying on the enforceable law of the democratic legislator. Politics, and not capitalism, is responsible for promoting the common good.[64]

Of course, the reasons for the European democratic deficit run much deeper than the recent crisis. The EU is a highly unconventional political object, characterized by shared sovereignty, intricate political negotiations and decision-making procedures that involve twenty-eight different polities. This makes the task of articulating a European common good in which a majority of European citizens can believe particularly challenging.

More fundamentally, the very notion of a common good is one which

---

64 Jürgen Habermas, 'Lessons of the Financial Crisis', in *Europe: The Faltering Project* (Polity Press, 2009), p. 184.

modernity has rendered problematic: to some extent, the crisis currently facing the EU has to do with a much broader crisis of politics and democratic representation, which has seen hierarchies of values about the good life fading out of liberal public discourse in favour of highly individualized conceptions of the good.

This was very well captured by Max Weber over a century ago when he described the modern condition as resulting in two closely interrelated developments: the process of 'rationalization', of ever greater knowledge specialization and technical mastery which, in late modernity, peaks in an 'iron cage' of bureaucratic routine; and the process of 'disenchantment', ending with the individual's abandonment to a radical 'polytheism' of conflicting values, none of which can claim rational superiority.

Such a process is intensified by the dynamics of today's global capitalism, which encourages social atomization. Yet, however bold and demanding the exercise may be, it is of the utmost importance that we think about the ways in which moral-ethical enquiry can contribute both to the public economic discourse and to the deepening of democratic practice in Europe. As Jacques Delors once put it: 'Rekindle the ideal, breathe life and soul into it, that is the essential imperative if we intend to give shape to the Europe that we so dearly wish for.'

This should not be seen as an exercise aimed at selling a new opium to the masses. Europeans can draw on a great tradition of scholarship; they can draw on and remember a model of society based on a balance between the state and the market, between the individual and society, and a post-war history of international relations based on negotiation and the recognition of interdependency rather than forceful intervention. Indeed the 'European model' is often identified by envious outsiders not just as an 'economic model', but as a way of life. And we must be careful that the current policy of 'firefighting' – however essential the securing of the Eurozone's financial stability may be – does not end up in a social race to the bottom.

One of the questions raised by *How Much is Enough?* is precisely that:

What is growth for? Has growth become an end rather that a means? Growth remains central to the Skidelskys' analysis, but they elevate the debate by encouraging us to define the kind of growth that is best able to deliver the basics necessary for the good life – growth that is socially useful and ethically justifiable.

Public policy needs to make more ample use of those indicators which, perhaps more adequately than crude notions of GDP, are designed to measure social well-being. My own suggestion is that in seeking new indicators for the welfare of their citizens, member states of the European Union might well assess the vulnerability of their economies to predatory asset-stripping by speculative funds.

As we consider the social aims and ethical grounds of European economic policy, I believe that a focus on the future of work must be central to our discussions. It is another great merit of *How Much is Enough?* that it places work at the heart of the argument.

Indeed the question of 'good work' remains one of the defining issues of our times: are workers to be seen as isolated units of labour, or can work be conceived of as a wholesome activity within a social context? Can the life of a worker be reduced to a labour cost whose fluctuations are ever more defined by casualization? How do conditions of work in contemporary capitalism impact on demand in the wider economy? What should the respective roles of the state and the market be in regulating working hours? What is the social impact of arrangements that encourage employers to hire fewer people working longer hours?

All these questions are complex, and whatever the answers to them may be, I believe that the Skidelskys make an important claim in placing work in the wider frame of 'the good life'. Indeed, can a worker hope to lead a flourishing life to whom, as the philosopher Simone Weil put it, 'no good is proposed as the object of his labour except mere existence'?

At our best in Europe we have seen how a healthy balance between competition and cohesion, an economic policy serving agreed social aims as an instrument of popular will, can achieve prosperity and harmony. Such necessary balance between economic competitiveness and social cohesion is present in Jacques Delors's famous triptych: 'Competition that stimulates; co-operation that strengthens; and solidarity that unites.'

We should never forget that the single market and cohesion policy were instigated almost simultaneously and were designed to relaunch European integration in the mid-1980s. The creation of the cohesion policy was presented by Delors as a vital counterpart to the 'four freedoms'. This was underpinned by Delors's philosophical interest in social catholicism and the personalist movement, for whom people are not atomized individuals – abstract and easily transferable units of labour – but 'persons' engaged in active relationships with others, and situated in actual social and territorial communities.

Today this 'cohesion pact', which for several decades has been one of the foundations of the *affectio societatis* between European citizens, is under threat, partly because the current crisis has called into question the principle of solidarity between the various regions of the EU.

European integration is now a fragile project, torn between the requirements of fiscal adjustment and increasing social discontent. We must all be concerned by the widening gap, described by Paul Gillespie in a recent paper, between deeper financial, regulatory and economic integration on the one hand, and the social solidarity required to give these policies popular legitimacy on the other.

I personally believe that the privileging of expertise and technocracy over democratic debate is a perilous one for the future of European democracy. There is nothing wrong with technical efficiency. The danger arises from a conception of economic policy governed by the narrowest instrumental criteria of 'efficiency' and 'success', which are immune to moral-normative considerations.

We need to locate the role of expertise within an accountable system where its function is to clarify choice, not serve as a substitute for the collective deliberation of citizens who are dismissively assumed to be economically illiterate. To achieve this, one possible option might be to devise a policy frame grounded in pluralist scholarship, rather than drawing too heavily on a narrow version of economics that has severed its ties with its ethical and philosophical sources, except for those deriving from the utilitarian tradition.

The portrayal of ethics as 'soft' in contrast to the 'hard science' of economics is a form of intellectual trivialization. Indeed the invitation to view the world as made up of rational, calculating utility maximizers has inflicted deep injuries on our moral imaginations, on our relations with others and on our natural environment. And the recent economic and financial upheavals have thrown a glaring light on the shortcomings of the intellectual tools provided by mainstream economics and its key assumptions about the sustainability of self-regulating markets.

Responding to this intellectual failure requires more than an adjustment of the forecasting tools used by most economists, or a tightening of banking supervision. It requires, I suggest, the member states of the European Union to address their citizens' concerns on unemployment and growing inequality. This is both urgent and important.

I believe that an appeal to make a fresh start in the crafting of our shared European space could have a unifying force. We will inevitably have to discuss, in the coming decades, not just integration in its fullest sense, but also such issues as the nature of work itself. Let me quote Simone Weil again, from *Gravity and Grace* (published 1947):

> Man's greatness is always to re-create his life, to re-create what is given to him... Through work he produces his own natural exis-tence. Through science he re-creates the universe by means of symbols. Through art he re-creates the alliance between his body and his soul. It is to be noticed that each of these three things is something poor, empty and vain taken by itself and not in relation

to the others. Union of the three: a working people's culture (that
will not be just yet)...

Those words were written seventy years ago; now we must take our responsibilities. We must do our work in our different ways – in intellectual,
manual and artistic work; in politics and science. *How Much is Enough?*
makes a significant contribution to a renewed economic discourse for
Europe, one that does not lose sight of ethical ends.

On such grounds, we can start a fresh discussion about the kind of
prosperity we wish to bequeath to future generations of Europeans, so that
they may indeed live up to the hopes Keynes had for his 'grandchildren'.

Drawing Water from the Same Well

<hr />

The Central Importance of UNESCO in Building Peace through Recognition of the Power of Culture

UNESCO, PARIS

19 FEBRUARY 2013

R AN GCÉAD dul síos is mían liom mo theanga fein a úsáid, agus mé á rá go bhfuil an áthas orm bheith anseo inniú le mo bhean chéile, Sabina.

It is a very great pleasure and honour for me to be here today at UNESCO. The language I have just spoken is one of the oldest in the world, a language which almost went out of existence but was saved by, among others, a man who later became the first President of Ireland, Dubhghlas de hÍde. The Irish language itself is used every day in my office.

It is a pleasure for me to be at UNESCO. The importance of UNESCO was recognized from the earliest days of the United Nations. People sometimes tend to forget that Eleanor Roosevelt chose UNESCO to consult with organizations, nations and peoples on the drafting of the Universal Declaration of Human Rights.

I am so pleased to be here because UNESCO matters. It matters if we are to shape a world that will not only deliver peace, but the fruits of peace and all of the products of the imagination in our shared future.

This is the first time that a President of Ireland has come to UNESCO, and it is my dearest wish that my visit marks a new and positive departure in my country's relationship, and the people of Ireland's relationship, with your Organization. I am also conscious that I am coming at a time when Ireland holds, for the seventh time, the Presidency of the Council of the European Union. And I hope also that my visit signifies a commitment to placing culture at the heart of the debates about the future of the Union.

UNESCO has always been an important part of the United Nations project. It is probably more important now, at the time of an economic crisis rooted in a radical move away from production and the real economy into the realms of speculation on virtual financial products – an economic model that has delivered so much disaster in so many different parts of our world.

The mandate of UNESCO may have been at times perceived by some to be idealistic. At the time of Eleanor Roosevelt's initiative, there was a sense that after the horrors of the war a moral nadir had been reached, as well as a sense of urgency, almost of a desperate anxiety to ensure peace. The sentence 'wars begin in the minds of men, it is in the minds of men peace must be created' reflects this anxiety.

But I think it is important for us to remember that there is no necessary clash between idealism and pragmatism, between interests and moral principles. We all have an interest in living in peace, prosperity, security, respect and dignity. And while we may differ on the sources of such moral principles, as to whether they are derived from an enlightenment in one continent, in one period, or whether they are divinely revealed to us, this should not deflect us from the task of securing the universal acceptance of such interests as rights.

I want to congratulate you, Director-General, on the spirit and the vision that are contained in the speech that you delivered in Milan in 2010 when you spoke of a new 'Humanism for the twenty-first century'. And I want to applaud your recent visit to Mali; for your solidarity and the solidarity of UNESCO with the people of Mali who have suffered so much, and who are so much at risk from extremism. Like you, I am shocked by the deliberate targeting of culture as a weapon of war, for example the destruction of libraries, monuments and mausoleums in the historic city of Timbuktu. The attack on the culture of Mali is of course primarily an attack on the people of Mali and the generations yet to be born in that region. However, we must remember that an attack on the culture of one of our members, in a UNESCO of 195 members and associate members, is an attack on the culture of us all, who share the culture of humanity.

UNESCO's most fundamental task is the disarmament of the mind of war and aggression. As I paraphrase the preamble to your Constitution I also want to suggest that a peace based exclusively upon political and economic arrangements could not secure the unanimous, lasting and sincere support of the peoples of the world. True peace requires a form of consciousness that not only eschews all forms of violence but also envisages the rich fruits of peaceful life together in all its utopian diversity.

Madame la Directrice générale, you quoted a line from my poem 'Of Memory': I should tell you that I wrote that poem in honour of the French philosopher Paul Ricoeur, and when I did so I was acknowledging his enormous contribution to the politics and ethics of memory.

We must be able to place the narratives of our origins and our history side by side with respect for others. And as Paul Ricoeur wrote, we should try to achieve such an amnesty in our view of past conflicts that it does not disable us from living with a sense of humanity in the present and, most important of all, prevent us from imagining the futures that we can share together. That kind of thinking is embodied in the phrase I see written on the wall of UNESCO that invokes 'the memory of the world'.

The memory of the world – yes, there are various versions of it, but it is important that it does not become a place of arid contestation but rather one in which an ethical exchange of narratives can enable and emancipate our common future.

It is very important that our ethical aspirations be adequately communicated and I congratulate UNESCO on its great publications. I think, for example, of *Many Voices, One World*, a report published in 1980 which caused such conflict in its day because of the simple suggestion that in our world, a voice in any part of the most remote areas was as important as any in the more developed world if you wished to acknowledge the dignity of the human person. One world, many voices, many stories: that was the message of this powerful UNESCO publication. I was proud to participate as a contributor to *In from the Margins*, which was a regional contribution through the Council of Europe to *Our Creative Diversity*. This was UNESCO's attempt to explore how culture can be used to form the mind of peace.

We need to use all of our intellectual resources if we are to build the mind of peace through culture. For example, it is striking that the discipline of anthropology was not consulted in the drafting process of the Universal Declaration on Human Rights.

But we need now to include all of the different intellectual instruments that we have, and take steps on the path towards new models of economy embedded in culture, to put human rights at the heart of development, and to think of human rights themselves in such a way that the discourse of reason and of different faith systems can live together on the common assumption that their protections of the human body and of the person must never be relinquished.

Real peace must be founded upon 'the intellectual and moral solidarity of humankind', as the founding texts of UNESCO state. And it is to the achievement of that peace that UNESCO has devoted itself, with some success, over the past sixty-seven years.

In making this contribution today I recognize with humility the great minds who have contributed in the past, and continue to guide UNESCO's discourse and ideas: Albert Einstein, Leon Blum, Rigoberta Menchú,[65]

---

65   1992 Nobel Peace Prize winner and UNESCO goodwill ambassador Ms Menchú is a Guatemalan national who has campaigned for the rights of indigenous peoples.

Nelson Mandela, Kuniyoshi Obara,[66] Sarvepalli Radhakrishnan, to mention but a few. And I think that while their influence has been of immense value, it must be turned into something more than a moral or theoretical influence. The words must be driven into policies. The need for policy reform must be brought home to the member countries and the words must turn into actions.

I am especially aware that the Chilean poet Pablo Neruda, whose work I have so often quoted, and whose home in Isla Negra I recently visited, spent some of his last days here at UNESCO as Ambassador of Chile in 1972, and in those late writings of his passionately reminded us all of our obligations to the people of the world as human beings.

At the end of last year, the President of the Republic of Peru was here to discuss the great World Heritage project of the Qapaq Nan, the main historical Andean route between the peoples of that region, which is now being rediscovered and re-explored.

I was delighted to read that Argentina, Bolivia, Chile, Colombia, Ecuador and Peru are working together to present this initiative to the World Heritage Committee for Qapaq Nan. What a splendid act of cultural co-operation this is. It illustrates the power of shared cultural legacy in contributing to building and re-enforcing peace between nations, and it is UNESCO that is providing the opportunity for this. Recently in South America I described all of these countries which are experiencing change as symbolically being rather like the pilgrims in *The Canterbury Tales*. They are all on pilgrimage, but each has a different story. Sometimes it is change led by movements in civil society, sometimes by workers in unions, with an overwhelming number of women involved; sometimes it is about the rights of indigenous peooples. But they all share one view – the awareness that their continent is moving and changing from the base – and this is such an extraordinary development, let us all recognize,

---

66 Japanese educationalist and first President of the UNESCO World Education Fellowship.

in countries that not long ago were dominated by military regimes that trampled on human rights.

The World Heritage Programme of UNESCO is one of its great visible achievements. But there are many more UNESCO achievements that have been feeding unknowingly into our daily lives – from the way we approach education and science to how we recognize, protect and celebrate the cultural diversity of humankind.

We in Ireland were very pleased that Dublin was designated UNESCO City of Literature in 2011. I thank you for your references to James Joyce and Samuel Beckett, and indeed I should say that we have added the architect and designer Eileen Gray as our third great modernist, whose exhibition is on in Paris at the present.

The work of these three artists tells us something about the exilic mind: it is work that emerges from the experience of migrants – people who have left the comfort of the familiar and the sedentary, who have renounced the security of property and have gone on to use their creativity in the pursuit of freedom. In the case of Joyce, the work breaks open an art form and rethinks its possibilities; in the case of Beckett it poses radical doubts about the adequacy of words themselves, and addresses our humanity, reduced to the point, but also celebrated at the point, where words are insufficient; and in the case of Eileen Gray it involves continually moving on, migrating from one form of invention to another through materials and design and shapes.

That is the story of the modern world. We must build into our knowledge, incomplete as it is, the morality that comes from the transience of the mind, the experience of the migrant, and the careful reflections of those who have used exile as the prism through which to look at their own pasts, their own people and their own futures.

I am aware that when UNESCO in its Constitution states, 'Since wars begin in the minds of men, it is in the minds of men that the defences of peace must be constructed', it is not doing so in any merely defensive way. It is also seeking to celebrate the possibilities of the peace that is thus secured. In establishing the UNESCO Chair in Education, Pluralism, Human Rights, Democracy, Education and Conflict at the University of Ulster in Ireland, and in working together with another third-level institution in Ireland, NUI Galway, to create a chair in Children, Youth and Civic Engagement Development, the Organization is taking that stated aim and turning it into practice. These are practical examples of UNESCO's work in Ireland on post-conflict resolution and reconstruction.

I am well aware that UNESCO faces particular funding challenges today, but I am confident that it will follow a balanced and focused programme of reform – one that meets your needs, but one that also safeguards the future of the Organization. Those of us who have looked at the United Nations as our hope for the future, and who made the case for reform of the UN, also know how essential is the work of some of the other UN agencies, not only of UNESCO but, for example, the Food and Agriculture Organization. Change in those organizations must be driven by the moral purposes of their founders. It must not be a case of shrinking back with some nods to efficiency in an administrative sense. It is about making sure that the fundamental purposes are secure.

Madame la Directrice générale, what I read in the Milan speech, which you gave sixty-five years after UNESCO was established, deeply moved me. I think it was so important to insist on a consideration of values in the work of the review. The building of a human community, of a humanist ideal, means building bridges between north, south, east and west. It means guaranteeing access to quality education for all, so that everyone may make their voice heard. It means encouraging scientific co-operation networks, establishing research centres, disseminating information to accelerate the sharing of ideas. But, as you know, it is not about the sharing of a single idea.

We need to re-establish again in the public intellectual world the importance of a plurality of ideas. And at the same time as we are defending this plurality of ideas, we also need to make a claim for the sovereignty of the imagination. To achieve this, I suggest, it is important that the economy is once again embedded within a cultural framework.

We should remember that Einstein and other great scientists saw science and technology as instrumental for the achievement of fundamental human and moral purposes. We must not surrender to those who say that culture and science and the creative industries should be available only to those who want to invest in them for such profit as they will yield and that alone. It is easy, on this view, to see how hunger and food shortages are becoming an opportunity for speculative investment.

Speaking in Ireland recently, I quoted Professor Howard Stein's paper on world famine. While countries such as Ireland give a great deal voluntarily – indeed give more per capita than most countries – and while 20 per cent of our Irish aid budget goes on relieving world hunger, other members of the global community decide, when they see a shortage of wheat or other staple food, to seize an opportunity for profit irrespective of human values. Thus, according to Professor Stein, in 2011 61 per cent of wheat futures were owned by hedge funds, the comparable figure in the 1990s being 12 per cent.

So our world has that moral contradiction, between those who would use words, and rightly so, to draw attention to the dying and the hungry and the vulnerable of the world, and those who feel it is more important to leave intact a model that suggests it simply does not matter how you make a speculative profit.

And we can see this conflict at work in the history of UNESCO. UNESCO was defeated in many of its aims in the past by those who regarded education as 'the next best thing', and water as 'the next best thing' for speculative profit. The same could happen in relation to the cultural industries unless we are very careful. That is why I am so pleased that UNESCO is having a conference to look at the creative industries and how they may best develop in an ethical way, that recognizes that the cultural object is not simply a commodity and that it expresses a people's remembered and imagined life, and that it is the labour of a human creator.

We do need a debate on culture, one that takes into account its history as a concept and above all its transformative capacity for peace, inclusion and democratic development. In the European Union, culture is not recognized very much in the founding treaties: there is a single reference to it in the Maastricht Treaty. This is in part perhaps explained by the assumption that the Council of Europe would do the work of cultural encouragement. But culture also had a bad name because of its abuse by ideological extremists and racists. One cannot, however, abandon the area of culture as if it were peripheral.

At this time the greatest scar on the European Union is the high unemployment rate, particularly among young people, which puts at risk not just social cohesion but the very legitimacy of the Union itself.

I think that in the European Union in particular we should urgently recognize that the cultural space is wider than the economic space, and that even if you lose your capacity as a consuming unit in an economy, it should never be the case that you lose your cultural rights to participate in the wider society. We must also recognize that culture is never fixed or frozen, but that it is continually reworked through different impulses and in new conditions.

In 1996, as President of the Council of Culture Ministers of the European Union, I sought to develop such a debate on access to culture as a right of citizenship. I also suggested that it was even more important that in times of recession you nurtured a flourishing culture, because it is in the public world, in the spaces in which you can share and exchange your vulnerabilities as much as your successes, that true democracy and citizenship are defined.

UNESCO cannot afford to fall into any dated pseudo-romantic trap of believing that devoting less resources to the broad cultural space is in any sense beneficial to creativity. Starving artists in attics may make for entertaining operatic librettos, but such a myth is as destructive of social value as it is of the individual artist's life. Poverty is not the route to great art.

We must also accept that culture helps us to develop the capacity not just of tolerating difference, but of being able to value a common democratic discourse. We must be able to see the threats to a vulnerable democracy as they emerge, so that we are able to listen with respect to those whom we oppose, and gradually put ourselves in a position of taking on the narrative of the other, and encourage our opponents to do likewise.

We are in the throes of great change. As I have said, the hubris of unregulated markets and speculative growth, based on virtual products invented by the financial markets, and fuelled in the recent period by property inflation – that model is of the past. From its disastrous consequences we are seeking to recover, and open a new chapter in our lives.

The world of today is very different from what it was sixty-seven years ago when UNESCO was founded. Yet the fundamental issues remain the same. I think that it is very important for us to remember, for example, what Sarvepalli Radhakrishnan called for at your first General Conference in 1946. He was appalled at how much time was wasted, how much human life was wasted, in false and foolish divisions, and he described those past illusions of certainty as the 'intellectual narrowness and rigidity of revelatory creeds'.

We must, I suggest, approach issues of development by placing human rights at their centre. We must continue our efforts at discovering human rights that we might agree to be universal. We must make our way with patience towards these aims. We must realize that in development it is important not simply to see developing countries as potential markets, but as places to which we can transfer technology and science, so as to enable them genuinely to deal with us as equals.

I believe that while we recognize the challenges in this time of uncertainty, it is important for us also to remember that we are not at the 'end of history'. We must be vigilant that our transformative moment is not stolen from us. Very recently, the film-maker David Puttnam reminded me of a phrase in T. E. Lawrence's *Seven Pillars of Wisdom*, which Lawrence wrote in 1926, looking back on the shattered dreams and the broken promises that followed the Allied victory in World War I: 'The moral freshness of the world-to-be intoxicated us... we were wrought up in ideas to be fought for... yet when we achieved, and the new world dawned, the "old men" came out again and took our victory – to re-make it in the likeness of the former world they knew.'

We have the opportunity of taking this global economic crisis and making from it a new world driven by the kind of values that are expressed in the founding constitution of UNESCO. We must not allow our world to regress to old conflicts. We must not lose the opportunity to put the stamp of our shared humanity on these changes. We must not capitulate to that which has failed us, which has been imposed on us, or which has falsely been described as inevitable.

UNESCO has been given an opportunity to work in order to achieve this humane outcome, and members of the United Nations must support it in this role.

You, the Ambassadors and Delegates of member states, have a particular responsibility to help make our new dialogue more open than it has been in the past. Of course we must represent our own peoples and their concerns in constructing a better world order, but we should also ask our governments to look to the deeper needs of humankind so that the discussion here at UNESCO can genuinely illuminate decision-making in the years ahead.

I see this new global community as very achievable. UNESCO is well placed to advance these debates that we so badly need in human rights, development theory and practice. I also think that the commitment to UNESCO of individual member countries must not rely solely on support from education departments, because education is very often a reserved space for the narrow interests of a particular state. Education is of course important and must be included, but other things matter – such as justice and human rights and equality. And resources do matter. UNESCO knows what it means to have lost a significant portion of its budget, and I wish you well in filling that gap, but I am convinced that you will not be defeated by it.

May I also appeal to the Delegates and representatives of countries, as a matter of urgency, to have active and regularly renewed UNESCO committees, so as to be able to communicate to new generations the importance of UNESCO's ideas.

Our goals for development must take not only political and civil but also economic, social and cultural rights into account. We need a more inclusive intellectual framework than we have had in recent years. There is a huge contrast between the way in which issues of a moral and public kind were embraced in previous decades. Perhaps it is the case that in our lapse into postmodernism, as a critique of modernism, we lost the capacity to make the moral critique that is necessary in our very unequal world. I hope that in the debate on culture this most important argument will take place, and that our intellectual recovery can spring from that source.

Thomas Carlyle said: 'Culture is the process by which a person becomes all that they were created capable of being.' George Bernard Shaw said: 'Imagination is the beginning of creation. You imagine what you desire, you will what you imagine, and at last you create what you will.'

May I suggest, finally, that you must ensure that when you are producing a document on creativity, one that will succeed the UNDP's *Creative Economy Report 2008*, that it is genuinely a citizens' document. It is important for us all to recognize the employment opportunities that are there in what is called the creative industries, but it is even more important for us to realize that those industries are most sustainably based on cultural policies that are inclusive. In music, film, or software and technology, all citizens should have access to them and they will then go on to yield a rich harvest, in employment, exports or economic growth. I think that an inclusive cultural policy is so much better than seeing culture simply as an engine creating new pools of consumers, which is likely to generate a new cultural colonization of the less powerful by the strongest.

These are debates which I have followed with great interest from my home in Ireland: How can we bring culture in from the margins, to the centre of policy formation, to the heart of public administration; How can we ensure that culture is not administered in the same way as any other commodity; How can we ensure real freedom of expression, ensuring protections to those who need them, protections that must never be traded away in the name of cultural difference? No cultural contingency should ever be used as a shield for trampling on a right of protection of the body, or of a person's right to a belief, or of speech. We should go on to ask how we can create a form of work that is fulfilling and sustainable. How can we reconcile the arts and sciences and restore the unity of our thought within diverse inheritances of ethics and knowledge?

All of these themes, I believe, are inextricably linked. And all of these, I humbly suggest, are themes for the future agenda of your discussions here at UNESCO. They are intellectual and moral encounters which do not weigh heavily on your scarce resources, but they can be the source of enormous wealth for humankind as we grapple with the challenges before us.

Going back to my native language: *Gúidhim rath agus beannacht ar or obair UNESCO.*

Finally, may I also take this opportunity to address the importance of public intellectuals, who can support the dialogue we desperately need if we are to have a constructive engagement between our different systems of thought – a dialogue, for example, between modern Western thought and moderate Islam. If we are threatened by the extremes of any distorted failed system, it is often because we have not had the conversation we need with those who see the truth, the beauty, the promise that is at the heart of some of these beliefs. The West has neglected its conversation with moderate Islam. And there are many Muslims who must speak to us too if we are to save the world from the consequences of extremism. Let us recognize and accept that the legacies of our civilizations are not separate from each other.

While there may be a great many gloomy economic commentators in this part of our shared fragile world at the moment, I believe that the potential for all of humankind is so much more positive. We live in times of change and opportunity – opportunity to advance the real development of humanity. Again and again, not just as President of Ireland, but long before that, when I was struck by new art or literature or music in any part of the world, I saw the sheer power of expression and the ability to transcend borders and conflicts and take in the wounds and the grief and joy of others as part of one's own experience. That is a truly human experience. That is the power of culture, and that is the importance of an organization such as UNESCO.

The Irish Launch of
the European Year
of Development

DUBLIN CASTLE

22 JANUARY 2015

T HE DECISION BY the Foreign Affairs Council of the European
Union to designate 2015 as the European Year of Development
could not have been more timely. Indeed 2015 is a seminal year:
the nations of the world have engaged in two processes of negotiations of
immense and interrelated importance: one on the UN's post-2015 development agenda and the other on climate change.

The choices that will be made will have a real impact on this and future
generations. Our decision-makers have a unique opportunity to address
the most urgent and fundamental needs of millions of people around the
world, people who have the right, and seek the means and the freedom, to
live their lives in dignity. And all of us must use whatever means we have
at our disposal to ensure that the governments who represent us conduct
the negotiations with commitment and a sense of urgency.

Last week, addressing a gathering of Irish Ambassadors and Heads
of Mission in this same venue, former President of Ireland Mary
Robinson told them how, in her view, 2015 is comparable to 1945, a year
of reconstruction and hope when new institutions were designed, new

texts drafted and new declarations adopted for humanity's shared future. Referring to the very tight schedule of both streams of negotiations, she talked not of the 'road' but of the 'race' to Paris and New York.

Of course the two processes are profoundly interconnected. Recent years have seen the food security and livelihoods of millions of men, women and children seriously undermined by unusually severe floods, droughts and rises in sea levels. Beyond its obvious scientific aspects, we should also look at climate change in a holistic way, in terms of its consequences on the realization of human rights.[67] Indeed it is becoming increasingly obvious that the effects of extreme weather threaten the effective enjoyment of a range of basic human rights, such as the right to safe water and food, and the right to health and adequate housing.

These connections between climate change and human rights have been emphasized by, among others, the UN Secretary-General's Special Adviser on the post-2015 development goals, Ms Amina Mohammed, whom I had the pleasure of welcoming to Áras an Uachtaráin last Thursday. Referring to the hellish violence that is devastating the lives of the people – and those of women and girls in particular – in her region of origin, North-Eastern Nigeria, Ms Mohammed explained to me how she saw a link between the destruction of agriculture, the resulting unemployment and young people's disenfranchisement and resort to violent action. Thus the climate change agenda is deeply intertwined with that of development.

Another key discussion for 2015 concerns the unlocking of the necessary financial resources available at global level. The outcome of the International Conference on Financing for Development – to be held in Addis Ababa in July of this year – is of crucial importance: should governments, NGOs, the wider civil society and business sector

---

67   Climate change is largely the field of environmentalists and natural scientists, who do not always do justice to the people-centred perspective associated with the human rights approach.

entities fail to agree, the chances to deliver this agenda will be gravely imperilled.

I am delighted to say that Ireland is well positioned to make a constructive contribution to these critical talks. Our country has solid experience of multilateral negotiations; our membership of both the European Union and the UN Human Rights Council endows us with additional leverage; and Ireland has a well-respected aid programme, of which all the civil society organizations represented here this afternoon are important co-actors. Furthermore, as a European country without a colonizer's legacy, Ireland also enjoys particular empathy with, and sympathy from, many non-Western countries.

Ireland's appointment, together with Kenya, as one of two co-facilitators of the negotiations on the post-2015 UN development agenda is, therefore, both an honour and a critical opportunity for our country to help advance a strong global agenda through a process that gives voice to those most affected by global inequalities.

In doing so, my view is that we – elected representatives, academics and practitioners in the field – must start by revising our traditional definitions of development, with their undertones of enduring divisions between the North and the South. We need instead a new narrative telling us of humanity's shared future on this fragile planet.

Too often has the term 'development' been used interchangeably with the terms 'aid' or 'charity'. Development was presented as something that needed to happen in the so-called 'developing' world, outside the sphere of industrialized nations and remote from the daily existences of Western citizens. Such a binary view can all too easily slide into a sense of condescension grounded in unspoken feelings of superiority. At the very least, it divides the world in two, with one side depicted as helpless victims and the other as their well-meaning saviours.

Development – the possibility of flourishing in one's community and culture, and access to the means to do so – is not simply a gift to be meted out by a gracious benefactor; it is both a right and a moral obligation.[68] Development should be driven by well-informed citizens who insist that their governments implement sound policies grounded in normative imperatives of justice, equality and dignity.

Moreover, simplistic oppositions between 'Northern' and 'Southern' countries risk obscuring the fact that, in many ways, elements of 'the South' are now in 'the North', and that, vice versa, some features of 'the North' have migrated to 'the South'. Indeed the high levels of youth unemployment experienced in many European countries, the recent debt crises, the existing and looming poverty and the consequences of externally imposed fiscal rectitude are but some of the phenomena which must prompt us to interrogate the relevance of old distinctions between 'developed' and 'developing' worlds. Food security, gender equality, dignity are core universal values.

The climate challenge and the urgency of other global environmental and social issues (such as, for example, the scale of the refugees problem), further expose the need to go beyond thinking in binary terms of 'us' and 'them'. All of us are called on to adjust our mindset and discourse – to take part, not just in a North–South conversation, but in a conversation about our humanity itself. As the great leader and visionary Nelson Mandela put it: 'Our human compassion binds us the one to the other – not in pity or patronisingly, but as human beings who have learnt how to turn our common suffering into hope for the future.'[69]

We can only rejoice, then, at the universal scope of the development goals currently in the making at UN level. Contrary to their predecessors, the Millennium Development Goals, which were targeted at poorer

---

68 Cf. Simone Weil: 'It is an eternal obligation towards the human being not to let him suffer from hunger when one has the chance of coming to his assistance. This obligation being the most obvious of all, it can serve as a model on which to draw up the list of eternal duties towards each human being.'

69 Nelson Mandela, 'Address at Healing and Reconciliation Service: The Healing of Our Land', Johannesburg, South Africa, 2000.

countries, these new post-2015 goals do not only concern the world's nations: they are about the crucial task of building new forms of living together, here and there. It is an agenda everybody can own and contribute to. In the North as in the South, the legitimacy and soundness of the dominant paradigms of development and growth that we have inherited are being challenged.

We cannot avoid tackling the root causes of the blatant and growing inequalities that plague our world. During my recent visit to Africa I was impressed by the achievements of many African countries in improving access to education and health services, building up their agricultural and food production sector, and protecting the rights of women. Yet I also witnessed first-hand the many basic needs and fundamental rights that are unfulfilled. Indeed the overall – and most welcome – improvements in global human development indicators should not mask the great poverty and suffering that exist in many parts of the globe, including, as I have just said, in the world's more affluent countries.

Most of you here will be familiar with Oxfam's latest research on inequality, which warns that, on current trends, the richest 1 per cent in the world will own more than 50 per cent of the world's wealth by 2016. This is but the last in a series of recent studies which have convincingly shown that the contemporary trends in inequalities are underpinned by a concentration of financial capital in the hands of a few. One problem which is central to the future of international development is that posed by the encroachments of highly mobile speculative capital on to the 'real' economy. This is a concern that faces all nations, and – alongside other global issues such as the use of natural resources, gender equality and the provision of jobs for young people – it requires concerted action at the global level.

The destructive effects of unregulated global financial markets are particularly evident in relation to what remains the most pressing of challenges, namely food security. In addressing this we must indeed consider the global infrastructure of commodity trading and the alarming level of control that speculators have acquired over the commodities futures market. According to a paper my friend Professor Howard Stein presented at a conference at Trinity College Dublin in 2012: 'It is estimated that 61 per cent of the wheat futures market was held by speculators in 2011 compared to only 12 per cent in the mid-90s prior to deregulation.'[70]

The problems posed by the financialization of the economy have been identified by a multitude of scholars and analysts, and denounced with renewed urgency since the global financial meltdown of 2008. This perhaps indicates that the heyday of a particularly strident version of neo-liberal economics lies behind us, and I very much welcome the fact that, after many decades, the role of the state is again being recognized as essential for responding both to novel global challenges and the destructive effects of self-regulating financial markets.

There are, then, many encouraging signs that a radical rethinking of our economic models is under way, not least in the UN Secretary-General's preparatory synthesis report, *The Road to Dignity by 2030*,[71] which refers to the need to control international finance and suggests alternative measurements of growth.

All of us can also benefit from the critique of the failed paradigm of development expounded by non-Western countries, as analysed, for example, by Vijay Prashad in his book *The Poorer Nations: A Possible History of the Global South*. In this book Professor Prashad documents in particular the manner in which 'Third World' countries have progressively been confined to a marginal role in the multilateral system, and how the most powerful Western countries sought to undermine (and to some degree succeeded in doing so) international institutions such as

---

70   H. Stein, 'The Neoliberal Policy Paradigm and the Great Recession', *Panoeconomicus*, 4 (2012), pp. 421–40.
71   United Nations, December 2014, *The Road to Dignity by 2030: Ending Poverty, Transforming All Lives and Protecting the Planet*, Synthesis Report of the Secretary-General on the post-2015 Agenda.

the UNCTAD, whose policy-framers are known to have been particularly vigorous in their defence of an alternative to neo-liberalism.

There is a new, multipolar world emerging. There are real opportunities to depart from the biased practices such as those described by Vijay Prashad in order to deliver a new architecture of legitimate and well-resourced multilateral institutions – based on genuine representativeness, an ability to translate agreed principles into action and a recognition of the intergenerational nature of our responsibility towards the planet.

This will be an essentially political process, with governments playing the central role. But it will only succeed if it is nurtured by the energy, creativity and legitimacy of a wide range of social actors. Parliaments and citizens must not avert their gaze. They must hold governments to account to ensure that decisions are truly based on the needs of the people, including those who are marginalized and most vulnerable. I believe that all of you who are here this afternoon, and all of Ireland's NGOs who are concerned with global justice and development, can, each in their own way and according to their own means, bring about the right atmosphere for such a transformation – a new moment in global relations that can yield a new integrated and culturally sensitive version of development.

All of you here know that there is no single correct model of development; you fully appreciate the importance of context and place. The idea of a linear path to progress and modernity is one that has created much damage in the past, as the former UN Secretary-General Kofi Annan recognized in his speech in acceptance of the Nobel Peace Prize: 'The idea that there is one people in possession of the truth, one answer to the world's ills, or one solution to humanity's needs, has done untold harm throughout history.'[72]

The majority of the solutions to poverty reduction and climate change

---

72   Kofi Annan, 'Nobel Lecture on the Occasion of Accepting the Nobel Peace Prize', Oslo, 2001.

lie outside the Western world, in those countries where infrastructure must be built; where more food has to be produced for an expanding population; where natural resources, and in particular our planet's largest forests, are located. Let us, then, do everything that we can to support those countries as they craft their own development path.

The year 2015 presents us with huge challenges and opportunities. It will require brave and wise decisions from world leaders. It will also require vigilance and activism among Ireland's NGO workers, parliamentarians, public intellectuals, academics and beyond, to ensure that our policies are sourced in global welfare and that our policymakers deliver on their promises.

I feel confident in saying that the actions undertaken by Dóchas and other civil society organizations throughout Ireland and the European Union will be of immense value in making 2015 a milestone in the history of humanity's development, and I wish you all the very best in these endeavours.

Go raibh míle maith agaibh go léir.

Recovering Possibilities

IIIIIIIIIIIIIIIIIIIIIIIIIIIIIIIIIIIIIIIIIIIIIIIIIIIIIIIIIII

THE ROYAL IRISH ACADEMY, DUBLIN, FOR THE LAUNCH OF THE CENTRE FOR THE STUDY OF THE MORAL FOUNDATIONS OF ECONOMY AND SOCIETY

13 NOVEMBER 2015

I AM DELIGHTED TO be here with you to launch the Centre for the Study of the Moral Foundations of Economy and Society, a joint academic and intellectual venture between University College Cork (UCC) and Waterford Institute of Technology (WIT).

Today's launch represents the culmination of a long process that began at a round-table discussion in Áras an Uachtaráin in November 2013, when the idea of creating an academic programme dedicated to studying the moral underpinnings of economic and social life was first mentioned.

I had invited the representatives of all of Ireland's third-level institutions, as well as the Royal Irish Academy, to that meeting. I wanted to hear their contributions to a national discussion on the values by which we might live together more ethically as a society. That was at the very earliest stages of the President of Ireland's Ethics Initiative – and it is especially fitting that one of the final public events of that Initiative will be the launch today of this Centre, a key legacy of the Initiative.

I am confident that the intellectual work produced by this Centre will contribute, over the years to come, in tackling the deep injuries inflicted upon our moral imaginations by the extraordinary ascendancy in recent decades of a narrow version of economics that has severed the ties between economics and its ethical and philosophical sources.

The connections between economics, ecology and ethics have been at the centre of my Presidency because I believe that they are essential to understanding the situation in which we find ourselves – in Ireland, in Europe and in the wider world. Furthermore, I believe that we must engage with these issues if we are to meet the great challenges we face in the years ahead: the challenges of global poverty, deepening inequality, climate change and sustainability.

The questions which will be addressed by this Centre, then, are not peripheral – they are essential concerns of our time; and they are concerns that require the deep consideration that can so appropriately be undertaken in centres of learning.

In my speeches at home and abroad I have again and again emphasized the crucial role that universities should play in crafting a response to these great intellectual challenges. As seats of pluralist scholarship, universities can significantly enrich the public debate on our notions of 'prosperity' and 'the good life.' As institutions dedicated to intellectual speculation, they can contribute to carving out a much-needed space for innovation in theory and policy at a time of great upheavals on our planet. We turn to them for critiques of the paradigms of thought that affect our lives. On them we rely for guidelines that can lead away from failing models to the new policies that we need.

Such a role for universities – and particularly public universities – as places of intellectual freedom, creativity and pluralism cannot, of course, be taken for granted. Today academics struggle to defend the moral purpose of emancipatory scholarship – a scholarship that is sensitive to ideals of justice and dignity; a scholarship that is concerned with the state of the world and the lives of others around us.

Academics are also challenged in their ethos as caring teachers in an environment which, far from being impervious to the trends at play in wider society, is infused with highly individualistic values, and inappropriate and artificial measurements of performance and productivity. Younger scholars face intense competition and increasingly precarious working conditions.

In this context, I think that we can all welcome the creation of the Centre for the Moral Study of Economy and Society as a worthy attempt to hold together the analytical (the descriptive) and the ethical (the prescriptive). Indeed its mission is not just to study the various ways in which the principles driving our current economic system can, as the founders of the Centre have described it, 'damage the very tissue of social life'; it is also to accept the task of 'imagining a better Ireland'.

The Centre already harbours an interesting variety of research projects. Some are of a rather classic sort; others focus on the training of students, such as the Economy and Society Summer School. Other projects are more unconventional in their methods, such as the 'Community Voices for a Renewed Ireland'.

The work of the Centre will have a relevance far beyond the areas of economic and social policy treated as discrete areas of study. The question, for example, of how we remember the past – as individuals, in our families and communities, collectively as a nation, and as Europeans – has great pertinence as we commemorate the centenary of the formation of the Irish State.

Commemoration is, of course, also an eminently ethical question. It concerns our lives in the present – the manner in which we relate to others of a different class, nation, religion or political conviction. It also relates to the manner in which we give a future to past events by remembering them in transformative ways. Indeed, following Paul Ricoeur, one can view the past as a repository (Ricoeur says 'a cemetery') of 'promises which have not been kept'. In Ricoeur's own words: 'the past is that which lives in the memory thanks to arrows of futurity which have not yet been fired or whose trajectory has been interrupted'.

The late John O'Donohue's work on 'possibility' made a similar point: 'The consideration of possibility as a force of transformative invitation enables us to recast our perspective on what facts actually are. Facts are not as lonely as they appear. Possibility is the mother of facts. Each fact is a former possibility.'

Such a reflection on the past is relevant, I believe, to our task today. It is legitimate to wonder, for example, what shape our economy and society would have assumed had our fellow citizens kept alive, during Ireland's recent economic boom, the cultural, philosophical, political and moral motivations that underpinned the Irish national revival, or the spirit of other historical movements for social reform such as the co-operative movement. How might these elements of the past now inform our vision of the Irish future? What should we retain and what should we discard? What is the purpose of our State?

It is my view that we have neglected the contribution of the co-operative instinct to our social cohesion and indeed the role that the co-operative movement played in the great debates that preceded the establishment of the state. That neglect is one example of the reflective choices we have avoided in our modern history, and we will have ample opportunities to explore such questions as we commemorate the Easter Rising.

For now, I would like to concentrate on a concept that is central to the intellectual ambition of the Centre we are launching today – namely, the concept of 'moral economy', a concept with a rich history and heritage of its own.[73] This notion of moral economy evokes different periods in the history of social sciences – for example, a time before the fall of the Berlin

---

73   The study of 'The anthropological foundations of a moral economy' is the object of one of the research projects developed under the Centre's first research themes entitled 'Recovering the Anthropological Foundations of Social Life' and led by Professor Arpad Szakolczai.

Wall, an era when the emancipation struggles of the oppressed were still widely believed to hold the key to a better world order. It also evokes the period from the late 1980s to the present when the role of the state has been reshaped by the demands of a financialized global economy.

Those who studied sociology or history in the 1960s and 1970s, as I did, were very engaged with studies such as Eric Wolf's on Latin America's armed resistance movements, or Sidney Mintz's work on the exploitation of sugar plantation workers in the Caribbean. Past economic forms and surviving oppressions were central to the discipline. Recently we have witnessed a revived interest in global poverty and deepening inequality, but we have not seen in the academic work of late much questioning of the significant changes in institutional economic decisions and responses that need to be placed in a philosophical or moral framework.

As many in this audience will know, the concept of 'moral economy' was first formulated by the British historian Edward P. Thompson, in an attempt to introduce a moral dimension to a Marxist (and, in his eyes, overly materialist) reading of the social history of the popular classes, a critique which I share. Although the expression 'moral economy' appeared in Thompson's book *The Making of the English Working Class* in 1963,[74] it was his essay on the 'food riots' of eighteenth-century England, published in 1971 in the journal *Past & Present*, that fully articulated the idea.[75]

Thompson's concept was later utilized by, among others, James C. Scott, who introduced it with great success to anthropology. Scott's work looked at the moral economies of South-east Asian peasants.[76] His research opened the way, in the early 1980s, to very good work on

---

74   E. P. Thompson, *The Making of the English Working Class* (Penguin Books, 1968), pp. 68 and 222.

75   E. P. Thompson, 'The Moral Economy of the English Crowd in the Eighteenth Century', *Past & Present*, 50 (1971), pp. 76–136.

76   James C. Scott, *The Moral Economy of the Peasant: Rebellion and Subsistence in Southeast Asia* (Yale University Press, 1976).

protest movements and social mobilizations among the rural populations of developing countries.

In some respects, the early work on strategies of defence used by peasants against those who held power reversed Gramsci's notion of false consciousness. Peasants, in certain Marxist accounts, were seen as hopelessly in thrall to reactionary ideologies imposed from above. James C. Scott's own interest lay in the 'subsistence ethic' of South-east Asian peasants. He described how these peasants, who constantly hover on the edge of famine, seek not to maximize their profit – as a liberal economist would expect – but to minimize the risk of loss.

This makes the important point that rational behaviour cannot be understood as the exclusive property of utility theory. A deeper version of rationality, rooted in instinct and cultural experience, is reflected in the tactical conclusion that it is better to minimize risk in confrontations with power, and to assess the opportunities for challenging that power or even rebelling against it.

This concept of moral economy is worth reactivating in the current intellectual climate. E. P. Thompson's study of food riots in eighteenth-century England offers a brilliant refutation of the notion that people's behaviour can ever be described as a simple response to economic stimuli.

Deriding those scholars who view the riots as mere 'rebellions of the belly', as 'compulsive, rather than self-conscious intrusions of the common people upon the historical canvas', Thompson warns us against what he calls a 'spasmodic view of popular history'. According to him, these eighteenth-century riots were never the mechanical result of soaring food prices and hunger. They operated within a popular consensus as to what were legitimate, and what were illegitimate practices in, for example, the marketing, milling and baking of bread. This consensus, in its turn, was grounded upon – I quote:

A consistent traditional view of social norms and obligations, of the proper economic functions of several parties within the community, which, taken together, can be said to constitute the *moral economy* of the poor. An outrage to these moral assumptions, quite as much as actual deprivation, was the usual occasion for direct action.[77]

E. P. Thompson's study thus grasps the confrontation between the two economic models described by Karl Polanyi at the historical juncture of what he called the 'great transformation', when liberal reason undercuts traditional reason and the capitalist ethic challenges the ethos of the poor. The moral economy of the dispossessed reminds us that alternative forms of exchange are possible; that despite the ideological revolution then under way in England, older principles of justice, respect and dignity still mattered, and continue to matter.

The difficulty for us now lies in interpreting the degree to which a cohesive collective morality has survived in a deeply fractured society where the public world has shrunk in comparison with privately consumed experience. Even in the sphere of communications, public service broadcasting, which assumed a shared story and national consensus, has been replaced to a large extent by privately consumed entertainment.

Nevertheless, I believe that this idea of a moral economy can still enlighten our current situation. Forms of civic resistance and popular protest, which have developed recently in a number of European countries such as Greece and Spain, fit the Thompson model in that such protests are not just an automatic response to deplorable levels of unemployment and deteriorating material circumstances – though that reality must be recognized and understood. There is more to them – and this 'more' has to do with the breakdown of trust between citizens and their institutions,

---

77   E. P. Thompson, 'The Moral Economy of the English Crowd in the Eighteenth Century', in *Customs in Common* (The Merlin Press, 1991), p. 188. (This chapter was first published as the aforementioned 1971 article in *Past & Present*.)

and with the rupture of the democratic pact between political parties and those they represent.

The present institutional structure of the European Union surely reflects the distribution of political power in recent decades, decades that have seen the emergence of a new financialized global order, where unaccountable forces removed from democratic oversight or control can impose their will on nation states.

Scholars such as Dr Srinivasan Raghavendra, the author of 'Economics, Politics and Democracy in the Age of Credit Rating Capitalism', show us the impact of monetarist orthodoxy in its new guise of New Consensus Macroeconomics.[78] Dr Raghavendra raises questions that flow from the tyrannical effect of credit ratings on national economies: 'Their power does not merely stop at inhibiting the State or its agencies from borrowing from the market, it goes beyond the markets into the realm where it is beginning to reshape the palettes of representative democracy in the conduct of the fiscal affairs of the State.'

Dr Raghavendra mentions two instruments that resulted from the Maastricht Treaty – 'Transfer of Competition to Community, Rules-based Co-ordination' and 'Soft Co-ordination' – as being central to this process. These changes surely deserve more attention than they have received so far for their effects on democratic accountability within, and between, the countries of the EU.

The alternative path is for European democracy to retain its full meaning, and for our decision-makers to remain attentive to expressions of the moral economy that still animates our citizens, and in particular to the concerns of the most vulnerable amongst them. This view demands that our fellow citizens should never be seen merely as 'consumers' of public policies, driven by their sectional interests. They in fact harbour deeply held moral views as to what is legitimate and what is not in

---

78   *Economy and Political Weekly*, Vol. XLVIII, No. 5 (February 2013).

matters of economic relations, and these views should be listened to and respected.

Thompson's argument is also interesting in that it colourfully exposes the intellectual bias involved in endorsing the analytical framework proposed by Mauss or Malinowski when looking at so-called 'traditional societies' – whether they are located in the distant past or in faraway lands – while forgetting all about these authors as soon as we look at modern Western society. Here it is worth quoting E. P. Thompson at length:

> We know all about the delicate tissue of social norms and reciprocities which regulates the life of the Trobriand islanders, and the psychic energies involved in the cargo cults of Melanesia; but at some point this infinitely complex social creature, Melanesian man, becomes (in our histories) the eighteenth-century English collier who claps his hand spasmodically upon his stomach, and responds to elementary economic stimuli.[79]

Paraphrasing Thompson, this infinitely complex social creature becomes (in twentieth-century neoclassical theory) the self-regarding, choice-making individual whose only concern is the maximization of his utility. He or she has become an abstraction.

The moral economy approach powerfully undermines the 'abbreviated view of man' as mere *homo economicus*. It invites us to reassess the relevance of moral sentiments such as care, trust and friendship, and to reassert the centrality of mutuality, redistribution and co-operation in our social and economic life.

We are left with a choice between a mechanistic view of the individual on the one hand, and a rich, complex and social view of humanity on the other. At the present time, these are not ideas that are treated equally in

---

79   Ibid., p. 187.

academic discussions, let alone in the mainstream media. Yet if the future possibilities of our citizens are to be realized, we will need a pluralist scholarship and an open space for different discourses.

We need to rediscover, with joy and hope, the full meaning of our interdependence as human beings – an interdependence that is international as well as inter-generational, with those who came before us and with those who will come after us; an interdependence that also extends, we increasingly realize, to all the non-human beings with whom we share this fragile planet.

The President of Ireland's
Ethics Initiative National Seminar

ÁRAS AN UACHTARÁIN

28 MARCH 2015

YOU ARE ALL very welcome to Áras an Uachtaráin for this National Seminar, as we draw together the various events that have made up the President of Ireland's Ethics Initiative.

This Initiative was designed to ask the Irish people to engage in a national conversation about ethics. It started with an appeal I made to Irish third-level institutions and to community and advocacy groups, to discuss the values by which we might wish to live together as a society, in the wake of a crisis that requires us to interrogate our vision of social bonds and our notions of 'prosperity' and 'the good life'. As President of a society which has been affected acutely by the recent global financial meltdown, I consider it crucial that we reflect on the structural, and indeed moral and philosophical, questions raised by this crisis in order to ensure that we learn from the experience.

My starting point was that it is not possible to change economics or politics without addressing the values and assumptions that underpin them. That such a change is necessary has been acknowledged at the global level by many eminent scholars. Kaushik Basu of Cornell University, who is currently Chief Economic Adviser and Vice-President at the

World Bank, and was formerly Chief Economic Adviser to the Ministry of Finance of the Government of India, is among them. In his seminal book *Beyond the Invisible Hand* Professor Basu wrote of his rejection of the norms that prevailed in the Bengali household of his childhood: 'To think of such norms and shared beliefs, and the social pressures that they place on individuals, as trivial or inconsequential to the functioning of the market would be a great mistake. On the other hand, taking account of those properly is an extremely difficult job.'

Examining the underlying values behind failed policies is indeed difficult. In Ireland we might ask, for example, how property ownership and the individualism on which it is based influences our views on the ethical quality of government policy. Across Ireland, there are many such conversations under way, conversations that explore the means by which we might transform our society and the world around us. To a certain extent, these conversations are informed by a real anxiety that is often inchoate, but they are producing a profusion of ideas, projects and activities that suggest avenues for change.

By inviting all those interested to take part in the President of Ireland's Ethics Initiative, my purpose was to give recognition to these many positive endeavours; it was also to provide a catalyst to those already engaged in crafting more solid foundations for our shared present and future, and to inspire, perhaps, new activities and new collaborations.

Many of you who are here today have been directly involved in the Ethics Initiative, through your participation in events hosted by universities, civic society organizations, or in the wider community. Others have written to me directly to express a personal interest in the Initiative and outline their own views on the challenges of living together ethically at the beginning of the twenty-first century. To all of you I wish to convey my sincere appreciation for helping to make Ethics Initiative a vibrant experience over the past year, and for coming here today, on a fine Saturday in spring, to continue this discussion with me and with each other.

When I was elected as President, I committed myself to shape my Presidency as one of ideas and transformation. In my inaugural address, I outlined how:

> It is necessary to move past the assumptions which have failed
> us and to work together for such a different set of values as will
> enable us to build a sustainable social economy and a society
> which is profoundly ethical and inclusive. A society and a state
> which will restore trust and confidence at home and act as a wor-
> thy symbol of Irishness abroad, inviting relationships of respect and
> co-operation across the world.

The encounters I had throughout the presidential election campaign, and the visits I have made since taking office to so many villages, towns and cities across Ireland, as well as to foreign countries, have only strengthened my conviction that there is a groundswell of popular demand for a re-examination of the assumptions that underpin the dominant economic and political discourse of our times.

Ethics offers a language that is useful, I suggest, in capturing these diffuse demands and in connecting ongoing discussions about dignity, human rights, education, quality of life and social and community values – all of which are neglected in the mainstream public discourse.

At a moment of great loss, when trusted institutions have failed the citizenry, and when values of social responsibility are shown to have been neglected or even abandoned on a grand scale, it might be tempting to respond to the question 'Is it possible to live ethically in the contemporary world?' with despondency, fatalism and even cynicism.

It would be easy, too, to diagnose the cause of our difficulties as being merely rooted in failures of compliance, individual failures or misdeeds which could be named and punished while we continue as before. It is not enough to say, for example, that the upheavals caused by an unprecedented banking collapse and property bubble can be fixed if the right supervision and regulatory mechanisms are put in place.

As I emphasized in my first speech dealing explicitly with the topic of ethics in September 2013, 'the proliferation of ethical manuals and codes of conduct in the various professional sectors will be of only limited consequence if we do not also ensure that their purpose is embraced and understood by, and not just enforced upon, those for whom they are designed'.

The current crisis has moral and intellectual ramifications that run very deep. It calls for an interrogation of our vision of what it is to be human, and the conception of human relations that animate us as a society. The risk, as I see it, is that if we do not tackle the assumptions that have inflicted such deep injuries on our moral imaginations, we will indeed resile to a position of 'business as usual'. We must not, then, miss this opportunity to seek, together, a new set of principles by which we might live ethically as a society.

In that regard, I am happy to observe that the Irish people's response to the economic crisis has not been, in my view, one of fatalism or reaching for simplistic solutions. Beyond issues of accountability, and notwithstanding divergent views on specific policy questions, Irish citizens have shown a deep desire to examine the root causes of what has happened and to reconnect what has been sundered in our society.

This radical demand stems from a growing frustration with existing institutions and with the mostly unstated ideologies which have contributed to the economic and political meltdown of recent years, but it also carries with it a constructive willingness to think and act in different ways, even if the way forward is not yet defined but must be fashioned through enduring intellectual work and social action.

I would suggest that our current moment is defined by challenges which established modes of politics are ill-equipped to meet, and the nature and scale of which demand a radical rethinking of how we live and how we organize our national and international systems of governance. This means that it is not only possible to live ethically in our contemporary world, but it is, in fact, imperative that we re-engage with ethics if we are to survive and flourish and meet these great challenges.

There is firstly a need to revive political economy, and to reconnect economic thinking to its ethical foundations. We should never forget, for example, that the Adam Smith of *The Wealth of Nations* is the same person who wrote *The Theory of Moral Sentiments* some years earlier; and that the two texts are deeply connected. Out of the instability and the material and social losses suffered by many across Europe in recent years, is springing a demand for sustainable and secure models of socio-economic development which are accountable to elected governments, rather than being at the mercy of remote financial fluctuations, or 'externalities' presented as being events akin to natural disasters. If we are to construct a stable and prosperous future for our people, based on sound foundations, and avoiding a replay of the errors of our recent past, then we must engage directly with those issues of ethics that have become marginalized in our economic and fiscal discourse.

One step, for example, towards what might be called a re-peopled concept of economics would be to treat essential social goods such as housing, health and food differently from other commodities in their relation to the market. All across Europe the consequences of the economic crisis have been visited disproportionately on the poor and the marginalized.

It is my conviction that we cannot meaningfully address poverty in our communities without reflecting on the unacceptable current levels of inequality – inequalities that threaten to be transmitted from generation to generation, with very serious consequences for our peaceful co-existence. Indeed the current levels of inequality pose nothing less than a fundamental challenge to the legitimacy of institutions and the morality of the state.

Homelessness is just one of the manifestations of this inequality

– perhaps the most pressing of all in Ireland today, and one which I have sought to highlight throughout the past year. In this area we see writ large the consequence of a commodification of social life and social goods, whereby policy has been cut off from what should be its ethical grounding in a conception of the fundamental requirements of the dignity of individuals and families. The social blight of homelessness calls for, at both individual and collective level, not just the impulse of charity as an immediate response, but also a recognition of the requirements of social justice in the way we design our policies and make our political choices.

The relevance of ethics is also immediately apparent in the area of work. We need to interrogate current conceptions of the worker as being a mere unit of labour, rather than a human being and an active citizen engaged in a range of activities and social relations. Any consideration of the ethical and social dimensions of work and the workplace must challenge such an atomized view of the individual; it requires us to see the worker and his or her productivity, in his or her fullness as a citizen, connected to others through family, community, participation in public or political endeavours, and by living a full life which includes work, play, culture, spirituality and study.

Climate change is a threat to life on this planet and presents a compelling case for the impossibility of persisting with our current models of economic development or indeed, for those of us in the wealthy parts of the world, with some parts of the lifestyles we have recently acquired. The ecological reality of our fragile planet exposes the fallacy of growth models that ignore the human and environmental context in which goods are manufactured and traded. This challenge of marrying ecology, economy and ethics is very pressing in the case of farming, land use and global food production – and that great aspiration of providing nutrition to all of humanity without discrimination.

In the relations between peoples and nations, we cannot ignore changing forms of conflict and the rise of extremism in many regions, including on the fringes of Europe. This calls for a new kind of diplomacy, one that reaches beyond the narrow pursuit of national interests. This may entail the creation of new global institutions, accompanied by new agreements and perhaps even new systems of international law, as well as the restructuring of existing institutions.

The last great moment of international institution-building, in the period immediately after the Second World War, was founded on a clear ethical bedrock: in that case the drafting and approval of the Universal Declaration of Human Rights. Were the international community to succeed in the great tasks it currently faces – in relation to conflict, shifting power relations, extreme intolerance, climate change, migration and inequality, to name but a few – then it must once again ground its work in a strong ethical framework.

As we tackle all of these great challenges, challenges which are public and political in nature, we must recognize that the very sphere of 'the political' itself has been undergoing a very profound crisis over the last few decades, and that this has far-reaching consequences.

Political participation itself is generally in decline across the Western world. There is now a widely shared realization that much of what has gone wrong, and has weakened and eroded our society, has involved the alienation of political choices from the people affected by them. We have witnessed, in public commentary, in the media, including the social media, a reduction of issues that are crucial for our society to the status of merely technical problems, sometimes presented as the sole competence of experts drawn from a very narrow field where, very often, context is ignored, theoretical assumptions undeclared, and ethical reasoning bracketed off. In order to counter this trend we urgently need, I suggest, to develop among our citizens an inclusive economic literacy that will demystify what is too often presented as being too complex for them.

Against this backdrop, the President's Ethics Initiative has aimed to stimulate the kind of intellectual reflection that might suggest ways of tackling these challenges and identify opportunities for solutions. This Initiative was intended to be, at its heart, about democracy and empowered citizenship, about recapturing the public space so as to reinvigorate discussions around the issues that matter most to our citizens.

Very deliberately, this Ethics Initiative was not presented as a prescriptive enterprise, in that I did not seek to pre-empt the issues or themes which might be addressed. Neither was it designed to come up with a single strategy for how any one set of values or views on society should be realized. Rather, it was about opening up a national discussion centred on values, with the conviction that a national conversation grounded in ethical reasoning could lead to better social outcomes, and that a more ethical society can indeed be fashioned by citizens joining together.

To address this crisis of legitimacy in our politics requires that we as citizens claim a space for discussion in which everyone can participate. It has been widely welcomed, but it has also found itself, in certain circumstances, having to force its way in, and to create a space where such a reflection might be allowed. It requires, I repeat, citizens to be empowered, to be given the tools to participate effectively in that discussion, particularly in the sphere of economics.

It was my view at the time of my election as President, and this view has been affirmed throughout this Ethics Initiative, that if we rekindle ethical thinking, Ireland can take advantage of being at the cusp of a radical transformation. However, this will require being willing to take a bold step forward – of both an intellectual and a practical kind. I consider such a collective examination of ethics in our society to be an expression of hope and an effort to utilize the strong moral core at the heart of our community.

The purpose of today's seminar, then, is to reflect back on what we have learnt through the past year, and to discuss the steps we have identified, or might consider, so as to lay the foundations for an ethical society. The seeds sown will, I hope, continue to take root and flourish into the future.

We will hear from the different constituencies that have been part of the Initiative, who will share their experiences and reflections. The first panel, this morning, will be composed of representatives of some of the third-level institutions which have been most active in the Initiative.

I have, on several occasions, described the crisis of recent years as being an intellectual as well as an economic one. We are therefore forced to consider what role our public intellectuals and our institutions of learning can play in the building of a republic of ideas. By inviting the various universities to take a leading role in the President's Initiative, my intention was to assist in that process. There is an unashamedly intellectual dimension to the job of work that has to be done and that is why the university sector, with its human capital and resources, was at the centre of this Initiative in its early stages.

The task of reimagining our society from an ethical perspective requires reflection and open debate, and the sixty events in the various universities have had interesting results. I have been most impressed by the creative quality of what has taken place in the universities. Interestingly, where the results were most positive they were driven by those willing to give leadership on the project, to break down the barriers between disciplines, between institutions and between the academy and the community. I had the feeling, too, that academics, often within the same institution, were taking the opportunity to become aware of each other's work on these issues.

The university events themselves have identified some large themes which map a set of priorities for future action, and others where considerations of ethics had previously been marginal. Among the themes identified, and this is far from an exhaustive list, are:

· The role and duties of professional bodies and other stakeholder bodies in society;
· The ethical challenges posed by emerging technologies in the social and biological areas;

- The ethical questions raised by urban planning and the built environment;
- Ethics in journalism and in the mass media;
- Religion in public life;
- Housing, homelessness and direct provision;
- The role of the State in present conditions of economic, social and political change and the growing gap between economic policy and the standards contained in treaties such as the Revised European Social Charter;
- The future of democracy in Europe and the fragility of the concept of Union in the European political landscape;
- Human rights and their relevance to the social issues of our time;
- The nature of contemporary conflict and the related challenge of building peace;
- The position of the conscientious objector and the ethical issues arising from that stance.

I am happy to see that many of these academic endeavours and initiatives are continuing or have inspired further projects, and I hope that the Initiative will also continue to inspire collaborations between scholars and schools in the institutes of education. We need a pluralist intellectual environment and an activism that is radical in its moral reach and able to engage in public debate in an open-ended way.

University College Cork has made particular efforts in this regard which I want to acknowledge, through the establishment as a response to this Initiative of a Centre for the Study of the Moral Foundations of Economy and Society, which I will be opening in May, and through inter-institutional collaboration with Waterford Institute of Technology. Several other institutions have advanced inter-disciplinary co-operation and I commend them for that.

There can be no doubt that, in some quarters, a utilitarian view of education as a commodity and as an instrument of economic policy has, in recent years, sought to assert itself, often at the direct cost of academic integrity and academic freedom. Indeed this has been the specific topic of some of the events that have taken place under this Initiative, such as the Workshop in Critical Pedagogy hosted by the University of Limerick. This is also an issue I addressed at the beginning of my Presidency in a paper to the London School of Economics and it is one which I have returned to on several occasions since then, and I believe that the denigration of intellectual engagement in politics and policy formation is in fact one of the great ethical issues of our time.

At the level of the broader education system, we must also probe the deficiencies of a model of education that has become excessively instrumental in focus, emphasizing a conception of the student as a future worker rather than as an active citizen. In an earlier speech on ethics I said: 'Our schools' curricula and pedagogical methods reflect the kind of humanity our society seeks and nurtures. The society we so dearly wish for will not take shape unless we acknowledge the need for an education of character and desires, the need to encourage and support critical reflection and a more holistic approach to knowledge.' While I made this point with specific reference to the value of teaching philosophy in our schools, it is also relevant to the wider question of social and economic education.

Bridging the gap between the academy and the community, in both its teaching practices and its research, is one of the questions that is being addressed by the Community Voices project, which has been initiated by a partnership between the University of Limerick, UCC and Limerick IT. It is a strong example of how this can be achieved and I look forward to hearing about the outcome from this university–community project this afternoon. This is one of many of the projects which I am pleased to say will continue beyond this Presidential Initiative and will provide a future source of inspiration.

Finally, this afternoon, we will hear from civic society organizations, whose mission has always been to promote responsible values in our society and in our politics. To many there is nothing new in this, but it is worth restating that the community and voluntary sector has always had its roots in an ethical worldview, often based in religion or in the traditions of human rights and equality.

Civic society – that is the joint enterprise between groups of individuals around shared values and shared public objectives – is the lifeblood of a healthy community and a healthy nation. Participation in civic society, in the public space, is the opposite of individualism, atomization and isolation. The continuing vibrancy of this sector, despite the great challenges it has faced in recent years, is itself an expression of how ethics and a concern for the dignity of others infuses the social action and the work of so many individuals and organizations in our society.

Five national community and voluntary organizations have responded to the President's Ethics Initiative with their own projects and events, and we will hear more about them this afternoon; they reflect some of the most pressing issues of our time.

Work and the position of the worker is the subject of the Irish Congress of Trade Unions' 'Ethical Workplace Initiative', which is seeking workers' views on the relevance of ethics to contemporary labour.

Poverty and inequality was the theme of my address to the Society of St Vincent de Paul Annual Conference in September 2014 and the Society has responded by making the Initiative the main focus for the work of the Vincentian Partnership for Social Justice in 2015.

The challenge of achieving equality and the protection of women's rights was the theme of a major international conference hosted by the National Women's Council of Ireland and the Irish Human Rights and Equality Commission in February.

Development, ecology and sustainability and our place in the world are the focus of the European Year of Development, which is being run in Ireland by Dóchas, and I addressed the launch event of the European Year in January.

The occasion of the centenary of 1916 inspired The Wheel to undertake a national consultation process entitled 'The People's Conversation', seeking to stimulate discussions about community values in a wide range of places and institutions, including in prisons.

The response to this Initiative has demonstrated an appetite for deeper debate and also for the project of renewing our society in a more ethical and sustainable way.

In my first speech on the topic of ethics, I said that my Presidency would seek to develop an ethical discourse that places human flourishing at the heart of public action. In my Presidency, I have found that the framework of ethics has been a very useful mechanism for engaging with themes of concern to citizens. What I have sought to do is to bring an ethical perspective to the centre of the Presidency, for example addressing the present decade of commemorations from the perspective of an ethics of memory, and engaging with global affairs during my official visits to other countries, where I have tried to discuss issues of development, climate change and human rights in terms of sustainability and justice.

I invite you all to join with me in an open-minded and open-hearted discussion about the values on which we might build a better future for our people. I believe that hope can only be fulfilled if bold changes are made in many aspects of our thought and our institutions. As we approach the centenary of the founding visionary document of our nation, this is an ideal moment to set about this ambitious task.

The European Union

Towards a Discourse of Reconnection, Renewal and Hope

THE 11TH ANNUAL EMILE NOËL LECTURE, NEW YORK UNIVERSITY SCHOOL OF LAW

28 SEPTEMBER 2015

T HE TITLE I have given to my lecture is a response to what I feel is a great contemporary democratic challenge, one of a regional kind insofar as its focus is the European Union, but one that is also global – delivering and deepening democracy. I am convinced that the challenges of connecting citizens, of creating a space for vision and innovation in scholarship, theory and policy, of offering hope at a time of great change on a planet scarred by a growing inequality, are also global in nature.

The discourse that prevails in relation to European issues at the present time, including the contributions of distinguished, but at times lonely, academic voices, refers to a crisis of legitimacy in an institutional sense. The roots of this discourse on the legitimacy gap are, of course, as old as the Union, but they have acquired an increasing urgency due to the fiscal crisis of member states, the response of different governments and the effect of those responses on citizens.

If we are to respond to this issue of legitimacy, it is useful I believe to look to the social sciences, remembering that all policy at some point bases itself, or at least seeks to justify itself, in terms of theoretical assumptions. In doing so, we need to test the transparency, the adequacy and the power of such assumptions. I suggest that the discourse I seek in the title of my lecture assumes a pluralism of scholarship which has been in decline for some time.

As a consequence we are, as flies in a jar of honey, trapped in a single paradigm of thought in the social sciences and above all in economic theory from which we are finding it difficult to escape. We perceive the need for thinking that will inspire policies that address the human challenges of social inclusion, poverty elimination, gender equality, public health and security in its widest sense; we perceive this need, but we seem unable to act. We often wait for rating agencies to indicate what the future has in store for us.

That single paradigm of thought has a historical location. It comes from a moment of hubris that suggested that literally all aspects of life could be fitted within an explanatory frame of extreme market theory. Citizens came to be redefined as consumers who were assumed to rationally calculate how to maximize their satisfactions.

That this model is now in crisis is evident in the social statistics that we gather from developed, developing and so-called undeveloped societies. That we need a new model is acknowledged even by conservative institutions, for example in the *World Development Report 2015 – Mind, Society and Behaviour* – published by the World Bank Group. That report, in describing the current paradigm, quotes Milton Friedman's famous work of 1953, *Essays in the Methodology of Positive Economics*:

> The individual actor could be understood as if he behaved like a dispassionate, rational and purely self-interested agent since individuals who did not behave that way would be driven out of the market by those who did. The assumptions of perfect calculation and

fixed and wholly self-regarding preferences imbedded in standard economic models became taken for granted beliefs in many circles.

But the Report goes on to suggest that:

> Economics has come full circle. After a respite of about 40 years, an economics based on a more realistic understanding of human beings is being reinvented ... [T]his Report shows that a more interdisciplinary perspective on human behaviour can improve the predictive power of economics and provide new tools for development policy.

Such a statement acknowledges the inadequacy of the prevailing model of economic theory, one that is usually associated with the Chicago School.

It may be obvious in the history of theoretical physics, but I believe it can happen in every area of thought: paradigms of thought do change. Modernization Theory in sociology is a good example. It is almost fifty years since I passed through New York for the first time on my way to study at Indiana University, Bloomington. I was in my early twenties and one of the first Irish graduates to be offered an opportunity of postgraduate study in the social sciences in the United States. Sociology was enjoying a renewal, different from its nineteenth-century springtime that included Weber, Marx and Durkheim, and was perhaps even moving into a moment of hubris in that autumn of 1966.

Many like me were introduced to Modernization Theory in the great canonical assertions of the Princeton studies of Gabriel Almond, Lucian Pye and Samuel P. Huntington, with their binary and evolutionary concepts of modernity and tradition, civilization, progress and development. Their perception was that the cultural traditions of traditional society hindered progress, and they saw peasants in traditional society as lacking 'achievement orientation', as David McClelland put it.

In time, such narrow frameworks did come to be questioned and were deconstructed by scholars such as Orlando Fals Borda, particularly so in the fields of political science and anthropology.

As to method, there was great excitement at the new possibilities of quantification based on large-scale surveys, on sampling, and the capacity for analysis of a newly introduced large computing facility. The social sciences increasingly focused on individual 'opinion' and 'preferences' rather than the 'discourses' and 'politics' that shaped those preferences. Preferences, it was assumed, preceded cognitive discourse, and could be directly modelled in 'rational utility terms'.

Missing from the narrative of the times was any analysis of the form or the location of power. At the edge of the academy, C. Wright Mills's *The Sociological Imagination* stood as an accusing text to the self-satisfied times.

It was a decade later while teaching at Illinois that I read, for the first time, Alvin Gouldner's *The Coming Crisis of Western Sociology*, and I have had that work ringing in my head through all these years, in particular the emphasis Gouldner placed on the need for good scholarship to adhere to the discipline of declaring what he called one's 'domain assumptions'. The framework one took for granted as the given, the normal, had to be acknowledged, presented explicitly as a paradigm. Good scholarship required one to be open, and to allow that one's taken-for-granted reality underlying the research should be open to question.

I look back to that time when the possibility of what we called paradigm articulation, shift and change seemed to offer a set of possibilities that would make pluralist scholarship the norm. Its scholarly hypotheses would help to generate a diversity of policy options. Sadly, so many academic institutions have recoiled from a commitment to that pluralist scholarship.

This stands as a background, as a global background in intellectual terms, to the concerns we must face, including those confronting the European Union. There are, of course, particular issues that arise within the Union, urgent ones as to whether it will be possible to have an institutional integration, which most commentators agree is necessary if the Union is to prosper, and also a parallel social integration that would receive the support of the citizens of the Union. The assumptions of theory as it informs discourse are perhaps even more important here, because they define what is possible and what can be imagined. They determine the way in which issues such as integration are approached. Unchallenged theoretical frameworks and failing paradigms can disguise reality, and contribute to the separation and indeed the alienation of citizens from their political institutions.

If the current crises within Europe, as I have suggested, have an intellectual as well as political and economic dimensions, we must recognize too that the European Union has within it the capacity to bring into being a new discourse that achieves a fairer, more inclusive Union, one that we can come to know, understand and will into being.

I believe that the political will which would enable a new vision of the European future can already be glimpsed among European citizens. The public response, for example, to the plight of refugees from Syria has, for the most part, demonstrated a deeply humanitarian instinct. A change of consciousness at a global level also seems possible, with, for example, overwhelmingly positive public attitudes to action on climate change. Is it not also possible, then, to aspire to a response, at a European and a global level, to the threat to democracy that is posed by increasing global inequality and a largely unaccountable financialized world economy?

Let us consider for a moment the context in which the positive view of Europe, developed and advanced by Emile Noël and others, was conceived. The memory of war and the near-extinction of European culture were ever present in the minds of the pioneers of the Union. Their vision was one of peace and prosperity based on core values of reconciliation and solidarity. In that vision, the role of the state, and of the inter-state institutions that were being constructed, was to act as mediators: balancing, as they did, the historical tensions between the interests of capital and labour, or as Wolfgang Streeck has defined it in more recent times, balancing the objectives of social justice and market justice.

That balance defined the post-war boom, and also served as context for significant social progress in the United States, spurred on by works like Michael Harrington's *The Other America: Poverty in the United States*. However, the balance would be irrevocably upset in the period beginning in the 1970s, as growth slowed and the view took hold that prosperity and the balancing of interests could only be sustained by a weakening of the state.

In a relatively short period the widely disseminated views associated with Friedrich von Hayek and Milton Friedman took a powerful grip on intellectual life. That hegemony was achieved in a conscious exercise of institutional power. It insisted on a very concrete set of political principles, and it set the terms for the position Europe and other regions find themselves in today. Over time, policy became ensnared within a single hegemonic model built on the assumption of the human actor as a utility maximizing rational being. These intellectual assumptions were the source of an economic policy that was the antithesis of the Keynesianism of the post-war decades. As to work within the academy, dissent and heterodoxy would be silenced or marginalized.

Far beyond Europe, especially after the fall of the Berlin Wall, one can trace an ideological drift that redefined language. For example, 'freedom' in the public discourse becomes 'freedom' from state regulation. Support for the concept of public goods and public services, for the public world, for the enrichment of the public space, for culture and broadcasting as a shared public activity, was put under pressure from a populism based on radical individualism, all of it predicated on an assumption of infinite economic growth that carried no burden of ecological concern. The state as an institution, which after the Second World War had been used as an instrument to set about the rebuilding of Europe, offering healthcare, decent housing and social protection to its veterans, their families and their successors, came to be regarded as an institutional obstacle to growth and prosperity.

Aspects of state regulation did survive for a while, but the financial-ization of the global economy was now well under way. In the process, the profoundly ideological notion that state regulation was an obstacle to freedom came to achieve a tacit acceptance. In the United States and Europe, the stripping-away of regulation can be shown to have shifted power to the beneficiaries of a growing inequality. Over the period since 1980, gaps in income and wealth have widened hugely.

Thus our present circumstances in Europe are dominated by different forms of crises: the crisis of debt, the crisis of unemployment and economic stagnation, and institutional crises at several levels including some that challenge the integrity of the Union itself.

The centrality of debt to the European economic crisis and to the wider questions of integration has been neatly summarized by Claus Offe. Giving the title 'Europe Entrapped' to his recent article in *Eurozine*, Offe's response to the present crisis is critical of European Union strategies to date:

> A central problem for the euro rescue scheme is that the banking crisis became a state budgetary crisis, which then became the cri-sis of European integration we have today. This in turn is a crisis of renationalising our sense of solidarity, a crisis in which the rich countries of Europe impose saving packages upon their poorer neighbours which are supposed to win back the confidence of the finance industries.

If we take perhaps the most troubling of the contemporary problems – that of scandalously high levels of youth unemployment – we see writ large the profound consequences that the deregulation of finance has had on social cohesion and indeed, as research has shown, on productivity at a personal and social level.

For the EU-28, the most recent Eurostat figures disclose youth unemployment running at 20.4 per cent, compared to 10.9 per cent of the general population. In some of the worst-affected countries, the picture is of course much bleaker. Spain has an unemployment rate of 22 per cent, but a youth unemployment rate of 48.6 per cent. Greece has an appalling rate of unemployment of 25 per cent, but its youth unemployment rate is currently running at a catastrophic 51.8 per cent, and Croatia and Italy also have youth unemployment rates of over 40 per cent. The life prospects of an entire generation of young people are withering, and confusion and populism are the inevitable response.

By any measure, these are stark figures and demonstrate the impact of the banking and financial collapse of 2007–2008, and the linked issue of unsustainable public debt in many states. In Ireland, unemployment is falling and currently stands at 9.5 per cent, but further progress will be contingent on a wider European recovery, which remains fragile.

At those times within the Union when growth, however poorly defined, produced surpluses, citizens would often be encouraged to compete with each other in terms of individual consumption. Now, however, as governments are forced to cut services and suspend infrastructural investment, fear and tension are the consequences. These consequences fall most heavily on the poor, and within society hope is eroded among the young whose expectations, after all, were formed in a debt-fuelled financialized economy rather than in a real economy that emphasized skills and creativity delivered in a socially purposeful way.

Recognizing this intellectual and public policy context is important for coming to terms with the disconnect between the citizens of the European Union and their representative institutions.

Democratic participation is now at historically low levels across the continent. In times of economic contraction and reduced state expenditure on services, elected representatives take the hit of public anger as they are the nearest available sources of authority, while at the same time they are perceived as powerless to act. Politics itself and the status of governments and parliaments have been eroded, as crucial decisions that affect people's lives are increasingly taken outside such accountable institutions. This is the real legitimacy crisis that we are facing.

Indeed this grounding question of legitimacy is a primary focus for thinkers such as Jürgen Habermas, Wolfgang Streeck and Claus Offe, who all share the view that the weakening of politics that we are witnessing in Europe has been fundamentally affected by the political changes that came about in the 1980s and 1990s.

A growing gap has opened between, on one hand, the advocates of a Social Europe who simply wish to protect aspects of democratic solidarity, parts of which, such as the British National Health Service or Scandinavian social protection, are iconic political achievements of the past; and, on the other hand, those who under the mask of 'labour market flexibility' seek the surrender of hard-won rights in the workplace as the entry qualification to a radically unregulated global economy. The outcomes of this conflict result in our shared world being scarred by a growing inequality – an inequality that has implications for health, housing, work, participation, for life itself. That is what concerns the European Street.

There might once have been a range of political responses to such a crisis, but it has been dampened by the squashing of electoral competition into what is regarded as the political centre, a centre of course that, in recent times, has had to function under the shadow of dangerous populisms.

There is nothing uniquely European about our position, although it may be that in the multi-level structure of the EU the tension between democracy and global markets is particularly pronounced. We may be living through the birth of a new form of global capitalism, which existing democratic institutional arrangements are simply failing to render accountable: a capitalism without democracy. Where discussion of redistribution, of poverty-proofing, of reducing inequality, were once possible, these issues are now presented as very much secondary to the management of the newly socialized public debt.

As parliaments lose capacity, as the realm of the social state shrinks, the feeling on the street is that more and more the people are being asked to adjust themselves and their lives to fiscal policies, which it is suggested are beyond the ken of ordinary folk. The adjustment of the citizenry to debt costs and forecasts may be called 'austerity', but what is masked by such a term is perceived by many as simply a submission to forces that are not under any democratic control, and are at the same time delivering a transfer of wealth to private creditors.

The scale of the debt problem and the ongoing economic difficulties facing Europe are enormous, and as governments struggle with these great questions, diverse proposals have been brought forward by scholars and political scientists. Jürgen Habermas makes a case for a new institutional 'transnationalism', while acknowledging the scale of the democratic challenge this would present. Wolfgang Streeck seeks, as an alternative, an exit from a dysfunctional version of monetary union, which was badly planned and implemented. Claus Offe takes a more pessimistic view and highlights the gap between what he sees as fiscally necessary in terms of debt-sharing, and the political obstacles to the changes that would be necessary across the Eurozone to make this happen. Offe suggests that the only possible solutions may lie in the area of social policy.

Teasing out the various policy options at this difficult moment is the very onerous work of national governments, rather than for me as a non-political Head of State. I would suggest, however, that their efforts at economic and institutional reform will not, if they are taken in isolation, for example in the fiscal sense, address the deeper issues of legitimacy facing Europe, unless they recognize the changes in the contemporary forms of capitalism and also the need to revisit the relationship between economic and social policy in a fundamental way.

This is not to say that there are no grounds for hope. The crisis at an economic and at a political level is deep, but crises can provide an opportunity for a new strategic direction. For a start, we need to break free intellectually so as to be able to see the possibilities that our sustainable future demands, but breaking with paradigms can be painful. In a passage near the end of his *The History of Development*, published in 1997 , Gilbert Rist wrote of the difficulty of arriving at a new paradigm in intellectual work and policy:

> Only a new paradigm can alter, not the way things are, but our way of conceiving them. That is, it can make it possible for us to think what is today unthinkable. History shows us a series of turnarounds that have changed the face of the world.
>
> What value today have the certainties of Galileo's adversaries, of the Inquisitors hunting down witches, of the colonisers so full of their sacred trust of civilisation?

We are not living in circumstances that cannot be changed. Inequality at global, regional or national level is not some form of natural law. Many heads of state, government legislators and people active in civil society are now recognizing that distributional issues must be addressed if we are to restore the legitimacy that is needed to achieve European integration; but the need for reform has to be primarily directed at the needs of the Union and its citizens, and only within that can the institutional change needed in relation to the banking sector, the currency and economic stability be achieved.

As to how we can act in response to economic issues such as youth unemployment in the short term, there are proposals available to us in such works as that of Professor Anthony B. Atkinson, who will chair the new Commission on Global Poverty. In his recent book *Inequality* he makes the following observation: 'Crucially, I do not accept that rising inequality is inevitable: it is not solely the product of forces outside our control. There are steps that can be taken by governments, acting individually or collectively, by firms, by trade unions and consumer organisations, and by us as individuals to reduce the present levels of inequality.'

Professor Atkinson goes on to make some proposals for policy which I believe could be implemented within the present structures of the European Union. The proposals would build a 'social floor' for the European Union but would also have a global reach in addressing inequality. These are Professor Atkinson's proposals, not mine, but their central claim is that addressing inequality, arresting its deepening, breaking the cycle of exclusion and alienation are truly achievable.

In this regard, I have previously pointed to the existing treaty obligations under the Charter of Fundamental Rights and Freedoms and the Revised Social Charter of the Council of Europe as providing an existing rights framework for such a social floor. Such proposals could serve as a beginning for the rebuilding of a Social Europe, and do so within existing constitutional arrangements. I find such a contribution attractive and valuable. I ask myself, however, could this ever make its way into the current discourse in the European Union at a political level?

We should remember the great achievements that have been made possible in the past. At its periods of greatest achievement and progress, the European Union has inspired the loyalty of its citizens because of the hope it represented of a better society. If it is to survive and flourish, Europe must regain the power to inspire and to offer hope. The Union has much to be proud of and to celebrate and European Union membership has given impetus to so many inclusive reforms in member states. In the Irish case, membership of the Union has been a powerful impetus towards gender equality, for example. Its influence on environmental responsibility has been immense, and it has been used as both source and shelter for Government decisions on sustainability.

The principle of free movement of peoples was once seen as a core value to be celebrated rather than merely as a labour market instrument or a legal rule to be circumvented. It was a cornerstone of the idea of Europe that enabled cultural and social interaction on an unprecedented scale.

For example, in the area of education, the ERASMUS scheme allowed young European people to study and work in other member states, exposing them to a different linguistic and cultural environment at a formative period in their lives. Since 1987, three million Europeans have taken part in ERASMUS, with 40 per cent going on to settle abroad and one-third marrying a citizen from another state. The Commission has estimated that there have been one million babies born of ERASMUS – in what Umberto Eco has described as a 'sexual revolution' sweeping Europe, which he has argued should be extended beyond students to workers also. Travel is the nourishment for integration.

In the task of fostering political will for reform, the importance of symbolism should not be underestimated. When intergovernmental meetings are called, they usually conclude with a joint statement and what is called the family photo, an image of jovial European leaders in a happy reunion. But on the street very often what citizens believe they are hearing is not the necessary invitation to any new understanding of economic circumstances. For many citizens, when the conditions of life itself cannot be reconciled with the image of authority and care on offer in the family photo, they are pushed to ask the question: Have things spun out of control? Has a new and unbridgeable fissure between the public and those in power emerged?

In responding to this current crisis some public intellectuals speak of what they see as an irreformable reality, of the need for a new moment of confrontation and total change when existing institutions must be swept away. This may be heady stuff, but there are those who see the human costs of such an outcome; who see how old badges of difference, ethnicity and belief, the bankrupt certainties of the past, could quickly fill the vacuum that would be created by a weakened parliamentarianism or shrunken state, how easily our publics could drift into old hatreds.

I remain committed to the European vision and to the founding principles of Europe, which can offer the basis for a renewed and strengthened Union. Yet to provide hope at this crucial moment, I believe we must rediscover the enabling and inspiring principle of solidarity: solidarity within the Union and solidarity with the wider world.

When Europe was in ruins after the war it was impossible to avert one's gaze from the destruction. When European growth rates were achieved within a social model modest redistribution took place, and it may not have seemed necessary to encourage widespread economic literacy. Assuming all was well, many could drift away from political participation. Debates about living conditions could be about the disposal of the fruits of growth; and a debate on poverty was possible. We should remember too that period of the European Union's history when solidarity mattered within a European scheme aimed at tackling poverty. Combat Poverty in Ireland was established under the administration of the Irish Minister for Social Affairs, the late Frank Cluskey T.D. Combat Poverty, established in the 1970s, looked at the structural sources of urban and rural poverty.

It is well within the capacity of the European publics to craft new policies and a new institutional order which combine social cohesion with competitiveness. The danger at the moment is that progress has stalled because there is so little connection between economy and society. The further danger is that without the political support of its people, the necessary institutional and policy changes will become ever less possible.

Rebuilding a Social Europe may require greatly increased tax and spend capacities on the part of the EU institutions. At present, the political will for such policies and for the necessary ceding of sovereignty from the national level does not exist.

An active European citizenship requires participation by citizens, facilitated by an economic literacy. May I suggest that if literacy was an essential tool in securing the right to vote in a previous century, in contemporary conditions an economic literacy that can demystify banking, fiscal and real economy crises surely seems necessary now? The vacuum that is emerging and will grow will otherwise be filled with populist extremes, and old and dangerous fundamentalisms. Bogus certainties are resurrected to justify exclusions, create fears and revive hate.

We can, I believe, save the European vision, and in doing so would be saving a model in which the peoples of other continents have placed their hopes. At general level, the perception of our interdependency can be the basis for joint action on issues such as climate change, the elimination of global poverty, the ending of gender violence and a restructuring of global debt.

Reviving solidarity also offers the best prospect of re-engaging electorates. Reflect, for example, on what would be the response among its publics if the European Union agreed to implement a social agenda derived from the economic, social and cultural rights articulated by the Council of Europe. Imagine the value of a meaningful guarantee of rights to food, shelter, education and health.

A reconstituted European Union can be part of a new global discourse that builds on commitments on issues such as sustainable development and climate change. Europe can embrace these and other challenges in conscious rejection of an old legacy that many of its members share, one of imperialism, of economic exploitation, political manipulation, gender and cultural exclusion.

Recent developments and global challenges can be turned in a new direction by building a Union that will be an exemplar for other regions, presenting new global and regional choices, alternative connections between society and economy, ethics and ecological sustainability.

The European Union can, in its response to the present migrant and refugee flows from the neighbourhood of the Union, create a model for appropriate response to such crises. If it does not do so, the evidence is that such an issue can confound the best European values and that new xenophobic parties will be the beneficiaries. When we see the overwhelming popular support for compassionate and generous policies at this time, we should be left in no doubt that solidarity both within the Union and with our neighbouring regions is possible and can be a powerful unifying value.

Within the economic sphere, by redefining work itself as a human activity the European Union can stem the creation of the 'precariat' that is emerging at a global level, a mass of part-time, unorganized workers on zero-hours contracts. At times, this growing phenomenon of insecure work sails under a flag of convenience called 'labour market flexibility', but it is really about deregulation and the erosion of rights and benefits painfully gained over generations. This is a universal issue, one not confined to the European Union, but one where, again, given the political will and its strong legal framework and tradition, the Union could be exemplary.

The glaring inequalities of our world must be recognized as the threat they are to democracy everywhere. If what is called 'democracy within capitalism' continues to change its form into 'capitalism without democracy', and, I repeat, if politics becomes hollow, if economic literacy is not provided as a necessary tool in public discourse, the argument on legitimacy will not simply be an economic one. It will be about democracy itself.

We are at a defining moment. The scale and complexity of the challenges we face are daunting, but we have great resources with which to face them: the rich and profoundly ethical intellectual heritage of Europe and of the founding visionaries of European co-operation such as Emile Noël.

The tasks we must undertake are political and institutional, but they are also intellectual and moral in nature.

We have together, at global level and in the European Union, an opportunity to define our interdependency in terms of human vulnerability and care. We should seize our opportunity, and that would be very European indeed.

REMEMBERING THE PAST: COMMEMORATION AND FORGIVENESS

Remembering the
1913 Lockout

Its sources, impact and some lessons

THE 2013 MICHAEL LITTLETON MEMORIAL LECTURE

18 JUNE 2013

I T IS A great pleasure to be able to return to social history, even for a little while, and it is an honour to have been asked to deliver the 2013 Michael Littleton lecture.

The Littleton lecture celebrates a life devoted to public service broadcasting at its best. Michael Littleton was Head of Features and Current Affairs at RTÉ and sadly left us all too soon in 2002. It is acknowledged by many that Michael Littleton was responsible for the modernization of current affairs reporting in Ireland, and thus can be credited with having enhanced our capacity as citizens to engage in an informed manner in debating and shaping the way we live.

In the role of Editor of Arts, Features and Drama for RTÉ Radio 1, he forged links with a wider programme-making community in Europe and further afield. At a personal level, Michael is remembered by colleagues as a great teacher and mentor. A highly strategic thinker, he expressed that skill in public, and in private too – after all, he played chess for Ireland. I know he is missed by his colleagues, his many friends, and by his family.

Tonight the Littleton lecture takes as its focus the Dublin Lockout of 1913. I would like to reflect, in my brief time, on its significance, its impact on those involved, and the response it evoked. I am indebted to the now considerable literature on the topic, and I would like in particular to thank Diarmaid Ferriter for assistance that enabled me to develop tonight's lecture by taking into account the newly digitized census material of the period.

In May 2013 another valuable resource was launched. The Century Ireland online project, as part of the government's commemoration programme, is producing a fortnightly online newspaper with contemporary accounts of what Ireland was like at the time; it includes documents, photographs and contextual essays and interviews. By 2023, this will be an unparalleled resource for archives relating to the revolutionary period.

Many here will no doubt remember the Lockout through James Plunkett's novel *Strumpet City*. Many more will have seen the RTÉ series adapted from the book for television by the late Hugh Leonard. In a decade of centenaries, however, it may still be necessary to outline how the Lockout of 1913 came to happen.

In 1988, on the occasion of the seventy-fifth anniversary of the Lockout, Alan MacSimoin described the beginning of what would be remembered as the most acute confrontation between workers and employers in the history of the Irish trade union movement, personalized in the confrontation between trade union leader Jim Larkin and the leading Irish owner of tramways, newspapers and property, William Martin Murphy:

> On August 21st nearly 200 men and boys in the parcels office of the Tramway Company received the following notice: '*As the directors understand that you are a member of the Irish Transport Union, whose methods are disorganising the trade and business of the city, they do not further require your services. The parcels traffic will be temporarily suspended. If you are not a member of the union when*

traffic is resumed your application for re-employment will be favourably considered.'

On the morning of August 26th, the first day of Horse Show week, Murphy got a shock. At ten o'clock in the morning the tram drivers took out their union badges and pinned them in their buttonholes. They then walked off their trams, leaving them stranded in the middle of the road. The strike was on. Their demands were reinstatement of parcels staff, and equality of hours and wages with the tramway workers of Belfast.

The Lockout had begun. The dispute would last from 26 August 1913 to 18 January 1914, and is generally seen as the most severe and significant industrial dispute in Irish history. The right of workers to organize was central to the dispute.

William Martin Murphy was thirty years older than Jim Larkin and was regarded as the most successful figure in Irish business at the time. From modest beginnings in Cork as the son of a building contractor, he showed an early ability for business. He established his wealth through ventures that were at first most successful in London but which extended as far as Africa. For many years before the Lockout he had been admired as one of the great successes of native Irish capital. A Home Ruler and anti-Parnellite, he supported the movement for a native government but one that would, as he put it, 'retain the jewel of a connection with the British Crown'. By 1913 he was the owner of the *Irish Independent*, the *Evening Herald*, *The Irish Catholic*, Clery's Department Store, the Imperial Hotel and the company where he would choose to mount his fight, the Dublin United Tramways Company.

He had been somewhat disillusioned with the decision by an overwhelming majority of the Committee of the Federation of Dublin Employers to enter into a Conciliation Board for employers and employees. This had arisen as a result of previous strikes that were a result of Jim Larkin's efforts on behalf of the Irish Transport and General Workers' Union (ITGWU) members and others. Murphy persuaded more than 400 Dublin employers to seek a pledge from their employees that they would cease their membership of the ITGWU if they were existing members, and give an assurance not to join in the future, if they had not already joined.

The employers in question agreed to lock out all workers who refused to sign the following pledge: 'I hereby undertake to carry out all instructions given to me by or on behalf of my employers and further I agree to immediately resign my membership of the Irish Transport and General Workers' Union (if a member) and I further undertake that I will not join or in any way support this union.' Within a fortnight the larger farmers in the Dublin region had sought a similar declaration from their workers.

William Martin Murphy wished to defeat what he called Larkinism, which he saw as a form of syndicalism and a threat to the basic structures of employer–employee relationships, and indeed basis of any future Irish State. Murphy's main antagonist was Jim Larkin, who in the years before the strike had a number of successes in organizing workers and improving their wages and conditions.

Larkin's reputation was achieved principally by the extraordinary power of his oratory and what was perceived by his members to be a fearless commitment to the moral rights of workers. His view of the worker was a utopian and deeply ethical one. His aim was a commonwealth of co-operation. He was deeply opposed to the abuse of alcohol and had drawn criticism on account of his interventions on the subject of wages being squandered by dockers, for example, on drink. The cultural events organized by Liberty Hall, and the union's social outings, were alcohol-free.

For Seán O'Casey, with whom he retained a close friendship and to whom he remained a hero to the end, he is the major figure of the period.

On the day of his death O'Casey wrote: 'It is hard to believe this great man is dead... for all thoughts and all activities surged in the soul of this labour leader. He was far and away above the orthodox Labour leader, for he combined within himself the imagination of the artists, with the fire and determination of a leader of a downtrodden class.'[80]

Larkin was much more than an orator, as David Krause, Seán O'Casey's friend, noted:

> Although he became known as the great strike-leader, it was his aim to organise unions, not strikes, and it was the absolute refusal of the employers even to enter into open negotiations that invariably led to the strikes which Larkin himself deplored and accepted only as labour's last resort. But he was a marked man in Dublin, feared by the capitalists he had come to scourge, and even assailed by the Catholic clergy who at that time had little sympathy with the trade union movement. In spite of the fact that he was denounced by many priests and by the Catholic press, Larkin boldly insisted that he was a Catholic and a Socialist at a time when *The Irish Catholic* newspaper was frantically warning the people that Socialism was tantamount to Satanism. Shortly after the union was forced to strike in late August 1913, that newspaper came out with a leader called 'Satanism and Socialism', warning the strikers to listen to their priests and go back to work, to renounce Larkin who was referred to as 'that Moloch of iniquity'. The editorial also introduced a political note when it stated that Larkinism or Socialism was the enemy of Ireland's national ideals as well as Christianity: 'From beginning to end Socialism is anti-Christian and un-patriotic. There is scarcely a single national ideal long cherished by our people

---

80   Seán O'Casey, *Drums under the Windows* (Macmillan 1945).

of which the Socialism now daily and nightly preached at Beresford Place is not the negation.'

In attempting to recover the atmosphere of the Lockout it is useful to consider how these two men have been represented. Earlier historical evaluations were inclined to ask succeeding generations to choose between two heroic figures: on the one side a founding figure in the struggle for workers' rights, and on the other a hero of native business. More recent scholarship has avoided such extremes and has offered us a more complex account of the period, the motivations, the social forces and, above all, the contradictions within the groups of participants on each side of the conflict.

We also now have available some fine studies of the working life of the people of Dublin, including the lives of those in the tenements, work such as that of Kevin C. Kearns's *Dublin Tenement Life: An Oral History*. The Lockout took place in a city marked by poverty and hunger, and it was a city deeply divided by class. In 1913 Sir Charles Cameron, the Medical Inspector for Dublin, reported: 'it is certain that infants perish from want of sufficient food'. Overall, the average death rate in Dublin in 1911 per thousand people was 22.3. In London it was 15.6.[81] With a totally inadequate sewerage system, Dublin was described as having its own distinct smell to complement the 'social decay and economic stagnation'.[82] In those conditions, TB and other illnesses took a savage toll.

Many years later, Seán O'Casey would recall his life in the tenements and describe a similar scene:

> Then, where we lived, with thousands of others, the garbage of the ashpit with the filth from the jakes was tumbled into big wicker baskets that were carried on the backs of men whose clothing had been

---

81   Catriona Crowe (ed.), *Dublin 1911* (Royal Irish Academy, 2011).
82   Ibid., p. xxi.

soaked in the filth from a hundred homes; carried out from the tiny back yards, through the kitchen living-room, out by the hall, dumped in a horrid heap on the street outside, and left there, streaming out stench and venom, for a day, for two days, maybe for three, till open carts, sodden as the men who led the sodden horses, came to take the steaming mass away, leaving an odour in the narrow street that lingered till the wind and the rain carried trace and memory far into outer space or in the heaving sea. Hardly a one is left living now to remember how this was done, or the work remaining behind for the women to purify the hall and kitchen so that the feet felt no crunching of the filth beneath them, and the sour and suffocating smell no longer blenched the nostrils.[83]

The death rate in Dublin in 1913 was worse than Calcutta, and child mortality was high, with almost a fifth of deaths in the city in 1908 being of children under a year old. [84] It is hard to believe today that about one-third of Dublin's population lived in these appalling conditions.

The census of 1911, to which I have referred, depicts a Dublin of great contrasts: at the exclusive Kildare Street Club, there were six visitors on census night, including a landowner, a land agent, a retired colonel, the official starter at Irish race meetings and Lord Fermoy. Thirty-two staff attended to their comfort. The German waiters from the Shelbourne Hotel lived nearby on Kildare Street, while W. B. Yeats and Lady Gregory were staying around the corner in Nolan's Hotel on South Frederick Street. The census also describes the vast number of servants required to keep the viceregal lodge in the Phoenix Park ticking over for the benefit of the Lord Lieutenant Lord Aberdeen and his wife Lady Aberdeen, the women's rights activist and founder of the Women's National Health

83   Seán O'Casey, *Feathers from the Green Crow*, p. 239, quoted in D. Krause, *Seán O'Casey: The Man and His Work* (Macmillan, 1975), p. 6.
84   http://multitext.ucc.ie/d/Dublin_1913Strike_and_Lockout

Association. There is, notably, no return for a number of well-known Irish feminists, including Hanna Sheehy Skeffington, as she and a number of other suffragettes refused to co-operate with the census in protest at women's lack of the vote.

But perhaps the greatest value of the census records is the detailed picture of ordinary people living their lives and, unfortunately, experiencing the death and deprivation of loved ones. The 1911 census asked a new question of women: How many children had been born to them, and how many remained alive? Their answers on the census forms bring abstract statistics about child mortality right down to the household level. Particularly in the inner-city tenements, you can see terrible attrition, with many families losing over half of their children. For example, ten families lived at 24 Gloucester Street in 1911, most families occupying one room. At that address, forty-seven-year-old Annie Doran had given birth to eight children; only three survived. Her neighbour in the same house, forty-four-year-old Katherine Cavanagh, had lost four of her ten children, and another neighbour, Catherine Taylor, had lost two of five.

I myself once talked to a woman who had lived in the tenements and spoke of a woman in a neighbouring room putting her dead baby in a shoebox, placing it on the top of a press and waiting for assistance for its burial.

The Dorans and the Taylors, each family numbering five, lived in one room apiece, while the Cavanaghs, with six, had two rooms. Twenty-six thousand families in Dublin in 1911 lived in one-room dwellings, making Dublin the most overcrowded city in Europe. The decay of Dublin was epitomized by Henrietta Street, on the north side of the city, where an astonishing 835 people lived in just fifteen houses. The street had once been salubrious and home to a generation of lawyers, but by 1911 was overflowing with poverty.

At 10 Henrietta Street, the Sisters of Charity ran a laundry with more than fifty single women living in the house. Members of nineteen different families lived in number 7. Among the 104 people who shared the house were charwomen, domestic servants, labourers, porters, messengers, painters, carpenters, painters, a postman, a tailor and a whole class of schoolchildren. Out at the back there was a stable and a piggery. It is from such tenements that workers emerged to do what was, for many, casual and uncertain labour.

When the workers who were locked out, or who had gone on strike in support of them, received their ultimatum from the employers, they refused to give up their membership of the ITGWU. They were immediately dismissed by their employers, and by September 1913 20,000 workers in hundreds of businesses were locked out.[85] Events took a dramatic turn, particularly following the arrest, imprisonment and release on bail of Jim Larkin and the holding of a public meeting that had been arranged by James Connolly and others in Sackville Street. With the help of some actors such as Helena Molony, Jim Larkin addressed supporters from the balcony of the Imperial Hotel.

In the response to the meeting an interesting division is revealed between progressive and conservative nationalists. Among those attending the meeting were Constance Markievicz and Thomas MacDonagh. Both would comment later on the clash between those attending the meeting and the police, after Larkin had been rearrested. Most commentators were in agreement that the Dublin Metropolitan Police, assisted by the RIC, had reacted with unnecessary violence. Ireland experienced its first Bloody Sunday – 31 August 1913 – as a result of which James Nolan and John Byrne would later die of their injuries, and over 500 other people were injured. Sixteen-year-old Alice Brady would also die after contracting tetanus from a gunshot wound in the wrist. Both James Larkin and James Connolly gave short speeches at her funeral.

---

85   http://www.irishlabourhistorysociety.com/pdf/Saothar%204.pdf

That is the context in which James Larkin and James Connolly sought to build the ITGWU which, they hoped, would speak not only for Dublin workers but would usher in a commonwealth of co-operation and transform Irish society.

While these leaders who brought a new militant trade unionism to Ireland had a commitment to improving the lives of working people, they also had to grapple with the role of labour in the wider independence movement. It is important to recognize the significance of the new language they were using. In retrospect, there seems to be an extraordinary optimism in the way they spoke. Revolution was in the air, great changes were coming that would sweep away the old order.

The late Donal Nevin,[86] a committed and painstaking chronicler of Irish labour history, suggests that there is in the writings of James Connolly between 1896 and 1903 a messianic fervour and an expectation that the collapse of the capitalist system was imminent. Nevin also remarked that the moment of the Lockout has to be looked at in a broader international context. James Connolly and Jim Larkin were not alone in fervently believing that a workers' republic could be brought about in a relatively short space of time: the American socialist Daniel De Leon and John Leslie in Scotland (who is said to have converted Connolly to Marxism) shared his optimism and brought a corresponding sense of urgency, vigour and commitment to changing society.

In Ireland this was a time of fervent organization on a number of fronts, a cultural revival, a nationalist revival as well as a labour awakening. Diarmaid Ferriter notes that it became possible for the first time to use the words 'Irish Republican' and 'socialist' in the same breath. It did not seem necessary to wait for middle-class endorsement in order to bring about a new form of socialist existence.

The Lockout, and particularly the events of Bloody Sunday, encouraged

---

86   Donal Nevin, *Between Comrades: James Connolly: Letters and Correspondence 1889–1916* (Gill & Macmillan, 2007).

artists to respond to the crisis they saw unfolding around them. Nelson O'Ceallaigh Ritschel charts how writers such as George Bernard Shaw, George Russell and James Connolly, coming from different traditions, agreed that the Lockout and particularly the police response to the meeting of Sunday, 31 August was a disgrace. O'Ceallaigh Ritschel writes of how Patrick Pearse, who had reacted so badly to John Millington Synge's *The Playboy of the Western World*, now defended the sacked workers. In response to the shocking scenes on Sackville Street, Pearse began to develop an economic critique of British imperialism. At the height of the Lockout, Pearse wrote in *A Hermitage*:

> Twenty thousand Dublin families live in one room tenements. It is common to find two or three families occupying the same room: and sometimes one of the families will have a lodger! There are tenement rooms in Dublin in which over a dozen persons live, eat and sleep. High rents are paid for these rooms, rents which in cities like Birmingham would command neat four-roomed cottages with gardens. These are among the grievances against which men in Dublin are beginning to protest. Can you wonder that protest is at last being made? Can you wonder that the protest is crude and bloody? I do not know whether the methods of Mr James Larkin are wise methods or unwise methods (unwise, I think, in some respects) but this I know, that here is a most hideous thing to be righted and that the man who attempts honestly to right it is a good man and a brave man.[87]

Following the reaction of the police and the RIC to the meeting Larkin had addressed on 31 August, Pearse was moved to write: 'An employer who accepts the aid of foreign bayonets to enforce a lock-out of his

---

87   UCC Multitext Project in Irish History, p. 15.

workmen and accuses the workmen of national dereliction because they accept foreign alms for their starving wives and children… [is] a matter for a play by Synge.'

W. B. Yeats, too, was forthright in his denunciation of the Dublin nationalist newspapers who demonized the workers:

> I charge the Dublin nationalist newspapers with deliberately arousing religious passion to break up the organisation of the workingman, with appealing to mob law day after day, with publishing the names of workingmen and their wives for purposes of intimidation… Intriguers have met together somewhere behind the scenes that they might turn the religion of Him who thought it hard for a rich man to enter the Kingdom of Heaven into an oppression of the poor.

The *Irish Times*, which took a consistent anti-Larkin line, was nonetheless prepared to publish Yeats's poem 'September 1913' and George Russell's (AE's) polemic, 'Open Letter to the Masters of Dublin':

> We read in the dark ages of the rack and thumb screw. It remained for the twentieth century, the capital city of Ireland to see an oligarchy of 400 masters deciding openly upon starving 100,000 people and refusing to consider any solution except that fixed by their pride. You masters asked men to do what masters of Labour in any other city in these islands had not dared to do. You insolently demanded of those men who were members of a trade union that they should resign from that union; and from those who were not members you insisted in a vow that they would never join it. Your insolence and ignorance of the rights conceded to workers universally in the modern world were incredible and as great as your inhumanity.[88]

---

88   *Irish Times*, 7 October 1913.

George Russell was not the only public intellectual or writer to be galvanized into action by the Lockout and the repression of the Sackville Street meeting. He, and others, were now writing and speaking with an increasing social militancy.

At the major meeting in solidarity with the strikers outside Dublin, Russell shared a platform with James Connolly, whom Russell described as 'a really intellectual leader', and with George Bernard Shaw at a meeting at the Royal Albert Hall in London on 1 November. Russell's speech was again highly critical of State and Church authorities, particularly the police and William Walsh, Archbishop of Dublin. The speech caused fury in the constitutional nationalist press; the *Freeman's Journal* accused AE of hiding anti-Irish sympathies in his socialism. The response in the media is clear evidence that for many a nationalist, independence need not carry the burden of workers' rights.

There was also an exchange of views in print between Russell and Connolly, each reading and responding to the other's theories of social and political organization as laid out in the columns of the *Irish Homestead* and in Connolly's books on labour in Ireland. Each offered the other a constituency difficult to reach – in Russell's case the urban worker, in Connolly's the farm labourer and smallholder.[89] This was an alliance that was unfortunately stillborn even in the later decades of the new State.

These exchanges give us a glimpse of radicals with a utopian vision who were nonetheless meaningfully engaged with the society around them. They were clear that suffering humanity was at the core of the crisis. For example, running through the speeches on the Lockout are references to hunger and starvation. Here is James Connolly, for example:

> You cannot build a free nation on the basis of slavery. We are against
> the domination of nation over nation, class over class, sex over sex.

---

89 Nicholas Allen, *George Russell and the New Ireland: 1905–30* (Four Courts Press Ltd. 2003).

> But if we are to make Ireland the Ireland of their dreams and aspi-
> rations we must have a free and self-respecting and independent
> people. You can never have freedom or self-respect whilst you have
> starvation, whether it is the green flag or the Union Jack that is fly-
> ing over our head. If there is nothing in your stomach it matters
> mighty little what flag is flying.

This reference to starvation is something that unites James Connolly and Patrick Pearse. But the absence of food for one's dependants, and the fact that employers and those who stayed at work would eat while those on strike would be hungry, was also a feature of William Martin Murphy's address to 700 of his tramway workers.

As mentioned earlier, many of us this year will have read or reread James Plunkett's *Strumpet City*, first published in 1969. In its pages we see life as it was lived and suffered by convincingly drawn ordinary people. Neither propagandistic nor sentimental, James Plunkett remained true to his belief that 'the duty of a good writer of fiction or drama is not to preach. It is to absorb, to observe, to distil and to reveal – gently.'[90]

Plunkett drew among other sources on Arnold Wright's *Disturbed Dublin: The Story of the Great Strike of 1913–14*,[91] which was published as defence of the employers' side in the Lockout, and in which workers are referred to as 'damaged material' due to their low standard of living and low energy levels born of poverty, a reminder of the extremity of the views being expressed at this time. However, in fairness to Arnold Wright, *Disturbed Dublin* acknowledges the horror of the atrocious housing conditions of the tenements.

Plunkett's book is faithful to history in its depth and detail. The book creatively recasts the collapse on the evening of 2 September 1913 of two houses in Church Street, which killed seven people and injured many

---

90   *Irish Times* obituary of James Plunkett, 31 May 2003.
91   London, 1914.

more. This avoidable tragedy exposed the vulnerability of the tenement dwellers crowded into the rooms of once great and now neglected houses.

Both official nationalism and the Church were challenged by the Lockout. Some nationalists such as Thomas McDonagh, Thomas Ashe, Tom Clarke and Patrick Pearse supported the Lockout, but Arthur Griffith and his Sinn Féin paper were frankly hostile. Indeed, during the summer of 1913 Douglas Hyde, President of the Gaelic League, attempted to expel Thomas Ashe and Patrick Pearse from the language organization on account of their support of the locked-out workers.

As for the Church, the most serious clash between the locked-out workers and the clergy occurred following the offer of supporters in Britain to host suffering Irish children for the duration of the strike. The confrontation led to a battle for the children travelling between Westland Row and the boat at Kingstown. It opened with cries of 'throw them in the Liffey' addressed to Dora Montefiore and Lucille Rand, promoters of the scheme, and when the departure had been successfully blocked, Montefiore and Rand were arrested on charges of kidnapping. The protest involved a large number of priests and a crowd who had been swayed by their hostile sermons. 'Faith of Our Fathers' and 'Hail Glorious St Patrick' rang out as the children were returned to their homes in the tenements. Archbishop Walsh opposed the children's journey not just on religious grounds, but also because it would make them discontented with the homes that they would inevitably come back to sooner or later.

During the Lockout food ships sent by the British TUC had helped to sustain morale. That assistance would have a value, in today's terms, of about €10 million. The TUC, however, would not take the further step of sympathetic strike action. The style of Jim Larkin's leadership in advance of a special TUC conference that was called to discuss the matter had further antagonized his opponents within the trade union movement. When the time came to vote at the conference, it was 2,280,000 votes against and 203,000 in support of a strike in solidarity with the locked-out Irish workers.

After four months, the men's children starving and their families in dire hardship, the Lockout came to an end in January 1914. The workers were defeated. James Connolly wrote in *Forward*: 'And so, we Irish workers must go down into hell, bow our backs to the lash of the slave driver, let our hearts be seared by the iron of his hatred, and instead of the sacramental wafer of brotherhood and common sacrifice, eat the dust of defeat and betrayal.'

But while William Martin Murphy had won a victory in the short term, he was not successful in his greater aim of smashing the ITGWU or organized general trade unionism. Through the heroic efforts by members and organizations it had recovered sufficiently to defeat a further attempt at lockout in 1915 as other employers, recalling the cost of 1913, refused to throw in their lot with Murphy. By 1919 the International Labour Organization would establish as basic international labour law some of the principles that he opposed. While membership was initially decimated, by 1921 the ITGWU was organizing 120,000 workers throughout the country. The union had survived. A Housing Commission was set up following the strike and it provided incontrovertible evidence of poverty and slum conditions near the heart of Empire.

The role of the Irish labour movement and its leadership in shaping Ireland's democracy is acknowledged by writers on the Lockout. One of the most interesting things about the writing on Irish labour history over the last ten to fifteen years is that the published books go beyond hagiography and demonology; they attempt to restore the real complexity of individuals who were trying to make a difference.

Today, any consideration of James Connolly must include knowledge of his temperament, his frequent displays of volatility and the confusing and ambiguous relationship he had with Ireland. Larkin was inspirational in many ways, but he was exceptionally difficult as a collaborator. William O'Brien has often been presented as somebody who was a very destructive and malign force in the labour movement for his later opposition to Larkin. However, Tom Morrissey[92] reassesses him as a much more rounded character, emphasizing his contrariness and the fact that he died widely honoured but not widely liked, but also stressing the important intellectual role that he played and what he characterizes as O'Brien's deep humility.

We must always respect what James Connolly and Jim Larkin brought to the trade union movement and what they faced in the Lockout of 1913, the social forces that combined to defeat them. It was, however, people like William O'Brien in the decades after 1916 who focused on the actual mechanics of trade union organization: not a glamorous job, but one that was crucial in keeping labour organized in the 1920s and 1930s.

The impact that the Lockout had on the development of trade union consciousness in Ireland was vital. Dermot Keogh has argued that 1913 is important because of its contribution to that process, but that such a consciousness was not necessarily socialist, let alone revolutionary.[93] This may be one reason why, ten years after 1913, a TUC Annual Report referred to the fact that working-class electors still did not see the importance of having independent working-class representatives.[94] This highlights the great dilemma facing socialists in the 1920s and 1930s: how were they to appeal successfully to these voters? The electorate that was unionized seemed to think that trade unions were good for looking after their economic interests, but that their other main concern, nationalism, could be catered for by centrist or conservative political parties. This was the great difficulty in a country that did not have a very advanced industrial society and was, in any case, cut off from its industrial base in North-East Ulster.

In the 1930s and 1940s there was some progress, but also some less progressive developments. Some of the important legislation of the 1930s,

---

92   Thomas J. Morrissey, *William O'Brien, 1881–1968* (Four Courts Press, 2007).
93   Dermot Keogh, *The Rise of the Irish Working Class* (Appletree Press, 1982), pp. 245–50.
94   Donal Nevin (ed.), *Trade Union Century* (Mercier Press, 1994), p. 50.

the Workmen's Compensation Act and the Conditions of Employment Act, for example, were designed in some respects to limit exploitation, and the setting-up of the Agricultural Wages Board was another enlightened development. But during the Second World War, the Wages Standstill Order was a backward step, as was the highly restrictive Trade Union Act of 1941, which led to a split in the union movement.

One question that has to be asked is whether or not there could have been a more rapid improvement or even a healing of these divisions in the early 1950s, if so many people had not emigrated. As we have seen, in 1913 Archbishop Walsh had opposed the proposal that strikers' children go to England for relief. There were similar concerns over emigration a few decades later. In the 1940s and 1950s, the young people who emigrated generally did not return. But the permanence of their absence was not always clear.

During the Second World War, there was an interesting exchange of memoranda between the Department of External Affairs and the Department of Industry and Commerce about the threat that might arise if the emigrants did come back. There was no guarantee that Britain would continue taking in Irish immigrants if the labour market contracted. In a revealing document from the Department of Industry and Commerce in 1942, the author expressed a fear about 'the dumping home of workers who no doubt will have imbibed a good deal of "Leftism" in Britain'[95] and wrote about possible contingency plans for this.

According to this document, it was quite clear that the threat of social revolution was going to be at its highest in the late 1940s and 1950s, with a whole swathe of unemployed individuals who, it was feared, would not take their situation lying down, who were actually going to fight to assert their right to challenge the status quo and perhaps demand the social

---

95   National Archives of Ireland, Department of the Taoiseach, S11582A, 'Irish Labour Emigration', 18 May 1942; Diarmaid Ferriter, *The Transformation of Ireland* (Profile Books, 2004).

provisions they had enjoyed in England with the emerging welfare state.

Women were also blazing a trail in the labour movement in the early twentieth century, with considerable vigour, vitality and commitment. Delia Larkin announced in 1911 that Irish women workers were as wide-awake as male workers. The strike action in Jacob's biscuit factory saw 3,000 women withdrawing their labour to achieve their aims, which they did after a week, and though the laundryworkers' strike lasted three months it achieved two weeks' paid holidays for working people, pioneering a norm for most industrialized workers. This trail went cold in the early 1920s. Female trade union membership continued to grow, but it was largely in mixed unions, which did not press the case for equal pay or career progression with any great force.

The 1930s and 1940s saw a more hostile climate for female workers. In the Conditions of Employment Act of 1936, along with sections designed to limit the exploitation of workers, there were provisions restricting the jobs available for women. When you look at the response of some of the organized women to these restrictions you sense a seething and understandable anger. The Joint Committee of Women's Societies and Social Workers suggested that the Act was one of the most reactionary pieces of legislation of its time, and it placed Ireland at the head of an International Labour Organization blacklist that highlighted countries actively discriminating against women in the workforce. But when the Irish Women Workers' Union went to look for the support of the Labour Party and the trade unions in its campaign against the Act, none was forthcoming.

It is also true that politicians, most notably Seán Lemass, who introduced the Conditions of Employment Act, were clever enough to link their concerns about women in the workforce with ones that were already being expressed within the labour movement. In referring to the ferocious reaction that had greeted his Act, he used what was called the 'Derry card': Did they want a situation such as prevailed in the Derry textile factories, where the men stayed at home minding the babies and the women went to work? This particular rhetoric was bound up with the broader debate about the mechanization of industrial workplaces and the proper place of women. What were traditional male roles? What were contemporary female roles? Lemass's comments echoed exactly the comments of Senator Tom Foran, President of the ITGWU at the time: 'Do we really want this in this holy island of ours?'[96]

However, in 1953, when the Irish Women Workers actually brought an equal pay agenda to Congress, it is clear that its spokespersons were also keen to distinguish between different women within its ranks. They were not looking for equal pay for unmarried workers, for example. Indeed, female trade unionists like Louie Bennett were not great feminist liberators in that context. They were women of their era and they had concerns about certain classes of men being replaced in the workforce and doubted whether this was a good idea. There was nevertheless a huge growth in female trade union membership: by the 1970s, there were about 150,000 women members. This decade and the 1980s saw the shedding of some of the more patriarchal attitudes in the trade unions.

The influence of the Catholic Church in labour questions was significant, particularly in the 1930s, and deliberate scaremongering on the evils of socialism coloured discussions of workers' rights. Even though it was not successful, the primary school teachers' strike of 1946 was important in demonstrating what organized professional workers could achieve. The teachers' strike was significant, too, in what it revealed about the role played by the Archbishop of Dublin, John Charles McQuaid, who initially supported the claims of the teachers but then encouraged them to back down. This was typical of the practised ambiguity of the Catholic Church towards labour and trade union questions during the post-war era.

The Church promoted the idea that it was in favour of a 'just wage',

---

96   *Seanad Eireann Debates*, 27 November 1935.

but it would not define what constituted such a wage, and conveniently deemed this to be a matter for the professional economists. In a sense the Church appeared to give with one hand only to take back with the other. Its spokespersons sometimes maintained a very blatant denial of the extent of poverty, unemployment and destitution in Ireland. For example, one Catholic social theorist, Seamus O' Farrell, in a contribution to the Jesuit journal *Studies* in 1951, wrote about 'the stupid propaganda of the calamity mongers' who were determined to drive Ireland into Communist slavery because they kept emphasizing poverty. He suggested that poverty fifty years previously had been real, but was now only relative: if actual destitution was to be found in Ireland, it was rare and avoidable.[97] Highlighting the concerns of the unemployed would lead Ireland into Communist radicalism. The denial of poverty was not confined to the hard years before and after the war. Indeed, poverty would only be 'rediscovered' by the Church in the 1970s.

The decades of social partnership that followed warrant a separate treatment. As a form of partnership or a type of new corporatism, it had its achievements; but it also blunted competing interests in not entirely positive ways.

I should also mention, perhaps, that historians might consider whether there has been too much focus on wages at the expense of broader social issues. Pádraig Yeates has said that one of the key lessons of 1913 is 'the need to broaden the agenda from work place issues to the wider social, political and economic situation'.[98] Such a lesson has a moral significance today as we reflect on the increased drift and acceptance of economic models that lead to deregulated work, new forms of casual labour, extreme individualism and an economic and social crisis from which we

---

97 Diarmaid Ferriter, 'The stupid propaganda of the calamity mongers: the middle-class and Irish politics, 1945–1997', in Fintan Lane (ed.), *Politics, Society and the Middle Class in Ireland* (Palgrave, 2011), pp. 271–89.
98 *Irish Times*, 25 August 2003.

are struggling to recover.

The Lockout also compels us to ask questions about our role in the wider international world of work: we are challenged to respond to the workplace disasters of south Asia, where European and American corporations make many of the clothes we all wear. In Pakistan 300 textile workers were killed in a single fire, and more recently in Bangladesh over 1,000 textile workers were crushed in the collapse of a badly maintained, overcrowded building. Today we learn about such disasters even more quickly than citizens in Ireland's countryside learnt of the collapse of Dublin tenements in 1913. As global citizens we should respond to such disasters, informed by our own Famine-haunted past, but conscious too of the benefits we have achieved through the efforts of those who a century ago had the courage to struggle for the rights of workers.

In conclusion, I believe that it is vital that a new generation has a deep understanding of the 1913 Lockout. Eric Hobsbawm, the great British historian who recently died, expressed concerns late in his career that:

> The destruction of the past or, rather, of the social mechanisms that link one's contemporary experience to that of earlier generations, is one of the most characteristic and eerie phenomena of the late 20th century. Most young men and women at the century's end grow up in a sort of permanent present lacking any organic relation to the public past of the times they live in.[99]

Without good history teaching, there can be no shared idea of a public past. Now, more than ever, during the commemoration of our own fascinating and difficult past, we need to empower all our citizens with an appreciation of how we got to where we are. This is not to invoke the cliché about learning the lessons of history; rather, it is about seeing

---

99   Eric Hobsbawm, *Interesting Times: A Twentieth Century Life* (Abacus, 2002).

history as essential to understanding who we are today and who we might be in the future.

Knowledge of history is intrinsic to citizenship. To have no knowledge of the past is to be burdened with a lack of perspective and a lack of wisdom. Knowledge of history allows us to debunk myths and challenge inaccuracies as well as to expose deliberate amnesia or invented versions of the past. It enables us to understand the significance of diversity, nuance and context. This decade of commemorations is an opportunity to use the new resources available to professional and amateur historians, to all of us, in the exploration of our past and the strengthening of our idea of citizenship.

As part of that exploration, we might reflect on the plight of the working families of Dublin a century ago who were courageous participants in and victims of the struggle between capital and organized labour that we now know as the Great Lockout of 1913.

At a
Symposium Entitled
'Remembering 1916'

MANSION HOUSE,
DUBLIN

28 MARCH 2016

*I*S MÓR AN *phléisiúr dom tús a chur leis an gcomhrá seo tráthnóna ar an eachtra ríthábhachtach a bhí in Éirí Amach na Cásca 1916. Tugann sé sásamh faoi leith dom go bhfuil an ardán á roinnt agam inniu le scoláirí den scoth - gach duine acu, trína saothair agus taighde, a chur go mór lenár dtuiscint maidir leis an tréimhse sin inar saolú ár Stáit.* (It is my great pleasure to be opening this discussion on the seminal event in the history of Ireland that was the Easter Rising of 1916. I am especially pleased to be sharing this exercise in collective reflection with such a distinguished panel of scholars – all of whom have contributed to enhancing our understanding of the founding moments of our State.)

I want to pay tribute to the work of the many historians, in Ireland and abroad, who – with the benefit of newly available archival material – have enabled us to gain a deeper grasp of the cultural and intellectual ebullience that stirred Ireland in 1916, the overlapping loyalties and passions that animated the men and women of the time, the influences of the Enlightenment, romanticism, mysticism, suffragism, socialism, pacifism – all the complexities of the wider global context of which they were part and from which they drew.

It is especially fitting that we undertake this discussion here, in this Round Room of the Mansion House, where, in January 1919, the first meeting of the First Dáil was held. This was a key moment in our history, when the revolution of 1916 took on the form of a parliamentary democracy.

The presence of eminent historians here today also reminds us of the complicated relationship between the act of commemoration and the discipline of history. History and commemoration operate, of course, in different registers. Commemoration inevitably involves a selection of events, and it requires a dialectic between remembering and forgetting that is mediated through the prism of contemporary concerns.

There is always a risk, then, that commemoration might be exploited for partisan purposes, and good historians have rightly warned us against the perils posed to historical truth by any backward imputation of motives, any uncritical transfer of contemporary emotions on to the past.[100] Commemoration can also lead to a form of public history aimed at securing the present, whether by invoking an 'appropriate' past or, in desperation, by encouraging a form of amnesia that might allow a bland transition to the future. Such approaches are often those that least discomfit those who wield power.

As Diarmaid Ferriter has shown, each anniversary of the Easter Rising has had a different focus, a distinctive way of looking back at the past. These anniversaries tell us at least as much about the zeitgeist of each commemorative period, and perhaps about those who controlled the process of commemoration, as they do about the events of 1916 themselves.

---

100 These risks are brought home to us, for example, in the following remark by Timothy Snyder, eminent historian of the Holocaust and the Second World War: 'With commemorative causality, the boundaries of history are set by the contingencies of empathy.'

Conscious of these risks, my emphasis as President of Ireland has been on the challenge of remembering ethically in this decade of commemorations – not just the Easter Rising, but other defining events such as the Great Lockout of 1913, the outbreak of the First World War, the War of Independence and the Civil War.

There are several aspects to such ethical remembering. On one level, it entails the inclusion of the voices of the marginalized and the disenfranchised in our recollections of the past, a willingness to do justice, for example, to the essential part played by women and the working people of Dublin in the Easter Rising. The ethics of commemoration also entails an openness to the dissonant voices and stories of 'the other', the stranger, the enemy of yesterday – a disposition described by the philosopher Paul Ricoeur as 'narrative hospitality'. In speeches I have given in the North and South over the last few years, I have often drawn on Ricoeur's suggestive conceptual work, and I have emphasized in particular the importance of avoiding any comforting amnesia.

Ethical remembering does not dispense with historical empiricism, acknowledging as it does that the exclusion of inconvenient facts can close doors to reflection and research. Furthermore, while commemoration is always a process of selective remembering, ethical commemoration seeks to respect context and complexity, as well as the integrity of the motivations of the men and women of the past.

Crucially, and perhaps most importantly, there is an introspective dimension to ethical remembering, inviting us to revisit critically the collective myths and beliefs by which we have defined ourselves as a nation. Commemoration provides an opportunity to address the assumptions of competing foundational mythologies, mythologies that have at times turned our historiography into a bitterly contested space.

A critical examination of the nature of nationalism as it prevailed at the time of the Rising is the subject of my address today.

Such an examination of nationalism does not imply a disqualification of national pride or national feelings. Quite the contrary: my purpose is to seek those elements within Ireland's nationalist tradition that are most meaningful to us today – elements from which we might draw; elements whose emancipatory potential, once retrieved, might better enable us to rekindle the purpose of our living together as a nation.

Of course, a critique of Irish nationalism as it manifested itself at the turn of the last century is a task that many have already undertaken. By relocating the Easter Rising within the frame of the First World War, but also in the context of the wider currents of ideas that then stirred the world – movements such as socialism, feminism, but also militarism, imperialism and racialist ideologies – there has been a great critical reassessment of aspects of the Rising and, in particular, of the myths of redemptive violence that were at the heart, not just of Irish but also of Imperial nationalism.

The latter has not, perhaps, been revisited with the same sharp edge as the former. Indeed, while the long shadow cast by 'the Troubles' in Northern Ireland has rightly led to a scrutiny of the Irish Republican tradition of physical violence, a similar sceptical review of militarist imperialism needs to be more fully achieved. In the context of 1916, this imperial triumphalism can be traced, for example, in the language of the recruitment campaigns of the time, which evoked mythology, masculinity and religion, and glorified the Irish blood that had 'reddened the earth of every continent'. But that is a task for another day.

Today I would like to offer a brief but, I hope, constructive, appraisal of Irish nationalism from the point of view of the egalitarian tradition that manifested itself before and during the Easter Rising, but which was progressively and, I would argue, consciously repressed in later decades.

What is the nature of our nationalist movement, and where is its egalitarian element? Why and how has the flame of equality and social justice been quenched? What republicanism can we speak about in Ireland? Can these centenary commemorations be an occasion to redefine what constitutes a real republic, a polity that allows for a more meaningful co-existence, reaching back to the generous aspirations of the men and women who preceded us – to the 'unfulfilled future of our past' – and reaching forward to the generations who will succeed us?

In tracing the journey which took us from the promises of equality contained in the Proclamation of 1916 and in the Democratic Programme of the First Dáil, through to the socially conservative clauses enshrined in the Constitutions of 1922 and 1937, it might be useful to consider in more detail the sequence of events that led to these changes.

One of the great milestones of Ireland's egalitarian tradition is, of course, the Lockout of 1913, which galvanized the Irish trade union movement and led to the formation of the Irish Citizen Army as an organization whose members distinguished themselves, among all the formations that took part in the Easter Rising, by their commitment to equality and revolutionary social transformation.

The coming-together of public intellectuals and activists in the events surrounding the Lockout was an extraordinary one. It included people who differed on many issues and on questions of tactics, for example George Bernard Shaw and James Connolly; but they were united in an appeal for justice that was far greater than what divided them.

It was their response to the Lockout that brought James Connolly and Patrick Pearse closer together, as attested to by Pearse's references in his letters of the time to the appalling living conditions in the slums of Dublin. This rapprochement was made explicit in the lines on equality woven into the Proclamation of the Republic that Pearse read out from under the porch of the GPO on Monday, 24 April 1916. If I may quote those lines which remain with us as, perhaps, the most meaningful promise bequeathed to us by the men and women of 1916: 'The Republic guarantees religious and civil liberty, equal rights and equal opportunities to all its citizens, and declares its resolve to pursue the happiness and prosperity of the whole nation and all of its parts, cherishing all the children of the nation equally....'.

Addressed to Irishmen as well as Irishwomen, in years when few women in the wider world had yet secured the right to vote,[101] the Proclamation was, for its time, an exceptional document. It was not a description of the actual state of Irish society, but a compelling vision of what it might become. And while we might, nowadays, choose to forget some of the other formulations contained in the Proclamation, its emancipatory appeal is certainly one that still resonates strongly with us a century later.

This call for egalitarianism was repeated in another, and too often neglected, founding document of our State, the Democratic Programme of the First Dáil. This Programme, which was drafted in January 1919 by Labour leader Tom Johnson, with the help of William O'Brien and Cathal O'Shannon, and with some final editing by Seán T. O'Ceallaigh, proclaimed the equal right of all citizens to essential social goods. As I have written elsewhere, the Democratic Programme of the First Dáil was:

> The shining evidence of a possibility being expressed at the birth of a State, a vision that was powerfully egalitarian, celebratory, asserting a deep humanity, and linked to an international movement that was pushing for a great change towards a socialist version of politics, economy and society…
>
> The Democratic Programme gave a glimpse of the possibility of dealing with the injustices that motivated the founders of Labour – the elimination of poverty, inequality, the exploitation of vulnerable workers; advancing the rights of women and children, and ending inadequate access to education and healthcare, amongst other things.[102]

---

101 It would be 1918 before women over thirty would get the vote in Ireland, and proposals to extend the voting age to twenty-one were defeated in the new Dáil.
102 Michael D. Higgins, *Renewing the Republic* (Liberties Press, 2011), p. 68.

The Irish Republican Brotherhood, however, did not approve of the Programme, and indeed there were some in the IRA leadership who were determined to suppress it. Kevin O'Higgins later referred to the text as 'largely poetry', while the leader of Sinn Féin, Arthur Griffith, who was in prison and prevented from attending this historic meeting of the First Dáil, not only objected to the principles of the Programme, but criticized it eloquently before the meeting. Their responses were but a few of the signs that presaged a wider rolling-back of the aspirations for equality in the decades following the Easter Rising.

Before I describe in more detail the nature of that conservative reaction, it is important, I think, that we remember the process of socio-economic transformation in rural Ireland in the years preceding the Rising. These changes helped to form the particular ideology of nationalism that triumphed in the first decades of our independence. This ideological influence thoroughly shaped the character of the new State.

I believe that Irish historiography, with some notable exceptions, has insufficiently addressed the way in which the later development of the State was shaped by the social differences that were deepening in Ireland at the turn of the twentieth century; especially the differences between an impoverished urban working class and a rural Ireland from which so many of the marginalized had been forced to emigrate.

More specifically, it is important to recall how the implementation of the Land Acts, a great achievement for parliamentary action in combination with rural agitation, had turned tens of thousands of rural tenants into peasant proprietors. Famine and later emigration saw to the virtual disappearance of the class of land labourers. A new grazier class emerged, often in alliance with professionals and with those who controlled rural commerce and credit. These were the classes who would rise to power in the new State.

By the time of the Easter Rising, this native class of landowners, many of whom defined themselves as nationalists, had largely replaced

Anglo-Irish landlords. The ideas of class, property and respectability animating that new body of native landowners were to have a huge influence on Irish political life throughout the 1920s and 1930s. And while there were many socially transformative dimensions to Irish nationalism – expressed, for example, in the movement for women's suffrage, in the labour movement, and in the explosion of creativity that characterized the cultural revival – this ascendancy of the more conservative trends smothered the call for equality expressed in both the Proclamation of 1916 and the Democratic Programme of the First Dáil.

We should not forget, however, that for a brief period after the Rising, ordinary men and women did seek to make the principle of popular ownership a living reality. Between 1918 and 1923, five general strikes and eighteen local strikes occurred in Ireland. Workers took over the running of more than eighty workplaces, and established 'workers' soviets' at the Cleeves factory in Limerick, in the neighbouring coalmines of Castlecomer, and at the foundry in Drogheda. The West was particularly awake. A network of popularly elected, local arbitration courts sprung up, sometimes to decide the terms of land redistribution. But these bold moves resulted in the country's wealthier landowners turning from Westminster to the Sinn Féin Party to put an end to 'agrarian Bolshevism'.[103]

The debates around the drafting of the Constitution of the Irish Free State in 1922 further signalled the gradual retreat of conservative nationalist leaders from what might be regarded as any dangerous ideas of redistribution. The suggested inclusion of the Proclamation's lines on equality were dismissed as 'Bolshevist' by the British authorities, to whom the draft 1922 Constitution was submitted. The words were dropped.

The rejection of egalitarianism by some members of the Provisional Government was sometimes expressed in the most brutal manner. Hugh

---

103 Thomas Murray, 'Igniting fire in minds of Irish men and women', *Irish Independent 1916 Collection*, Thursday, 3 March 2016.

Kennedy, the Provisional Government's senior law officer, argued, for example, that popular disorder would have to be overcome by 'utterly ruthless action'.

Similarly, when the Labour Party, appalled by what was happening, threatened in 1922 to withdraw its nineteen members unless the Dáil was called into session – so that peace terms might be discussed and the horrific Civil War brought to an end – the response from the Irish Republican Brotherhood members of the War Council was sharp. As Eoin O'Duffy put it in a letter to Michael Collins on 19 August 1922: 'I believe the Labour element and the Red Flaggers are at the back of all the moves to make peace, not for the sake of the country but in their own interests.' The letter also made it clear that a military victory would give notice as to how any future egalitarian movement would be dealt with: 'When the National Army have entered this conflict with such vigour,' O'Duffy wrote, 'labour realised that there would be much more vigorous action to crush any Red Flag or Bolshevist Troubles.'[104]

The Constitution of 1922 did, admittedly, make space for some innovative political ideas. It contained certain provisions for direct democracy, allowing for citizens' initiatives in the drafting of legislation. But later governments amended the Constitution to prevent any such subversive provisions from coming into effect, with the result that the new Constitution was ultimately a minimalist document which belied the radical proposals in its early drafts. There are, of course, constitutional theorists who defend minimalism in constitutions, but in the Irish case I suggest that the why and the how of such minimalism is of historical interest and significance.

A further sign of the conservative reaction in Ireland after the Easter Rising was the muting of cultural creativity during those years. While the period 1890–1910 had witnessed an extraordinary output of new

---

104 From Ferghal McGarry's 'O'Duffy' at p. 111, cited by John M. Regan in his *Myth and the Irish State* (Irish Academic Press, 2013).

ideas and debates and literary forms, reflected in a remarkable flood of publications, the new State established a chilling censorship that derived more from the authoritarianism of the war period than from the cultural creativity of the Revival years. From the 1920s onwards, anti-conformism and cultural innovation were encouraged to express themselves abroad.

Many women who had participated in the Rising, such as Kathleen Clarke or Helena Molony, vehemently opposed the inclusion in the new Constitution of 1937 of the articles that limited the participation of women in the public sphere.

But despite such efforts, new levels of bigotry, censorship and a subjugation of the State to hierarchical and patriarchal values were achieved in the 1930s. A property-driven conservatism took hold, at the expense of any wide-ranging transformation of an egalitarian kind. The fetishizing of land and private property, a restrictive religiosity and a repressive pursuit of respectability, affecting women in particular, became the defining social and cultural features of the newly independent Ireland.

How, then, to remember 1916? The question has often been raised during these commemorations as to whether we have lived up to the ideals articulated in the founding events of the Irish Republic. This is, as I have suggested, an inadequate question. Indeed we must never forget how Irish society as a whole was in those years neither equal, nor ideologically drawn to egalitarianism. It was and it remains a challenge to create a society that will enable all of its members – children, women and men – to flourish.

There was no descent from a paradise of equality into inequality; but the inequality that has existed throughout our history is today growing even deeper. The early years of our State did not represent an idyll of liberty and freedom – but the study of the revolutionary moment does offer us a moment of idealism and hope, the promise of what our nation might yet become. Let us put it positively: the joy of making equality the central theme of our Republic is for us to achieve.

Agus muid ag tabhairt faoin saothair seo, b'éigean dúinn, i mo thu-airim, athchúirt a dhéanamh ar an tuiscint atá againn ar cad is brí le fíor Phoblacht; Poblacht ina mbeadh smaointe maidir le dlúth-pháirtíocht, an Pobal agus an réimse poiblí ina cheartlár.; fíor phoblacht a aithníonn go bhfuil an Stáit féin ina fhreagracht do chách, agus a thuigeann an ról lárnach atá ag an Stát chéanna ar mhaith-eas a saoránaigh ar fad.

(As we set to this task, we are also called to revisit our conceptions of what constitutes a real Republic – a Republic that would have solidarity, community and the public good at its heart; a Republic that would acknowledge the State as a shared responsibility, and recognize, too, its vital role in achieving the welfare of all citizens.)

This conception of the State and the Republic is so much richer than any limiting, individualistic definition of citizenship – and it is also, I suggest, closer to what the leaders of 1916 had in mind. They were advanced thinkers, selfless women and men who took great risks to ensure that the children of Ireland would, in the future, live in freedom and enjoy their fair share of Ireland's prosperity.

The passage of 100 years allows us to see the past afresh, free from some of the narrow, partisan interpretations that might have restricted our view in earlier periods. We have a duty to honour and respect that past, and retrieve the idealism which was at its heart. But we have a greater duty to imagine and to craft a future illuminated by the unfulfilled promises of our history.

Address at an Ecumenical Service to Commemorate the Children Who Died During the Easter Rising

ST PATRICK'S CHURCH, RINGSEND

5 MAY 2015

*I*S CÓIR, AGUS *muid i mbun deich mbliana dírithe ar chuimhneacháin, áird a thabhairt ar iadsan nach déanadh machnamh orthu - fiú gur caileadh iad i mbláth a n-óige i 1916 agus iad ach amháin i mbun imeachtaí an oige.*

(It is fitting, as we undertake our decade of commemorations, that we remember those whose loss in 1916 has been less thought about and less spoken about, even though they were killed in their full flush of youth, while they went about the pursuits of children.)

Engaging with the past is rarely a simple or easy process. It can involve a complex negotiation of the memories, hurts, legacies and emotions of all those affected by events; most of all the cataclysmic events such as the Easter Rising and the response to it, whose consequences were profound.

The 1916 Rising is, of course, a seminal event, preceded by both parliamentary and military actions at home and abroad, and driven by a vision of independence for Ireland which, many believed, might be built on the foundations of equality, justice and respect for all.

The history of 1916 is, of course, made up of many different stories, and today we are invited to remember the neglected stories of the children who lost their lives during the final days of April 1916.

We are, as a nation, greatly indebted to Joe Duffy and to all those who assisted him in reclaiming the memory of the children who were mourned so silently in the days and months following the Easter Rising, their deaths often unknown to later generations of their families, their names absent from the history books and from our foundational stories as a nation.

Many years and decades now separate us from April 1916, and it is critical that we not only recall that past, but remember it in a way that is ethical and honest, that is inclusive of the stories of all people, including those who played and made friends on the streets of Dublin at that time.

Commemorations such as this have a great significance, and indeed should not be seen solely as formal occasions or sombre ceremonies; but rather as an encouragement for citizens to come together and to remember collectively, and with feeling, the people and events of the time.

Today we remember, by individual name, each of the forty young citizens whose tragic deaths in 1916 did not bring forth memorials or plaques, or songs or poetry. This is an occasion of recovery, of reclamation and it is not one of recrimination. We are invited to recall the loss of these young lives in a way that will grant us the freedom to deliver the best versions of ourselves in the present, and we hope that it will allow our past to inspire a moment of grace and even of healing; and for some, perhaps, of forgiveness.

Today we have an important opportunity to reflect on citizenship, the importance of each individual member of our community, and of our own duty and responsibility to seek to play a role in the creation of a fair and equitable society, one in which all citizens have the opportunity to flourish.

Ní an óige amháin a bhí i gcoitinne ag íobartaigh dearmadta 1916. Ba chuid den aicme oibre iad. Bhí cónaí ar formhór dóibh i dtionóntáin i lár na cathrach, go leór dóibh ag roinnt tithíochta den sort sin le hiliomad clainnte eile sna coinníollacha tithíochta ba mheasa san Eorap. B'fhéidir gurb é sin an chúis gur déanadh dearmad orthu féin, ar a mhuintir agus ar a aicme agus muid a macnamh ar scéalta Éirí Amach na Cásca.

(Some of the forgotten victims of 1916 shared more than youth. Many of them were working-class. Most of them lived in inner-city tenement buildings, many of them sharing such accommodation with several other families in some of the worst housing conditions in Europe. It is perhaps for this reason that they, and their parents, and their class have remained obscure in stories of the Easter Rising.)

The children, like so many children in the world today, were left to be the survivors of the street. Many were simply going about the tasks of generosity and care that come so naturally to children. It is also true to say that children, at that time, were not given a childhood as contemporary society knows it. They had to learn the tasks of survival early. In our own time, allowing an equality of citizenship to our children has been a slow process and for many children and their families achieving equality of opportunity is an, as yet, unfinished task.

The tragedy of the loss of a child is twofold: it is the gravest of all possible hurts to those who love the child, and it is also the quenching of possibilities before they have the chance to blossom.

The children we celebrate today were denied their potential. We now restore to those forgotten children their rightful place in the story and the celebration of that founding moment of our State that was the Easter Rising. We can, perhaps, best honour their memory through the rebuilding and renewal of our society and the creation of an ethical foundation on which our Republic can grow and thrive, and, most importantly, by making ours a country in which our children can fulfil their potential in peace and security, in health and in happiness.

A century has passed since the Easter Rising, and many more chapters will be written in the story of our independent nation. We have recently faced times of great challenges; challenges that have left us wounded as a society. This experience should have encouraged us to recognize the assumptions which have failed us, of the need to close a chapter on what was not the best version of ourselves, and invite us to start a new chapter based on a different version of our Irishness.

Today, as we recall the innocent lives that were lost during the traumatic events of the founding period of our nation, let us all redouble our efforts to ensure that we fashion together a Republic of which they would have been proud.

To the Relatives of Those Who Participated in the Easter Rising

MAIN HALL, ROYAL DUBLIN SOCIETY (RDS), BALLSBRIDGE, DUBLIN 4

26 MARCH 2016

MAY I COMMENCE by thanking the many descendants and relatives of the participants in the 1916 Rising who have gathered here today to honour their brave ancestors. All of you here this evening share, and represent at a unique and personal level, the significance of the actions taken by those with whom you have a relationship. While this occasion is one of pride in citizenship for you it is also an intimate family occasion. Yours is a special relationship with the founding moments of our State and with the creation of the independent Ireland we now enjoy. I am privileged to share this event with you.

Some of you present are related to the leaders of the Rising, now immortalized as the signatories of the Proclamation, or as leaders of the participating organizations. Others among you represent the many quiet, unsung heroes who moved around the streets of Dublin on that seismic Easter Monday. Names like Lily Kempson, Walter Bell, James Maguire, Daniel Brophy, Margaret Quinn and Patrick English may not have been perpetuated in the names of our streets and buildings, or in songs, poems and films of the period, but they and many others, of every rank and skill, played their own unique and significant role on the streets and in the buildings of Dublin during that April week.

Whatever the valued memory or connection that has brought you here, all of you in this room share a direct link to the people who, some with more preparation than others, took to the streets of Dublin on Easter Monday 1916 to make a demand for independence and to call for an end to empire. Those who participated were men and women who risked everything in their different ways, by occupying buildings in the city, by carrying ammunition around its streets, dodging snipers in order to carry messages or transport food and medical supplies to where they were needed, and undertaking many other essential tasks in a city fighting for freedom.

For all of us citizens today theirs are stories of great bravery, vision and determination; but they were also, for their loved ones and dependants, stories tinged with sadness, loss and separation. The human price paid should not be forgotten, should remind us of the great debt of gratitude we owe to all of those who risked their lives 100 years ago so that future generations could grow up as citizens of a free and independent State.

Across a distance of time there is the danger that we might lose the human essence of the lives of the men and women who changed the course of our history. Tonight we have the opportunity to give proper place to the intimate human dimension of the Easter Rising and the sacrifices made by so many of those who helped to build our nation.

A chúin an cothéacs as a thagann ár bhféidireachtaí d'inniu agus don todhchaí.

I often think of Lily Connolly's words to her husband James when she and her daughter Nora visited him on the eve of his execution: 'But your beautiful life James...'.

Cuireann bhur láithreacht i gcuimhne dom an baol agus na híobairtí a ghlac na fir agus na mná a raibh páirteach san Éirí Amach orthu féin.

Ní rabhadar cinnte faoin toradh a bheadh ar an Éirí Amach agus ní rabhadar ag súil le maireachtáil chun an toradh sin a fheiceáil, is é sin Éire saor.

(Your presence calls to mind the risks and sacrifices of the men and women who became involved in the Rising. They may have been uncertain of its outcome and without expectation of living to see what could subsequently be achieved in the name of Irish freedom.)

An occasion such as this gives us the opportunity to shine a light on an often forgotten chapter in the story of 1916 and the War of Independence, the layers of grief and loss and the final farewells that had to be borne and cast long shadows across families for so many years.

For example, when we remember Thomas MacDonagh we should not just recall his role as Commandant taking control of Jacob's biscuit factory, but we should remember him as a young man and father whose daughter woke up and put her arms around his neck as he said his last goodbye to her on Easter Sunday night.

Patrick Pearse's final words to his mother before he was executed , 'I will call to you in my heart at the last moment', are words that for many will echo as strongly across the years as the memory of his reading of the Proclamation in front of the GPO at four minutes past noon on Easter Monday afternoon.

Má smaoinímid orthu mar aithreacha agus mar dhearthaireacha, mar iníonacha agus mar leannáin, mar a dhéanaimid anocht, tá sé níos éasca orainn tuiscint a fháil ar a saolta roimh an Éirí Amach agus le linn an Éirí Amach féin.

(Thinking of them as fathers and brothers, daughters and lovers, as we do tonight, allows us to place ourselves more easily in their lives and to appreciate the experiences they lived through in the lead-up to, and during, the Rising.)

The actors in the Rising were not abstract or mythical figures; they were living, and particularly conscious and engaged, men and women. They were poets, academics, journalists and civil servants; city clerks and shopkeepers; rural farmers and labourers; Catholics and Protestants, whose voices made the call for a new and reimagined Ireland.

When we read the first-hand accounts that have been made available to us, we are presented with a sense of what it was like to live in Dublin in the early twentieth century.

That period between the 1910s and the 1920s, the 'revolutionary decade', was a vibrant episode in Irish history. Far from the image of a homogenous and insular Ireland with which we are often presented, the Ireland of that time was a hotbed of creativity, in which were articulated demands for civic participation. It was a time of passionate public discourse; but it was also an Ireland that was deeply divided in terms of class.

The teeming tenements in the abandoned Georgian sections of the inner city were locations of the worst poverty in the empire whose capital was less than a half day's travel away; 5,000 tenements were home to 87,000 people, comprising 26,000 families. Of those families, 20,000 lived in apartments of just one room. In the suburbs the previous occupants of Georgian Dublin, many of them landlords charging rents that would secure a small house in Britain, in the words of Patrick Pearse, 'prepared for Summer tennis'. In rural Ireland consolidation of land-holding was under way and a grazier class was seeking political influence.

Today we view the Rising as being synonymous with republicanism, but that of course was not a dominant ideology at the time; it was deliberately included in the Proclamation by Pearse and Connolly, who were very well aware of its historical significance and of its emancipatory promise.

Some of those who sought independence, we should remember, were seeking an Irish freedom that would have facilitated the expansion of commerce without a republic. Even amongst the ranks of the Irish Volunteers, whose rhetoric was republican in tone, many were honestly motivated by a desire to counter the unionist threat to Home Rule, or to secure their recent and invaluable gains in security of land tenure, holdings that had been achieved against a backdrop of insecurity, poverty and involuntary emigration.

Some of the rebels recorded their surprise when they learnt that a republic had, in fact, been declared in the Proclamation. The signatories understood the spirit and meaning of what was a republic in the sense of the Enlightenment, the French Revolution and the American Revolution.

The loss of Patrick Pearse and James Connolly – who had brought an egalitarian, workers' rights emphasis into the relationship between the Citizen Army and the Volunteers, whose coming together is reflected in the language of the Proclamation – would be felt all the more keenly in the years that followed, with the difficulties that obstructed the drafting of the Democratic Programme of the Dáil in 1919, the minimalism of the 1922 Constitution which did not incorporate the language of Pearse and Connolly, and indeed the deep institutional conservatism of the early decades of the State.

The Ireland of the early twentieth century was a place where the shops, restaurants and back rooms of radical Dublin were alive with the conversations of feminists, socialists, radicals, nationalists, anti-imperialists and the many other ideologists compelled, in their different ways, to dream of a new and better Ireland, and they cared for each other.

They were able to differ with dignity and respect for each other's views. Constance Markievicz would ask her sister Eva Gore-Booth to visit Agnes Mallen because she had a house full of children and would need help. Eva would in turn write to Hanna Sheehy-Skeffington, who while a pacifist still brought provisions to those involved in the Insurrection.

Some of you here today may be related to the nationalist families who socialized in the church halls and pub rooms around Clanbrassil Street and Harold's Cross, others to the middle-class radicals, pacifists, suffragettes and feminists such as the Sheehy Skeffingtons I have mentioned, others to the cultural radicals such as the MacDonaghs and the Pearses who lived in the neighbouring suburbs of Rathmines, Rathgar and Ranelagh. Others may be related to figures such as the cultural and artistic literati clustered around Harcourt Terrace, such as Dubhglas de hÍde or Sarah Purser, who had language and cultural rights as their priorities, key to the vibrant Irish Revival which they had sought to build and which inspired much of the idealism that was at the heart of 1916.

All of the participants in 1916 had come to recoil from what was a constant theme in the assumptions of the imperialist mind: that the subordinate people in any colony such as Ireland were lesser in human terms, in language, culture and political rights. The historical evidence for this critical view of imperialism was all around, in housing, hunger, emigration, exclusion and language loss. The cultural freedom on offer was a freedom to imitate and ingratiate.

Our road to independence stretched beyond the capital city, and let us not forget revolutionaries such as the Waterford Quaker Rosamund Jacob, the Cork journalist Liam de Róiste or Maria Carney from Belfast, friend and confidante to James Connolly, amongst the many other activists across the country.

Some young revolutionaries were coming from and continuing a strong family Fenian tradition, others owed allegiance to a parliamentarism that had many successes in achieving land reform and in seizing opportunities to make the case for Home Rule. For others, such as the younger Giffords, the Plunketts and the McSwineys, this was too slow a route and they rejected the constitutionalism of their elders in favour of revolution and a war of liberation.

Even within individual families loyalties were often divided in a deeper sense with, for example, Eamonn Ceannt's brother William fighting with the British Army in France, while Eamonn fought against that army in Ireland. In both cases they had expectations, most profoundly and ethically held, of a better Ireland.

It is critical to our understanding of the Rising that we view it in the broader historical context of the First World War. This was, together with the Lockout of 1913, an important prelude to the Rising. By the early twentieth century, a pinnacle of imperialist expectation and arrogance had been reached, and the unassailability of the great European empires, assured a century earlier at Vienna, was now under attack by insurgent nationalisms – Czech, Polish, Yugoslavian, Arab and many others. The Boer War had been widely viewed in Ireland as an anti-imperial struggle, while the First World War reinforced a perception that imperialism was drawing its final breath; six empires entered the war, only two would emerge. The world was in a turmoil of expectation. As Maurice Walsh puts it in his recent *Bitter Freedom*: 'Why would Ireland have been different? According to Czech leader Tomáš Masaryk, the War had turned Europe into "a laboratory atop a vast graveyard". '

Ireland's rebellion therefore had a global significance, acting as an inspiration for independence movements around the world throughout the twentieth century, particularly in other British colonies. As Conor Mulvagh has noted, V. V. Giri, who would become the fourth President of India (1969–74), came under suspicion, as a young Indian law student studying in Dublin between 1913 and 1916, and had, he claimed, a deportation order served on him.

Culture was a central element of the Rising and an inspiration for those who took part. In the years leading up to Easter 1916, the Irish had become an increasingly literate people, publishing and reading newspapers which allowed an alternative culture to emerge in the shape of provocative and radical Irish journalism. Journalists including Bulmer Hobson, Helena Molony, Arthur Griffith and Hanna Sheehy-Skeffington contributed polemical work to publications such as *Young Ireland* and *United Irishman*. Such papers were frequently banned by the British authorities.

To borrow from the title of Diarmaid Ferriter's most recent book, the cultural leaders of the revolution were concerned, not just with military or political victory, but with the elevation of the Irish people, long considered a 'rabble', to the status of a nation.

The Irish literary revival was of course part of a much wider progressive movement, which had seen the founding of the Land League, the Gaelic Athletic Association and the Gaelic League, as a generation of Irish men and women sought through such organizations simultaneously to retrieve their heritage and fashion an alternative Ireland. Myriad and intertwined connections existed between these groups at both executive and grass-roots levels, and it was such mutual affiliations that created the networks of the political movement which led to Easter 1916.

The breadth of their intellectual work, combined with activism, is astounding. James Connolly could write a play, be familiar with George Bernard Shaw's or Ibsen's work while busy with the tasks of organization and agitation.

Bhí timpeallacht chultúrtha thar a bheith saibhir ann ag an am le leithéidí W.B. Yeats, Jack Yeats, James Joyce, George Russell agus Sean O'Casey. Ealaíontóirí agus smaointeoirí ab ea iad a bhí flaithiúil agus a bhí tiomanta do shaol an phobail. Náisiúnaithe, poblachtaigh, sóisialaithe, feiminigh agus idirnáisiúnaithe ab ea iad fir agus mná an ré sin. Theastaigh uathu Éire nua, radacach a chruthú, Éire ina mbeadh an sean-stair agus an sean-chultúr le braith inti.

(W. B. Yeats, Jack Yeats, James Joyce, George Russell, Sean O'Casey: these were artists and thinkers who were committed to the life of the public and the life of the community. Nationalist, republican, socialist, feminist, internationalist – the great men and women of the period typically lived many of these roles. They dreamt of creating something new and radical in Ireland, something which would also be continuous with a distinct Irish culture and history.)

All of these strands of the Rising are present in the idealism of the

Proclamation, which offers us a generous social and political vision, one that can still inspire us today. We should never forget that it was addressed to the nation's women as well as its men in equal terms, two years before women over thirty were allowed to vote, as it called forth a Republic that would guarantee: 'religious and civil liberty, equal rights and equal opportunities for all its citizens'. On that matter, Hanna Sheehy Skeffington was fulsome in her praise of James Connolly for including the equality of women, regarding it as a first in an emancipatory document drafted by men.

During the passage from the Proclamation to the 1930s that egalitarian emphasis would weaken. Women would have to struggle for their equality, and in that struggle they would invoke the women of 1916. This was particularly the case in the debate over *Bunreacht na hÉireann* in 1937, with its regressive view of women's place in society.

Our nation has journeyed many miles from the shell-shocked and burning Dublin of 1916. But we can also see that in many respects we have not fully achieved the dreams and ideals for which our forebears gave so much.

A democracy is always and must always be a work in progress, and how we use the independence we have been gifted will continue to challenge us, morally and ethically. We must ensure that our journey into the future is a collective one; one in which the homeless, the migrants, the disadvantaged, the marginalized and each and every other citizen can find homes.

So this evening, let us look to our past in a way that is transformative. Let us recognize all that was powerfully suggestive in that past as we set about constructing the foundations of a new and better Ireland.

Let us remember, with respect, not only those who have called us here today, or the leaders whose names are indelibly etched into Irish memory, but also all those who lost their lives during the 1916 Rising.

Let us remember the sung and unsung heroes of 1916, those who fought for Ireland and those who were caught up in the events on the streets of Dublin.

Let us remember all those who died or were injured in Dublin, the majority of them civilians. Of the 485 people who died, over half were civilians and forty of those civilians were children aged sixteen and under; children forgotten for almost a century, but in recent years reclaimed by the work of Joe Duffy and others.

We reflect and recall the loss suffered by all families. We recall and respect all the families who lost sons, fathers, brothers, sisters or daughters.

Inniu, tá sé de dhulgas orainn ar fad Poblacht a shamhlú agus a chruthú as a mbeadh na bunaitheoirí bródúil; náisiún cróga, le fís agus le spiorad fial daonnachta.

(Today we are all charged to take on our own responsibilities in imagining and building a Republic in the fullest sense, one of which our founders would be proud; truly representative of a nation rooted in courage, vision and a profound spirit of generous humanity.)

The Glencree Centre for Peace and Reconciliation

27 JUNE 2015

IT IS FITTING that we should come together here in Glencree to consider the challenge of how we should reflect on the legacy of 1916. For forty years the Glencree Centre for Peace and Reconciliation has provided a space for dialogue, and opportunities for people to come together and quite simply talk; and, even more importantly, to listen to each other and at times come to understand a previously opposing and challenging perspective.

While Glencree's mission has been very directly focused on building a better future for all the people on this island, it has always done so with a respectful consideration of the legacies of the past.

The term of my Presidency coincides with what has been referred to as the 'Decade of Commemorations', and addressing the challenge of this broad programme of anniversaries and remembering was an important theme in my Inaugural Address in November 2011. Beginning with the Lockout of 1913, and responding to anniversaries such as the beginning of the First World War, the founding of *Cumann na mBan*, the death of O'Donovan Rossa, the sinking of the *Lusitania* and the military campaign at Gallipoli, I have had many opportunities over the past three and a half years to reflect and speak on the theme of memory.

In addressing the need to 'remember ethically' I turned to the philosophical writings of Hannah Arendt, Paul Ricoeur, Avishai Margalit and Richard Kearney, among others. I was also aware of the published contemporary work of Johnston McMaster, Onora O'Neill and others from whom we will hear today.

When I began a first consideration of these concepts, I had been reading some relatively recent works on Hannah Arendt, notably Marie Luise Knott's *Unlearning with Hannah Arendt* and Elisabeth Young-Bruehl's *Why Arendt Matters*. A consideration of forgiveness was central to her work. I was also aware of the centrality of the concept of forgiveness to the circumstances of our time in an international context, and I had available to me the very valuable book entitled *Memory, Narrative and Forgiveness*, edited by Pumla Gobodo-Madikizela and Chris Van der Merwe.

Invited to speak at the launch of the International Meeting of the Institute of Conflict Transformation and Social Justice at Queen's University Belfast in October last year, I gave my paper the title 'Remembering, Forgiving and Forgetting', to which I added on the night a fourth concept, 'Imagining' – for if we imagine a future released from the burdens of distorted past memories and seemingly insurmountable present difficulties, we can find the energy to create a more empowering and moral kind of memory.

While a terrible and heinous act cannot be dissolved or forgotten, it is only through an act of imagination and creativity that we can prevent that tragic memory from colonizing the future. We have to make an important distinction when we talk about the future, stressing that our 'future' is not merely utopian, but that it is achievable.

In preparing for this afternoon's consideration of 1916, I took that reflection as my point of departure. In attempting to recall 1916, we must remind ourselves that individual memories survive and take shape through a relationship with others, evolving over time and open to reinterpretation as we strive to transact a relationship that will release us from the weight of past wrongs; and that will allow a moving-forward, however tentatively, to new beginnings by loosening the lid on the mouldering jar of 'memory'.

The softening of hearts involved in recollection is more easily caught in literature than in politics. Yet softening hearts require not just good instincts but also the provision of opportunities, and spaces such as Glencree, which allow us to yield to each other in mutual respect – to recognize that our fears, insecurities and vulnerabilities can only be assuaged by actions of mutual generosity.

All societies emerging out of conflict wrestle with the legacy of the past and how to address it. They must consider not only what is consciously recalled by an individual act of memory, but what is unconsciously transmitted, often through uncritically accepted versions of the past. What to remember, and how to remember it, carries the inescapable implication of ethics. It is important that any approach to dealing with the past recognizes the complex relationship that exists between memory, ethics and forgiveness.

While dealing with the legacy of the past is an enormously complex task, it is also one that has the potential to transfigure (in the most positive sense) the relationships between and across the peoples of these islands, and how we relate to our shared and overlapping histories.

Some people argue that the burden of the past is too heavy, too painful, and that we are not capable of providing adequate answers to the multitude of questions still afflicting those directly affected by the violence of the Troubles. Yet, however great that task may seem, it is now widely accepted that embracing amnesia is not only counterproductive but is, in its consequences for victims and their relatives, an amoral position. There is, of course, the more subtle danger of an unconscious amnesia, a turning of the eyes of history away from what is disconcerting.

The desire to remember, however, goes beyond a need for catharsis and a duty to 'not forget' in order to avoid repeating the mistakes of the past. While to ignore the past would be a betrayal of those who lost their lives, we must also ensure our remembered past is not allowed to overshadow the issues of moral significance in the future to which we aspire.

There are many questions that must be asked in any process of remembering. How do we distinguish between shared memory and common memory and set about unravelling the truth that might lie between? How are we to properly consider the context of the times in which the recalled event took place? And how can we remember in a way that has the potential to release us from past wrongs if such remembering can carry crystallized versions of hurts, recriminations and revenge?

Artists, as I have said, may be better at answering these questions and at reflecting on the contradictions involved, but it is on the shoulders of courageous women and men in the public world and politics that the burden most immediately falls. How we remember, how we may come to forgive and forget, and what is open to reconsideration – this must lie at the heart of any aspiration for a peaceful, fair and truly reconciled discourse across this island.

In considering 1916 we have to respond to the seismic events of both the Rising and the Somme. This requires generous effort, and reaching an accommodation with conflicting versions of the past is only a stage in the journey to the destination of forgiveness for past hurt, neglect or omission – a destination which, in so many areas of conflict, at home and abroad, past and present, the participants may not reach. Yet, as Hannah Arendt has written, 'Forgiveness is the only way to reverse the irreversible flow of history', and it is only through such an ethical remembering that we can avoid revisiting the blinding categories of revenge and bitterness.

Remembering Easter 1916 certainly poses challenges for all of us as individuals, as communities and as a state. How do we mark this important moment on our road to independence, and honour those who died fighting in that cause, appropriately and inclusively? How are we to properly recover the context of the times?

These are difficult questions, but they are fundamental ones, and we should approach them in a spirit of openness, using the process of commemoration, which has now commenced, to emancipate and empower us, and others.

It may be that the first step in understanding 1916 in an authentic way is to identify what has been excluded or marginalized in the official orthodoxy of the period. In their editors' introduction to the recently published *Handbook of the Irish Revival*, Declan Kiberd and P. J. Mathews warn against an uncritical acceptance of the narratives of those who sought to establish a rationalized version of the decades leading to independence. Of the government authorities of the new State, the editors express the view: 'those who commemorated often sought to control the discourse in ways which made them the social successors. In that process much was forgotten – Connolly's socialism, the dead in World War I, the role of radical women, the part played by the 1913 Lockout.'

For too long our understanding of 1916 and the surrounding period was hindered by an assumption that we can more easily make sense of events, and indeed our own sense of individual and national identity, if we keep historical narratives simple and homogenous. We must challenge this urge to oversimplify.

If we consider in the first instance the relevance of the First World War, we can see that in more recent years there has been progress in engaging with the experience of the war, and now we can take into consideration more easily its impact on our interpretations of 1916. As new materials including first-hand testimonies became more widely available, we can perceive the catastrophic impact that the first of two global wars in the twentieth century had on our own island and on Irish attitudes and allegiances. For so long, however, commemorating, or even acknowledging the memory of the First World War did not seem to fit into the mainstream narrative of Ireland's path to independence or was left to the Unionist community or those from a Protestant background.

In seeking to gain a fuller picture of the Rising itself we also have to recall not only the participants in war and rebellion, but also to recognize all of those who suffered in its midst and in its wake. As Declan Kiberd has written, 'the stories of the past had celebrated the wrong people: the smiters of the world rather than the smitten'.[105]

Seán O'Casey too, of course, wrote passionately, if not angrily, of the marginalized victims of these conflicts. Tellingly, it is the names of O'Casey's fictional characters, Bessie Burgess or Nora Clitheroe, that are more familiar to us today rather than those of the real victims of the violence, many of whom have remained anonymous, unrecognized and unremembered. In this regard the response to such omission in the work of Joe Duffy in remembering the children killed during the Rising deserves special praise.

When we seek to recall not only the Rising but also the Somme, we are required to ask, from what conditions did the participants come? For many it was deprivation rather than faith or beliefs that led to action. It was poverty that drove some to rebel against the British state and it was poverty that drove others to fight on its behalf in the trenches of Flanders and France.

A young Indian law student, V. V. Giri, who was in Dublin during the Easter Rising, wrote in his memoir of the 'grinding poverty and squalor in the areas of Dublin inhabited by the working class'.[106] Indeed, in 1916 Dublin's infant mortality rates were worse than those of Calcutta in Giri's homeland.

We should bear in mind that Giri was lectured by Thomas MacDonagh and that he met with Eamon De Valera; yet it was James Connolly and the Irish labour movement that he drew on for his real inspiration. James Connolly, of course, saw the Irish labour movement, and a

---

105 Declan Kiberd, *Inventing Ireland: The Literature of a Modern Nation* (Jonathan Cape, 1995), p. 222.

106 V. V. Giri, *My Life and Times* (Macmillan Company of India, 1976), quoted in Colm Keena, 'An Irishman's Diary', *Irish Times*, 5 January 2008.

new Irish Republic, in a wider international context. In *Socialism and Nationalism* he wrote: 'The Republic I would wish our fellow-countrymen to set before them as their ideal should be of such a character that the mere mention of its name would at all times serve as a beacon-light to the oppressed of every land'.[107] Giri would go on to become involved in the Indian labour movement following his expulsion from Ireland in 1916, many years before he became the fourth President of his country.

Although the labour movement linked the workers of Ireland with working men and women in other lands, other leaders of the 1916 Rising also saw the Irish struggle for independence in a wider colonial context. But nationalists differed in what they sought. Some wanted a form of autonomy, some desired commercial freedom, some sought forms of independence within the empire. Within all of this, the flame of egalitarian Republicanism was a wan light, a light that would in the succeeding years find quite a scarcity of supporting oil.

We must remember too that the shared story of the 1916 Rising and the First World War also coincides with the beginning of the end of the previously insatiable global empires. In the years following the 1916 Rising, the demand for democracy in its various forms was well under way in colonized nations across the globe. The Boer rebellion in South Africa, defeat for Russia in its war with Japan and the establishment of an independent China had each, in their own way, dented the myth of the invincibility of empire even before the outbreak of war. The disastrous conduct of the war in its early stages had undermined the moral and political standing of the old regimes, and revolutionary sounds were growing louder across Europe.

When we consider the international context of the Irish Revolution, we may sometimes underestimate the influence that this assertion of

---

107 James Connolly, 'Socialism and Nationalism', in Peter Berresford Ellis (ed.), *James Connolly: Selected Writings* (Pluto Press, 1997), p. 122.

independence against empire in Dublin was to have on the world. The work that Glencree has undertaken in sharing the lessons from conflict and resolution in Ireland with those facing similar problems in other parts of the world is a clear indication that rarely is a political event so unique that its processes cannot be revelatory to others.

There are other significant omissions to be undone. The story of the women who participated in the Easter Rising is yet another strand in the overall story of this time that is now being let into the light. The political activism of women led to the extension of the franchise two years later, in 1918. Of course the sight of women at polling stations caused alarm for some, while others took a more progressive view. On 14 December 1918, the *Irish Times* editorial made the following – and somewhat patronizing - recommendation: 'If any woman pleads domestic engagements, her husband should tell her that on this one occasion his dinner is less vital than her vote.'[108]

Notwithstanding such culinary self-sacrifice, in the years following the Rising the crucial role of women during the Rising was disregarded, and not only in the historical accounts, but where it mattered most – in relation to the most basic income due to participants in the Rebellion.

Margaret Skinnider, a member of *Cumann na mBan* who was shot and injured while in command of five men during Easter Week 1916, was refused a pension in 1925 because the law was 'applicable to soldiers as generally understood in the masculine sense'. The army's legal advice was that a 'person' was, in fact, 'referable only to the male sex'.[109]

Remembering 1916 100 years on provides us with the opportunity to acknowledge, even if belatedly, that Irish women have always played, continue to play, and should be supported in playing a central, active and direct role in shaping the great issues and struggles of the day.

---

108 Quoted in Maurice Walsh, *Bitter Freedom: Ireland in a Revolutionary World 1918–1923* (Faber and Faber, 2015), pp. 15–16.
109 Genevieve Carbery, 'Women played key and courageous role in 1916 Rising', *Irish Times*, 17 January 2014.

I have referred elsewhere to the work of Richard Kearney in this area of remembering ethically and to his astute observation that engagement with the diversity of various narratives could, over time, contribute to a culture of forgiveness.

All of the dead, including those Irish who died abroad, at the Somme and elsewhere, deserve our respect. At a community and political level, acts of shared remembering of the various iconic events of the other traditions have played an important part in our journey towards healing and reconciliation. This is especially true in sharing moments of grief and bereavement.

We have seen so many great gestures of forgiveness over the past forty years, grounded in what I have referred to as a kind of existential generosity as old as humanity and its greatest writing and as captured most eloquently by Michael Longley's poem 'Ceasefire', to which I have often referred. The act to which that poem refers did not save Troy, but it restored for a while, between antagonists, the respect called forth by grief.

Most recently, Prince Charles in Co. Sligo – at the site of a place of great personal and collective sorrow on Irish soil – out of his own anguish in the loss of his great-uncle, said that he understood 'in a profound way, the agonies borne by so many others in these islands, of whatever faith, denomination or political tradition'.

In April I represented Ireland at the centenary commemoration of the Gallipoli Campaign in Turkey. During the Commonwealth and Ireland Service at the Helles monument, it was moving to hear an extract from one of the last letters written by a young Dublin man – Patrick Tobin – who fought and died there. Running along the sandbanks in the intense heat, just days before he was shot and killed, he thought of what he called his beloved 'Alps of Dollymount', the strand near his home in Clontarf.

As the personal testimonies of combatants, in Flanders, Suvla and in Dublin, have become more freely accessible we have all been moved by the images of the violence imposed by war, and the destruction of young lives. War takes the young away from home, from what is intimate and what is remembered. When the false heroics of war are re-enacted, we should counter them with the terrible reality that it is the children of the poor who have always paid the price of the pretensions of empire and the godfathers of violence.

To understand 1916 as it was experienced, let us imagine the Dublin of those years, among the survivors of the Lockout, where revolutionary conspiracy is taking place on the very same poor streets where dreaded telegrams are arriving from the front. The emotions of the city and the country are feverish as the horror behind the rhetoric of the recruiting posters becomes apparent. Dublin, with a population of perhaps a quarter of its present size, lost hundreds of young men at Gallipoli alone in 1915 and, when one combines this with the losses on the Western Front, and then the losses at home of hundreds more in the Rising and the subsequent executions, one can see how these dreadful multitudes of lost lives changed the city utterly.

The sharing of moments of grief, even at a distance, allows us to remember both the Somme and the Easter Rising in a manner that can deepen reconciliation rather than seek to perpetuate conflicting versions of different identities.

At the same time, we must recognize too that exemplary violence is of the worst kind, above all when it is violence by the state. One of the most iconic episodes of the Rising occurred in its aftermath – the executions at Kilmainham Gaol. Most historians accept that this moment had a profound and radicalizing impact on Irish politics, the Irish people, that it changed the nature of popular discourse. As Yeats famously wrote:

> *O but we talked at large before*
> *The sixteen men were shot,*
> *But who can talk of give and take,*
> *What should be and what not*

While those dead men are loitering there
To stir the boiling pot?[110]

Considering the decade of commemorations in its full context, we must allow too for the fact that it is through the prism of the War of Independence and of the Civil War that we now see 1916. Considering these later events in a spirit of forgiveness will pose particular challenges for all of us in the coming years.

Is our process of commemoration to be approached with trepidation, looking downwards to pick our way through the pitfalls and offences that might be committed, or does remembering 1916 offer us hope and sustenance for our future? These are the basic questions we must answer.

We must perhaps be encouraged by the fact that the shared process of commemorations thus far has contributed to the building of peace and trust on our island. The rediscovery of lost accounts, diaries and letters, the sharing of remembered grief and bereavement, and all of the fumbling towards forgiveness have strengthened and reinforced a peace which was so hard-won. That knowledge should encourage us to continue on this path, always knowing, as Václav Havel put it, 'that words can kill, and have killed, as well as making us free'.

As I mentioned earlier, in my speech at Queen's last year I added to these three concepts of remembering, forgiving and forgetting, that of 'imagining'; 1916 was a moment in our history informed by an emancipatory view of the world and the possibilities of freedom. While there may be, and will always be, debate about the motivations and strategies of the revolutionaries and their contemporaries, I suggest that the enduring relevance of their Revolution is in their idealism.

It is also surely helpful that, as we in Ireland attempt a reimagining of our State in the wake of severe economic and political failures, we

---

110   Yeats, 'Sixteen Dead Men', in ibid., p. 154 (Macmillan Press, 1991).

acknowledge that we have much to learn from the idealistic visionaries of this period. Lest we be moved to judge others retrospectively, we must ask ourselves if we have taken our opportunities to break away from old and failing paradigms of thought, or perhaps we should acknowledge that we have lacked the moral courage and intellectual commitment to bring the world we need, sustainable and equal, into being.

This work of commemoration should invigorate rather than discourage us. It is in imagining a future released from the burdens of present difficulties, falsely presented as insurmountable, that the energy is found for constructing what might be an ethics of life we are living. It is only through acts of imagination that we can prevent forms of tragic memory from colonizing the future.

The revolution of 1916 was, as Diarmaid Ferriter has described it, 'while propelled by much idealism and courage, also multilayered, complicated, messy, brutal and sometimes compromised as a result of competing impulses, tension between the labour and republican movements and the use of the revolution as a cloak to try and settle grievances over land, class, the distribution of power and status'.[111]

I agree, and perhaps that quote is even more apt for the War of Independence, and particularly for the Civil War, whose commemoration awaits us. For all its complexity, the Rising was undeniably foundational in nature. Speculation as to what might have happened otherwise had it not happened is just that – speculation. There can be no doubt that the protagonists themselves saw their actions as unavoidable and necessary, and that the independence of Ireland directly followed from these events.

In a way that could not be achieved on the fiftieth anniversary of the Easter Rising, in the 100th year we can now acknowledge the diversity of our past. The process of commemoration we share and to which we welcome each other, no longer as strangers or in fear, can facilitate a

---

111   *Irish Times*, 30 August 2014.

deepening of the bonds of empathy and healing between all those who remember the different strands and truths of our shared history.

We have had in the past few years moments which powerfully deny authority to the distortions of the past; and such moments have the ability to release us from a history viewed through the prism of a single or exclusive narrative; moments which remind us that while we have a duty to those gone before us to remember, no person or nation must be forever defined by any single version of the actions of their antecedents; that it is only by a constant will to release each other from the consequences of recalled past deeds that we can move forward, beyond the collision of competing certainties. While some very significant gestures can be, and have been made by those in leadership roles, it is in popular consciousness that the most significant and enduring change must take place.

Unlearning the comfort, and solace too, of familiar versions of our life and past is a necessary and preliminary task. However difficult it may be for us, we have to realize that unlearning is a crucial preparation for the journey of reconciliation. Marie Luise Knott tells us of Hannah Arendt: 'In the difficult work of unlearning, Arendt drove out her own "opinions" on the concept of forgiveness as in many previous cases she "forgot" the unexamined prejudices that keep us from thinking.'[112]

There is a headline in this for all of us.

Happily, closeness and warmth have been the hallmark of relationships between these islands in recent years. We owe this transformation not least to the hard work and courage of those who, across generations and borders, dedicated themselves to peace in Northern Ireland. Their unflinching determination reversed what too many had thought irreversible. At a community and political level, respectful and courageous acts of shared remembering, and of the acknowledgement of the iconic moments in the stories of the other tradition, have also

---

112 M. L. Knott, *Unlearning with Hannah Arendt* (Other Press, 2011).

played an important part in our journey towards a future released from vengeful reaction.

At the State Banquet at Windsor Castle last April, an event that brought together leaders from all four corners of these islands, I said that 'We owe a duty to all those who lost their lives, the duty to build together in peace; it is the only restitution, the only enduring justice we can offer them.'

Má tá síocháin bhuan agus chóir le bunú, ní mór dúinn dul i ngleic leis an stair. Ní bheadh sé eiticiúil ná infheidhme neamhaird a dhéanamh de ná an díth cuimhne a ligean orainn; ní dhéanfadh sin ach an mhímhuinín agus an naimhdeas a chothú amach anseo.
(An enduring and just peace requires us to engage with the past. To ignore it or to pretend amnesia would neither be ethical or workable; it would merely sow the seeds of future distrust and enmity.)

Engaging with the past is never easy. It involves a complex negotiation of the manifold stories, memories, hurts, legacies and emotions of all who recall 1916 or were affected more recently by the Troubles. Finding a fair and comprehensive way of dealing with the past, one that will win the confidence of all, will be a huge challenge – but a challenge that cannot be shirked. In facing up to that challenge, let us at least ensure that our approach is characterized by a will to view forgiveness as a true release from the past, and to move forward unburdened as much as possible by any bitter memory of that past, in conditions of an enduring peace.

Thank you for your attention.

I want to thank William Devas, Glencree's staff and board for their invitation to speak today.

At the Dedication of the Cross of Sacrifice

GLASNEVIN CEMETERY, DUBLIN

31 JULY 2014

HIS ROYAL HIGHNESS, THE DUKE OF KENT
WAS THE PRESIDING SPEAKER

I T IS IMPORTANT that the First World War, and those whose lives it claimed, not be left as a blank space in Irish history. Today therefore is a significant day, as we dedicate this Cross of Sacrifice – the first such Cross to be erected in the Republic of Ireland.

On an occasion such as this we eliminate all the barriers that have stood between those Irish soldiers whose lives were taken in the war, whose remains are our responsibility, and whose memories we have a duty to respect.

San iliomad uaigheanna ar fud na hEorpa, tá glúil de fhir óga curtha taobh le taobh, agus is sna huaigheanna sin ar fad ina n-iomláine atá íospartach an chogaidh sin.
(In so many graves across Europe, the flower of a generation lie together, and all of their graves taken together hold the victims of that war.)

We cannot give back their lives to the dead, nor whole bodies to those who were wounded, or repair the grief, or undo the disrespect that was sometimes shown to those who fought in that war or their families. But we honour them all now, and we do not ask, nor would it be appropriate to interrogate, their reasons for enlisting. If they could come back no doubt they would have questions to ask as to how it came to be that their lives were taken.

To all of them in their silence we offer our own silence, without judgement, and with respect for their ideals as they knew them, and for the humanity they expressed towards each other. And we offer our sorrow too that they and their families were not given the compassion and the understanding over the decades that they should have received from their fellow Irish men and women. The suffering visited upon our own people at home had perhaps blinded our sight and hardened hearts.

As His Royal Highness, the Duke of Kent, just said in his speech, the Cross of Sacrifice stands in cemeteries in the care of the Commonwealth War Graves Commission throughout Europe, indeed across the world – from Flanders to Gallipoli to Mesopotamia. As one in a web of many others, this monument reminds us that the First World War was a global war that affected every part of the European continent – and that Ireland is an integral part of that history.

In recent years, an increasing number of writers and scholars, religious and political leaders have redirected our gaze to the complexity of the Irish engagement with that war, allowing for a more inclusive remembering at public level. As we turn to that past, we are also making progress in our understanding of the complicated intertwining of loyalties that made up Irish identities at the turn of the twentieth century.

This is facilitated by easier access to, and a renewal of interest in, the writings of Irish soldiers who fought in the war – their diaries, notebooks, letters and poems. The line 'not for flag, nor King, nor Emperor' in the sonnet that Thomas Kettle dedicated to his three-year-old daughter Betty four days before his death during the Battle of the Somme, or the poem

Francis Ledwidge wrote in honour of his close friend, the doomed rebel Thomas MacDonagh, while recovering from his wounds in Manchester in 1916, lend us a better sense of those men's complicated sense of belonging.

Such writings throw light on the complex motives and circumstances that led so many Irishmen to join the British Army. Whether it was a true belief in the ideals for which the army fought; or whether it was driven by unionist or nationalist feelings, and within that, many different versions of each; or an escape from poverty; the search for adventure; a friendship network, or the continuation of a family tradition – it is not for us to judge those who fought and their motivations. We should seek, rather, to show respect for this complexity without sinking into relativism, a glossing-over of differences, some of them enduring and not easily reconcilable.

A century after it began, the First World War remains something of an enigma. Its origins are mysterious. So is its course. Why, when the hope of bringing the conflict to a decisive conclusion was dashed within months of its outbreak, did the combatant states decide to persist, to mobilize for total war and eventually to commit the totality of their young manhood to mutual destruction?

If all wars are an object of infinite sadness, this war also remains as an inextinguishable source of bewilderment.

But while historians still struggle to ascribe a definite meaning to the First World War, we now see more clearly what it is that was sacrificed: health, both mental and physical; youth – life itself. Huge destruction was inflicted on families and communities; a whole generation was destroyed that could have furnished their countries with workers, farmers, scholars, artists, administrators and political leaders.

Not only did the First World War bring human devastation and economic ruin to Europe, it also shattered the notion of progress; it put an abrupt end to the aspirations for happy modernity and human improvement harboured by Europeans for the previous forty years: 'Never such innocence again', as Philip Larkin put it.

Today, on the eve of the centenary of the outbreak of the war, we are invited to remember the sacrifice of so many Irish men and women who fought alongside British and Commonwealth soldiers. We should break once and for all from the myths of redemptive violence that infuse all of Ireland's main political traditions, go beyond disputes as to the legitimacy of the various causes embraced by those men, in order to reflect, together, on what was lost for everybody.

We are here to remember with respect and dignity the great human loss of those years. Our duty is to mark the graves of all who have lost their lives, wherever they may be – and I salute the invaluable work carried out by the Commonwealth War Graves Commission and the Glasnevin Trust to ensure that this duty is fulfilled.

The wall that stands before us lists 166 Commonwealth burials from the First World War. I invite anyone who reads those names to reflect on the individual stories that go with them. Each man had parents and friends; many had a wife, or a lover, children, siblings.

Indeed, beyond the staggering statistics associated with the First World War – a war whose casualties number in the millions – it is important, I believe, that we do justice to the dead by endeavouring to recover the human dimension of the experience of war, the tragedy of each single death, of every life shattered.

And while it is hard for us to imagine what life in the trenches was really like, it is only through reading the writings of the soldiers themselves that we can gain a better sense of the experience of those who fought and lived on the battlefields – the cold and damp, the confined space, the insipid food, the rats and lice, the deafening din of shelling for days on end, the fear, the stench of rotting flesh, the muddy wasteland all around, the barbed wire and the burnt villages.

In the letters of soldiers, in the memoirs some of them wrote after the war, we understand the harrowing character of a mechanical, industrial war. We also see the great humanity those soldiers felt for each other in the face of incredible carnage. In those letters the combatants confer the award of courage on each other, thus commanding us, today, to ascribe agency to the men and women of the past, to honour their choice and to abstain from portraying them as mere passive victims.

The writings of the soldiers also remind us of our responsibility not to allow the power and energies of nations, their formidable industrial capacity, to be unleashed for mutual destruction.

Finally, let me say how the progress of our understanding, in Ireland, of the First World War has also given us a deeper empathy with the British people, for whom the war forms such an important element of their identity and mythology. It is an honour to host a monument to that memory.

Like those soldiers who had to leave behind the idiom of the nineteenth century – that language used for over a century to celebrate the idea of progress – we are invited today to leave behind some of the familiar terms and concepts of the twentieth century, with its grammar of divisions between 'the enemy' and 'us'. The time has come for us to embrace a kind of narrative hospitality to replace our past 'entrenchments' – that awful word bequeathed to us by an era scarred by total war.

I want to thank you, Sir, for your presence and for your words of recognition for the Irish men and women who were killed during the First World War.

The ability to share sombre and profound national memories is an important statement of friendship and respect: as friends we, both Irish and British, share this moment of remembrance; in mutual sympathy we dedicate this monument to the memory of all those who lost their lives during the long, dreadful years of 1914 to 1918.

Let us now, together, cultivate memory as a tool for the living and as a sure base for the future – memory employed in the task of building peace.

Of Myth-Making and
Ethical Remembering

THEATRE OF MEMORY SYMPOSIUM,
ABBEY THEATRE, DUBLIN

THURSDAY, 16 JANUARY 2014

I T IS A great honour to have been asked to open this symposium, which calls upon all participants to critically reflect on how we, in Ireland, might engage with memory and commemoration, including that of the defining historical events which stirred our country 100 years ago. And what better place to do so than the Abbey Theatre, linked as it is with the cultural movement and the men and women who responded to Ireland's socio-economic and political condition at the turn of the twentieth century?

As an introduction to the 'Theatre of Memory' held here, I would like to consider briefly the relationship between myth-making and ethical remembering. Rather than speculating in the abstract, I prefer to reflect on a particular, momentous event, the outbreak of which is being commemorated throughout the world this year – the First World War.

The First World War is of immense significance for so many nations. A century later, its causes and its political, economic, social and cultural legacy present an inextinguishable source of interrogation and investigation, not only for historians and social scientists worldwide but also for theologians, writers, poets and many individuals who are simply concerned with the history of their family.

In the Irish context, the First World War as a subject for commemoration poses the difficult issue of Ireland's divided, or even divisive, memories. It casts the Battle of the Somme, so central to Irish Unionists' identity, versus the 1916 Rising as our Republic's founding myth. For years the war has stood as a blank space in memory for many Irish people – an unspoken gap in the official narratives of this state. Thousands of Irish war dead were erased from official history, denied recognition, because they did not fit into the nationalist myth and its 'canonical' lines of memory.

Of course, contemporary Irish historiography has largely departed from such nationalist historical tradition. Recent years have witnessed a critical reassessment by historians of the complexity of Irish engagement with the war. And the powerful symbolism of particular acts of public commemoration – such as when former President Mary McAleese stood alongside Queen Elizabeth at Messines in Belgium in 1998 – has allowed for more inclusive remembering at a public level.

Yet so many questions remain, the exploration of which can feed our reflections during centennial commemorations that will run until 2022. How might we, in Ireland, remember the First World War in a way that is ethical? What ought we remember and, perhaps, forget? What is open to revision? What method should we follow? What sources should we draw on? And what might all this mean for our shared Irishness in the present and future?

As to the act of 'remembering', the use of the term itself, I would like to draw on the distinction established by the Israeli philosopher Avishai Margalit in his recent book *The Ethics of Memory* between 'common memory' and 'shared memory'.[113] In Margalit's definition, 'common memory' is an aggregate notion that combines the memories of all those people who remember a certain episode which each of them experienced individually.

---

113 A. Margalit, *The Ethics of Memory* (Harvard University Press, 2002).

'Shared memory', on the other hand, is not simply the sum of individual memories. It is an indirect memory – a memory of memory – which requires communication and seeks to integrate into one version the different perspectives of those who might have directly remembered a given episode. In other words, it goes beyond the experience of anyone alive, and thus we might ask: Is it inescapably ideological – as ideological as any enforced or induced amnesia?

According to Avishai Margalit, modern societies are characterized by a division of mnemonic labour. Shared memory in a modern society travels from person to person through institutions such as archives, historiographic texts and communal mnemonic devices such as speeches by public representatives, monuments and the names of streets. All of these reflect a distribution of power.

Shared memory is what I believe we are concerned with in this symposium. The choice of what is to be remembered, and how, are unavoidable issues in the progression from the simple urge to recall to what become designated acts of commemoration. Commemoration involves a choice between events and historical actors, motivations and consequences, and its purposes may be as elusive and complex as the original impulses to remember. In other words, only 'interpretations of memory' are collectively remembered and commemorated.

Among the competing sources for commemoration are myths and historiographical discussion. As Avishai Margalit puts it, 'modern shared memory is located between the push and pull of two poles: history and myth'.[114] This notion of shared memory as being torn between two worldviews can be likened to Max Weber's contrast between, on the one hand, seeing the world as an enchanted place, the locus of myth or, on the other as a disenchanting place, subject to critical history.

This does not amount to stating that memory is torn between

---

114 Ibid., p. 63.

seeking truth and seeking 'noble lies'. When I speak of myth I am not just speaking of false beliefs about the past which may be invested with symbolic meaning and charged with powerful emotions. I speak of myth as a founding, integrated source from which to interpret the past or anticipate the future.

Today, while it may be suggested that the spell of the enchanted world is vanishing under the combined assaults of scientific rationality and critical history, I believe that the two worldviews co-exist, that they both continue to be of unrealized value in the way we remember the past, live the present and imagine the future – in other words, realize our possibilities.

The Irish culture of commemoration shares with other cultures an emphasis on 'living myths' of the heroic dead. The Reverend Johnston McMaster has, in an interesting paper, referred to the 'myth of redemptive violence' which infuses Ireland's main political traditions. Such a myth is central to the popular understanding of the Easter Rising, largely interpreted as a necessary sacrifice for Ireland's freedom, and also to the commemorative practices that invoke the blood sacrifice of the 36th Ulster Division, slaughtered at the Somme – a sacrifice which, it is argued, morally obliges Britain towards Ulster loyalism.

In nations who were party to wars, commemoration often takes the form of rituals intended to revivify the war's events and heroes. Avishai Margalit names such rituals 'revivication rituals' – rituals surrounding mythic heroes, those in-between creatures who belong both to the world of mortals and to the world of immortals.

Revivication can even take the form of the living being called upon to assume the roles of their fallen comrades, as is captured for example in the final stanza of the Canadian poet John McCrae's piece entitled 'In Flanders Fields' (1915):[115]

---

115 Ibid., p. 68.

Take up our quarrel with the foe;
To you from failing hands we throw
The torch; be yours to hold it high.
If ye break faith with us who die
We shall not sleep, though poppies grow
In Flanders fields.

What sense are we supposed to make of such instances of myth-making sourced in war and the experience of it? Does Irish reconciliation with the memory of the First World War involve an accommodation of such myths; and what might this mean from an ethical perspective?

The First World War also gave rise to a brand of literature and poetry which radically undermined the link between patriotic duty and heroic death. Many war poets have related in a direct, almost hyper-realist, fashion what life in the trenches was really like – the forced intimacy between soldiers, the noise, the screams and the dazzling light of exploding shells. The war fostered the affirmation of the singularity of the poet's voice in the face of collective slaughter. It also engendered a new poetical diction, based on the rejection of the orderly formalism of pre-war versification.

The demise of idealism is manifest, for example, in the writings of Franz Rosenzweig, who before the war had completed a dissertation on Hegel. The experience of war in the Balkans led Rosenzweig to reject idealism and the Hegelian philosophy of history, which justifies individual death in the name of higher causes. Countering this, Rosenzweig asserted that only what is singular can die.

Poets such as Robert Graves or the French novelist and poet Blaise Cendrars, for example, have also strongly refuted such idealist dualism, the supposed ability of the human spirit to overlook everyday reality and bodily suffering. In 'The White Goddess', Graves tellingly abandoned the radiant figure of Apollo for that of Dionysus, the suffering god.

Cendrars, who lost his writing hand in the war, explicitly refused to be a penholder for heroic death. In his memoir entitled *The Severed Hand* (1946) he wrote: ' "*It is sweet and fitting to die for your country…*" isn't it? Do you believe yourself to be at the theatre, Sir? Have you lost any sense of reality? You are not at the Comédie-Française here. Do you know what hides beneath this alexandrine? War is an ignominy.' The alexandrine in question is the translation of a line from Horace's ode 'Dulce et decorum est pro patria mori', words which were widely quoted before the war.

The English poet Wilfred Owen also derided this same line in his poem 'Dulce et Decorum est' (1917), in which the Horatian motto is juxtaposed to a vivid description of the horrors of a gas attack. 'Dulce et Decorum est' includes these lines:

> *[…]*
> *Gas! GAS! Quick, boys! – An ecstasy of fumbling*
> *Fitting the clumsy helmets just in time,*
> *But someone still was yelling out and stumbling*
> *And flound'ring like a man in fire or lime…*
> *Dim through the misty panes and thick green light,*
> *As under a green sea, I saw him drowning.*
> *[…]*
> *If in some smothering dreams, you too could pace*
> *Behind the wagon that we flung him in,*
> *And watch the white eyes writhing in his face,*
> *His hanging face, like a devil's sick of sin;*
> *If you could hear, at every jolt, the blood*
> *Come gargling from the froth-corrupted lungs,*
> *Obscene as cancer, bitter as the cud*
> *Of vile, incurable sores on innocent tongues,*
> *My friend, you would not tell with such high zest*
> *To children ardent for some desperate glory,*

The old Lie: Dulce et decorum est

Pro patria mori.

Such depictions of the personal experience of the tremendous suffering generated by war were not to everybody's taste. In his *Oxford Book of Modern Verse 1892–1935*, Yeats famously made the controversial choice of excluding all of the First World War combatant poets, stating that 'passive suffering' is not a material for good literature. In his Preface he wrote:

> I have a distaste for certain poems written in the midst of the great war… The writers of these poems were invariably officers of exceptional courage and capacity, one a man constantly selected for dangerous work, all, I think, had the Military Cross; their letters are vivid and humorous, they were not without joy – for all skill is joyful – but felt bound, in the words of the best known, to plead the suffering of their men. In poems that had for a time considerable fame, written in the first person, they made that suffering their own. I have rejected these poems for the same reason that made Arnold withdraw his *Empedocles on Etna* from circulation: passive suffering is not a theme for poetry…
>
> If the war is necessary, or necessary in our time and place, it is best to forget its suffering as we do the discomfort of fever, remembering our comfort at midnight when our temperature fell, or as we forget the worst moments of more painful disease. Florence Farr returning third class from Ireland found herself among Connaught Rangers just returned from the Boer War who described an incident over and over, and always with loud laughter: an unpopular sergeant struck by a shell turned round and round like a dancer wound in his own entrails. That too may be a right way of seeing war, if war is necessary; the way of the Cockney slums, of Patrick

Street, of the *Kilmainham Minut*, of 'Johnny I hardly knew ye', of the medieval *Dance of Death*.

In Yeats's view, then, the crude reality of human suffering was not to be remembered by posterity; I suggest otherwise. These mundane myths, these 'minor' stories, as Yeats would have it, of human suffering, of resilience and friendship can, I contend, nurture groundbreaking historiography as well as prompt new forms of myth-making, ones that are not simply underpinned by glorious idealism and grand narratives but that confront the ugly reality of experience.

These stories can be an inspiring source for present-day myth-makers, memory-tellers and historians alike. One of the fields in which new Irish historiography has recently made much progress is that of the study of violence, its sources, and of how the first decade of the twentieth century brought about a militarization of Irish politics that sprang from different groups of memory which projected divergent futures.

Even with the years of distancing, we have not fully examined the consequences of the First World War in Ireland. The long shadow cast by the conflict in Northern Ireland has not made it easy for us to face up to our own culture of violence and to draw conclusions which might prove disturbing.

A respect for such complexity as does not sink into relativism is another benefit to be gained from engaging with the writings of Irish First World War soldiers. We need to better understand these men's multilayered senses of belonging and the complex motives and circumstances which led them to volunteer to join the British Army. It is well known, for example, that Thomas Kettle enlisted to further the cause of Home Rule.

Another example is Francis Ledwidge, an Irish nationalist and poet who was born in Slane in 1887, the son of a poor labourer. Despite his initial reluctance to enlist, Ledwidge believed that by joining the British Army he could advance the cause of Irish independence from Britain. Ledwidge learnt of the Easter Rising and the executions of nationalist leaders while recovering from his wounds and – testament to the complex intertwining of loyalties which characterized Irish involvement with the First World War – wrote one of his best-known poems in honour of his close friend Thomas MacDonagh. Ledwidge was killed in Flanders on 31 July 1917, as he was drinking tea in a shell hole with five comrades. He is buried in Boezinge alongside the Welsh-language poet Hedd Wyn, one of the 31,000 Allied soldiers who died on that same day.

Contemporary work such as Sebastian Barry's novel *A Long, Long Way* can also inspire us to respect complexity and allow for contingency, as we move to examine more closely the entanglements between the Easter Rising and the Somme and the great dilemmas of those who were involved in these events.

While it is essential to recognize the complexities of Irish identity at the turn of the twentieth century, indeed as today, there are also dangers in an ideology of 'inclusiveness at any price'. It is crucial not to gloss over differences and to acknowledge what it was that separated people in the various ideological groups in Irish society; one example of such complexity, is the Citizen Army and its relationship to the Irish Volunteers and differences with the National Volunteers.

We must also be aware of the potential pitfalls contained in the injunction to accept the Somme as the 'memory of the other' in the name of reconciliation. The Somme is equally the battle of those Irish nationalists who fought alongside Ulster loyalists.

It is important, too, not to deny agency to the men and women of the past. Those who voluntarily engaged in the armed conflict were not just passive victims, as a currently widespread trend in European commemorative language suggests. Finally, any critique of nationalist excesses should not be equated with a dismissal of national pride or its place.

What conclusions can we draw from all this that might help us define a tentative basis for what I call an 'ethical culture of commemoration'?

The first important point is, I think, that commemoration should never jeopardize historical accuracy. Timothy Snyder, an eminent historian of the Holocaust, has warned us against a culture of commemoration which 'requires no adequate explanation of the catastrophe, only an aesthetically realizable image of its victims. As cultures of memory supplant concern for history', he wrote, 'the danger is that historians will find themselves drawn to explanations that are the simplest to convey.'[116]

This observation corroborates the French historian François Furet's views on the bicentennial of the French Revolution's celebrations in 1989, when he outlined the dangers of 'commemorative history' wherein that which is most elegantly commemorated becomes that which is most felicitously narrated. Indeed, commemoration often runs the risk of projecting the contemporary emotions of the present on the past. Or, as Timothy Snyder succinctly put it: 'With commemorative causality, the boundaries of history are set by the contingencies of empathy.'[117]

As we commemorate events which unfolded 100 years ago, it is therefore crucial that we endeavour to do justice to the complexity of the historical context as outlined in contemporary historical research, while also recognizing contingency and refraining from reading history uncritically from any contemporary ethical standpoint. The conventional wisdom of the time – ideologies such as militarism, theories of race, the Protestant theology of empires or the Catholic mystical blood sacrifice – need to be engaged as carefully as possible, with respect but also with rigour, and utilizing scholarly discipline.

Commemorative practices might gain, too, from making clear the possibilities and limits of what Paul Ricoeur calls the 'historiographical operation', including how the tools used by historians to apprehend past

---

116 T. Snyder, 'Commemorative Causality', *Modernism-Modernity*, Vol. 20, No. 1 (2013), pp. 77–93.
117 Ibid.

events – archives, testimony and so forth – are actually deployed, and within what boundaries.

We must also overcome the currently widespread preference for internal, psychological and national history over external, sociological and transnational history. In this regard, recontextualizing the Irish experience of the First World War within a European framework is an important first step.

The unfolding decade of centenaries presents us with a wonderful occasion to reappropriate the repressed parts of our history, to include in our narratives the forgotten voices and the lost stories of the past – those of the First World War Irish poets, but also the points of view of women, or, for example, those of the 1913 Lockout workers who decided to join the British Army because the king's shilling was more generous than a worker's wage in Dublin in the 1910s.

As we are in a theatre we might recall Bertolt Brecht's 'Questions from a Worker who Reads', with its wonderful lines:

> *The young Alexander conquered India.*
> *Was he alone?*
>
> *Caesar defeated the Gauls.*
> *Did he not even have a cook with him?*
>
> *Philip of Spain wept when his armada went down.*
> *Was he the only one to weep?*
> *[...]*
> *Every page a victory.*
> *Who cooked the feast for the victors?*

I have referred to the 'dangers' inherent in commemoration, but I also want to insist on the many opportunities these centenaries offer us: opportunities to add, to restore, to revise; to recollect the excluded, such as the life of Eva Gore-Booth, or Seán O'Casey's version of the history of the Citizen Army, already mentioned; to depart with a new set of responsibilities.

Ethical commemoration need not be extraneous either to historical understanding or to myth-making. And I would like to reiterate the call that I made in New York in 2012 for a new myth-making that would be both contextualized historically and emancipatory, respecting the right of unrealized dreams to be remembered as well as the facts of failure.

Indeed it is to be hoped that our old narratives of betrayals and failures will not determine the agenda for the future. We need new myths that not only carry the burden of history but fly from it, evolving afresh. Old myths, reworked, can become a vehicle for something contemporary and mould-breaking, for what nervous silences had sought to cover, for intimacies forbidden, racisms thinly disguised and faiths no longer trusted but then not easily discarded either, and never forgotten.

This decade of centenaries is an opportunity to consider how Ireland has been – and must now again be – renewed through memory and imagination. In that task we are invited to go beyond what is calculable, what is even seemingly reasonable. We have the opportunity to move along the arc of a heroic encounter with the morality of forgiveness and love, as artists in different generations have moved us. I am fond of quoting Michael Longley's beautiful Homeric poem 'Ceasefire', which addresses the difficulty of overcoming the past, of breaking the cycle of violence:

> *Put in mind of his own father and moved to tears*
> *Achilles took him by the hand and pushed the old king*
> *Gently away, but Priam curled up at his feet and*
> *Wept with him until their sadness filled the building.*
>
> *Taking Hector's corpse into his own hands Achilles*
> *Made sure it was washed and, for the old king's sake,*

Laid out in uniform, ready for Priam to carry
Wrapped like a present home to Troy at daybreak.

When they had eaten together, it pleased them both
To stare at each other's beauty as lovers might,
Achilles built like a god, Priam good-looking still
And full of conversation, who earlier had sighed:

'I get down on my knees and do what must be done
And kiss Achilles' hand, the killer of my son.'

Go raibh míle maith agaibh go léir.

Ba mhaith liom buíochas a ghabháil le Fiach Mac Conghail as ucht a chuireadh agus a fhocail deasa, agus libh uile as ucht bhur fíorchaoin fáilte. (May I thank Fiach Mac Conghail for his invitation and his generous words of introduction, and all of you for your warm welcome.)

Acknowledgements

All extracts from the poems quoted here are gratefully acknowledged as are their use originally in the speeches as delivered.

Excerpt from Philip Larkin, 'Home is So Sad' from *Collected Poems*, the Estate of Philip Larkin and Faber and Faber Ltd

Excerpt from John Hewitt, 'An Irishman in Coventry' from *Selected Poems*, Blackstaff Press

Excerpt from Seamus Heaney 'Bogland', from *Door Into the Dark*, the Estate of Seamus Heaney and Faber and Faber Ltd

Excerpt from Harry Clifton, 'Deep Ulster' from *The Holding Centre*, Bloodaxe Books

Excerpt from Sinead Morrissey 'Between Here and There', from *Between Here and There*, Carcanet Press

Excerpt from Nuala ni Domhnaill 'Ceist an Teangan', The Wake Forest Book of Irish Women's Poetry, translation by Paul Muldoon, Wake Forest Press

'Free Soul' by Patrick Kavanagh, Trustees of the Estate of the Late Katherine B. Kavanagh, through the Jonathan Williams Literary Agency

Excerpt from 'To a Blackbird' by Patrick Kavanagh, Trustees of the Estate of the Late Katherine B. Kavanagh, through the Jonathan Williams Literary Agency

'Pegasus' by Patrick Kavanagh, Trustees of the Estate of the Late Katherine B. Kavanagh, through the Jonathan Williams Literary Agency

'Shancoduff' by Patrick Kavanagh, Trustees of the Estate of the Late Katherine B. Kavanagh, through the Jonathan Williams Literary Agency

Index

‖‖‖‖‖‖‖‖‖‖‖‖‖‖‖‖‖‖‖